Words From the Champs

Table of Contents

Foreword………………………………………………………………………3

Introduction: A Word From the Champs……………………………………...4

Chapter 1: How We Did It……………………………………………… 5

Chapter 2: My Spelling Bee Experience……………………………………...7

Chapter 3: The Spelling Bee and Me……………………………………..33

Chapter 4: Precis…………………………………………………..43

Chapter 5: Jigsaw…………………………………………………103

Chapter 6: Stallion……………………………………..…………140

Chapter 7: Galaxy…………………………………………..…..204

Chapter 8: Cosmos……………………………………..…………313

Chapter 9: -ible Words……………………………………………337

Afterword………………………………………………..…..340

Foreword

Welcome to the spelling bee! Everyone must learn a language to communicate with family, friends, or society. We go through school learning how to speak, read, and write correctly. Whether we want to realize it or not, English is an important form of communication in the 21st century. With its eclectic vocabulary, its tendency to "borrow" words from other languages, and its quirky spellings, English does not have the best reputation among students scrambling to retain SAT vocabulary words or applicants seeking to proofread every last mistake in their résumés.

However, there is certainly some beauty that comes with the English language. Its eclectic vocabulary provides more detail in conversation or texts. With different words being used differently, one can better understand the situation at hand. And most certainly, English's unique borrowing style lends to some pretty fantastic competitions.

With Jairam climbing to victory at the 2016 National Spelling Bee, we found inspiration in writing a book to share some of our experiences. Because people have been asking us about our strategies to prepare for the spelling bee in the weeks after, we figured it would be easier to lay out our strategies on how we were able to win.

This book is meant for people of all ages, interested in the spelling bee. Students who are interested in getting involved in the spelling bee can learn about what it takes to succeed at each level of the hierarchical network. Those seeking to understand more about how the spelling bee works and how to get involved can find answers in this book. Moreover, students who seek to prepare and are already involved in the spelling bee can take advantage of the tips and strategies offered in addition to over 10,000 words from lists that we have accumulated over the years.

And lastly, we have an exciting collaboration project with the educational company Albert, where you can quiz yourself on some of the words in this book. We recognized that spellers may have trouble in quizzing themselves and assessing which words they know, so on Albert, you can go through words distributed by level of competition/difficulty (local, regional, national, and Olympic). The platform is chapterquite simple to use, and it gives instant feedback on whether you have correctly spelled the word or not. The tests are divided into groups of 25 words, similar to the format of the National Spelling Bee, so that you can develop and hone your skills on the words that you missed. Moreover, whenever you miss a word, an explanation for how to remember the word pops up, so it serves as a self-coaching tool as well. Each word has the information necessary for spellers, including parts of speech, definitions, and etymologies. The link to the website is https://www.albert.io/humanities/spell-for-success. The words have been chosen by Shreyas Parab, a former speller, and Sriram Hathwar, so our tool will hopefully be one way for you to hone your skills and learn new words.

Best of luck on this journey!

Introduction: A Word From the Champs

Interest. Talent. Practice. Challenge. These are the four most essential elements to achieving any goals in life. Having an interest in something is the first step to setting a goal. You must want to succeed. Next, you find whether or not you have a talent for what you want to pursue. You need to gauge where you are already in terms of reaching your goal so you can analyze your strengths and weaknesses. Next, you have to work hard and follow a plan. You have to set up a time regimen and practice until you succeed. And perhaps, most importantly, you have to take it as a challenge. Anyone can put in time to do something, but if you do not feel you have to do it, then you will just keep procrastinating and never actually realize your dream.

This is a simple formula to success. It works for any field or discipline. Say you want to run a marathon. You begin researching what it takes to run 26.2 miles and learn about different running techniques. Then, you see where you stand currently. You try running as far as you can in your neighborhood. You realize you can run maybe a couple miles before tiring out. Then, you develop a daily routine that you will run 2 miles everyday for a week to build up stamina. You do some training exercises to help develop muscles in your calves and legs. And finally, you say that you must be able to run 26.2 miles in one year, so you can run in the local marathon.

Similarly, this formula can be applied to doing well in spelling bees. You declare that you want to win your school spelling bee. So, you begin by learning a little bit more about what a spelling bee actually is and what you can do to start learning some words. After getting some resources to study, such as the school study guide, you look at how many words there are and try to see how well you know the words on the list initially. After gauging your talent, you begin to practice the words that you had not seen before and try to look up their origins or definitions to aid in retaining the word. Soon enough, you realize that your school bee is coming up in two weeks, so you set aside a schedule to go over all the words in the school study guide and master them within the given timeframe. When the school bee finally comes around, you may not do as well as you expected, but your performance will more or less reflect the amount of interest and practice you put into studying each day.

Studying for the spelling bee is quite a long-term goal. Learning and committing to memory all the words in the dictionary in one night (or in an entire lifetime) is simply not feasible. To study for the National Spelling Bee, you have very limited time to prepare and try to win the trophy. Hence, it is imperative that you develop a routine quickly so that you can make the most of the time you have. This book is meant to facilitate that process. In the beginning portion of this book, we have provided some context for our wins and what it took for each of us to reach our goals. By reading our stories, you can perhaps get a sense of the extensive time and effort it took for us to achieve our goal. However, we want you to do your best and try to win the spelling bee in a shorter time than it took the both of us. Because of the experience we have had in going through the dictionary, we recognized the importance of providing some words from the dictionary that we have found tricky and written down over the years. So, at the end of this book are over 10,000 challenging words that we feel could appear in the National Spelling Bee.

Chapter 1: How We Did It

At first, the spelling bee can definitely feel like a daunting task. It takes hard work, dedication, and a passion for the English language. To a newcomer, who is just curious on where to start, it can be very difficult to know where to start. There are some noteworthy resources out there which we used that will be benefical to you as well. Fortunately, more and more resources for the spelling bee are being produced, which makes it easier on you, the speller. The key is to go step by step, and one list after another. Here is a detailed explanation of how we won.

Step 1: School Spelling Bee Study List

The class spelling bee is normally composed of everyday, commonly misspelled words that your teacher wants to get ingrained in your head. Normally the study list provided is your grade's level in the school study list, which composes of 1st - 8th grade words. Still, study the school study list as well, in case your bee exhausts all your grade level equivalent words.

Step 2: myspellit.com

This study list is what is normally asked at your regional bee. It is composed of words from different languages, along with frequently misspelled words, commonly confused words, homonyms often misused, and even language patterns for each of the languages. This resource is very important because if your school competition runs out of their pronouncer guide, this is the next most likely list they will select their words from. Go through the Now You Try portion because one of the words nearly brought Jairam's downfall at the National Spelling Bee.

Step 3: How to Spell Like a Champ

This book contains quite a few good words and language rules. It teaches you those pesky homonyms and commonly misspelled words that can trip you up at any point during the competition. It has many exercises to enhance your vocabulary and spelling skills. Its wide range of difficulty of words makes for a great transition to harder words and lists to come.

Step 4: Consolidated Word List (CWL)

The *Consolidated Word List* is composed of approximately 23,500 words divided into three sections. Words appearing frequently, words appearing with moderate frequency, and words appearing infrequently. Some of the words included are extremely simple, though there are definitely still national finals' level words. It was issued from Scripps, and is a compilation of about 100 past national spelling bee words. Sadly though, more than half of the words don't have the pronunciation, definition, part of speech, language of origin, or sentence provided, but the good side is that it makes you look them up for yourself, which drills it into your head.

Step 5: Words of Wisdom

The book entitled, "Words of Wisdom" is a phenomenal study resource for the national spelling bee, which was written by a former finalist at the Scripps National Spelling Bee. Its wide variety of words is ideal for any speller who wants to succeed in the spelling bee, although it is more focused on the difficult words asked at the national spelling bee. It has different sections where he provides roots, language patterns, spelling tests etc. The whole book is claimed to have about 11,000 words.

Step 6: Dictionary

At this point, my brother and I didn't quite take the conventional route. Although there are other lists out there, like Hexco products or Rebecca's List, we felt that our previous knowledge was good enough, so that we wouldn't be overwhelmed by completing the dictionary. The way we did it was to break apart the dictionary into 14 littler books (one book for two letters, plus an additional book for the Addendum section). We took a highlighter and dove into the dictionary, word by word. It definitely wasn't an easy endeavor. After every word he crossed over, we highlighted and noted the word down either on a piece of paper, or a computer. The first time we completed the dictionary took us a couple months. It wasn't that easy. We then kept on going through the dictionary in search for new words, which we had not passed over the previous time. Consequentially, we ended up maximizing our time and got very efficient while we were diving into the dictionary. It was a percentage game, so we knew that to win you had to be confident with at least 90% of the words.

What next?

There isn't any larger list than the dictionary, so you are done with the curriculum! If you still don't know what to do even after you've mastered around 90% of those words, then keep improving. It will only increase your chances of doing well in the competition, and it doesn't hurt, so why not? When my brother, Sriram, won the national competition, he knew about 97% of all those words. When I won, I knew around 92% of those words. So if you are in that range, you definitely have a good chance for bringing home the trophy.

By this time, you should feel very confident with what you have studied. When you walk into the ballroom of the national competition, you should know that you've done whatever you could, and the rest was destiny. A large portion of the spelling bee competition has to do with luck, and if they wanted the truly best speller, they could just conduct a 100 word written test composed of the most difficult words in the dictionary to find the winner, but that isn't the way how the spelling bee's designed. There are bound to be upsets, but it is how you deal with them that makes you the real champion. So even if you don't win in the end, you should feel tremendously proud of yourself. Why? The reason being is that you can have the distinct honor of saying that any word that could be asked at any point during the competition, you had studied before.

Chapter 2: My Spelling Bee Experience

Written By: Sriram Hathwar

Early Years

As the son of two Indian immigrant parents, I grew up learning my family's tongue, Kannada, as my primary language. With relatively little exposure to the rest of the world, I only knew to communicate with my parents in Kannada, as that was all I needed. From when I spoke my first words to about the age of three, I only knew Kannada. So, when my parents first took me to daycare, I was a bit behind, surrounded by kids who only knew how to speak English. At the age of three, I still had the ability to pick up a language rather quickly. Hence, I did. So, soon enough I was learning from my parents and daycare teachers. Seeing any new word would be an opportunity for me to write down words in my composition book. "Astronaut." "Hippopotamus." I was increasing my vocabulary conversation-by-conversation, sentence-by-sentence, word-by-word. Soon, I would serve as a reference guide in my class for how to spell words.

Developing Interest

When I moved on from daycare to kindergarten at the Chemung Valley Montessori School, I would continue to have a passion for learning, especially English. While I enjoyed playing with Legos or kicking a ball as much as the next guy at a young age, I also had a great passion for English. Interested in learning new words and quirky English spellings, I would continue to write down any unique words. My love for words would continue well into first grade. I would ace every word on my weekly spelling tests. Because of the individualized and self-paced Montessori curriculum, my teachers always wanted to make sure I was being challenged. With much free time after completing all my assignments, my teachers would give me additional spelling tests. At one time, I had 100 word list spelling test in one sitting! To this day, I still remember the two words I missed- **genealogy** and **gymnast**. It's funny how even after all these years, spellers still remember the words they get wrong.

With some family friends recognizing my love and interest for words, they invited me to watch their daughter compete in the regional spelling bee. At that time, it was sponsored by our local newspaper, *The Leader*. On the first Thursday night of March 2007, the bee was conducted in a nearby high school auditorium, with about 20 spellers. There were two representatives from each school participating, my friend being one of the Montessori delegates. Sitting with my mom and my friend's mom, I would try to write down every word just for fun, to challenge myself. Kids would approach the microphone, trying to get their word correct each time. My friend was successful in this, as she kept advancing to the next round after spelling each of her given words correctly. She ended up placing third after misspelling **kahuna**. The champion was another Montessorian student, who won on **teriyaki**. After he won, he was given a large dictionary onstage. The announcers then explained that he had earned a ticket to the Scripps National Spelling Bee in Washington D.C. in May that year. Following up on that, impressed with the nature of the spelling bee, I told my mother that I would like to participate next year…

2007-2008

Translating Interest into Results

When I entered the second grade, my mother had approached the upper elementary English teacher regarding whether I could join the mock competitions conducted among the 4th, 5th, and 6th graders. In the 3 months leading up to the school spelling bee, we had little weekly spelling bees conducted rather informally with about 10-15 students per session. Every Tuesday afternoon, I would head up to the upper elementary classroom with two third graders who were also interested. In any given week, we would cover words solely from one language in the *SpellIt!* curriculum. One week, we had a spelling bee, where the words asked were only of Arabic derivation. The next week, a Latin one. Then a French one, and so on until we covered just about every language. So, in the beginning bees, I would just observe my older peers spell words like **azure** and **accommodate**. Interested, after a few sessions, I had asked my teacher whether I could actually participate. She was very supportive of me, so I started to study the assigned word lists and compete each week. My mother was the entire reason that I was able to do so well. She would quiz me on the words that would be asked the following week to make sure I knew the words in and out. The first week when I attended, I spelled every one of my words correctly. Many of my older friends were quite impressed with my skills. It was through these little mock competitions that I was able to expose myself to enough words and develop enough confidence in myself to give a try for my school bee.

On one February morning in 2008, all the 10 or so students participating in the school competition were seated onstage in the auditorium. Even though the pronouncer was the English teacher, with whose voice we had gotten familiar, everyone was still quite anxious and shaking in their seats. Of course, their nerves were not calmed by the fact that the lower grades came into watch the competition as well. So, for my older friends, not only did they have to worry about spelling their words correctly, but also keeping cool in front of an audience. However, as a second grader, I was the youngest one competing, so I was not as fazed by the spotlight as some of my other fellow spellers. My friends were watching me, cheering me on. My mom told me that she would take off time from work and come to watch me compete. Before the competition started, she came to wish me good luck. When all of us got up onstage, in accordance with spelling bee etiquette, we were all silent as each speller approached the microphone. I got up to spell my word. Without a doubt, I rattled off the letters, throwing all "unnecessary" information to the wind. My logic was, "Why waste any time?" As the competition progressed, more and more of my friends misspelled, ending their chances of winning the school bee. After a few rounds of correctly spelling my words, I had come to the top two with another 6th grader. At this point, I was elated with the results, for I knew that I had earned a spot to the regional competition. Beaming with joy, I continued to ace my words. After about 45 minutes from the inception of the bee, my fellow speller missed his word **semolina**. This meant that I had the opportunity to become champion! I was given my potential winning word. Hearing **coati**, I was **exuberant**. Without asking for any information, I enunciated each letter. It was this word that made me win my first spelling bee!

With many cheers and celebrations from my friends and parents, I had advanced to the regional competition, which was to be held in two weeks' time.

My teacher informed me that the curriculum for the school competition, *SpellIt!*, was the same for the regional bee, so if I learned all the 1000 or so odd words, I should be fine. My mother continued to quiz me daily for about 30 minutes to ensure I knew every word. **Commensurate**. **Philhellenism**. **Schadenfreude**. These were just some of the words I had to master. Sure, they might not seem too difficult now, but in the second grade, it was quite a feat. What I had also come to realize while studying this list in its entirety is that all the words in the 2007 regional bee were from this list. **Odori**. **Kahuna**. Even **teriyaki** was in this list. I began to wonder what was so difficult about remembering 1000 words. I had been writing words down in my composition book, and they had not seemed difficult to memorize. The days before the bee, I would not miss a single word when my mom quizzed me.

The day of the regional spelling bee came. Again, the competition was held on the first Thursday night of March, as it always is in our area. It was finally my turn to sit onstage where my friend was, in the previous year. As we drove to the high school where the bee was to be held, my parents tried to calm me down. Not because I was nervous, but because I was too excited. My father told me to keep cool and accept whatever results may come, while my mother told me to focus on the words while I was onstage. My 5-year old brother, Jairam, wished me good luck. When we reached the site, I met my teacher and she would sit next to my parents, rooting for me to win. Also sitting next to my parents were my best friend and his family. I was quite happy that I had received so much support not only from my family, but also from my friends and teachers. I looked through the competition guide before the bee began, and I had seen a familiar name. A representative from another school was last year's champion. I was about to spell onstage with a National Spelling Bee participant!

As the announcer declared that all spellers should report onstage, I quickly hugged my parents and brother. I then walked up onstage and sat in my respective seat, wearing my placard. I was one of 20 spellers who had a shot at winning. To an extent, it felt as if I was representing Montessori as well. Before the competition began, the pronouncer tried to calm us down by asking us to take deep breaths and relax. He proceeded to read the rules thoroughly, explaining the "speller's rights"- how we could ask for the sentence, etymology, definition, part of speech, and alternate pronunciations. But finally, the moment all families in the room were waiting for, the start of the bee, had come. The room was silent, and the spotlight was on us, the spellers. The first speller was asked to come to the microphone. With each speller, everyone was in awe as to whether he or she would correctly spell the word. This was also the first spelling bee my whole family had actually seen me compete in, so they were quite intrigued as well. After spellers came and went, it was soon my turn to approach the microphone.

When I went up, I realized how bright the lights were, and how I could not really see anyone in the audience, just the pronouncer and panel of judges in front of me. Recalling how much I prepared, I felt ready. I was given the word **quiver**. Without hesitation, I recalled the letters within 30 seconds. I was shocked at how easy my spelling bee experience had been so far. As the rounds continued, I kept knocking off each letter of a word, but sadly some of my other spellers did not. As the night grew, I had seen myself go from the top 10 to the top 5 to the top 3. It was me, the other Montessorian kid, and, of course, last year's champ.

Once my peer was eliminated on another *SpellIt!* word, it was just me, a 2nd grader; and last year's winner, a 6th grader. After a couple rounds of us acing our words, the pronouncer declared that we would now be entering the portion of the bee with words outside the provided list. Later I would learn that this was the first time this would happen since the inception of the regional competition in our area in 2003. **Tarmac. Ambitious. Pamphlet.** Retrospectively, these words seem very easy and in fact quite hackneyed in daily conversation, yet both of us just kept missing our words. I had never seen any of these words used before, even with the number of books I had read. At the time, it's a bit sad to say that both of us had only memorized the words, not realizing how to apply rules to given words. Right or wrong, we shared a strategy of spitting out the sequence that first came into our minds, throwing asking questions to the wind. I would use an 'f' in Greek words, which almost always use the "ph" letter combination to represent that sound, or he would not recognize common Greek roots. We both missed our (simple!) words for four straight rounds before the pronouncer decided to return to the *SpellIt!* lists. When we returned to these words, both of us annihilated our words. No-brainers like **glockenspiel**, **Bildungsroman**, and **dungaree**, we just knocked out of the park. After four round of 'insider' words, the pronouncer returned to the off-list words. And we returned to our incorrect spelling bout. **Metabolism. Enclave. Conspiracy.** He and I were missing sitters. It not only tired us out, but also the audience, for the competition had gone on for over 90 minutes, painstakingly long considering there were only 20 spellers initially.

However, after my fellow speller had misspelled **krypton**, I had finally received a word I knew. In math class, we were learning more about different shapes and properties, so I had come across the word **parallelogram** in school. It is a fun word to spell, keeping in mind the correct sequence of 'l's in the word. Once I punctuated each of the 13 letters of the word in a matter of seconds, I headed back to my seat. At this point, the pronouncer called me back up to the microphone, informing me that were I to spell my next word correctly, I would be declared champion. Standing on a stool at the podium, I reached to bend the microphone down to my level. I heard the word, but had never seen the word before. **Impervious.** My thought process was very simple: just spell it as it sounds. So, I did. **I-M-P-E-R-V-I-O-U-S.** The judge indicated to me that I was correct, and the crowd jumped to their feet to applaud me. During the standing ovation, I nonchalantly walked down the stairs to be greeted by a bear hug by my mom. I was congratulated by my friends briefly before being asked to return onstage. When the announcer gave me my prize of the official Merriam Webster Unabridged dictionary, he joked whether I could even hold it, because it is one huge resource. Much more seriously, he proclaimed that I would be heading to the National Spelling Bee in the last week of May!

When I got offstage, my family and I were interviewed by a reporter about my performance and my thoughts on spelling. I was obviously stoked to go to Washington D.C., but at the same time, I did not quite grasp the gravity of the situation. I was the youngest person ever to qualify for the National Spelling Bee at the time, which even the reporter remarked. I was just quite happy that I had won. So, frenetically, I answered the remaining questions so that I could meet my friend before he left. He expressed how proud he was and even gave me a nice book. When we drove home, my family began to discuss how to go about preparing for the national spelling bee. But the coolest part of it all was being in the local newspaper headline the next day.

For the National Spelling Bee, there were no words that were given in 2008. Thus, I needed a new approach to prepare for the competition instead of just memorizing a set list of words. My mother found a great resource, *How to Spell Like a Champ*, online, which we purchased soon after my win. When we got the book, we saw that it included many words, language patterns, roots, exercises, and even past spellers' experiences. It was a great resource to get me exposed to more spelling patterns. For instance, I learned that the "sch-" letter combination is used for the \sh\ sound in German, and that the Greek root "crypt-" means hidden. Quite honestly, we had very limited background in how to train for the spelling bee at the national level, for my parents and teachers had never competed or knew of additional resources. What is quite unorthodox is my mom was never involved with spelling bees, but she became my coach. So, my mother and I edged through every single lesson the book had to offer, learning more words related to sports, medicine, music, etc. In the meantime, I was busy with other activities, as I was a kid still, so we had to juggle in some time for spelling in between piano lessons, basketball games, baseball matches, swimming lessons, and just spending downtime with my family. So, we did the best we could to prepare for the National Spelling Bee in May, which was coming up soon.

In the couple of weeks leading up to the competition, both my grandmothers had flown in from India. So, we were all healthy and prepared to travel to Washington D.C., with my two grandmothers! I was excited that they could come and watch me spell, and my cousin from Virginia called and told us that he would like to come and watch as well! Even early on, spelling became somewhat of a family tradition, involving everyone.

Because I was the youngest speller of the time, it became a little bit of a sensation in the media that I was able to compete. We got phone calls to come to ABC and Fox studios for live interviews. But once again, while I was excited, I did not take them quite seriously, for I was still just an 8-year old. So, we drove down 6 hours south to stay at the Grand Hyatt in DC the week of Memorial Day. Not exactly a story typical of an 8-year old. The Sunday when we arrived, we arrived in a huge hotel in downtown D.C., with several floors and a cool water fountain in the mezzanine. We headed to the registration table and several nice staff welcomed us to the National Spelling Bee. I got a "Beekeeper," a book containing bios of every single speller. With this, we were supposed to collect signatures of all the other spellers, though with 280+ spellers, that was quite an onerous task. These goodies made me even more excited for the week.

That Monday, there was a Bee barbecue in a park in Virginia. Almost every speller tries to attend, so waiting in lines for the buses that morning, I was able to see some of my fellow orthographers and try to collect their signatures. I got to meet many new spellers, and get new contacts. At the spelling bee, I learned very early on the sense of camaraderie and sportsmanship that comes with the competition. Everyone is each other's friend and everyone is bound by a shared interest in the English language. It is inspirational that everyone, regardless of age or size, is competitive enough to vie for the trophy, yet all are friendly and cheer others on.

After tons of fun activities at the park, including inflatables, soccer, volleyball, and eating with some of my new friends, I had some interviews to attend later that day. My mother and I were invited to the studios where we were asked questions such as "How did you get started?" and "What is your favorite word?" At that time, I was infatuated with the word **archaeopteryx**, because of its 'ae-' letter combination and its '-yx' ending, and also because I really liked dinosaurs, so I went ahead with that Greek word.

That Tuesday, there was a computerized test with 50 words, though only 25 were to actually be used in determining a preliminary Round 1 score. This was to produce the effect of randomness, so nobody could tell another speller what some of the words are before their allotted time slot. When taking my test, I felt much more challenged than in any other competition. Setting aside the fact that it was a national competition, I had expected that with my preparation, I would do rather well. I guess this spoke to how high my expectations were. Some words were as simple as **mustard** and **altogether**, but others were as obscure as **Appaloosa** and **cacoethes**. Coming out of the room to greet my anxious parents, I told them I felt I fared decently. Encouraging and supportive of me, my parents told me they were proud that I had come this far and to just have fun with it all. Later that day, we decided to have some fun and visit the Smithsonian Air and Space Museum. Riding on simulators and seeing space exhibits were enough to distract me.

In the typical bee week, the Wednesday is when the oral preliminary portion is given. Every speller was given one word onstage to make the trips of spellers, who had come from places as far as Japan or New Zealand, well worth it. I was to spell a little later in the second portion of the group. When I entered the ballroom for the first time, I felt I was entering a game show. Large lights, cameras, and showy stages deviated from my perceived image of the spelling bee. However, the preliminary rounds were not aired on television, so many spellers could breathe easier. Exposed at a young age to these media, I would not really feel nervous approaching the microphone even in my later years. Before I was called in with the second group to come onstage, I met my 2-year old cousin, Srivarun, and family. With a quick hug from all my extended family members, I was ready to hit the stage.

The words given in Round 2 were not from any provided list, so I had to rely on my 'new' strategy of asking for the etymology and definition before spelling the word. I put 'new' in quotation marks because this did not really influence my spelling much, for I would go with the first sequence of letters that came to my head regardless of what Dr. Bailly, the pronouncer, would say. So, it was my turn. As one of the 15 or so New Yorkers in the bee, I was alphabetically in the middle of the geographically ordered spellers, at number 165. I walked to the microphone and pulled it down a good 2 feet to adjust to my mouth, which elicited a few laughs from the audience. My first word on the national scene was **elicitation**. Using my new trick, I asked for the etymology (Latin) and the definition (provocation of a feeling or sentiment). I then spelled each letter and heard, "That is correct." Unfazed, I returned to my seat as if nothing had happened. I sat in my seat until the last speller went on, after which I met my parents.

My dad had received my written score. I missed quite a few words, which was expected. But in the moments when the pronouncer stated the 90 names of spellers who would advance to Thursday's quarterfinals and did not hear my name, I was quite disappointed. I let out a decent cry as my dad lifted me up to his shoulders. Upon leaving the ballroom, our local news station WENY conducted an interview. Though I was quite dejected, I was rejuvenated and cheered up by the reporter. In a few minutes, I was climbing up and down the escalators as a giddy child, almost forgetting I had even come to compete in the spelling bee.

This would not be the end of my spelling experience though. We watched some of the rounds from our hotel room TV the next day, for those 90 spellers were on ESPN. **Aulos**. **Rhumb**. **Rankine**. These words are short, but difficult. I got really excited for these spellers. We continued to watch the semifinals the next day. After a few rounds, 12 finalists were determined, who would be spelling live in prime time on ABC. This was incredible that I could see so many great spellers onstage. One by one, these great spellers rattled off extremely tough words, including **nacarat**, **taleggio**, and the infamous **numnah**. As the competition dwindled down, there were just two spellers left, a 7th grader, Siddharth Chand, and an 8th grader, Sameer Mishra. **Esclandre**. **Introuvable**. **Kulturkampf**. These were cakewalks for them. But finally, Siddharth missed **prosopopoeia**, leaving Sameer to his victory word **guerdon**. With him correctly recalling this sequence, he had secured himself the title of champion. We had seen someone win in real life! This is what would inspire me to continue improving my spelling skills so that one day I could lift the trophy for myself.

After meeting up with some families of the top spellers, we learned about some resources that would serve to ameliorate my preparation for next year. They told us about the *Consolidated Word List*, a study tool containing circa 25,000 words which serves as the bread and butter for some of the more preliminary rounds of the spelling bee. Additionally, they referred us to *Prefixes and* Suffixes, which is conducive to spelling many Latin and Greek words of which one may not have heard. Most valuably, they brought to our attention an additional spelling bee circuit organized by the North South Foundation in which I could potentially compete. We were eager to get on board, and we decided to give it a try in the upcoming year. By then, we had some more guidance in how to approach preparing for spelling bees, for which we were truly grateful. Though that was the end of my first bee week, it was not the end of my spelling ambitions.

In fact, later that summer I was invited to compete in this brand new event called the South Asian Spelling Bee. The founder of the competition, Rahul Walia, had asked me to come and participate in the New York City regionals. Seeing this as an opportunity to expand my exposure to words and the spelling bee format, my parents took me to the competition site one Saturday in July. Here I met a good friend, Arvind Mahankali, who would go on to win the National Spelling Bee in 2013. Through this extra circuit, I could see more friends and learn more words to help me prepare. In this incipient bee, I would end up placing eighth after misspelling the fairly common word, **appraise**. It was rather humbling to know that I still had much to learn. So this only inspired and motivated me to pursue a better finish the following year.

2008-2009

Going into third grade, I began to study more systematically. Rather than approaching the dictionary head-on, I had more of a track to follow. To study for next year, we had printed out the *Consolidated Word List*, or CWL, to prepare. The 25,000 words are distributed unevenly among three lists categorized by purported frequency of appearance in the National Spelling Bee: Frequently Asked, Moderate Frequency, and Infrequently Asked. These three lists would serve as the de facto curriculum for the preliminary and semifinal portions, though it was certainly no guarantee all words would be derived from here. Regarding these words as bread and butter for succeeding at the national scene, we made it a goal to master all words in these lists.

As these words took up roughly 800 pages on paper, we created binders dividing the lists into portable study tools. One thing that is quite interesting with the CWL is that only about 40% of the words actually have definition, etymologies, and sentences provided. So, for the rest of the words, my mom was awesome enough to go through the CD provided with the large dictionary that I had won. Over a span of weeks, my mom would continue to write in the definitions for these words. In the meantime, I would try to study the pages she had already finished. Some of the words were quite easy, and I was surprised that they would even be included in the lists. I saw *hand* and *banana* in there, but they were scattered among words like **nastaliq** and **Rabelaisian**. Certainly, I had a full plate ahead of me.

Throughout the school year, I was completing all my assignments in school, so I still had much time at home to study. During this time, I would try to study 10 pages every day so that my mom could quiz me on them. Some days, when the words were easier, I would do much better, while other days, I had a real tough time. My mom would mark, either by underlining or circling, the words that I would miss everyday so that I could review them afterwards. This preparation took about 30-45 minutes every day. Gradually, I was becoming better and better with these words. The first time when we finished Frequently Asked Words, which was a whopping 341 pages, it seemed as if we had climbed up Everest. It took a long time, and **piecemeal**, we were able to cover the curriculum. Covering the other two lists felt more **Augean**, for the words were less relatable and there were many more words. Despite being shorter, there were many more definitions, languages, and sentences lacking, which made it harder for me to remember the words.

As the year progressed, I became much better with the words and began to get a handle over CWL. It took us a decent 4-5 months to cover all the words once. Some days, it would feel as though we were drudging through, because my attention was somewhere else. But many other days, I would do well and be quizzed quickly. My mom was so helpful to me being able to remember these words, for she would provide rationales and tips for me to remember the words.she would do so by helping me link it with another word,I knew.

Sooner or later, bee season was getting into gear again, so I would once again travel to the upper elementary classroom for the mock sessions. With some experience, I began to feel more familiar with the words. I had already memorized all the words in *SpellIt!* the previous year, but it was always good practice to follow spelling bee etiquette. Again, each week leading up to the school bee, 10-15 spellers would come and spell words from a certain language.

At home, my mother and I continued to go over the CWL. In addition, we went through *Prefixes and Suffixes* rather quickly, so I could learn some basic roots and combining forms for some of the compound Greek and Latin words. Because I was learning these, my strategy began to change. I would come to realize the importance of asking for the definition and the language to actually figure out some clues to help me spell the word. From this point on, I would actually listen to what the pronouncer was saying to hear any buzzwords for roots or language patterns. After finishing this compilation of all roots in the dictionary once, we decided to go through the CWL again, which we amped up to studying 20 pages a day. Though I was improving, I was still missing some of the same words. Practice, practice, practice. This was my mantra well into the spelling bee season. This time when the school bee came around, I was already somewhat of a veteran, so I was less concerned with the format and what words would be asked. I would go on to win my school spelling bee with relative ease, placing myself once again in a position to compete in the regionals. This time around, I was certainly more about business, as I had clear goals of making it to the national competition and passing the preliminary rounds.

The two weeks before the regional bee were a bit more of cram time. Each night, we would try to get through even more words in the CWL so that in the chance that we get more off-list words, I would be prepared. After all, the list advised by the National Spelling Bee contained a decent number of the words in the preliminary and semifinal rounds, so perhaps some of the easier one could appear in the regional competition. The day before the regional bee in March, I had about a 70% mastery rate over the words in CWL, which was rather decent considering I had only started a few months before. We went over *SpellIt!* one last time before the bee.

When the competition came, again, everything seemed quite trite. I had done this before, but my parents kept reminding me to keep focus on my words, for one incorrect letter anywhere in the competition could lose my chance to compete in Scripps again. My teachers and some of my mom's friends came to watch again in the audience. After the pronouncer read all the rules, we jumped into *SpellIt!* These rounds became quite boring, for I had studied these words so many times. I was beginning to wonder why so many people were still missing given words. Even my other Montessorian got out! It seemed that more people were casually competing than actually seeking to go to nationals. I had realized how important spelling had become in my life. Soon, there were just two spellers left: me and an 8th grader.

Once again, we went outside the list. However, this time, I had much more experience, so I was getting some of the words correctly. In fact, some of the words actually were from the CWL! It was certainly worth it to have gone through that list before regionals. Notwithstanding, I still managed to miss a few words. But once again, my fellow speller did as well. Interestingly enough, in the rounds where I managed to spell my word correctly, she would, too. And when I misspelled, she would, too. This would become a common theme in my spelling career.

Eventually, after five or so rounds of 'battling' between the two of us, she misspelled **resin**. I had the opportunity to win and once again advance to Scripps. Adjusting the microphone, I articulated each letter of my championship word **binoculars**, (quite unrepresentative of the difficulty of the bee), to victory. Once again, the crowd cheered after a long competition and I got a new dictionary. The newspaper interview was easier, with it not being my first rodeo.

So, my parents took off work to go to D.C. again for Bee Week in May. I was excited to meet my friends again and make new ones. But I was also more focused on improving my ranking and getting as far as I could. Preparing for the national competition this time was a little different. My mom would quiz me on words in the CWL and train me with prefixes and suffixes. In these couple months, I was getting much better, and felt much more prepared to get farther into the competition this year. In mid-April, Scripps had announced some new changes…

In order to appeal more to viewers and provide airtime for the best of the best spellers, Scripps announced that there would no longer be a quarterfinal portion in the spelling bee. This meant that from the preliminary rounds, only 50 spellers would advance to the semifinals. This certainly raised the bar for who would qualify. Additionally, Round 3 became a preliminary round with a list of 400 provided words, with Round 2 becoming a round for *SpellIt!* words. This was no problem, for learning it made the oral rounds much easier. Quite less consequentially, ABC had dropped primetime status for the spelling bee, so ESPN was happy to fill in this spot. Though these were quite important changes, it did not really affect our study routine much.

When we drove down to D.C. this year, I got my new Beekeeper to get signatures of other spellers. This time around, I wanted to keep in touch with spellers, so when meeting new spellers, I would write down my email. I would continue this even into eighth grade, and I still manage to talk with spellers from Texas, California, and all around the world to this day.

Once again, the Monday was a fun barbecue day. We had typical (vegetarian) barbecue food on Memorial Day (basically salad and veggie burgers). The main event was that Tuesday, the computerized written test, so while I was having much fun at the barbecue, I began to pay attention to that when we returned to the hotel room. The next day, I entered the room and sat down to listen to each word, before typing in what I felt the right response was. I was so ecstatic that **civitas**, a Latin word for a city-state, was included, for I had studied that word in the CWL, but more because I liked the way it was pronounced ("kiwi-toss"). I felt pretty confident about my performance, but knew I missed a couple. We were hoping that those were just the dummy words that would not make the actual 25. That Wednesday, a long day, I aced both of my words, as they were from a provided source. So, when they were announcing the semifinalists in the ballroom upon the completion of the competition, we were all keen on seeing who would qualify to the televised semifinal rounds the next day. One by one, Mrs. Paige Kimble, announced names of advancing spellers in a random order. With 50 spellers advancing, we were quite nervous. Number 48 was called up. The number 49. So, there was only one spot left. And at last, I heard my name, "From Painted Post, New York, speller 169, with a perfect score, Sriram Hathwar!" This was too amazing, not only had I advanced, but I also managed to get a perfect score of 31/31 in the preliminaries! The experience felt all too surreal. Later that night, all the semifinalists' families were invited for a special dinner to be debriefed of what to expect the next day. Bee officials explained to us that we would be on television, but to just focus on the word Dr. Bailly was to give us. After meeting some of the others who had advanced, I had an ESPN interview which would be used as a bio clip to show during the competition. We then headed back to our hotel room, though none of us really got much sleep.

When we entered the ballroom the next day, we saw it in a whole new way. There were large swiveling cameras and more glitzy lights. Cameras were stationed in the back. Head judge Mary Brooks would ring the bell if anyone misspelled. A champion would be declared on that red stage that night. So, the competition was to start and once again, my extended family from Virginia had come to watch. My cousin, still in his stroller, wished me luck along with my uncle and aunt. All my relatives got to sit in a special premier location with all other semifinalists' parents so that ESPN could show my parents when spelling. Soon, it was time to begin. I hugged my parents and relatives, keeping my mother's counsel of focusing on the word in mind. As 10:00 approached, the ballroom was almost filled, as many non-advancing spellers sat to watch.

As the announcer called the first speller up to microphone, the whole room fell silent as nerves were getting the best of many. In fact, the parents were more nervous for their children than the spellers, as was the case with my parents. Lights. Camera. Action. Round 4 was officially broadcast live on ESPN, so people all around the world could see us spell. As a New Yorker, I was in the middle of the batch, and with commercial breaks and all, I had to sit for a grueling amount of time; I was fidgeting the entire time. Each speller came up to the stage to be greeted by a straight-faced Dr. Bailly and an earnest Ms. Brooks as well as a 2-minute timer. The other New Yorker from a little more upstate, who was the speller right before me, got up to spell. **Triquetra**. After asking roots, he gave the unknown word a shot. Ding. I was up next.

After an excruciatingly long commercial break, my ESPN interview in the typical egg chair aired before the TV guy called me up to my turn. The lights were on me, first time spelling on television. The word is **fodient**. A relatively simple word from Latin, meaning 'digging, especially of animals.' Trying to buy more time to think, I ask for these specific clues, but to not much avail. In my head, I had the beginning down. It was just between –ant or –ent ending. I ended up going with the first and hearing the bell as well. Escorted off stage, I was consoled by my mom briefly on a couch. ESPN interviewer Erin Andrews came over to me and asked whether I would do an interview. I was munching on a cookie, but she was quite eager to conduct live at that time, so I was answering the questions while eating a cookie, eliciting many a laughs from the audience. Later, I would also learn that 'fodient' was in Moderate Frequency, so we knew that I still had to master CWL more. Watching the rest of the competition, we saw Kavya Shivashankar climb to her well-deserved victory on **Laodicean**, with her proud dad/coach, mom, and younger sister, Vanya, who would claim the title for herself one day, all rejoicing.

Though done with Scripps that year, I still had opportunities to do well in other circuits. Having heard of the North South Foundation spelling bee I had gone through the regional competition and advanced to nationals at University of Maryland. I competed in the junior spelling bee (grades 1-3). After missing words on the written test such as **diminutive** and **aspersions**, I had advanced to the final 12, the oral portion. Here, I emerged victorious on the word **shrewdness**. It was one of my first major victories. I also competed in the South Asian Spelling Bee again, where I placed 2nd in my regionals on **epigonism** to advance to the finals, with 20 other spellers from around the country. I ended up missing early on **cornichon** after nailing a few words, but really, it was here where we saw the potential of Arvind Mahankali, for in fourth grade, he was able to place third! Motivated to perform better, I studied harder the next year.

2009-2010

Having gotten past the semifinals the previous year, I made it my goal to advance to the finals in fourth grade. This year, studying was more focused on mastering the words in CWL by reviewing the list more times. I had inspiration from a famous speller who was able to go through all 25,000 words within a span of 5 days, so I began studying more words at a time, so my mom could quiz me the entire CWL quicker. Studying throughout the summer and well into the start of school, we got through more words at a quicker pace. This year, I had entered upper elementary. Soon enough, time flew by to December, the start of mock bee season. Comfortable with all *SpellIt!* languages, these tended to be more of a breeze. Week after week, my mom and I would go through the CWL at home. But, once again, we had to build through the basics, going through the school competitions.

One February morning, we had our school bee. A seasoned veteran, I was able to get through each round with ease, though some of my friends misspelled words early on. It came down to me and a sixth grader. We both advanced to the regional competition. It seemed liked I was well on my way to pursue my ambitions. Studying each day before the competition, I felt ready for another trip to DC. I was in for a rude awakening that first Thursday night of March.

The competition had started normally with a boring reading off of the rules and 'speller's rights.' Most of the spellers missed words from the (given!) *SpellIt!* words. It was left to just me and the other Montessorian girl. For the third straight year, we had exhausted the *SpellIt!* curriculum to go over into the off-list words. **Opal. Peevish. Escrow**. Eventually, after rounds of going after our words, I was asked to spell **esotericism**. In my studies of CWL, I had come across the word **esoteric**, but had not really learned its definition that well. So, when I was confronted with this word, I stood in place in shock. I had quite a bad habit of freezing when I did not know the word. Not ringing any bells onstage, I entered panic mode and just threw out a sound-it-out spelling. Nope. I was completely off. I sat back down, hoping to be redeemed as I had in previous years. However, she was asked to spell **Dickensian**, and she got it right to win. I would not advance to Scripps that year. My heart sunk as I was in disbelief. I would not understand the consequences until I emailed my friends. They all sealed their spots at nationals, but I was left out. But, when my mom asked whether I was still interested in spelling bees, I resolutely responded yes. I loved spelling too much to be disheartened by a loss.

The next couple months were difficult because I had no real motivation to study as hard, for I was not competing in Scripps. I took this time quite lightly, just casually going through material. As Bee week came that May, I realized that all my speller friends were in DC, while I was in Painted Post still. I would miss out on the barbecue, the Beekeepers, and of course the competition. I took the written test online and found out I got a score that would have advanced me to the semifinals, which bummed me out. But,we tuned in to watch the spelling bee live on TV. My mom and I would record each new word and I would remember what each person got and missed. This would help me make associations to spell the word correctly. That year, Arvind Mahankali had advanced and nailed tough words, like **phenazocine**. We watched the killer round 6, in which 11 of the 19 spellers would end up missing.

The finals were one of the quickest in Scripps history. Typically, the event is booked for 2 hours and goes over the allotted time slot by about 30 minutes, but because Round 6 finished with only 8 spellers remaining, the competition went along quite quickly. Words like **conchyliated**, **juvia**, **confiserie**, and **ochidore** were indicative of the level of difficulty for the rounds, so many spellers misspelled quickly. Four people ended up tying for second place, with Anamika Veeramani triumphing to become the 2010 champion on **stromuhr**, a CWL word. I was extremely happy for her, as she had gotten a perfect score that year and placed in the finals the previous year after missing **fackeltanz**. However, there was a part of me that wished that I was there. It just was not my year yet.

That summer, I started to take more seriously learning dictionary words. My dad had the dictionary broken down into 13 separate sections, so that studying the curriculum would not be as tough. Taking each one of these booklets, I would highlight any interesting new words. And then, I would type these really cool words into my own lists, some of which are included in the back of this book. I found these bizarre words and found a new favorite word practically every day. After accumulating so many words, I became a much more serious speller.

The minor league spelling bees were starting up again. This time, the North South Foundation bee was held in Rowan University in New Jersey. What is nice about the NSF competition is that we could get campus tours and college visits at a young age. I ended up meeting many of my friends here, and this time I was competing against them in the senior spelling bee (grades 4-8), so younger kids had a bit of a disadvantage. After doing well on the written test, I advanced to the final rounds, the only 4th grader in the mix. The words in this portion were quite tough, to the extent that 8 of the 9 spellers, including me, all misspelled in one round, but the remaining speller missed his word, **Iturean**. So, we were all reinstated. **Mechlin**. **Latinxua**. **Carnacian**. **Oidiomycosis**. **Degu**. After getting mixed up with the word **bifara**, I misspelled **Biafran** to place fourth. It was a rather commendable performance. Sukanya Roy, who would win the 2011 Scripps Bee, ended up taking the trophy.

In the South Asian Spelling Bee, I had done much better. Because this bee, broadcast on Sony television, notoriously uses the most arcane words in the dictionary, highlighting tough words really came in handy. **Pelamyd**. This one word stunned the audience. When I got this word right, I felt quite happy, for I had written the word down in one of my lists. I kept advancing, doing much better than I had the previous year. I ended up missing **justaucorps** to place third. A great close to the summer, I was determined to get redemption at Scripps the next year.

2010-2011

With rejuvenated confidence and motivation, I began studying much harder throughout the year, and trying to go through more dictionary words. Learning prefixes and suffixes, and trying to learn more about roots was really my main goal so that I would not be as frightened by words that I had never seen before. I tried to go through more words in the dictionary and tried to make more lists of interesting new words. Still focused on CWL, I wanted to get better at the dictionary. So, my mother and I went through the arduous task of quizzing in the dictionary.

After the minor league circuits in August, my mom began to quiz me about 30 pages every day of the dictionary words; when I came home from school, I would briefly study the words that I had highlighted and look for new words as well. Some days, when my mom quizzed me, I did well, but other days, when there were many more words, it got a bit tougher. In life and in spelling bees, it is important to accept both of these **vicissitudes** equally and learn from your mistakes. So, my mom would highlight again any words that I had missed. This was a painstaking procedure. But after a few months we had finally finished, just in time for the school bee.

Going through the school bee was no big deal, though I had learned from the previous year not to take anything for granted. I had gone through the mock competitions, keeping in mind that the dictionary is my primary resource. So, I won my school bee, and then advanced to the regional competition again. Preparing for it harder than last year, I hoped to regain my spot at Scripps. The number of competitors steadily grew to about 30 spellers that year, so it was great to see more and more people get involved in the bee. Going through all the normal rounds, it had come down to me and last year's champ, so we had to go out of the provided words. We both nailed our words, until she had missed one. Thus, it was my chance to win. **Deceptious**. Well, quite straightforward, but I mixed it up with **discept**, a word in CWL meaning to debate, even though the definitions were not even related. So, both reinstated, we went through a couple more rounds, until she missed **brontophobia**. I got up to spell my winning word **vituperative**. Correct! Elated that I could go back to Scripps, the reporter captured my enthusiasm in the piece the next day.

More and more, we focused on roots and combining forms in the months leading up to the bee. Going through these words would really help me get farther in to the finals, which was my goal for that year. This year, Scripps slightly changed its format again. The written round would consist of 25 words, and all of them would count. All spellers would take the test by hand at once in the ballroom, so no one could tell another the words. This did not change my mentality, for I treated every word as my championship word, so going into Scripps, I was more careful. The venue was also changed to Gaylord Convention Center in National Harbor.

After a fun Monday barbecue, it was time to get serious on Tuesday, the day of the written test. Dr. Jacques Bailly stood in front of a room full of spellers and anxious parents, the same format used currently for Round 1. He pronounced each word, and we had a minute or so to write down each word after he gave the information. Immediately after, all the correct spellings were displayed on the board, so I knew I missed **jiggety** and **monodomous**. After talking with a couple friends, I saw they only missed one, **pinealectomy**. Though I had gotten that right, I became more nervous as to whether I would advance to the semifinals.

That evening, I started marking more words from the dictionary and writing them down in a notebook. Whatever I could get through, I wrote down. I had an important deadline, for the bee would be over in a couple days. I rushed to get through as many words as I could.

After a long and boring Round 2 and Round 3 with words that were given, we queasily awaited the announcement of advancing spellers. All of our hearts were beating rapidly. And then, the moment came, when we heard my name called. I got on to the stage, rejoicing. There were 44 spellers who would continue on to the next round and the cutoff was 29/31, so I had just barely made the cut. But, I knew from here that it was a clean slate, so I was not as worried. Enduring a long day, I had to do a short interview with ESPN in the egg chair again to air before I would spell. I then went back to the hotel room and tried to go through a few more words, but I needed some more rest for the long day that would come Thursday.

The morning when we woke up, I felt ready. I had to just focus on the words given at hand. As 10:00 am approached, my parents gave me the usual pep talk to be calm and focus on my words. Going on stage, the lights were on me again, and I was ready to show the world how much I had improved. When the first speller came up, I sat in my seat, waiting my next turn, hoping my word would be one I had encountered before. Once it came to my turn, I tried to maintain a poker face and just focus on the word given. I got up to the microphone and got a word I had seen before. After enunciating each letter correctly, I went back to my seat, and started to think of more words that I could be asked, while still trying to spell along with some of the words asked. The words were tough and the spellers were excellent, so the competition was getting much more interesting. Going into Round 5, many of the spellers were getting out on tougher words. My turn next. **Desmachyme**. I had immediately recognized the beginning and ending. It was just a matter of figuring out the schwa in the middle. Typically, in Greek the connecting vowel is an o, but because I had just recently studied the root desma- meaning ligament, I was able to apply that knowledge and spell the word correctly after receiving positive feedback for the root. Phew. I had survived the killer round. Normally, Round 6 is the last round of the semifinal competition, so I told myself that if I spelled my next word correctly, I would be in the finals! Wow, I was so close to being on primetime! My word was **dégringolade**. I had known that word since second grade. Without doubt, I spelled the word, and I was sure that I had made it. I was celebrating inside. However, because of how good all the spellers were, we had to enter Round 7 with 17 spellers. **Ceratorhine**. **Ocypode**. The words in this round were still tough. Luckily, I had gotten my word correctly. There were 13 spellers left at the end of the round, but to avoid having too few spellers in the finals, we all advanced. I threw my hands in the air. I was in the finals!

In the few hours that we had leading up to the finals portion at 8:00 pm, all the finalists had some interviews and a special dinner for the families. We went back up to the room to take a quick power nap and when we came back to eat dinner with the other spellers, I got to meet and get to know the others much better. Soon enough, we were taken from our parents to be escorted onstage. My family wished me good luck and sat on the left side of the stage. I was going to be on primetime television spelling words! Just the thought of being in the top 13 in a field which started out with around 11 million spellers was extremely hard to believe.

And we were off. I was in the middle again as a New Yorker and there was a Buffalo resident before me, and Arvind Mahankali, from New York City. So, New Yorkers made up 3/13 spellers in the finals, which was amazing. The ballroom was packed and we could see the confetti cannons which would explode when the winner was declared. As the first round went on, I got more nervous, but I kept my mom's advice of keeping calm. Soon, the ESPN coordinator called me up and I took a deep breath before approaching the microphone. **Exsufflation**. A simple word with roots. Latin ex- meaning out and suffla- meaning breathing, so forceful breathing. I nodded my head to each letter of the word, and got the signal I was correct from Ms. Brooks. I made it through the first round of the finals. Next turn, I got the word **dasylirion**. Now even though I had not seen the word before, I knew I had been exposed to it since I had gone through the dictionary, which has every single word in it. Plus, I knew that the Greek root dasy- meant woolly, so I could piece together the word. An educated guess, I was able to spell the word correctly, and returning to my seat, I gave my parents a look of wonder that I had gotten it right. Getting through Round 9, I knew that I had made the top 10. So, the next time I went up to spell my word, I got **polatouche**. This was not a word I had ever seen before, but after hearing that the language was French, which came from Russian, I figured out the beginning and ending. It was just the dreaded schwa, as is the trouble spot for most spellers. In my head, I had thought either an 'a' or an 'e.' Thinking of Russian spelling patterns, I went with the latter and heard the ding. I joined my parents on the other side of the stage, where I was consoled by my parents and brother. They told me how proud they were and that the word was tough. From here, I had watched the rest of the round, and learned that I had come 6th, tying with four other spellers. For five straight rounds, the remaining five spellers got their words correct, until one missed **zanja**. Another round went by until another missed **tailleur**. Arvind, a Canadian speller named Laura Newcombe, and Sukanya Roy, the NSF champion from the previous year were the last three left. A couple rounds later, Arvind got his German word **Jugendstil**, which cracked up the crowd because of the way he said the word. Though missing the word, the world really got to see how good this guy was. Soon enough, after words like **panguingue** and **Volkerwanderung**, Laura misspelled **sorites**. So after Sukanya got **periscii** correct, she got **cymotrichous** correct to win. The following night, at the awards banquet, all 13 spellers sat on the dais and were recognized in front of the crowd, before a great farewell party. It was a great bee, and I had to get back.

Once again, as summer started up, I began preparing for the other bees. After a nice trip to India that year, I had little time to prepare for the South Asian Spelling Bee regionals, but I still managed to place first. The next two weeks, I tried going through more and more words in the dictionary; the day before the finals, I got through 1000 pages in the dictionary by just skimming over each page. As the first speller, my word was **Ichabod**. Then **zebu**. And then **heretoga**. I had not seen the word before, so I ended up missing it. Within 3 rounds, I was out to place eleventh. **Coccagee**. **Phthirophagous**. Then the winning word was **schindylesis**. Though disappointed with my performance, I was ready to do better at the North South Foundation competition in San Francisco two weeks later. Many of the same competitors at the Sony (SASB) bee were here as well. After getting through the written round with words like **cossyrite** and **rutch**, I got through to the final rounds. I ended up placing fifth after misspelling a simple CWL word, **pumicite**. Missing a CWL word at this stage should have rang bells to me, but I took it as an anomaly more than something I needed to address. This would come back to bite me too soon.

2011-2012

With a sixth place finish in the National Spelling Bee and receiving all the congratulations and well wishes, I thought I was on the top of the world and that I would be ready to come back to nationals without re-covering the basics. Once again, throughout the year, I started going through the dictionary more intensely and tried to go through the dictionary more thoroughly. While I was investing much time in learning the more difficult words, I began to lose my grip over some of the easier words, such as those in CWL. Even though I had gotten up to just about 99% (about 250 words missed) mastery rate of the CWL leading into the previous Scripps bee, I had not covered some of those words in such a long time, that I started forgetting more and more words. After getting through the easy mock competitions in the weeks leading, I won my school bee after my mom quizzed me on *SpellIt!*. In these two weeks before the regional bee, we tried going through the CWL. After all, I had gotten so good at CWL words that my mom was able to quiz me the whole 791 pages in 4 days. So, in these couple weeks, we tried to go through it. However, I was quite arrogant in going through the words because I was acting as if I had already won and should just study the dictionary. Instead, of going through the bread and butter of the regional bee and writing down any words I missed, I said I would just remember. But with so many words and studying late at night, you tend to forget many words.

So, when the regional bee came around, I had gotten through the typical *SpellIt!* rounds. Soon enough, it came down to me, the other Montessorian, and one other girl. The three of us outlasted *SpellIt!* and ended up going through offlist words. The other Montessorian missed **exponentially**. As the middle speller, it was my turn next. I got up to the microphone to spell my word. **Limburger**. I asked for the definition, and turns out it was a stinky Belgian cheese. It was a simple word- my third grade brother knew it. However, I chose to put an 'e' instead of a 'u,' costing me big time. It was the other speller's turn , and she correctly spelled her word. She went on to win on **umbilical**. I had done so well the previous year, but I had missed out on such a simple word that year. I was so disappointed. I did not even feel like going to school the next day. Time felt very slow. When I went back to school the next day, I could tell my friends were a bit surprised. They wanted to watch me again, and now they could not. I got many emails from my friends who expressed their condolences for me missing the bee.

It truly was a rude awakening. It turns out the word was in CWL, and I had missed that word in our most recent quizzing session. I had learned the hard way how important it was to listen to my mom and make sure I cover the basics. So, I developed more respect for my coach's words. The months leading up to Scripps were tough because I had less motivation to study. When Memorial Day came around, we would not be at the barbecue in DC or preparing for the written test. Instead, we would be home. The next Thursday, I chose to go to school instead of watch the semifinals since I could always just see the round results online. After a long day at school, I was eager to watch the finals that night, seeing if I could spell along. **Porwigle. Mauka. Aguinaldo.** All words I had seen before and could have gotten right. I saw Arvind once again in the top three. He got **schwannoma**, another German word. Soon, there were two spellers, and the second place finisher, Stuti Mishra, was the girl who won last year at NSF on **iruska**. She ended up getting **schwarmerei** incorrect, allowing Snigdha Nandipati of San Diego to win on **guetapens**. Yet another great competition, but I could not be part of it. Although I got some redemption in the state geography bee, where I placed sixth out of all New Yorkers, I still felt out of place with not being in Scripps. So, I was determined to do better in the other bees that year.

As summer rolled around, I began going through CWL words more thoroughly and wrote down words that I had misspelled. I got much better at it this time, retaining more and more words. I ended up winning the regional competition again for the SASB bee, but we soon learned that the nationals of SASB, which is always held in New Jersey, would clash with NSF nationals, which would be held in Detroit, Michigan. It was impossible to attend both competitions, so I made a decision to only go to NSF that year. Many of my other friends went to SASB, so I was one of the only "major" competitors that year in NSF. I was also competing in the vocabulary bee at NSF nationals, so it was a more practical decision for me. When we got to University of Michigan at Ann Arbor, I had learned about the results from the Sony spelling bee (SASB)which was held the previous night. I learned that Syamantak Payra, a great friend of mine, had won on **dghaisa**, a Malaysian boat, and the second place finisher missed **clook**. While I wished I could have been there, I had my own competition to worry about. After acing my written test and breezing through my three given oral words, I had advanced to the finals portion again. Most of the words were in CWL, and having come close to actually mastering it, I was in good shape. When it came down to two, the other speller missed **decalage**. So, I was able to win the NSF senior competition on the word **mendelevium**! I felt ecstatic, but I had the vocabulary bee later that day. I had managed to do well enough on the written test to make the finals. I got the word **keen**. I had learned the definition as being perceptive or eager, but the definition used was the ninth one listed in the dictionary, so the correct answer was 'to wail.' Oh well. The speller who came second ended up winning the vocab bee.

We had organized a vacation to Yellowstone from Detroit, so we flew out to Denver on vacation. While we were in a random town in Wyoming, we got an email from my former schoolteacher (I was to start seventh grade at a new middle school, ASMS). She had informed us that *The Leader* would be dropping sponsorship of the spelling bee due to budget concerns. This came as quite a shock, for it seemed as though the spelling bee would remain in our area forever. The pronouncer had already agreed to pronounce for the next year's regional bee if we found a sponsor. The registration deadline was running out for enrolling as sponsor. So, when we returned to Corning from our nice vacation, my mom went around the area, business to business. Luckily, we were good friends with a Rotarian, so we asked the Corning Rotary Club whether they would assume the leadership role as sponsor. They agreed, and the spelling bee survived in our area. Were it not for my mother's persistence in keeping the spelling bee in our area, neither I nor my brother could have won. This was a big victory that we could continue to do what we loved. I learned not to take anything for granted twice that year! With a new sponsor, the spelling bee in our area was saved.

2012-2013

As previously mentioned, I went into my second school ever in seventh grade, as I had been at Montessori for my whole education. At Montessori, they were highly supportive of me and my spelling pursuits and they were the ones who got me interested. In fifth and sixth grade, I was given some vocab and roots exercises intended for high school and college students in order to keep me challenged. But, I was entering a new stage in my life. So, going into seventh grade, much of my preparation continued to be out of school. My English teacher at my new school also turned out to be very receptive. This really facilitated and streamlined my preparation.

Throughout the year, I started to create more and more dictionary lists. Going through the dictionary, writing down the word, and including a definition, pronunciation, and language, I tried to make my lists look like CWL. It took a good 3 months for me to create my first list. I included all this information not only for my benefit, but also so that my brother could study as well when it was his turn to compete. After all I had been blocking him from competing since I was taking so long to win, so to speak. After making these lists, soon enough bee season was coming again, and that February, the school bee came. Even though it was a larger school, the bee still did not stray out of the given words until it came down to the top two. So, I advanced to the regional bee.

Seeking redemption for my previous year's loss, I went into the bee much more humble and focused than any other time. I approached every word as a potential to get out. Soon enough, we went off the provided list, and it came down to me and my brother at regionals. The two brothers. The competition was quite a crowd-pleaser, for they knew that a Hathwar was going to Scripps. My brother ended up missing **jicama**, and I ended up winning on **mobiliary**. I had advanced to nationals again, but this time through a new sponsor.

The week after the very last regional spelling bee, and all 280 contestants were determined, Scripps announced they would be introducing a vocabulary portion to the competition. Not only that, they would also have two written tests, so that they could vet the number of spellers that enter the finals. The vocabulary portion was ok, because I had kind of been learning definitions with the words I was studying, though the second written test was a bit frightening, for that would be the new Round 4. Studying for this new format put a little dent in my study schedule, for we had to go through the CWL much more precisely and thoroughly. My mom when quizzing me would skip over any word she figured I knew, though with vocabulary, no word could be unturned. So, I had to give the spelling and the definition, after having studied them of course. This turned out to be a more difficult task, especially for the words that are extremely obscure. After finishing this once, we went over the list of words that I had written down. It seemed as if I was writing another CWL, for remembering words was already so difficult, and then definitions made it even harder. But, because of my mom's commitment, we were able to progress through the words, and I was able to go through the dictionary on my own and create more lists.

When Memorial Day weekend came around, we were back in DC. It was great to be back at the barbecue and meet up with my friends again. That Tuesday, we had our once again computerized test with 24 spelling words, 24 vocab words, and two 3-point vocabulary words. However, only 12 of each of the spelling and vocab words actually counted, with the others being dummy words. The spelling words were up my alley, because there were words with more obscure spellings, such as **aurox**, **morel**, and **Ouagadougou**, the capital of Burkina Faso, something I had learned while preparing for the geography competition. However, I was a bit more concerned about the vocab portion, but it turned out to be much better than I expected. Many of them were fairly common words, or words that appear on the SAT. I remember feeling uncomfortable about a couple however. The next day, both of my preliminary words were once again from given lists, so I aced both of mine. I got my score report back and saw that I got 28/30. I missed one spelling **virucide**, and one vocabulary word **sublime**. However, I knew that I had spelled **virucide** correctly. My parents had gone to the speller and sponsor desk to address this. The word has a variant **viricide**, which was also accepted. I had spelled it **viruscide**, which was also in the dictionary. Thus, I had been re-awarded the point, and apparently a few other spellers spelled it the same way as I had. So, all three variants were accepted, and I ended up getting 35/36, accounting for the two 3-point spelling words onstage. Though that one word would have still allowed me to advance, it was certainly important that my score accurately reflect how I did, since it was not a clean slate quite yet. That night, we had our semifinals test. Many of the spelling words were up my alley, for I was good at the obscure words, such as **pohutukawa** and **katsura**. The vocabulary words were all roots, so the definitions were easy to figure out, like **xylophagous**, containing the Greek roots xylo- meaning wood and –phagous meaning eating. I ended up misspelling **Mertensia**. Many of my friends found the test extremely difficult.

The next morning for the semifinals, the words counted as three- pointers, but none of the words were given. I knew that if I got both my words correct, I would advance to the finals again. I managed to get two French words. This year, in school, I had begun to learn French, so it helped to know the language patterns. **Flaneur** and **surtout**. With acing these words, I would be back in the finals tied as highest scorer at 70/72. There were 19 spellers at the end of Round 6, but they took a cutoff of 12 people to advance to the finals. After getting off, we had the typical finals procedure of some interviews and the finals dinner. As the competition neared 8:00 pm, we were once again taken on stage, though our parents were in the audience this time. As the cameras started rolling, the ballroom fell silent. I got **singerie, catachresis, ushabti, mamaliga, thalweg**, and **bidonville** correct to get to the top three. I then got **ptyalagogue**. Even though I knew both roots, I hesitated about the schwa, ending up putting an 'o.' I had come third. After a couple more rounds, the other boy missed **cyanophycean**, Arvind Mahankali got **tokonoma** correct to get his anticipated championship word. **Knaidel**. Though it was a Jewish food, the word was of German origin. After correctly spelling his word, and the confetti fell on his nonchalant face, he explained that the German curse had become the German blessing. Friday night at the banquet, once again, I sat on the dais with the other finalists. It was quite fun and memorable, but I knew I had only one year left, so at that moment, I was determined to give it my all to win the next year.

When summer came, my brother and I both competed in SASB regionals. This time, my brother and I had gotten to the top three. I missed my word **quincuncial**. Jairam ended up doing better than I did! He ended up missing **phthirophagous** to place second. Since only the top two advance, he had earned a spot in the SASB finals! We were proud that he was able to do so well. However, once again, the SASB finals and NSF finals clashed on the same weekend and this time I attended the SASB.

Studying for the Sony finals was my forte, for I had to learn the obscure and arcane spellings. With all my lists, I became quite familiar with the really high-octane words. I was able to ace words like **spillflote** and **Weltschmerz**. Throughout the competition, the words were tough, including words like **kantele** and **mananosay**. SASB never fails to disappoint with nuclear words. After numerous grueling rounds, it came down to me and two other kids. In the same round, one misspelled **accidia** and the other missed **Quimper**. It was left to me to spell **phorminx** correctly. I immediately recognized the word. A Greek military unit. After enunciating each letter correctly, I was declared champion! With the sponsor being MetLife, 'Snoopy' came on stage for the awards presentation. I was given a large dummy check of $10,000. My heart was pumping too fast. It was unbelievable that I had just won another major bee. However, I had little time to celebrate even at the party after, for we had to drive down to Raleigh as I was enrolled in the vocabulary competition. So my parents took turns driving overnight to our destination: Duke university, 500 miles south of Rutgers. A couple other spelling bee families opted to do the same. Now, that is commitment. My parents drove overnight to see their kids succeed, for which I am truly grateful.

When we finally arrived in Duke at 9:00 am, I had made it in time to take the written portion of my vocabulary bee. My brother had already finished his written spelling test for the senior competition, and he felt okay about it. He got his three oral words right. However, we learned that Jairam had not advanced, though we knew he would do better the next year. The senior spelling bee was the main attraction however, which almost all families were watching, so we had to watch anyway. **Rhigolene**. **Oligidic**. The words were tough. After sorting out all the hubbub with the oral rounds of the vocabulary bee, I managed to get in with the help of my parents and advance to the final portion. I had to pick the correct choice out of four given. Round by round, I got my word correct, until I was the only one left. Getting my last word right, I felt relieved. I had won two competitions in one weekend! What a year!

2013-2014

My only goal was to win Scripps. While I was still involved in numerous extracurricular activities, such as jazz band, badminton, and basketball, I devoted much of my remaining time to studying. I still valued playing sports and hanging out with my friends, for no activity should fully take over your life. However, I had a deadline to meet, for there were no more 'next years.' This was my last shot. I had to give it my all.

In the months after my SASB victory, I began creating more and more lists of obscure words. The strategy was to be exposed to all the words in the dictionary at least once, even if I would not retain all of them. This way I could say that I studied every word in the dictionary, the source for all words of the bee.

As with last year, I typed many of these words into lists with definitions, etymologies, and pronunciations. Soon enough, with going through all these words, daily, I was becoming a master of the dictionary. What had taken seven years to complete was finally coming to fruition. When taking the 480,000 words at once, the task seems unfeasible. However, with assiduous dedication and dividing the dictionary into pieces and reviewing new words, the task becomes much easier. This was a long process, but this procedure worked for me and I felt more confident in knowing that I had covered all possible words.

Soon enough, the class competition came. The words were simple, for they were provided by Scripps. After becoming one of my two class delegates, I went onto the school bee later that day, where I was the last one standing. While these bees were certainly of lower caliber than the nationals, I had to be careful and not make any mistakes, so once again, I treated each word as my winning word. This mentality really behooved me throughout the rest of the year.

When the regional spelling bee came around, my brother was also a competitor from Montessori. I was proud to see my brother follow, and I knew that Jairam would have a good chance the following year regardless of what happened. Because of the extensive outreach of the Corning Rotary Club, the regional bee expanded to different counties and included altogether about 40 spellers. The fervor for the bee in our area was evident by the number of participants and schools present. As the competition began, I kept my mom's advice of staying calm and focusing on the word at hand. After the typical *SpellIt!* rounds, there were about 6 spellers remaining, which meant that kids were studying much harder. Soon enough, I was able to win on **maffick**. This meant that I was back to DC to compete for the last time. This time, there was no major addition or change to the Scripps format, especially considering how much of a surprise and short notice the incorporation of vocabulary into the bee was the previous year. After winning, my attention shifted to learning vocabulary. Once again, my mom painstakingly quizzed me on all the CWL vocabulary words, but with a year's worth of experience and extra studying, I was much better this time around. In the two months leading up to the bee, I was in full swing, and my friends at school were excited to watch me. Before I left, the school gave me a nice sendoff party. I felt more prepared than ever.

My mom had quizzed me a lot ever since I started spelling. I am truly grateful even to this day for all the time and effort she gave to helping me achieve my goal. However, especially in seventh and eighth grade, I began to study more independently, going through the dictionary and creating lists. My mom would continue to help me along the way, though I would try to become more self-sufficient. Through the spelling bee, you develop great life skills, and over the course of time, I was able to become more independent. Certainly, without my mom's help though, I could have never gotten as far as I had.

Reuniting with good friends that week, I felt great to be back. Plus, my grandmother came all the way from India to watch me compete in the national bee. I met up with friends who I had met throughout the years at the barbecue. This time as one of the seniors, I felt as though I would be a role model for the younger generation, just as Sameer and Kavya were to me. Entering the written test on Thursday, I felt focused and determined on my words. Going through the test, I was confident in my performance. After leaving the room, I learned that I had missed one spelling and one vocabulary question after looking up the words I had doubts on. I found out I had misspelled **tamborito**, and incorrectly defined **inscrutable**. The spelling was more of a shock, for it turned out to be in one of my lists, so that night, having missed that word, I went through all my lists very quickly, so that I would not make another mistake. All the 10,000 words that I had accumulated and written down over the last couple years, I tried to go through in one night. It was a long day, but I wanted to make sure that I would be prepared. After all, in two days' time, I would have to 'retire' from spelling.

The next morning, we had the typical preliminary rounds, and I got both of my words correct. I had advanced to the semifinals with a score of 34/36. After another long and uneventful day, I had the semifinals test, Round 4. When we were taken to our room for the computerized test, and given our login codes, we had 45 minutes to complete the test. When I started, I realized I knew every single word. I had no hesitation on any one of them, so I finished the entire test in 10 minutes and was the first one to leave. It felt great to know that I had done so well. I had gotten 30/30 on the test with words like the Hungarian **fizelyite** and words of other obscure origins. Feeling much better than Tuesday with my score, it was easier to sleep that night.

The next morning as 10:00 am approached, I felt some more pressure on me, for as the highest placing returner from the previous year, eyes were on me to see whether I would finish. I knew that if I spelled both of my words correctly, I would advance. And in the two semifinal rounds, I got lucky with words I knew, **favus** and **quatrefoil**. When the finalists were drawn from the remaining spellers after Round 6, I was the first one called up, and Mr. Loeffler announced that I got a perfect score in the semifinal test. When the airing finished, we were all escorted to the back lounge and dinner for the finalists and families. I went up to the room to take a quick nap and returned to eat dinner. After a couple interviews, 8:00 pm sneaked up on me, and I was ready to spell in primetime for my third time. The cameras were on, and thus my last bee commenced.

Going into the finals as an eighth grader, I definitely tried to be more relaxed and have a bit more fun. I tried to just soak in my last bee experience. **Detraque**. **Encastage**. **Hexerei**. **Criollismo**. **Bagwyn**. **Semmel**. **Lamentabile**. **Nocifensor**. With these words, I was back to the top three. I had known all the words so far, and felt great. Now, we entered the 25 championship-word list, meaning there were only 25 words left to ask in the competition. After acing **characin**, I was in the top two, so I had already improved my standing. The other speller was a Texan 7th grader named Ansun Sujoe. So, with just us two left, I approached the microphone, still as focused as ever. **Corpsbruder**. Hmm. I was taken aback. I asked for the definition and etymology, but I had no idea. Hearing that it was a French word taken from German, I was drawing a blank, but decided to go with a straightforward German spelling pattern. The clock showed 45 seconds left, and the stage lights switched colors, indicating I needed to spell. Giving it a guess, I went with K-O-R-B-R-U-I-T-E-R. Ding. The audience gasped, but I knew I was wrong. After hearing the correct spelling, still no bells rang. I figured it was the ending of my spelling bee experience. Then, Ansun went up to spell. He got his word **antigropelos**. He was evidently perplexed by the word. Having not seen the word before, he gave the word a shot, but ended up missing the schwa by putting an 'o' instead of an 'e.' This meant both of us were back in! At the national level, this was inconceivable, for the winner almost never misspells onstage. While I felt sympathetic for him missing his word, I was excited to have a new chance. I was reminded of second grade, when I went back and forth missing words. However, the bee would not end the same.

When I got back to spell in the next round, I joked, "A word I know this time, please," evoking a good laugh out of the crowd and Dr. Bailly. Luckily, it turned out to be a Sanskrit word I had studied, **skandhas**. Ansun got his word **Hyblaean** right in that round as well. For four straight rounds, we got words including **feijoada**, **augenphilologie**, **sdrucciola**, **holluschick**, **thymelici**, **paixtle**, **encaenia**, and **terreplein**, in order. It was my turn to spell again. I got my word **stichomythia**. Treating it like any other word, I asked for the definition and language, and enunciated each letter clearly. I returned to my seat. Dr. Bailly then announced something quite interesting; he declared that were Ansun to spell his next word correctly, we would be declared co-champions. I had not even kept track of how many words and rounds we had gotten through, for I was only focused on spelling my words correctly. I later realized that **stichomythia** would be my winning word. Ansun was then called up to the microphone, and I stood behind him. **Feuilleton**. It appeared as if Ansun had not seen the word before. The audience was on the edge of their seats, and we were all watching to see whether Ansun would spell correctly. He asked the typical questions about the word, but he took quite a long time to start spelling. The 45-second mark passed, then the 30-second mark, so Ansun could not ask for any more questions. The stage lights turned red, so he had to spell. After fumbling to pronounce the word correctly, he spelled F-E-U-I-L-L at a normal methodical pace before abruptly pausing. After a tense couple of seconds, he finished E-T-O-N very quickly to hear Ms. Brooks indicate he was correct. I pumped my fist in the air, and went up to him to shake his hand. We saw the confetti fall on our heads, and my mom and brother ran onstage to hug me. I felt on top of the world, that I had actually won. Extreme euphoria. Ansun's family soon came onstage, and then my dad, grandmother, and cousin's family came up. We were all sharing the excitement. Soon, Scripps CEO Rich Boehne came up to give us the trophy, which we both raised together.

After a couple minutes of rejoicing after our shared victory, ESPN reporter Kaylee Hartung came up to ask us a few questions onstage. She informed us of the rarity of a co-championship, a feat that had not occurred for 52 years. Asking us for our thoughts, I explained that we both knew the competition was against the dictionary and not against each other, so I was happy to share the trophy with him, as we both deserved it for our efforts. As we went off air, many more cameras and interviewers came onstage. We had finished the bee at around 10:40, and we were asked questions by reporters onstage until about 11:40. After posing for some more pictures and responding to their questions, we were taken to a room where we discussed what the next few weeks would look like. We were given a bodyguard for security reasons, so I felt like a movie star. The whole experience was quite surreal. After celebrating with my family, we headed back up to the hotel room at 1:00. But none of us could sleep, for we were all so happy and running on so much adrenaline. We were told to come back to the ballroom by 5:30 am, so we had little time to sleep, let alone getting any. We had no idea of how busy that Friday would be.

With just a few hours of rest, we were up by 5:30 for many of the morning interviews, including the Today Show, Good Morning America, FOX, and other television networks. We conducted these interviews in a makeshift studio in the ballroom. Soon enough, we completed all these 'call-in' interviews, and it was time for the studio tours in DC. We were taken to several studios, such as CNN, MSNBC, and Huffington Post, for even more interviews. Some were live while others were taped. It felt so amazing that we were actually on all these networks, and that too with so much energy, for we were running on only a couple hours of sleep. In our limo with our bodyguard, we went to studio after studio until about 5:00 pm. Though it was a long day, we were still not done, for we had to attend the awards banquet and deliver a speech. Changing into a suit, I had to be downstairs by 5:45 for the awards banquet. Once again, we were sitting on the dais. After eating our meals, some of our interview clippings were shown in front of the audience, and Ansun and I got to see ourselves from the other side. It then came to the time where I was called up by Dr. Bailly, who read a short bio of me and announced my prize of $30,000. After Merriam-Webster editor Peter Sokolowski announced Merriam-Webster's prize, I was to give a speech in front of the packed ballroom of spellers and families. I thanked everyone, especially my parents and sponsor, for all the support they gave me. After Ansun did the same, the awards banquet came to a close, and we headed to the farewell party.

In previous years, I would have been on the floor, dancing. However, Ansun and I were inundated by people asking for autographs in their Beekeepers or to take pictures. We had little time to let loose. I managed to get a fun photo with my friends in the end though. Another long day, but it felt great to have finished the spelling bee. We stayed up into the wee hours of the morning, just talking in the lobby. After coming back to our room around 4:00 am, we woke up a few hours later to go on the Ferris wheel at National Harbor. Just to relax, it was nice to talk and hang out with my friends before we traveled to our respective hometowns. That Saturday, we drove home, this time elated and rejoicing. I realized I would be done with competitive spelling, but I knew that it was only the beginning of a new chapter in my life.

Post- Victory

The next week was jam-packed. Coming back Saturday to New York, we got to spend the night at home. But that Sunday, we were to head to New York City for more interviews, including *Live with Kelly and Michael*. So, that afternoon, my mom and I took a 4-hour cab ride to NYC from home, arriving at our hotel in Times Square at 10:00 pm. We met with the Scripps communications manager Chris Kemper here, who would organize our interview schedule and all. Ansun and his dad flew in from Fort Worth late that night. My mom, a family friend, and I went to explore Times Square and eat out in the city. We just wanted to have some fun. In fact, I was just in the city a couple weeks before for our 8th grade class trip. But it's always fun to go back. The next Monday morning, we appeared on several networks including Fusion and E! The biggest highlight was going on *Live with Kelly and Michael* for another spell-off of co-champions versus co-hosts. It was really cool to meet a professional football player and see how tall Michael Strahan is in real life. When we went on air, Dr. Bailly pronounced, and Ansun and I just had fun with it. We ended up beating the two, and got a nice trophy. We also met Shailene Woodley, the lead actress in *The Fault in Our Stars*. In fact, that night, we got invited to the premiere of the movie in Ziegfeld Theatre, where we would meet the celebrities of the film and meet John Green. However, the next day, I had a math exam, so I had to return to school.

Returning late Monday, I had to go to school the next day, the first day back since I had won. The reception at my school was crazy. When I entered the school, my principal, congratulated me, and all the front desk staff expressed their pride and felicitations. When I entered my classroom, I met many of my friends and teachers, who also told me about how they watched the bee and were on the edge of their seats. I learned that my schoolmates were watching even the semifinals, so the teachers took off time to allow everyone to watch. It was really great that so many people were watching the spelling bee. Throughout the day, many people congratulated me. In the morning, we took our algebra exam, the reason I had to come back to school. During lunch however, the celebration continued, for my friends had organized a flash mob with my favorite song "I Will Survive," and they made a nice banner for me. It felt as if the whole school and all of Corning were cheering me.

The next day, I had to miss school again, for my mom and I flew to Los Angeles to appear on the most iconic interview of all, *Jimmy Kimmel Live*. Flying into LAX on Wednesday late, we rested and got up early the next morning. Meeting Ansun again at the hotel, we toured Hollywood Boulevard a bit and got to walk down the Hall of Fame. Later that day, we went inside the studio for *Jimmy Kimmel Live* and got to meet the comedian briefly before we had to air. After his monologue, we were introduced and were asked a couple of preliminary questions. Then, we got to business with a spelling bee. However, with it being a comedy show, the pronouncer was Guillermo, a parking lot security guard with a thick accent. So, he would pronounce every word obscenely wrong. We were just supposed to have fun with it all. I got 'juggernaut,' but he pronounced it like 'yargarno.' I managed to get it correct because he told me it was Hindi, but it was kind of a fluke. Jimmy and Ansun got tougher ones, so they missed theirs. But, we ended up winning. As a prize, we each got a trophy and an Xbox One. That was the end of our stay in LA and our weeklong tours. But, when we came back we had many local interviews.

Additionally, my local Congressman invited us to a tour of the Capitol Building and we got to see the room where the president addresses the Congress and Senate. I got a plaque of recognition from him in his office and a flag flown at the Capitol. It was all a lot to take in. The next week, we were invited to Albany to meet our state senators. Our senator and assemblyman gave us a tour of the building and I got recognized once again with a resolution. I met many of my state's representatives, the ones who decide New York's laws, so it was certainly a prestigious position to be in. The Corning Rotary Club, my sponsor, even had a "Spellebration" to celebrate my victory, so all my school friends, Rotarians, and even the mayor attended.

Even when we went to India to meet relatives and spend time with family, we got invited for interviews. News reporters from *Times of India* came to our house and wrote an article. Additionally, my whole family was invited for an hour-long news program on one of Bangalore's most renowned TV networks during primetime, so even in India the spelling bee was a great deal. Those living on the same street as my grandparents all were so proud. Even though the National Spelling Bee primarily consists of American students, it obviously has a global audience, and I am glad so many people around the world are interested in the English language.

When we came back from our nice vacation in India, we had many local events, including throwing the first pitch at a baseball game and watching the Watkins Glen International NASCAR race in the VIP lounge. Because I had expressed interest in becoming an ophthalmologist, the chief of Wills Eye Institute in Philadelphia, one of the best eye hospitals in the world, invited me for a tour of the building. It was awesome to see all the state-of-the-art equipment and technology. I even got to wear scrubs and see the room where ophthalmologists would perform cataract surgeries. It was truly an amazing experience, and all because I won the spelling bee!

One of THE most surprising and memorable visits of all, was getting an invitation to the White House. In the middle of August, we got an email from Chris Kemper saying the White House contacted him. Apparently, the President wished to meet both Ansun's and my family in the Oval Office! Back when Ansun and I had won, President Obama had sent out a tweet expressing how proud he was to watch the spelling bee, so as a follow-up, we were actually going to meet him! It was a wonderful opportunity, so in September of 2014, we drove down to DC to meet President Obama. After getting a tour of the White House with all its rooms and gardens, we went up to the West Wing and met the most powerful man in the world. After shaking his hand at the threshold, my family, Ansun's family, and a few Bee officials went inside the Oval Office. Here, we talked to him for a few minutes and he explained how he watched the spelling bee with his daughters and even tried spelling the two words Ansun and I had missed. He was just as unlucky as we were. We got to talk to him for about five minutes, and were given several goodies for our visit. It was a spectacular experience to meet President Obama.

That was essentially the end of my victory tour, per se. Into ninth grade, I was invited to speak at spelling bees in the area to help inspire younger kids. In fact, the regional spelling bee the next year would have about 60 spellers, a tribute to the expanded interest in our area. One of those spellers would be my younger brother Jairam, now a champion with a story of his own…

Chapter 3: The Spelling Bee and Me

Written By: Jairam Hathwar

I would always attend my brother's spelling bee competitions, yet I never was really interested in competing myself in the spelling bee. I thought that my brother would just beat me eventually, so why bother participate? I first competed in my school spelling bee in 3rd grade, even though I didn't study the list given by my teacher. I didn't really enjoy it that much, but my parents and brother told me that it would be a good experience. I ended up coming in 3rd place at the school bee, and was happy, overall, with my placement. Who knew that competing just for the exposure, would lead me to become the co-champion of the Scripps National Spelling Bee!

The next year I was prompted to participate again, and since my brother was in middle school, I didn't need to worry about him and the school bee. He, obviously, won his school bee and advanced to the regional competition. That year I tied for the first place at my school spelling bee, which meant that I would be advancing to the regional spelling bee as well. Once I qualified for the regional spelling bee, I was ecstatic, but I wasn't expecting to do well, since the regional competition only allowed one person to advance to the national competition. My brother proved his dominance, by winning the regional spelling bee, while I came in an exhilarating 2nd place. I was proud of not only my brother, but myself as well because I wasn't expecting to perform as well as I did. He later on advanced to the national spelling bee, and accomplished an invigorating 3rd place, but he still wasn't done yet.

The following year, my brother and I both triumphed in our school spelling bees, and since it was my brother's last year of participation, he was putting it all in. I was getting a little intimidated by the level of dedication that my brother showed into studying for the spelling bee. Soon enough, the regional spelling bee reached us again. My expectation was to come in 2nd place again, as I did the previous year. My brother conquered first place, while I achieved a disappointing 4th place. That taught me a very valuable lesson. You can never take any results for granted. My parents reinforced that concept because a lot of factors come into play for reaching your final placement.

In the meanwhile, my brother would be advancing to the 2014 Scripps National Spelling Bee, for the fifth time. His perseverance was a story of its own, through his rollercoaster of events. I would watch his study lists gain in size, starting with *My Spell It*, to *How to Spell Like a Champ*, to the *Consolidated Word List*, to *Words of Wisdom*, preceding the *Merriam-Webster's Dictionary of Prefixes, Suffixes & Combining Forms*, and finally the *Merriam Webster Third New International Dictionary*. His method of approach was to read from the hardcopy, which I personally knew I wouldn't enjoy to do. His determination to clinch the title that year was awe-inspiring, spending hours and hours day in and day out, starting out by being quizzed by our mom, to later being self-motivated to learn by himself. As the bee approached, his preparation only grew, by staying up late in the night just to study for this prestigious spelling bee. He was the favorite to win that year because of his previous year's achievements. It was amazing to see how he took it as a challenge, and put in the effort needed.

Once the bee arrived, I was awestruck by the words he would spell on the stage, but moreover the fact that he put in so much effort, yet didn't have any expectation in the end. He didn't let the pressure of being the favorite to win get to his head, which is what I admire the most from him. He took it round-by-round and finally won the bee. I will never forget that fantastic moment, but I would never have guessed what was soon to come. The following days, he would start his media tour around the country airing on large television companies, such as MSNBC, FOX News, CNN, Live with Kelly, and even Jimmy Kimmel Live. Just being a part of that was amazing, and at that moment, I wanted to follow in his footsteps. It was just icing on the cake, when my family was invited to meet the president in the Oval Office, at the White House.

Now that my brother was finally done with the spelling bee, I wanted to give it a good try myself. I was willing to put in the time and effort that I saw my brother put in, so half the battle was already over. As soon as I got back home, I hit the books. Now, it was my turn to take a shot at this.

2014-2015

Soon enough, a year had passed by, and the spelling bee had arrived once again. I breezed past the school level, and had reached the regional competition. Without my brother obstructing me, I wanted to go for the kill and advance to the national competition. I studied the *Spell It* and the *Consolidated Word List* and knew nearly all of it. I would soon to know that I missed a CWL word, but my opponent misspelled as well. I won the regional spelling bee on the word bandalore, which meant that I would be one among the 285 competitors at the 2015 Scripps National Spelling Bee.

I started studying intensely the way my brother did, by being quizzed by my mom, but I realized that I didn't learn the same way as my brother, and took a 180° turn. Since I had an aptitude for technology, my family encouraged me to enter words from my lists, my mom's lists, and my brother's lists into the computer, so I could quiz myself. Since my brother and I have totally different learning methods, my way of learning words was different than his.

Since I was sort of time-pressed, I had to rush to put in all of those words into my computer. I didn't manage to enter all of the words, but I did for the majority. I did have some difficulties in covering the whole curriculum, since the lists we made weren't comprehensive of the whole dictionary, so whenever I could, I would go through the dictionary and enter the words while I would also highlight it in the hardcopy dictionary. Once I finished entering all of the words, I had enough time to review them all about two times before the competition. I treated it as a percentage game. My goal was to get 70-75% of the words in those lists mastered by the time of the competition, and I was proud to achieve that goal. A month before the competition, I quickly reviewed the *Consolidated Word List* along with the vocabulary portion, since vocabulary was incorporated in the preliminary test of the competition. I also glanced over the *Merriam-Webster's Dictionary of Prefixes, Suffixes & Combining Forms,* and last but not least, the round 2 and round 3 word list, especially the vocabulary part, that the Scripps Spelling Bee gave upon successfully becoming the champion of my regional spelling bee.

Early enough, the 2015 Scripps National Spelling Bee had commenced. After weeks of hard work, I couldn't believe it came by so fast. It seemed as if just a week ago I had won my local bee. I had put in the effort needed, and the rest was fate. I was most proud that I finished the curriculum, so any word I would get, I would've seen before.

After a relaxing Monday at the barbecue picnic, I wanted to quickly review the list provided by Scripps for the next day's preliminary test. I was advised not to learn any new material because at that stage you won't really learn or retain much. The next day was the 26 question Scan Tron multiple choice test composed of 12 spelling words, 12 vocabulary questions, and 2 additional 3-point vocabulary questions, which were selected from the given list. One of the three-pointer words was from the *Spell It* and the other from a list that Scripps granted. I didn't feel confident at the end of the test, but I didn't lose hope. The rest of the day was spent preparing for the next day's onstage spelling words, which I ended up correctly spelling.

After properly spelling my two words on the stage, I had to anxiously wait for the announcement of the semifinalists. That wait was supposedly about 10 minutes, but felt like hours. The announcer called all of the contestants onstage, and one by one declared the semifinalists. I was fortunate enough to have the distinct honor of being deemed as a semifinalist, which also meant that I would have to take another test similar to the one I had taken in the preliminary round, except harder. The test was held immediately after the reporting of the semifinalists, and I ended up having the highest score out of the 48 other brilliant minds. Later that day, the bee staff sent out an email to all of the semifinalists' parents, where they would disclose all of the contestants' scores. I was tied for 7th place, which would mean I would qualify for the evening finals on Thursday, if I were to spell my 2 words accurately next morning.

The next day had arrived, the day where the champion, or co-champions, would be declared. Whatever sleep I got, I had to deal with through the competition. My family wished me good luck and I went on to the stage. I was number 152, so I would be in somewhere in the middle of the semifinals. I managed to endure through the grueling wait. My first word was noctidiurnal, which I aced. I knew that I only needed to spell one more word precisely to advance to the championship finals on ESPN. I had waited through the rest of the round patiently, until my turn arrived again. I walked up to the microphone and Dr. Bailly, the 1980 Scripps National Spelling Bee Champion, pronounced the word riegel. I was bewildered once I heard the word, since it didn't come to me immediately. I totally blanked out on the rules from German, and botched the word up terribly, which meant that my run at the 2015 Scripps National Spelling Bee was over, and I was eliminated from the competition.

At first it was hard to deal with such a devastating loss, coming so close to reaching the championship finals, but I later became proud of my 22nd place achievement, and was determined to do better the next year. Later that day, my friends and family went to go have frozen yogurt to celebrate, but I still didn't want to miss the championship finals because I wanted to cheer on my friends who had qualified for it.

The bee turned out to be a huge success, with co-champions declared once again. I was very happy for them, and congratulated them once all of the media dispersed. I had known both of the co-champions before, and I knew how hard they studied in the past years. Watching the finals just motivated me the most because I knew that I could do it too. So I decided to put it all in the following year, and tee it up high and hit it hard.

2015-2016

Once again, the class spelling bee had arrived, and the whole process was to be started all over again. I was as confident as ever. My class bee wasn't too difficult, yet it did seem to go on forever. The school bee was even longer, but I managed to pass through it, which meant that, once again, the regional competition was about to commence. As the defending champion, I had a little bit extra pressure than the previous year, but I wasn't trying to worry about that part of it. My brother told me to stay calm under pressure and eliminate other distractions, so I was keeping that in mind during the competition. I spelled round by round and ended up winning the bee again on the word elision. I was proud of myself to defend my title, and not misspell any of my words. But that win meant that I would qualify for the national competition, so it was back to studying again.

The day after I won the regional competition, my whole family gathered around and made a plan for what to study before the nationals. We had 18 lists, about 50,000 words that they suggested me to review about 4 times, and be at around 90-95%. It felt like a lot to do in just a short period of time, but I was willing to do it, since it is so difficult to return to the same stage of competition the next year. I had studied through all those lists including language patterns, since that was what cost me the previous year.

It was time for the 2016 Scripps National Spelling Bee. I felt that I knew those 18 wordlists about 85%. On the drive down to National Harbor, my brother quizzed me on some random, lucky words, that weren't in any of my lists, and disappointingly I missed every single one of them. I was disappointed with that performance, so we made a plan to somehow, go through the entire dictionary before the main day of competition on Thursday. As soon as we got to our room at the hotel, my brother gave me a marathon session of quizzing me on words that he felt were difficult, and that weren't in any of the lists we created.

On Monday, I had a blast at the barbecue and got to rejoin with my friends who I had been keeping in touch with throughout the year. Sadly though, it started to rain midway through the barbecue, which meant that we had to head back to the resort. As soon as we got back, my brother, my mom, and I reviewed through the dictionary, and I also studied over the list that the spelling bee provided, since the following day would be the preliminary test. The preliminary test would be slightly different than the previous year because one of two three pointer vocabulary questions, were not given, compared to previous years , where both were given.

The next day, the preliminary test was quite difficult. I managed to ace the spelling portion composed of 12 spelling words, but the vocabulary section posed some challenges. Out of the 12 vocabulary words, I has answered 8 properly, and I got perfect on both the three-point vocabulary words. I felt much more confident than previous year, yet I wasn't that happy with my score personally. My family and I thought that my score would suffice to qualify for the semifinals, or as they changed it, the finals, but,it wasn't over yet. I still had to spell 2 words onstage correctly, which used to be both provided from a given list to us, but now only one was.

It was Wednesday now, and I was about ¾ through the dictionary. My goal was to finish before the announcement of finalists, but first I had to survive through two crucial rounds on the stage. There were two batches of spellers, which were split evenly, and once again I was at the beginning of the second batch. I wasn't too worried about the first round, since I knew those words cold. I spelled my word, triglycerides, correct, and I had to wait for 130 or so other contestants. That became a bit tedious and obviously, and being in the front row didn't help whatsoever, making you vulnerable to cameraman to take pictures of you.

After quickly taking a bite for lunch, I had to head back to the stage for another nerve-racking round. This round was much more terrifying, since the words were straight from the dictionary, opposed to a given list in the previous years. I was fortunate enough to be in the second batch, so I could see on the spelling bee website what type of words they were asking, even though they, obviously, couldn't ask the same words as they previously asked. The round became delayed by a while, which was good for me, since I could squeeze in some more studying.

It was finally my turn up at the microphone again. I was extremely anxious because if I spelled my word correctly, I would move on to the semifinals (or finals 1). Luckily, I was one of the first 10 to go up to spell, so that would make me feel a little better, since I didn't have to deal with the nerves as much as the latter spellers. I went up to the microphone, and I got the word logopedics. I rattled it off effortlessly. This would mean that I would advance to the semifinals of the national spelling bee for the second time!

The rest of the round felt like forever, and it felt so good when it was over. It was just a few minutes before they would announce the semifinalists. I did feel pretty confident that I would make it, but definitely had butterflies in my stomach. Soon enough, they called my name and I received an aureate medal. While I was elated in accepting my medal, I heard that there was only one person who got a perfect score on the written test, and that was Nihar Janga. I knew Nihar for about a year now, and I wasn't surprised to hear that at all. I knew that he was going to be a very tough competitor, but it was all against the dictionary anyways.The rest of the day was just spent celebrating, instead of having to take a grueling semifinals test, a bit of studying, oh, and, finishing the dictionary as well!

I woke up the next morning feeling uncharacteristically nervous. I knew that was the long awaited day. The finals part 1 would be held in the morning this time, so as to let the finalists have some time to rest before the evening championship finals. The morning finals procedure was changed again. It was the same style as how they conducted it pre-2013, and now they incorporated it again. A total of 45 students advanced to the final competition. I was close to the middle of the batch, which meant that I was in the front row again.

The finals had arrived and one after another the spellers dropped. I was becoming increasingly nervous because the previous year's semifinals was nowhere near the caliber of this first round. After a few commercial breaks, I regained my composure, and fortunately the words seemed less difficult. Fortunately my word was from the *Consolidated Word List*, which I had been very well acquainted with. This first round had become a lawnmower round, even seeing some favorites get eliminated. More than half the competitors were eliminated just in the first round. As the rounds went on, more and more worthy spellers left the stage, as I seemed to get fairly simpler words. Most of mine were from CWL, until the last round.

I suspected that this would be the last round because there were only about 14 spellers left. The nerves were extremely hard to deal with. Once it got to my turn again, I was almost sure that I would advance to the championship finals, if I spelled my word correctly. My word was quinton, and I couldn't recall studying that word before. I did get very nervous because all my previous words were words I knew cold. This was the same way how I was eliminated from last year's competition, so I wasn't going to give up that easy. I asked for everything that I could get, and started to think about French rules. I knew that the ending was –on in French, and I connected it to a similar word quimper. I did my best educated guess and it turned out to be correct. I was ecstatic.

Once the round finished, a total of 10 were left on the stage. We were declared championship finalists! All of us were provided a lanyard with a unique schedule attached to it. I had a short intermission for about an hour before my first interview started. I immediately went to my room and got as much rest as I could, which turned out to be very helpful. I then had to go to numerous interviews asking how I felt, how I think I would do, and other questions that at that moment seemed a bit futile.

Finally, they called all of the finalists for dinner, which was one of my favorite bee experiences because I got to become such good friends with all of them. We even managed to squeeze in a little last minute cramming. I didn't feel that my chances of winning were high because three of the other nine had done better than me at previous year's competition. My brother had written down some words during all my interviews to review during dinner time, so one of my very good friends, Nihar Janga,and I went over them directly before the competition.

My parents, my brother, my cousin, my grandma, my friends, and my aunt and uncle all wished me good luck before the competition, and advised to stay calm in the bright lights, even when I don't know a word. All the finalists were soon taken behind the stage and were taking spellfies with a twitter mirror. We were introduced onto the stage, and were greeted by the other spellers who missed in the earlier rounds of the competition.

The competition had started! I was, finally, not in the first row at the finals, but it didn't really matter much now. The first word was myoclonus, and when Cooper Komatsu finished spelling the word just in the nick of time the crowd went wild. It was definitely quite away to start off the evening. All of the finalists were giving high-fives to each other whenever one of them got their respective words right. It was very fun spelling the words that were being asked because not only did it help to kill the nerves, it was also a good way to stay focused. Being in the finals was a totally different experience. The lights were brighter, and the crowd nearly doubled. It was finally my turn up to the mike. My word was chaussure. I spelled it right, then returned to my seat to be welcomed by more high-fives. A few more rounds went on like that, although seeing my friends being eliminated was very hard to see. All of a sudden, only four people were left. It was just Nihar, two other finalists from last year, and myself. I was very happy for making it that far, but I knew how much it took me to get there, so I took that as a motivation.

It was just four more rounds till it was down to just Nihar and me. We were really good friends even before the competition, and being the last two made it even more special. We both spelled our words correctly for multiple rounds, encouraging each other that there was a chance for us to become co-champions. After numerous rounds, I was asked to spell the word drahthaar. I had studied this word multiple times from the infrequently section of the *Consolidated Word List*, as well as *myspellit.com*, but I couldn't recall it whatsoever. I spent a lot of time thinking about the spelling of the word, but I just couldn't remember it. Sadly, my guess was incorrect, and I had to return to my seat because there was a chance that I could be reinstated if Nihar missed any of his two word. So many emotions were flowing through me at that moment. I finally could understand how my brother felt when he was in that exact position. I still knew there was a chance for me to keep going in the competition, but I wasn't that confident in that theory. I just took a deep breath and had to take whatever happened in equal stride. Nihar ended up spelling his word correctly, and Dr. Bailly announced that if he spelled his next word correctly, he would be the champion. I couldn't feel happier for him, since I knew how hard he had worked. He ended up missing his word. I felt absolutely bad for him.

The show had to go on! We both had to deal with it, but we were still both in it. A few more rounds went on, until once again I misspelled the word mischsprache. On hindsight, I have no clue what was going on in my mind on that word. It was just simple German, yet it just didn't click. I ended up missing the word, and once again, so many emotions were going through my mind. I couldn't be reinstated again. Could I? Well, guess what? Nihar missed his word again. We were only 2 more rounds away from the end of the 25 rounds. We knew that we could do it. My next word was zindiq, which I had studied many times. Nihar also responded with a correct spelling of euchologion.

Soon after, there was a pause. Dr. Bailly explained the protocol for ending the bee. If both of us spell our words correctly, we would be co-champions. If we both misspell our words, then we would also be co-champions, but if one of us spells our word incorrectly and the other one spells both their word and their championship word correctly, then that individual would be the solo champion. We both faced each other, and mentally congratulated/acknowledged each other.

I walked up to the microphone, and waited to get my word, while I was trying to avoid thinking of what would happen if I spell my word right, or wrong. The word was Feldenkrais. I knew it right away. All my hard work had finally paid off! I took a deep breath and concentrated as much as I could on the word. I asked for all the information, just to make sure what I was thinking was correct. It also helped me calm down.

Feldenkrais. F-E-L-D-E-N-K-R-A-I-S. Feldenkrais! I had done it. I had won the Scripps National Spelling Bee! I quickly glimpsed at my parents, watching them celebrating and it was a moment that I will cherish my whole life, although there still was a chance that Feldenkrais wouldn't be my last word. Nihar congratulated me profusely, but he still had to spell his word. His word was gesellschaft. I could tell he knew it instantaneously, although he didn't rattle off the definition like he did on a couple earlier on. He took his time as well, and letter by letter spelled gesellschaft to crown both of us Co-champions of the 2016 Scripps National Spelling Bee!

The celebration had begun! Both of our parents and siblings ran onto the stage sharing their excitement to both of us. Everyone was in such a cheerful mood, and it was just amazing! We then saw the CEO of the Scripps Company heading towards us, to hand us the championship trophy! Nihar and I both hoisted it up as high as we could in front of the humongous crowd, with hundreds of cameras shooting towards us. Soon after, the press and media bulldozed us onto the stage, asking us very similar questions as what they did before, except now that we were champions. What are you going to do with the money? What is next for you? Some of them, definitely were obvious answers, but you've got to let them do what they have to. After a couple hours of doing that, we finally got to return to our room. All our phones were being flooded with messages from our relatives and close friends. We had to wake up very early in the morning the next day, so I tried to sleep however much I could.

The next day we were bombarded with interviews all around the local D.C. area. We appeared on various news channels, radio stations, and newspapers, which ranged from CNN, to MSNBC, to NPR. In the middle of that, we had to juggle around writing a speech, obviously with some help, for that night's Awards Ceremony, and Farewell Party. The rest of the day went by in a jiffy, and by the time we finally got back to our room, it was time for us to go back to the Awards Ceremony. The Awards Ceremony and Farewell Party are always very fun ways to bond with the other spellers, and create long-lasting friendships.

The next week was, once again, filled with interviews. It started off on Monday, where we both appeared on Live with Kelly in New York City, where we did a friendly spell off with Dr. Bailly as the pronouncer. There were more interviews in the afternoon as well. The next day was very special because we got to ring the opening bell of the New York Stock Exchange, something that was new and unprecedented. That night we flew to Los Angeles to appear on Jimmy Kimmel Live that would happen the following day.

After that whirlwind week, I finally was able to return back home, but that was just the start of even more interviews. The next day, when I had to go back to school, as soon as I entered all my classmates were cheering for me, and they were all thrilled to be watching me while I was on stage. My whole locker was covered with bees, and they even made cookies to eat during class which had spelling bees on it as well. I had become, sort of, a celebrity in my area now because everyone wanted a picture taken with me. Little did I know, that so much more would happen. I would be invited to interviews for newspapers and even broadcasting stations while I was traveling in India. I even got to meet and participate in a spell-off, golf version, with my favorite golfer, Jordan Spieth, which was a very memorable moment. Lastly, I got to be invited by all of our local lawmakers and was honored by them at their respective places.

It definitely did take a while before everything finally settled down, but the whole experience was just wonderful. From the beginning to the end, throughout the rollercoaster run, every moment was indeed worth it. Even if you don't win ,in the end, you still learn so many valuable life skills that will stick with you the rest of your life, which was, hands down, my favorite part of the spelling bee!

Note to Spellers:

We have included 10,000+ words in the following chapters to facilitate the process of preparing for the higher levels of the spelling bee. Every time we went through the dictionary, we compiled a new list of words, which is why the words are broken down into separate lists. This should also help to make the challenge of going through such a large amount of words significantly easier for you. The pronunciation, etymology, and definition of each word are provided, with the definition being abbreviated to simply capture the main idea of the word's definition, which will help you prepare for the vocabulary portion of the spelling bee. Dictionary diving is a rather daunting task, so we hope that you can take advantage of this compendium of potential spelling bee words.

Best of luck!

Chapter 4: Precis

abacaxi
\a-bə-kə-ˌshē\
Portuguese
: pineapple

abaisse
\ə-ˈbā-sā\
French
: lowered in rank

Abbasid
\ə-ˈba-səd, ˈa-bə-səd\
Islam+English
: member of caliphs

abeigh
\ə-ˈbēk̲\
Old Norse
: cautiously aloof

abelmosk
\ābəl̲ˌmäsk\
New Latin
: bushy herb

abilene
\abəˌlēn\
Texan geographical name
: prehistoric culture

ablach
\ablək̲, ˈā-\
Irish Gaelic>Scottish Gaelic
: insignificant person

abogado
\abəˈgätō\
Latin>Spanish
: adviser

abrocome
\abrəˌkōm\
Greek+New Latin
: rodent

abrotanum
\əˈbrätᵊnəm\
Greek>Latin
: southernwood

aburagiri
\äbərəˈgirē\
Japanese+Japanese
: large tree

aburton
\əˈbərtᵊn\
English elements
: length athwartship

acaciin
\əˈkās(h)ēən, -shən\
ISV
: crystalline glycoside

acaleph
\akəˌlef\
New Latin
: coelenterate

acapu
\äkəˌpü\
Tupi>Portuguese
: timber tree

acesodyne
\əˈsesəˌdīn\
Greek+Greek
: pain reliever

Achaemenid
\ə-ˈkē-mə-nəd\
Greek+Greek
: Persian rulers

Acheronian
\a-kə-ˌrō-nē-ən, -nyən\
Latin+English
: dismal

achiote
\ä-chē-ᵊˈō-tē\
Nahuatl>Spanish
: seed of tree

achkan
\äch-kən\
Hindi
: tunic

achras
\a-krəs, -ˌkras\
Latin
: tree

Acoemeti
\ə-ˈse-mə-ˌtī\
Greek
: monks

acoine
\a-kə-ˌwēn, -wən\
German
: crystalline derivative

actinophrys
\ak-tə-ˈnä-frəs, ak-ˈti-nə-\
Greek+New Latin
: protozoan

acyloin
\ə-ˈsi-lə-wən, -ˌwēn; ˈa-sə-ˌlȯin, ˌa-sə-ˈlō-ən\
ISV
: ketone

adelantado
\a-də-ˌlän-ˈtä-dō\
Latin>Spanish
: military governor

addra
\a-drə\
African name
: gazelle

Adessenarian
\a-ˌde-sə-ˈner-ē-ən\
Latin+English
: believer of Christ's body

Adighe
\ä-də-¦gā\
Russian
: Russian native

adinole
\a-də-ˌnōl\
Greek>French+Greek>French
: rock

admi
\ad-mē\
Berber
: gazelle

adsum
\ad-ˌsəm, ˈäd-ˌsùm\
Latin
: indication of presence

Adullamite
\ə-ˈdə-lə-ˌmīt\
English+English
: seceders

advehent
\ad-¦vē-ənt; ˈad-və-hənt, -ˌhent\
Latin
: bear organs

Aeaean
\ē-ˈē-ən\
Greek>Latin
: Tyrrhenian native

aecium
\ē-shē-əm, -sē-\
Greek
: rust fungi

aedeagus
\ē-dē-¦ā-gəs, ē-ˈdē-ə-\
Greek>Latin
: male organ

aegagrus
\ē-ˈga-grəs\
Greek>New Latin
: wild goat

aegyptilla
\ē-jəp-ˈti-lə\
Latin+Latin
: gem

aeoline
\ē-ə-ˌlīn\
Greek+English
: soft organ stop

aetites
\ā-ə-ˈtī-tēz\
Greek>Latin
: eagle stone

affrettando
\a-frə-ˈtän-dō, ä-\
Latin+Italian
: faster in music

agapetae
\ä-gə-ˈpā-ˌtī, a-gə-;a-gə-ˈpē-ˌtē\
Greek
: spiritual women

agarwal
\ə-gər-ˌwäl, a-\
Hindi
: mercantile cash

aglaozonia
\a-glē-ə-ˈzō-nyə, -nē-ə\
New Latin+Greek
: brown alga

aguamiel
\ä-gwə-¦myel\
Latin+Latin>Spanish
: unfermented juice

aguardiente
\ä-ˌgwär-dē-ˈen-tē, -ˈdyen-tā\
Latin+Spanish
: alcoholic beverage

agunah
\ä-gü-ˈnä, ä-ˈgü-nə\
Hebrew
: deserted women

ahaaina
\ä-ˌhä-ˈī-nə\
Hawaiian
: banquet

Ahir
\ə-ˈhir\
Hindi
: cattle-breeders

ahuehuete
\ä-wē-ˈwä-tē\
Spanish
: cypress

aillt
\ī(-ə)lt\
Welsh
: servile class

ailsyte
\āl-ˌsīt\
Scottish+English
: rock

ainoi
\ā-nē\
Greek
: part of divine office

airan
\ī-ˈrän\
Turkish
: fermented milk

aire
\är-ə\
Gaelic
: Irish ranks

aischrolatreia
\ī-skrō-lə-ˈtrī-ə\
Old English>Greek
: worship of filth

aithochroi
\ī-ˈthä-krə-ˌwī\
Greek>New
Latin+Greek>New Latin
: red-brown skin

aizle
\ā-zəl\
Middle English
: spark

ajimez
\ä-ḵē-ˈmäth, -ˈmäs\
Arabic>Spanish
: twin window

akeley
\ə-ˈkē-lē\
New Latin
: plant

akhissar
\äk-hi-ˌsär, ˌä-ki-\
Turkish
: carpet

akhundzada
\ä-ˌkün-ˈzä-də\
Hindi+Hindi
: son of officer

akkum
\ä-kəm\
Hebrew
: star worshiper

akori
\ä-kə-rē\
African name
: porous coral

akule
\ä-ˈkü-lē\
Hawaiian
: big-eyed scad

alalus
\a-lə-ləs; ā-ˈlä-, -ˈla-\
Greek>New Latin
: lower order of man

alameda
\a-lə-ˈmē-də, -ˈmä-\
Spanish
: promenade

alamiqui
\a-lə-mə-ˈkē\
American Spanish
: insectivore

alant
\a-lənt, ə-ˈlant\
Latin>German
: sneezeweed

Alascan
\ə-ˈla-skən\
Polish name
: foreign protestant

alastrim
\a-lə-ˌstrim, ə-ˈla-strəm\
French>Portuguese
: form of smallpox

albacea
\al-bə-ˈsā-ə\
Arabic>Spanish
: designated person

albahaca
\al-bə-ˈhä-kə, -ˈha-\
Arabic name
: plant

albertustaler
\äl-ˈber-tə-ˌstä-lər\
Dutch+Dutch>German
: silver coin

albaspidin
\al-ˈba-spə-dēn\
ISV+New Latin+ISV
: crystalline

alcyon
\al-sē-ən\
Greek>New Latin
: coral

Alderney
\ȯl-dər-nē\
English name
: cattle

Alexian
\ə-ˈlek-shən, -ˈlek-sē-ən\
Roman name+English
: nurse

alferez
\al-ˈfer-əs, -ˈfir-\
Arabic>Spanish
: ensign

alguacil
\al-gwə-ˌsēl, -ˌsil\
Arabic>Spanish
: justician

alintatao
\älintäˌtau̇\
Tagalog>Philippine Spanish
: tree

aliter
\alətər, -ətər, -əˌte(ə)r\
Latin
: otherwise

alkavervir
\alkəˈvərˌvi(ə)r, alˈkavə(r)\
New Latin
: preparation

alkermes
\alˈkərmēz, -məs; alkərˈmes\
Arabic>Spanish>French
: Italian liquor

alliin
\ˈalēən\
ISV
: amino acid

alloeostropha
\alēˈästrəfə\
Greek+New Latin
: irregular stanzas

almaciga
\alˈmäsēgə, -ˌgä\
Spanish
: gumbo-limbo

almemor
\alˈmē, mȯ(ə)r\
Hebrew
: platform in synagogue

almique
\almə¦kē\
American Spanish
: tree

almirah
\alˈmīrə\
Panjabi>Hindi
: wardrobe, cabinet

Almoravid
\alməˈrävəd, alˈmōrəv-\
Arabic
: member of Muslim

almuce
\alˌmyüs\
Middle French
: hood

aloysia
\aləˈwish(ē)ə\
New Latin
: plant with lemon fragrance

alpujarra
\alpüˈhärə\
Spanish
: rug

alternat
\ȧlternä\
Latin>French
: diplomatic practice

aludel
\alyəˌdel\
Arabic>Middle
Latin&Spanish
: pear-shaped bottle

alurgite
\əˈlərˌjīt, alər-\
ISV+German
: mica

aluta
\əˈlütə\
Latin
: leather

Alypin
\aləpən\
Trademark
: amydricaine

amaltas
\əˈməlˌtäs\
Hindi
: extract from drumstick tree

amamau
\ämə¦mau̇\
Hawaiian
: tree fern

amassette
\amə¦set\
French
: scraping instrument

amatungula
\aməˈtəŋg(y)ələ\
Zulu
: bushy shrub

amauta
\əˈmau̇tə\
Quechua>Spanish
: wise man

ambay
\amˌbī\
Tupi
: timber tree

ambilanak
\ambə¦länə(k)\
Malay+Malay
: Sumatran marriage

ambitus
\ambətəs\
Latin
: periphery

ambrein
\amˌbrān, -brēən\
French
: alcohol

ambry
\am-brē; ˈäm-rē, ˈȯm-\
Latin
: place for keeping things

Amidah
\əˈmēdȯ, äˈ-, -dä; ˌämēˈdȯ\
Hebrew
: benediction

ammocoetes
\aməˈsētēz\
Greek>Latin
: larva

amphictyony
\am-ˈfik-tē-ə-nē\
Greek
: association of neighboring states

amphimacer
\amˈfiməsə(r), ˈamfəˌmās-\
Greek>Latin
: syllable

amphisbaena
\am(p)-fəs-ˈbē-nə\
Greek+Latin
: serpent

amydricaine
\əˈmidrəˌkān\
ISV
: anesthetic

anacahuita
\anəkəˈwētə\
Nahuatl>Spanish
: aromatic tree

Anacrogynae
\anəˈkräjənē\
New Latin
: liverwort

anagignoskomena
\anəˌgignəˈskämənə\
Greek
: Old Testament Apocrypha

Anakim
\anəˌkim\
Hebrew
: giants

anargyros
\äˈnäryēˌrós\
Greek
: thirteen saints

anaspalin
\əˈnaspələn\
Unknown
: mixture of wool fat

anatexis
\anəˈteksəs\
Greek+Greek
: process of dissolving rocks

anconeus
\aŋˈkōnēəs\
Latin
: muscle

anetha
\əˈnēthə\
Greek>Latin
: dried fruit

angelon
\anjəˈlōn\
Late Latin>Spanish
: plant

angico
\anˈjēkü, -kō\
Portuguese
: tree

anhima
\anˈhīmə; əˈnēmə, aˈ-\
Portuguese
: horned screamer

anisidine
\əˈnisəˌdēn, -dən\
French
: isomeric bases

anjan
\anjən, -ˌjan\
Hindi
: tree

ankyroid
\aŋˈkīˌrȯid, ˈaŋkə-\
Greek
: hook-shaped

Anomura
\anəˈm(y)ùrə\
New Latin
: crustaceans

anquera
\anˈkerə, aŋ-\
Mexican Spanish
: stock saddle tailpiece

anthraquinonyl
\an(t)-thrəˌkwēˈnōˌnil\
ISV
: radical

antichthon
\anˈtikˌthän, -ˌthōn, -thən\
Greek>Latin
: counterearth

apatheia
\apəˈthīə\
Greek
: freedom

apeiron
\əˈpīˌrän, -pā-\
Greek
: indefinite ground

aperea
\äˌperēˈä\
Tupi
: rodent

Aphthartodocetae
\afˌthärtōdōˈsēte, apth-, -sētē\
Latin>Greek
: Monophysitic sect

apocha
\apəkə\
Greek>Late Latin
: written receipt

apodeipnon
\äˈpȯdēpˌnȯn\
Greek+Greek
: divine office

apophyge
\əˈpäfəjē\
Greek
: curvature

appenzell
\a-pən-ˌzel, ˈä-pən(t)-ˌsel\
Swedish
: fine embroidery

aquafortis
\ä-kwə-ˈfȯr-təs, ˈa-\
Latin+Latin
: nitric acid

Aquilian
\əˈkwilēən\
Latin+Latin
: Roman republic

aragonesa
\arəgōˈnäsə, -äzə\
Spanish
: dance

aralkyl
\aˈralˌkil\
ISV
: radical

aramid
\a-rə-məd, -ˌmid, 'er-ə-\
Aromatic Polyamide
: polyamide material

araphorostic
\arəfə¦rästik\
Greek+English
: unsewed

aratinga
\arə'tiŋgə\
Portuguese>New Latin
: parakeet

Araucana
\əˌraůˈkänə\
Spanish
: chicken

archai
\ärˌk ī\
Greek
: things that were in the
beginning

arcifinious
\ärsə¦finēəs\
Latin
: naturally boundary

arête
\ˌa-rə-'tā, -tē\
French
: ridge

arisaka
\arə¦säkə, ¦är-\
Japanese
: rifles

Armagnac
\är-män-'yäk\
French
: brandy

arrant
\a-rənt, 'er-ənt\
Alteration
: wandering

arras
\a-rəs, 'er-əs *sometimes* a-
ˌras, er-ˌas\
French
: tapestry

arrastre
\ə'räˌsträ\
Philippine Spanish
: operation of unloading

arrau
\äˌraů, ə'raů, ə'räü\
American Spanish
: turtle

arrayan
\ä'rəyän\
Spanish
: tree

asarabacca
\asərə'bakə\
Greek>Latin+Spanish
: plant

asherah
\ə'shirə\
Hebrew
: wooden post

Ashkenazi
\äsh-kə-'nä-zē, ash-kə-'na-zē\
Hebrew
: Jewish speaker

askari
\askərē; ə'skärē, a's-\
Arabic
: native soldier

aspalathus
\a'spaləthəs\
Greek>Latin
: biblical shrub

asparaginyl
\aspə'rajənəl, -ˌnēl\
ISV
: radical

assythment
\əsithmənt\
Scottish
: indemnification for injury

aswang
\ä'swäŋ\
Filipino
: witch

atopy
\a-tə-pē\
Greek
: allergy

aubain
\ō'bān\
French
: alien subject

aubepine
\ôbəˌpēn, -bā-, -pən, ōbā'pēn\
French
: amisaldehyde

aufait
\ō-'fā\
Alteration
: ice cream

Aufklarung
\aůf-ˌkler-əŋ, -ůŋ\
Middle Dutch+German
: enlightenment

aumaga
\aů'mägə\
Samoan
: village organization

aumakua
\aůmə'küə\
Hawaiian
: family god

Aunjetitz
\aůnyəˌtits\
Czechoslovakian name
: Bronze Age

autacoid
\ȯ-tə-ˌkȯid\
Welsh>English+Greek
: active substance

autoette
\ȯtə¦wet\
Alteration
: 3 wheel motorbike

auwai
\au̇ˌwī\
Hawaiian
: watercourse

avadavat
\avədəˌvat\
Indian place
: weaverbird

avellan
\ə-ˈve-lən, ˈa-və-\
Italian
: like a hazelnut

avenin
\əˈvēnən, ˈavən-\
Latin>ISV
: glutelin of oats

avizandum
\aviˈzandəm\
Scottish
: private consideration

avondbloem
\ävənˌblüm\
Middle Dutch>Afrikaans
: bulbous plant

avourneen
\əˈvu̇rˌnēn\
Irish Gaelic
: darling

awanyu
\əˈwänyü\
Tewa
: serpent

awmous
\áməs, ȯməs\
Middle English
: alms

ayacahuite
\īyəkəˈwētä\
Nahuatl
: pine tree

ayah
\ˈī-ə; ˈä-yə, -yä\
Hindi>Portuguese>Latin
: maid

ayahuasco
\ī-ə-ˈ(h)wä-skō, -skə\
Quechua
: vine

Aylesbury
\ālzbərē, -brē, -i\
English name
: ducks

ayllu
\īlü\
Quechua
: socioeconomic unit

azafran
\äˌsəfrän\
Arabic>Spanish
: saffron

azarole
\azəˌrōl\
Arabic>Spanish>French
: shrub

azedarach
\əˈzedəˌrak\
French>Persian
: chinaberry

azon
\āˌzōn, āˌzän\
Portmanteau
: bomb

azoth
\a-ˌzȯth\
Arabic
: mercury

azrael
\azrāˌel\
Hebrew>Arabic
: angel of death

azulene
\azhəˌlēn\
Spanish>ISV
: hydrocarbon

azyme
\aˌzīm\
Latin>Greek
: unleavened bread

babacoote
\bäbəˈkütē\
Malagasy
: lemur

baboen
\bäˌbün\
Dutch
: timber tree

bacauan
\bəˈkäwən\
Tagalog
: mangrove

bacaba
\bəˈkäbə\
Tupi>Portuguese
: palm

bache
\bach\
Middle English
: valley

badian
\bädēən, badēən\
Persian>French
: fruit

baeckeol
\bākēȯl, bākēōl\
New Latin+English
: ketone

baggit
\bagȧt\
Scottish
: salmon

bagoong
\bäˈgȯʔˌȯŋ\
Tagalog
: sauce

bahadur
\bəˈhȯdə(r), -ˈhä-, -ˈhȧ-\
Hindi
: distinguished person

bahera
\bəhəˌrä\
Hindi
: tree

bailli
\bȧyē\
French
: military powers

baittle
\bātᵊl\
Old Norse
: rich nourishing

bakula
\bəkələ\
Sanskrit
: tree

Bakuninism
\bəˈkün(y)ȧˌnizəm\
Russian+English
: anarchism

bakupari
\bäküpəˈrē\
Portuguese
: tree

balaam
\bā-ləm\
Biblical name
: rejected magazine

balam
\bäləm\
Maya
: supernatural being

balancelle
\bälən¦sel\
Italian>French
: fishing boat

balangay
\bälən¦gī\
Ilako>Tagalog
: boat

baldie
\bȯldē\
Italian name
: double-ended boat

balian
\bälēən\
Malay
: medicine man

balinger
\balȧnjə(r)\
Middle French>Middle English
: ship

ballogan
\bäl(ə)gən\
Scottish Gaelic
: nipplewort

balmony
\ba(l)mənē\
Unknown
: turtlehead

balow
\baˈlō\
Scottish
: lullaby

bamboula
\bamˈbülə, bäm-\
Bantu>French
: drum

bambuco
\bamˈbükō\
American Spanish
: dance song

Banaba
\bä-ˈnä-bä\
Tagalog&Bisayan
: timber tree

bancal
\bäŋˈkäl\
Bisayan>Spanish
: tree

bancha
\bänchä\
Japanese
: tea

Bandkeramik
\bänt-kä-¦rä-mik\
French+Greek
: pottery

bangalay
\baŋ-ˈa-lē\
Australian name
: Australian tree

banghy
\baŋ-gē\
Hindi
: shoulder yoke

bankskuta
\baŋkˌskütə\
Norwegian+Swedish
: fishing craft

bantayan
\bänˈtäˌyän\
Tagalog
: signal tower

banuyo
\bəˈnüyō\
Tagalog
: tree

barani
\bəˈranē, -ränē\
Eponym
: trampoline stunt

barathea
\ber-ə-ˈthē-ə, ba-rə'thē-ə \
Trademark
: fabric

barbas
\bärbəs, bärbbəz\
Portuguese
: tree

baramin
\barəmə́n\
Hebrew
: created plant

barbasco
\bärˈbaskō, -rˈbä-\
American Spanish
: wild cinnamon

barde
\bär¦dā F bȧrdā\
French
: covered with salt pork

barff
\bärf\
Eponym
: protect with iron-oxide

bargham
\bärfəm, bärkəm\
Old English
: horse's collar

barit
\bəˈrēt\
Tagalog
: marsh grass

barmbrack
\bärmˌbrak\
Irish Gaelic
: rich currant bun

Barotse
\bəˈrätsə\
Afrikaans
: African cattle

barranca
\bəˈraŋ-kə\
Spanish
: deep gulley

Barsac
\bärˌsak\
French
: Bordeaux wine

barsom
\bärsəm\
Persian
: sacred twig bundle

baryta
\bəˈrītə\
Alteration
: barium compound

Bassalia
\bə-ˈsä-lē-ə\
New Latin
: abyssal zone

bassanelli
\ba-sə-ˈne-lē, bä-\
Italian
: double-reed instrument

basural
\bä-sü-ˈräl\
Spanish
: refuse heap

batitinan
\bätə'tēˌnän\
Tagalog
: Philippine tree

battue
\ba-ˈtü, ba-ˈtyü\
French
: drawing out from game

baumer
\bȯ-mər\
Eponym
: fabric impressed pottery

bavin
\ba-vən\
Unknown
: brushwood bundle

bayok
\bī-¦ōk\
Tagalog
: tree

bedikah
\bə-dē-ˈkä, bə-ˈdē-kä\
Hebrew
: ritual inspection

begti
\beg-tē, ˈbek-tē\
Bengali
: fish

begum
\bā-gəm, bēgəm\
Hindi>Turkic
: Muslim queen

beisa
\bā-zə, bā-zä\
Amharic
: antelope

bejel
\be-jəl\
Arabic
: disease

bekra
\be-krə\
Indian name
: antelope

belah
\bē-lə\
Australian name
: beefwood

benab
\bə-ˈnab\
Guianan name
: native hut

Bentinck
\ben-ti(ŋ)k\
British name
: sail

benzalkonium
\ben-zal-ˈkō-nē-əm\
Greek elements
: radical mixture

berairou
\bə-ˈrī-ˌraů\
Native New Zealand name
: tree

Bergama
\bər-gəmə, ˈber-, bər-ˈgä-mə\
Turkish name
: rug

bergapten
\bər-ˈgap-tən\
ISV
: crystalline

berimbau
\bā-ˈrēm-ˌbaů\
Brazilian Portuguese
: instrument

bethabara
\be-ˈtha-bə-rə\
Unknown
: timber tree

Beveren
\be-v(ə-)rən, ˈbā-\
Belgian
: rabbit breed

Bezpopovets
\bes-pə-ˈpȯ-vəts, bez-\
Greek+Russian
: priestless sect member

bevue
\bā-ˈvue\
Latin+French
: error due to ignorance

biacuru
\bī-ə-kə-ˌrü\
Tupi>Portuguese
: root

bickiron
\bi-kərn, -ˌkī-ərn\
Latin>Middle
French>English
: anvil part

bigae
\bē-ˌgī, bē-gē, bē-jē; ˈbī-jē\
Latin
: two-horse chariot

bijar
\bȯ-ˈjär\
Iranian geo name
: Persian rug

Bikaneri
\bikəˈnerē, bē-, -nirē\
Hindi
: breed of sheep

bikhaconitine
\bikəˈkänəˌtēn, -ən\
ISV elements
: crystalline alkaloid

bikkurim
\biˌküˈrēm, -ˈkůrim\
Hebrew
: ripe fruits

bilander
\biləndə(r), ˈbī-\
Dutch
: ship

bilimbi
\bəˈlimbē\
Konkani&Malay
: starfruit-like tree

billiken
\bilə̇kən\
Name
: comic figure

billywix
\bil, ēwiks\
Unknown
: tawny owl

Bilston
\bilstən\
English name
: enamelware

binghi
\biŋ, ī\
Australian name
: aborigine

biriba
\birēˈbä\
Tupi>Portuguese
: tree

birsle
\birsəl, ˈbər-\
Scottish
: broil, toast, dry

bisabolene
\bis, abəlēn\
ISV
: sesquiterpene

blaasop
\blä̇ˌsäp\
German>Afrikaans
: globefish

blaffert
\bläfə(r)t\
Middle High German
: silver coin

blaflum
\blaf(l)əm, blə'f(l)əm\
Unknown
: hoax

bleaunt
\blēənt\
Middle French>Middle
English
: medieval tunic

blesmol
\bles‚mȯl, -mōl\
Afrikaans
: rodent

blijver
\blīvə(r)\
Dutch+Afrikaans
: mixed blood

blimbing
\blimbiŋ\
Tagalog+Malay
; starfruit

blite
\blīt\
Greek>Middle English
: herbs

blore
\blu̇(ə)r, -u̇ə\
Middle English
: bellow

bluet
\'blü-ət\
Portmanteau
: cornflower

blype
\blīp\
Unknown
: shred of skin

bobachee
\bäbə‚chē\
Hindi
: male cook

bocal
\bōkəl, bō'kal\
Greek>Italian>French
: tube for mouthpiece

bocksbeutel
\bäks‚bȯitᵊl\
German
: wine bottle

bodach
\bōdək, 'bädək\
Irish Gaelic&Scottish Gaelic
: boorish old man

bodieron
\bōdē'irən\
Unknown
: sea trout

boekenhout
\bükən‚hȧut\
Middle Dutch+Afrikaans
: tree

boeotarch
\bēə‚tärk, bē'ō‚tärk\
Greek elements
: chief magistrates

bokadam
\bō-kə-dəm\
West Indies
: snake

bonaci
\bōnə'sē\
Spanish
: grouper

bonduc
\bän‚dək\
Arabic>French
: tree

bonxie
\bäŋksē\
Latin>Middle
French>Middle English
: great skua

boongary
\büŋgərē\
Australian name
: wallaby

borak
\bȯrək, 'bär-\
Australian name
: fun, ridicule

borderer
\bȯr-dər-ər\
Middle English
: London City member

boreen
\bȯr-'ēn\
Latin>Irish Gaelic
: country road

Borinqueno
\bȯriŋ'känyō\
Spanish
: Puerto Rican

borracha
\bə'räshə\
Spanish>Portuguese
: crude rubber

Bosjesman
\bäshəsmən, 'bȯsh-, -shəzm-\
Middle Dutch+Middle Dutch
: bushman

bosse
\bä¦sā, 'bäs, 'bȯs\
French
: leaflets

bosthoon
\bäs'thün\
Late Latin>Irish Gaelic
: boor, dolt

botogenin
\bō'täjənən, bätə'jenən\
Spanish
: sapogenin

botete
\bō'tätē\
American Spanish
: globefish

bouchal
\büǝk̲ǝl\
Greek>Irish
: herdboy

bouillotte
\bō'tätē\
French
: dance

Boulonnais
\bülǝ¦nā\
French
: horse breed

bourrelet
\bu̇rǝ¦lā\
French
: cloth worn on helmet

bouto
\bō-ˌtü\
Late Latin>Portuguese
: dolphin

boutre
\bütr(ᵊ), -t(rǝ)\
French
: coasting boat

bowkail
\bōˌkāl\
Scottish
: cabbage

bowssen
\'bau̇sᵊn\
Welsh
: duck in water

bowyang
\bōˌyaŋ\
English
: tied cord

boyla
\bȯilǝ\
Australian name
: native sorcerer

Brabancon
\brabǝnˌsän, brǝ'ban(t)sǝn\
Shortening
: horse breed

brackmard
\brakˌmär(d)\
Middle Dutch>French
: straight broadsword

braconniere
\brakǝn¦ye(ǝ)r\
French
: thigh armor

brasero
\brǝ'serō\
Spanish
: brick stove

brassard
\brǝ-'särd, 'bra-ˌsärd\
French
: armor

brattach
\bra-tak\
Scottish Gaelic
: banner, flag

braul
\brau̇(ǝ)l\
French>Romanian
: lively dance

braxy
\'braksē\
Unknown
: malignant edema

brayera
\brǝ'yerǝ, 'brāǝrǝ\
New Latin
: pistillate flowers

Bretwalda
\bret-wäldǝ\
Old English
: chief king

brewis
\brüz, brüǝs\
Old French>Middle English
: broth

briard
\brē-'är(d)\
French
: breed of dogs

brizz
\briz\
Middle English
: crush

bromidiom
\brō'midēǝm\
Portmanteau
: commonplace

bromsulphalein
\brōm-ˌsǝl-'fa-lē-ǝn, -sǝl-, -'fā-\
Trademark
: dye

bromvoel
\bräm̲ˌfüǝl\
Middle Dutch
: hornbill

brose
\brōz\
Scottish
: dish

brotchen
\brœtk̲ǝn\
German
: piece of yeast dough

brouillon
\brüyōⁿ\
French
: rough draft

bruang
\brü-äŋ\
Malay
: sun bear

brucine
\brü-ˌsēn, -sən\
French+French
: poisonous crystalline

Bruxellois
\brūēselwȧ\
French
: Brussels native

buaze
\bwäzē\
Nyanja
: woody vine

bubaline
\byübəˌlīn, -ə̇n\
New Latin+English
: antelope-like

bubonocele
\b(y)ü-ˌbä-n ə ˌsēl\
Greek
: inguinal hernia

bucare
\bükəˌrä, -ē, büˈkärē\
Spanish
: tree

buccinae
\bəksənē\
Latin elements
: trumpets

buchu
\ˈb(y)ük(y)ü\
Zulu
: dried leaves

buckshee
\bək-shē, bək-ˈshē\
Hindi
: gratuity

bugala
\büˈgalə\
Arabic
: dhow

bugloss
\byü-ˌgläs, -ˌglȯs\
Greek>Latin>Middle French
: plant

buirdly
\bu̇r(d)-li\
Alteration
: well-built

bullace
\bu̇-ləs\
Middle English
: plum

bulto
\bu̇ltō, bül-\
Latin>Spanish
: saint image

bungarum
\bəŋˈgärəm\
Telugu
: snakes

bunuelo
\bünyəˈwälō\
Catalan>Spanish
: semisweet cake

buplever
\b(y)ü-ˌplevə(r)\
Latin>French
: plant

bure
\ˈbürä\
Fijian
: large temple

burley
\bər-lē\
Name
: tobacco

butenyl
\byütᵊnəl\
ISV
: univalent radicals

buteonine
\byütēəˌnīn, -ən; byüˈtē-\
New Latin+English
: like short-winged hawks

butsudan
\bu̇tsəˌdän\
Japanese
: household altar shelf

butteris
\bətərəs, -ət(ə)rəs\
Middle French
: steel instrument

butyryl
\byütərəl\
ISV
: radical

buyo
\büyō\
Spanish
: masticatory

Buzain
\bu̇ˈzān, bəˈz-, -zan\
German
: reed stop

bwana
\bwä-nə\
Arabic>Swahili
: master

bycoket
\bīˌkäkət\
Middle French>Middle
English
: hat

byon
\bīˌän, -īən\
Burman name
: clayey earth

byrnie
\bərnē\
Old Norse>Middle English
: coat of mail

bysmalith
\bizmə‚lith\
Greek+English
: laccolith

bywoner
\bī‚vōnə(r), bā‚v-\
Middle Dutch>Afrikaans
: laborer

cabezon
\kabə‚zōn\
Latin>Spanish
: fish

cachaza
\kə'chäsə, -ȧsə\
Spanish
: press cake

cacotheline
\kə'käthə‚lēn, ka-, -lȧn\
French>ISV
: poisonous base

cafeneh
\kafə‚nā\
Turkish
: coffeehouse

caffetannin
\kafə̇¦tanȧn, -fē-\
ISV+French
: crystalline

cafila
\kafələ, 'kä-\
Arabic
: company of travelers

calabozo
\kalə'bōzō, -ōzə\
Spanish
: jail

calipee
\kȧl-ə- pē\
Unknown
: resin

calvados
\kal-və-¦dōs, ¦käl-, -¦dȯs, -¦däs\
French
: brandy

camauro
\kə'maùrō\
Italian
: velvet cap

cambaye
\kam¦bā\
Indian place
name>Portuguese
: cotton

canaigre
\kə'nīgrē\
Mexican Spanish
: dock

canajong
\kanə‚joŋ, -äŋ\
Tasmanian
: beach apple

canepin
\kanəpȧn, F kȧnpaⁿ\
French
: leather

capias
\kā-pē-əs\
Latin>Middle English
: legal writ

capuche
\kə-'püch, -'püsh\
Late Latin>Italian
: hood

caracal
\ker-ə-¦kal, ¦ka-rə-\
Turkish>Spanish>French
: cat

carceag
\kärsē‚ag\
Romanian
: sheep disesase

carey
\kə'rā\
Taino>American Spanish
: hawksbill

Carlowitz
\kärlə‚wits\
German
: red wine

caroome
\kə'rüm\
Irregular
: license

carrizo
\kə'rēzō, -sō\
Latin>Spanish
: reed grass

casaque
\kə'zak\
Middle French>French
: blouse

cassareep
\kasə‚rēp\
Akawai Galibi>Cariban
: flavoring

cassiri
\kasə¦rē\
Tupi>Carib
: drink

catasarka
\katə'särkə\
Greek
: altar cloth

catechu
\ka-tə-‚chü, -‚shü, -‚kyü\
Malay
: resins

catla
\kätlə, -ˌlä\
Bengali
: fish

catocala
\kəˈtäkələ; katəˈkālə, -ˈkalə\
Greek
: moth

caure
\kär, -ȯ-\
Middle English
: calves

cawquaw
\kȯˌkwȯ\
Cree
: porcupine

cebil
\səˈbēl\
American Spanish
: gum

cedriret
\sed(r)əˌret\
Greek>Latin>German
: quinone

cedula
\sāthəˌlä, ˈthāth-\
Late Latin>Spanish
: document

ceibo
\sābō\
American Spanish
: tree

celadon
\se-lə-ˌdän, -dᵊn\
French
: yellow-green

cenizo
\sə-ˈnē-zō, -sō\
Spanish
: shod scale

censitaire
\sänsēteer\
French
: vassal

centenier
\sentᵊnˌi(ə)r, -iə\
Latin>Late Latin>Middle French> Middle English
: police officer

cercle
\serkl(ᵊ), -k(lə)\
French
: district

cereza
\səˈrāzə, -āsə, -re-\
Latin>Spanish>American Spanish
: cherries

cerris
\serəs\
Latin
: oak

cervelat
\sər-və-ˌlat; -ˌlä, ˈser-və-ˌlä\
Obsolete French
: sausage

ceterach
\setəˌrak\
Persian>Arabic>Middle Latin
: scale fern

chacra
\chäkrə\
Quechua>American Spanish
: ranch

chaja
\chəˈhä, chä'-\
Guarani>Spanish
: screamer

chakari
\chäkərē\
Persian>Hindi
: clerical service

Chaldee
\kal-ˌdē, ˈkȯl-, ˈkäl-\
Latin>Middle French>Middle English
: vernacular

chaloupe
\shəˈlüp\
Old Provencal>French
: boat

chagoma
\shəˈgōmə\
New Latin+New Latin
: tumorlike swelling

chamma
\shamə\
Arabic
: toga

chanar
\chänˈyär\
Spanish
: tree

chantant
\shäⁿtäⁿ\
French
: tuneful

chalone
\kā-ˌlōn, ˈka-\
Greek
: secretion

chamar
\chəˈmär\
Sanskrit>Hindi
: fan

chambery
\shäⁿbārē\
French
: dry white wine

champlevé
\shäⁿ-lə-ˌvā\
French
: enamel work

chancre
\shaŋ-kər\
French
: ulcer

chandul
\chənd⁽ᵊ⁾l, -än-\
Unknown
: fiber

chappow
\chəˈpaủ\
Persian
: foray

chamaerrhine
\kaməˌrīn\
ISV
: broad-nosed

Charentais
\sharänˈtā\
French
: muskmelon

chaudron
\shō¦drōⁿ\
French
: antique red

chausses
\shōs\
Latin>French
: armor

chelinga
\chəˈliŋgə\
Sanskrit>Tamil
: boat

Cheltenham
\chelt(ᵊ)nam\
English
: printing types

chemawinite
\chəˈmäwəˌnīt\
Hudson Bay Indian name
: fossil resin

chersonese
\kərsəˌnēz, -ēs\
Latin+Greek>Latin
: peninsula

Chessylite
\shesəˌlīt\
English+French
: azurite

cheverel
\shev(ə)rəl\
Latin>Middle
French>Middle English
: leather

cheville
\shəˈvē\
Latin>French
: repetitive word

cheyney
\chānē\
Chinese>Persian
: fabric

chicozapote
\chēkōzəˈpōtē, -ōsə-\
Nahuatl>Spanish
: tree

chikara
\chə́ˈkärə\
Kannada>Dravidian
: gazelle

chilte
\chiltē\
Mexican Spanish
: tree

chiniofon
\kə́ˈnīəˌfän\
ISV
: yellow powder

chinotto
\kēˈnȯtō\
Italian
: sour orange

chiru
\chir-ü\
Tibetan name
: antelope

chocalho
\shüˈkalyü\
Middle Latin>Portuguese
: rattle

cholent
\chȯlənt, 'chəl- *also* 'sh-\
Yiddish
: dish meat and vegetables

chrotta
\krätə\
Welsh>Celtic>Late Latin
: harp

chrysazin
\krisəzə́n\
ISV
: compound

chuzwi
\ˈchəzˌwē\
Afrikaans
: waterbuck

cinquedea
\chiŋkwə́ˈdēə, -dāə\
Italian+Latin>Italian
: medieval dagger

cipolin
\sipələ́n, ¦sēpə¦laⁿ\
Italian&French
: marble

Circumcellion
\ˈsərkəm' selē ən\
Late Latin+Late Latin
: run away slaves

ciruela
\sirəˈwälə\
Latin>Spanish
: plumlike fruit

58

ciseaux
\sē'zō\
French
: ballet movement

citole
\sə'tōl, 'si͵tōl\
Greek>Latin>Middle
French>Middle English
: lute

civet
\si-vət\
French
: seasoned stew

clachan
\kla-ḵən\
Scottish Gaelic>Middle
English
: hamlet

clearcole
\klir͵kōl\
Greek+French
: white priming

cleruch
\kli͵rük, -lē͵r-, -rək\
Greek+Greek
: citizen

cleuk
\'kl(y)ük\
Middle English
: claw

clition
\klitē͵än\
Greek>Greek>New Latin
: median point

cloff
\kläf\
Alteration
: allowance

cloque
\klō-'kā, 'klō-kā\
French
: fabric

clyer
\klī(ə)r\
Dutch
: lymph glands

clypeus
\kli-pē-əs\
Latin
: shield

coaita
\kü͵ī'tä\
Tupi>Portuguese
: spider monkey

cobalamin
\kō-'ba-lə-mən, -͵mēn\
ISV
: vitamin B12

cobego
\kə'bēgō\
Malay
: flying lemur

cobia
\kō-bē-ə\
Unknown
: fish

cochin
\kō-chin, kä-\
Vietnamese place
: fowl

cocillana
\kōsə'lanə, -länə also -länə\
American Spanish
: dried bark

cocozelle
\͵käkə¦zelē\
Middle Latin>Italian>Italian
: squash

coenenchyme
\sə'neŋ͵kīm, sē-\
New Latin
: polyp

cofradia
\kōfrə'dēə, -rä'-\
Latin+Latin>Spanish
: laymen

cognac
\kōn-͵yak also 'kòn- or 'kän-\
French
: brandy

cohosh
\kō-¦häsh, kə'həsh\
Natick
: medicinal plant

coir
\kòir, kòi-ər\
Tamil
: stiff fiber from a coconut

colchiceine
käl'chisēən, -'kis-
;¦kälchə¦sēən, -lkə¦-\
ISV
: crystalline

collidine
\'kälə͵dēn, -dən\
ISV
: organic base

collochore
\kälə͵kō(ə)r\
Greek
: chromosome

colmar
\kōl-͵mär, kōl-'\
French
: fashion fan

colobin
\kä-lə-bən\
French
: monkey

colulus
\käl(y)ələs\
Latin
: organ

59

colza
\käl-zə, ˈkōl-\
Dutch>French
: annual herb

comble
\kōⁿbl(ᵊ), -b(lə)\
Latin>French
: acme

comes
\kō͵mēz, -mes\
Latin
: adviser

comital
\kämət°l\
Latin
: earllike

commandite
\kämən¦dēt, kōⁿmäⁿdēt\
Italian>French
: partnership

commot
\kä͵mät\
Middle English>Medieval
Latin>Middle Welsh
: territorial unit

Comnenian
\käm¦nēnēən\
Byzantine noble family
: 11ᵗʰ to 15ᵗʰ centuries

compital
\kämpət°l\
Latin+Latin
: broad intersection

Complutensian
\kämplü¦tenchən\
Latin+English
: biblical

compromis
\kämprə¦mē\
French
: national agreement

conchuela
\känchəˈwälə\
Spanish>Mexican Spanish
: flat green bug

concupiscence
\kän-ˈkyü-pə-sən(t)s,
kən- also ͵kän-kyü-ˈpi-
s°n(t)s\
Latin>Middle French
: ardent or strong desire

congou
\käŋ-gō, -gü\
Chinese
: Chinese tea

conicopoly
\känəˈkäpəlē\
Sanskrit+Tamil
; native clerk

connexivum
\känəkˈsēvəm\
Latin>New Latin
: abdominal border

conule
\kän°l, -nyəl\
Latin
: elevation

copaene
\kōpāēn\
ISV
: sesquiterpene

copain
\kȯpaⁿ\
French
: companion

coquecigrue
\käk-si-grü\
French
: monster

coquelicot
\käklə͵kō, ˈkōk-\
French
: poppy

corcass
\kȯrkəs\
Greek>Irish Gaelic
: marsh

corcir
\kȯ(r)kə(r)\
Latin>Scottish Gaelic
: violet dye

coremium
\kōˈrēmēəm, kə-\
Greek>New Latin
: fruiting body

corial
\kōˈrēˈä l\
Arawakan
: canoe

coriamyrtin
\kōrēˈəmərt°n\
French+ISV
: poisonous compound

cornemuse
\ˈkȯ(r)nə͵myüz or as F\
Latin>Middle French>Middle
English
: French bagpipe

cornettino
\kȯ(r)nəˈtēnō\
Italian
: 2 ft. organ

Cornwallis
\kȯrnˈwäləs, -wȯl-\
English Eponym
: muster

corpsbruder
\kōr͵brüdər, ˈkȯr-\
German+German
: comrade

Corregidor
\kə-ˈre-gə-͵dȯr\
Latin>Spanish
: magistrate

corrida
\kȯ-ˈrē-thə\
Latin>Spanish
: bullfight

corroboree
\kə-ˈrȯ-bə-rē, -ˈrä-\
Australian name
: nocturnal festivity

cortile
\kȯrˈtēˌlā\
Latin>Italian
: courtyard

coryneform
\kə-ˈri-nə-ˌfȯrm\
New Latin
: bacteria like

coscet
\käsət\
Old English+Old English
: peasnt holder class

costumbrista
\kōstəmˈbristə, käs-, -rēs-\
Latin>Spanish
: regional writer

coteaux
\kȯˈtō(z)\
Canadian French
: hilly uplands

cotele
\kōtᵊlˈā\
Latin>French
: broken outline

cothamore
\kōt(h)əˌmōr\
Irish Gaelic
: overcoat

cotrine
\kätrən, -ˌtrēn\
Unknown
: orange yellow

cougnar
\künˌyär, ˈkünˌ-\
Malay
: ship

coumarou
\k(y)üməˌrü\
Portuguese or
Spanish>French
: tonka-bean tree

courbaril
\kůrbərəl, kůrbəˈril\
French
: locust tree

couratari
\kůrəˈtärē\
Galibi>New Latin
: tropical tree

coussinet
\küsᵊnˌā, -ᵊnˈet\
French
: cushion

cowan
\kaůən\
Spanish
: unskilled worker

coyotillo
\kī-ə-ˈti-lō, kȯi-, -ˈtē-ō\
Mexican Spanish
: shrub

coxopodite
\käkˈsäpəˌdīt\
New Latin
: crustacean joint

crabier
\kra-byā\
Old English>Middle
Dutch>Middle French
: crab-eating bird

crannog
\kra-nəg\
Irish&Scottish Gaelic
: fortified island

cranreuch
\kran-růk̲\
Scottish
: frost

creaght
\krā(k̲)t\
Irish
: herd of cattle

cresol
\krē-ˌsȯl, -ˌsōl\
ISV
: crystalline

crissum
\krisəm\
Latin>Lithuanian>Welsh>Ol
d Norse>Latin
: bird part

Crocein
\krōsēən\
Latin>ISV
: azo dyes

crombec
\k::rämˌbek\
Middle
Dutch>Afrikaans>French
: warbler

cromorne
\krōˈmȯrn, krəˈ-\
French
: reed stop

croute
\krüt\
French
: slice of bread

crucethouse
\ˈkrüsətˌhaůs\
Latin>Old English
: medieval torture

cruiskeen
\krüsh¦kēn\
Middle Dutch>Scottish
Gaelic
:pitcher

crusie
\krüzē, -œzē\
Middle French
: iron lamp

cryoconite
\krī'äkə͵nīt\
Swedish>Greek
: glacier dust

cubeb
\kyü-͵beb\
Armenian>Middle
Latin>Middle French
: fruit

cucujo
\'kük-üyō, -üjō\
Spanish>Taino
: beetle

cuichunchulli
\kwēchən'chülē\
Quechua>American Spanish
: root

cuittle
\küt³l, 'kət-\
Unknown
: coax

culet
\kyü-lət, 'kə-\
Latin
: facet

culilawan
\külē'läwən\
Malay+Malay
: aromatic bark

culpeo
\kül'pāō\
Araucan>Spanish
: mammal

cumay
\kü'mäē, kümə'ē\
Tupi>Portuguese
: shrub

Cupisnique
\küpēz¦nēkā, -ē¦sn-\
Peruan place
: coastal section

Curete
\kyə'rēt\
Greek>Latin
: priest

cuttanee
\kə'tänē\
Arabic>Hindi
: goods of linen

cyamelide
\sī'amə͵līd, -ləd\
ISV
: compound

cyclas
\sikləs\
Greek>Latin
: tunic

cymatium
\sī-'mā-sh(ē-)əm, sə-\
Greek>Latin
: crowning molding

cynganeddion
\kənə'nethyən\
Latin>Welsh
: system of rhyme

daboia
\də'bȯiə\
Hindi
: viper

daddock
\dadək\
Unknown
: rotten wood

Daghestan
\dagə¦stan, dägə¦stän\
Soviet
: rug

dahoon
\də'hün\
Unknown
: evergreen

daikon
\dī-kən\
Japanese
: radish

daimen
\demin, 'dām-\
Unknown
: occasional

dambrod
\dam͵(b)räd\
Scottish
: checkerboard

dandiprat
\dandē͵prat\
Unknown
: silver coin

darabukka
\də'räbəkə, darə'bükə\
Arabic
: kettledrum

darrein
\də'rān, da¦r-\
Latin
: final

dartos
\där͵täs, -rtəs\
Greek
: contractile tissue

dartrose
\där͵trōs *also* -ōz\
Latin>French
: tomato disease

datiles
\dät^əl‿ās, -ätē‿lās\
Spanish
: tree

dattock
\datək\
Wolof
: tree

dauphine
\dòfə‿nā, ‿dōf-\
French
: mashed potatoes

davainea
\də'vānēə\
French
: tapeworm

defi
\dā‿fē\
French
: challenge

dehors
\də'(h)ȯ(ə)r\
French
: foreign to

deirid
\dīrəd\
Greek
: pair of papillae

delatynite
\də'lat^ən‿īt\
German
: amber

deleerit
\də'lērət\
French
: intoxicated

delthyria
\'del,thə,rēə\
Greek>New Latin
: opening between beak

dementi
\dā‿män‿tē\
French
: official

DeMolay
\dēmə'lā\
French
: secret society for boys

dempster
\demztər, -m(p)st-\
Middle English
: court official

dentex
\den‿teks\
Latin
: fish

dentil
\dent^əl, -n‿til\
French
: small block

derechazo
\derə'chäsō\
Latin>Spanish
: bullfighting

de rigueur
\dərē'gər \
French
: required by etiquette

desemer
\dāzəmə(r)\
Turkish
: ancient balance

Deseret
\de-zə-'ret\
Name
: one from Utah

dessous
\də'sü\
French
: underwears

detinet
\det^ən‿et\
Latin
: common law

deutzia
\d(y)ütsēə, 'dȯit-\
Latin
: ornamental shrubs

dhaman
\'dämən\
Sanskrit
: Indian tree

diallelon
\dīə'lē‿län\
Greek
: circle's definition

dieldrin
\dēldrən\
Eponym
: insecticide

diesnon
\dē‿ā‿snōn, ‿dī‿ēz‿nän\
Latin
: day with no business

disselboom
\disəl‿büm, -‿bōm\
Dutch>Afrikaans
: pole

Diveses
\dī‿vēzəz\
Latin
: rich men

doigte
\dwä'tā\
Latin>French
: fingering

dolosse
\də'läsə\
Afrikaans
: knucklebones

Doron
\dōrˌän\
French+English
: layered glass cloth

doucine
\düˌsēn\
French
: molding

doundake
\dünˈdäkē\
Wolof
: bark

dourine
\düˌrēn\
French
: contagious disease

douzainier
\düˌzänˌyā\
French
: member of a body of IZ

draisine
\drāˈzēn, drāˈzēnə, drīˈzēnə\
German+German
: dandy horse

Dreyfusard
\drīfəˌsärd, ˌdräf-, -f(y)üˌ-, -ˌzä-\
French+French
: defender

drostdy
\dròˈstā, -òsˈdā\
Middle Dutch+Afrikaans
: office

dudaim
\d(y)ü'dī, ēm\
Hebrew
: melon

dytiscid
\dīˈtisəd, dȯˈ-\
New Latin
: diving beetle

Fagara
\fəˈgärə\
Arabic>New Latin
: plant

Fameuse
\fəˈmyüz\
French
: apple

fanion
\fanyən\
French
: flag

fartlek
\färtˌlek\
Swedish
: endurance

fasciolae
\fəˈsēəlē, -sīə-\
Latin
: architrave

fatshedera
\fatˈsed(ə)rə, -tsˈhe-\
New Latin
: foliage plant

Feldenkrais
\feldənˌkrīs\
Trademark
: tension easing

felibrean
\fāˈlēbrəən\
French
: literary writer

fierasfer
\fīəˈrasfə(r)ˌ fēə-\
Latin>Provencal
: inquiline fish

fisetin
\fəˈzetˀn\
German
: crystalline

flaser
\ˈfläzə(r)\
German
: streaked lens

fletton
\fletˀn\
English
: brick

flindersia
\flinˈdərzēə\
New Latin+New Latin
: tree woody

fluavil
\flüəˌvil\
French
: yellow resin

flumerin
\flümərən, flüˈmərən\
ISV
: red powder

fluoxetine
\flüˈäksəˌtēn\
ISV
: antidepressant drug

folacin
\fōləsən, ˈfälə-\
ISV
: vitamin

fonio
\fōnēˌō\
French
: crabgrass

foram
\fòrəm\
New Latin
: protozoan

foresey
\fōrˈsī\
Scottish
: beef cut

formedon
\fȯrmə͵dän\
Middle Latin>Arabic
: former writ

fouette
\fwe¦tā\
French
: movement

foule
\fü¦lā\
French
: cloth

fourdrinier
\fu̇r'drinēər, -ē͵ā\
English name
: paper machine

fourragere
\fu̇rə¦zhe(ə)r\
French
: braided cord

fradicin
\fradəsən\
New Latin+English
: antibiotic

freddo
\frādō\
Latin>Italian
: passionless in music

Fribourg
\frē͵bu̇(ə)r\
Swedish
: cattle breed

frisolee
\frēzə¦lā\
French
: mosaic

furiant
\f(y)u̇rē͵änt\
German&Czech
: dance

fusain
\fyü͵zān\
French
: charcoal

gabbaim
\gä͵bīəm\̇
Hebrew
: gift collector

galanas
\gä'länəs\
Welsh
: fine for murder

galeeny
\gə'lēnē\
Latin>Spanish
: bird

gallivat
\galə͵vat\
Middle Latin>Portuguese
: ship

garancine
\garən¦sēn\
French
: dye with acid

gardyloo
\gärdi'lü\
French
: warning shout

garookuh
\gə'rükə\
Unknown
: fishing boat

garrot
\gȧrō\
French
: diving duck

gaspereaus
\gaspə¦rōs\
Canadian French
: food fish

gaspergou
\gaspə(r)¦gü\
Late French
: freshwater drum

gattine
\ga¦tēn\
French
: fatal disease

gaungbaung
\gau̇ŋ͵bau̇ŋ\
Burmese name
: headcloth

gaydiang
\gīdē͵aŋ\
Annamese
: boat

gayyou
\gā¦(y)ü, gī¦\
Annamese
: boat

gelada
\jelədə, 'ge-; jə'lädə, gə'-\
Arabic
: ape

gelilah
\gə'lēlə\
Hebrew
: rolling of scroll

gelinotte
\zhəlēnȯt\
French
: hazel hen

genistein
\jə'nistēən, -'ni͵stēn\
ISV
: colorless compound

geonim
\gā'ōnəm, gāō'nēm\
Hebrew
: intellectual honor

Ghibelline
\gibə͵lēn, -͵līn, -lən\
Middle High Greek>Italian
: political member

Gideon
\gidēən\
Biblical name
: organization member

gifblaar
\gif͵blär\
Afrikaans
: perennial shrub

gisant
\zhēzän\
Latin>French
: recumbent sculpture

glaucothoe
\glȯ'käthə͵wē\
New Latin
: hermit crab

gleization
\glā'zāshən\
Polish>Latin
: clayey formation

glenurquhart
\gle'nərkərt\
German
: twill pattern

gliadin
\glīədᵊn\
Italian
: simple protein

glochid
\glōkəd\
Latin
: barbed hair

glucagon
\glükə͵gän\
Greek
: protein

glutelin
\glütᵊlən, glü'tel-\
ISV
: protein

gnaphalioid
\nə'fālē͵ȯid\
Latin
: herb

gnetaceous
\nə'tāshəs\
New Latin
: fleshy fruit

Gobelin
\gōbələn, 'gäb-\
French
: tapestry

goitcho
\gȯichō\
Australian name
: weedy herb

golach
\gälək, -ə̱k\
Scottish Gaelic
: arthropod

Golconda
\gäl'kändə\
Indian name
: source of wealth

gommier
\gämē͵ā, 'gəm-, -m͵yā\
French
: Caribbean tree

goodwillit
\gu̇'dwilət, gœ̄'-, gūē'-, gi'-\
Scottish
: generous

goran
\gə'rän\
Bengali
: mangrove

gordiid
\gȯ(r)dēəd\
New Latin
: hairworm

gorevan
\gȯrə¦vän\
Iranian name
: rug

gorgerin
\gȯ(r)jərən\
French
: capital part

Gorsedds
\gȯr͵seth̲s\
Welsh
: mock institutions

gosmore
\gäs͵mō(ə)r, -äz͵m-\
Alteration
: European weed

gospodin
\gäspə¦dēn, -əd¦yēn\
Russian
: courtesy title

gossypitrin
\gä'sipətrən\
ISV
: glucoside

goujon
\güjən\
Louisiana French
: catfish

goundou
\gündü\
French
: swelling

gowiddie
\gō'widē\
Unknown
: evergreen

gowpen
\gəu̇pən\
Norse
: bowl hollow

granat
\granət\
French
: orange

gratins
\gra-t°ns, ˈgrä-\
French
: brown crust

gravata
\gravəˌtä\
Tupi
: cordage fiber

gridelin
\gridᵊlən\
French
: purplish red

griege
\grāzh\
Alteration
: gray yellow

grilse
\ˈgrils also -lts\
Middle English
: salmon

grivet
\grivət, grəˈvā\
French
: monkey

grotzen
\gròtsən\
German
: centerback strip

guadua
\gwädəwə\
American Spanish
: bamboo

guaican
\gwīˌkän\
Taino
: fish

guapena
\gwəˈpēnə\
American Spanish
: ribbon fish

guaraguao
\gwärəˌgwau̇\
Taino
: timber tree

guarri
\gwärē\
Native name
: fruit

Guastalline
\ˈgwästəˌlēn, gwäˈstälən\
English
: sisterhood

guayabi
\gwīəˌbē\
Guarani
: tree

guayule
\(g)wīˈülē\
Nahuatl
: subshrub

guazuti
\gwäzəˌtē\
Guarani
: deer

guereza
\gəˈrezə\
Native name
: monkey

guettarda
\gəˈtärdə\
New Latin
: plant

guillemet
\gē(y)əˌmā, ˌgiləˌmet\
French
: pronunciation

Guisard
\gēˌzärd\
French
: partisan

gulaman
\güˈlämən\
Tagalog
: Ceylon grass

gulsach
\gəls(h)ə(k)\
Norse
: jaundice

gumlah
\gəmˈlä\
Hindi
: pottery jar

gunyah
\gənyə\
Australian native name
: aboriginal hut

gympie
\ˈgimpē\
Australian geo name
: mettle tree

gynaeceum
\gīnē,sēum\
Greek
: apartment

gyronny
\jīˈränē, ˈjīrənē\
Middle French>Middle English
: heraldic change

haiari
\hīˈärē\
Guainan name
: fish poison

67

haiduk
\hī͵du̇k\
Hungarian>German
: Balkan outlaw

hallali
\halə¦lē\
Imitative
: bugle call

hameil
\hāməl\
Old Norse
: homelike

haupia
\hau̇ˈpēə\
Hawaiian
: pudding

heautarit
\hōˈtärət, hyüˈt-\
Arabic
: measured pressure

hedysarum
\hēˈdisərəm\
Greek
: African plant

heishi
\hēshē\
Unknown
: bead

Hercynian
\hər¦sinēən\
Latin+English
: mountain building

herola
\həˈrōlə\
Unknown
: antelope

hevea
\hēvēə\
Spanish>New Latin
: So. American herb

hircarrah
\hərˈkärə\
Persian
: spy

hookup
\hu̇k-͵əp\
Hawaiian
: celebration

houhere
\hōˈherə\
Maori
: ribbonwood

huerta
\wertä\
Spanish
: cultivated land

hurgila
\hərˈgēlə\
Hindi
: adjutant bird

hyoscine
\hīə͵sēn, -sən\
ISV
: alkaloid

Hypapante
\ēpə͵pänˈdē\
Greek
: feast

hyraceum
\hīˈrāsēəm\
New Latin
: African product

hystazarin
\həˈstazərən\
ISV
: yellow compound

icica
\əˈsēkə\
Portuguese
: tree

idant
\i¦dᵊnt, ˈī¦, ¦dant\
ISV+German
: structural unit

iguape
\ēˈgwäpā\
Brazilian geo name
: oily seed

ijolite
\ē(y)ə͵līt, ˈiyə͵-\
Swedish
: igneous rock

iliau
\ēlēˈau̇\
Hawaiian
: disease

imbirussu
\imbərə¦sü, -rü¦sü\
Portuguese
: tree

incarvillea
\in͵kärˈvilēə\
New Latin
: trumpet-shaped flowers

indienne
\andē¦en\
French
: cotton fabric

inguina
\iŋgwənə\
Latin
: groins

innomine
\inˈnämə͵nā, -͵nē, -ˈnōmə͵nā\
Latin
: composition

intertrappean
\intə(r)¦ˈtrapēən\
Middle English+Middle
English+Latin
: between lava flows

Intichiuma
\intēchē'ümə\
Australian name
: magical ceremony

intisy
\intəsē\
New Latin
: spurge

intocostrin
\intə'kästrən\
Trademark
: extract of curare

iodopyracet
\ī͟ͅōdə'pirə͟ͅset, ī͟ͅäd-\
ISV
: salt

iodyrite
\ī'ädə͟ͅrīt\
ISV
: mineral

iridosmine
\irə'däz͟ͅmēn, īr-, -mən\
German+New Latin
: mineral

isatin
\īsətən, -ətən\
ISV
: crystalline

ismene
\iz'mēnē\
Greek
: daffodil

isoetes
\ī'sōə͟ͅtēz\
Greek
: quillwort

ixodid
\iksə͟ͅdəd\
New Latin
: tick

ixora
\iksərə\
Sanskrit
: shrub

jangadeiro
\jaŋgə'dārō\
Portuguese
: tree

japygid
\jə'pijəd\
New Latin
: insect

jaquima
\hakəmə\
Spanish
: haller

jaragua
\zharə¦gwä\
Portuguese
: grass

jasey
\'jāzē\
Alteration
: wig

jermonal
\jərmə¦näl\
Hindi
: snow cock

Jezebel
\je-zə-͟ͅbel *also* -bəl\
Biblical name
: impudent woman

jirkinet
\jərkə¦net\
Alteration
: woman's jacket

jockteleg
\jäktə͟ͅleg\
Unknown
: large knife

jocote
\hō'kōtā\
Nahuatl
: purple-flowered plant

jocum
\hō'küm\
American Spanish
: tree

johnin
\yōnən\
ISV
: sterile solution

joree
\jə'rē\
Imitation
: bird

jorram
\yu̇rəm, yȯr-\
Scottish Gaelic
: boat song

jougs
\jügz\
Latin>Middle French
: iron collar

jowter
\jau̇tə(r)\
Unknown
: fish peddler

Jubilate
\yü-bə-'lä-tā, jü-\
Latin
: song

jubilatio
\yübə'lätsē͟ͅō\
Latin
: group of notes

Juglar
\zhü¦glär\
French name
: business cycle

jumbuck
\jəmˌbək\
Australian name
: sheep

jupon
\jü, pän\
Middle English
: tight-fitted shirt

kabaragoya
\kəˌbärəˈgōyə\
Unknown
: water monitor

kaburi
\kəˈbûrē\
Unknown
: crab

kachin
\kachən\
Alteration
: picture developer

kaempferol
\kempfəˌrȯl, -rōl\
German+English
: crystalline

kahikatea
\kīkəˌtēə, kak-\
Maori
: evergreen

kainga
\kīŋə\
Maori
: village

kaingin
\käˈēŋən\
Tagalog
: clearing land

Kaithi
\kītē\
Hindi
: alphabet

kakapo
\käkəˌpō\
Maori
: parrot

kakawahie
\käkəwəˈhēˌā\
Hawaiian
: flower-pecker

Kakiemon
\käkēˈ(y)äˌmän\
Japanese potter name
: enamel-decorated ware

kakortokite
\kəˈkȯ(r)təˌkīt\
Eskimo+English
: rock of variable
composition

kalam
\kəˈläm\
Arabic
: theology

kalema
\kəˈlāmə\
Portuguese
: violent wind

kallidin
\kalədən\
German
: vasodilator kinins

kallitype
\kaləˌtīp\
Greek>ISV
: photographic process

kalopanax
\kəˈläpəˌnaks\
Greek+New Latin
: Japanese tree

kalpis
\kalpəs\
Greek
: jug

kalua
\kəˈlüə\
Hawaiian
: oven-baked

kalumpang
\käləm¦päŋ\
Tagalog
: old world tree

kalunti
\kəˈlûntē\
Taw-Sug
: Philippine tree

kamao
\kəˈmäˌō, -maû\
Hawaiian
: bird

kamarinskaia
\kəˈmärənzkəyə, -mar-, -nsk-\
Russian
: folk dance

kamboh
\kəmbō, ˈkäm-\
Persian
: low caste member

kambal
\kəmbəl\
Sanskrit>Hindi
: blanket

kamerad
\käməˈräät\
Middle French>German
: used by soldiers

kanchil
\känchəl\
Malay
: deer-like animal

kaneelhart
\kəˈnā(ə)lˌhärt\
Dutch+Dutch
: tropical tree

Kangayam
\kaŋgə¦yäm\
Madras place
: cattle breed

kanin
\känən\
Tagalog
: boiled rice

kankrej
\kän͵krej\
Unknown
: cattle breed

kantiara
\kantē'a(a)rə\
Unknown
: spinose plant

kapote
\kə'pòtə\
French>Yiddish
: long coat

kapparah
\käpä'rä, kä'pòrə\
Hebrew
: ceremony

kapuka
\käpəkə\
Maori
: evergreen

karaka
\kärəkə\
Maori
: tree

karakurt
\karə͵kù(ə)rt\
Turkish
: venomous spider

karela
\kərələ\
Sanskrit>Hindi
: balsam apple

karez
\kə'rez\
Persian
: irrigation tunnel

kaross
\kə'räs\
Dutch>Afrikaans
: animal rug

karree
\kə'rē, -rā\
Dutch+Afrikaans
: plant

kascamiol
\ka'skamē͵òl\
Unknown
: gallinule

katel
\kätᵊl\
Malayalam>Tamil>Portugue
se>Afrikaans
: wooden hammock

kathal
\kət͵həl\
Sanskrit+Hindi
: jackfruit

Kathiawari
\kätēə'wärē\
Gujarati>Hindi
: horse breed

katuka
\kətəkə\
Tamil>Dravidian
: Russel's viper

kawaka
\kə'wäkə\
Maori
: timber tree

Kayasth
\käyəst\
Sanskrit+Sanskrit
: highest caste member

kebyar
\keb͵yär\
Balinese
: solo dance

keelivine
\kēli͵vīn\
Unknown
: pencil

Keemun
\kä¦mùn, kē¦mən\
Chinese
: black tea

Keewatin
\kē-¦wā-tᵊn, -¦wä-\
Canadian name
: Archeozoic division

Kegon
\kä͵gän, -gòn\
Japanese+Japanese
: Buddhist sect

kelep
\kə'lep\
Kekchi
: ant

kellion
\ke'lē͵än, -ē͵òn\
Greek
: religious house

kelty
\kelti\
Unknown
: glass of liquor

kempas
\kempəs\
Malay
: tree

kentrogon
\kentrə͵gän\
Greek+English
: larva

Keraulophon
\kəˈrôləˌfän\
Greek+English
: pipe-organ stop

keriah
\kəˈrēə\
Hebrew
: traditional act

kerril
\kerəl\
Indian name
: sea snake

ketimine
\kētəˌmēn, -mən\
ISV
: Schiff base

keurboom
\kərˌbüm\
Afrikaans+Afrikaans
: shrub

kevalin
\kävələn\
Sanskrit
: liberated soul

khalsa
\käl(t)sə\
Arabic>Persian>Hindi
: theocracy

khankah
\käŋkə\
Persian+Persian>Hindi
: monastery

Khlyst
\klist\
Russian
: secret sect

khoa
\kəˈwä\
Hindi
: milk product

khuskhus
\kəskəs\
Persian&Hindi
: grass

kikar
\kēkə(r), kik-\
Hindi
: gum Arabic tree

kilhig
\kilˌhig\
Unknown
: thick pole

killogie
\kəˈlōgi\
Middle English>Scottish
Gaelic
: sheltered space

kindal
\kindᵊl\
Indian name
: tree

Kinkaider
\kinˈkādə(r)\
Congressman
: free land settler

kinnor
\kēˈnȯ(ə)r\
Hebrew
: lyre

kioea
\kēōˈāə\
Hawaiian
: curlew

kiore
\kēˈōrē\
Maori
: rat

Kirillitsa
\kəˈrilətsə\
Russian
: alphabet

kirombo
\kə́ˈrämbō\
Malagasy
: bird

kirpan
\kirˈpän, kər-\
Sanskrit>Hindi&Panjabi
: dagger

kissar
\kisə(r)\
Arabic
: lyre

kistvaen
\kistˌvīn\
Welsh+Welsh
: grave

kitab
\kēˈtäb\
Arabic
: sacred book

kittereen
\kitəˈrēn\
Unknown
: carriage

Kizilbash
\kizəl¦bäsh\
Turkish
: Persianized Turk

klippe
\klipə\
Old Norse>Swedish>German
: lozenge-shaped coin

klystron
\klīsträn\
Trademark
: electron tube

knaidlach
\kəˈnäd-dlək̲\, ˈknä-\
Yiddish>Middle High
German
: dumplings

knaur
\nȯ(ə)r\
Middle English
: wood knot

knawel
\nȯ(ə)l\
German
: annual weed

knopper
\näpə(r)\
German
: gall

koban
\kōˌbän\
Japanese
: gold coin

kogasin
\kōˈgasən, kōˌg-\
New Latin+English>Greek
: liquid mixture

kohekohe
\kōēˌkōē\
Maori
: tree

koimesis
\kēmēsəs\
Greek
: church feast

kokan
\kōkən\
Hindi
: tree

kokerboom
\kōkə(r)ˌbüm, -bōm\
Dutch>Afrikaans
: quiver tree

kokoona
\kəˈkünə\
Singhalese>New Latin
: East Indian tree

kokowai
\kōkəˌwī\
Maori
: red ocher

kolattam
\kōˈlätəm\
Tamil
: folk dance

kolea
\kōˈlāə\
Hawaiian
: plover

kolek
\kōˌlek\
Malay
: canoe

koleroga
\kōləˈrōgə, käl-\
Sanskrit+Kannada
: disease

kolinsky
\kə-ˈlin(t)-skē\
Russian
: minks

kombu
\kämbü\
Japanese
: food

kominuter
\käməˌn(y)ütə(r)\
German+Latin>German
: ball mill in grinding

Komondor
\kämənˌdȯ(ə)r\
Hungarian
: breed of dogs

konditorei
\ˌkȯndētōˌrī\
Latin>Arabic>Italian>French
>German
: pastry shop

Kondratieff
\kənˈdrätēˌef\
Russian
: business cycle

konfyt
\kənˈfīt\
Middle
French>Dutch>Afrikaans
: preserves

konimeter
\kōˈnimətə(r)\
Greek+Greek
: dust estimation device

konjak
\känˌjak\
Japanese
: plants

konohiki
\kōnəˈhēkē\
Hawaiian
: headman

konseal
\känˌsē(ə)l\
Trademark
: sandwiched medicine

konze
\känzə\
Konde
: hartebeest

kooletah
\küləˌtä\
Eskimo
: caribou skin coat

koomkie
\kümkē\
Persian>Hindi
: female elephant

kootcha
\küchə\
Australian name
: honeybee

konini
\kəˈninē, -ˈnēnē\
Maori
: tree fuchsin

Koppelflote
\käpəlˌflātə, -
flātə,G ˈkȯpəlˌflœtə\
Old French>German
: open flute stop

korakan
\kōrəˌkän\
Sinhalese>Tamil
: cereal grass

korari
\kōrəˌrē\
Maori
: flax

korimako
\kōrəˈmäkō\
Maori
: bellbird

korin
\kōrən\
Unknown
: gazelle

kosin
\kōsᵊn\
ISV
: powder

kotschubeite
\kəˈchübēˌīt\
French+Russian
: rose-red mineral

kotuku
\kōtəˌkü\
Maori
: heron

kotwalee
\kōtˌwälē\
Persian>Hindi
: police station

kouprey
\küprā\
Cambodian name
: forest ox

kowhai
\kōˌwī\
Maori
: small tree

koyemshi
\kōˈyem(p)shē\
Zuni
: clown society

Kraepelinian
\krepəˈlinēən *also* -rap-\
German
: psychiatry

krapfen
\kräpfən\
German
: bismarck

kreef
\krāf\
Dutch>Afrikaans
: crawfish

kreittonite
\krītᵊnˌīt, -rāt-\
German
: zinc oxide mineral

krex
\kreks, ˈgr-\
German
: grumble, complaint

krieker
\krēkə(r)\
Dutch+English
: sandpiper

krubi
\krübē\
Sumatran name
: aroid

Kuan
\gwän, ˈkw-\
Chinese
: pottery

Kulah
\küˈlä\
Turkish place
: Turkish rug

kumarahou
\küˈmərə-how\
Maori
: woody plant

kumbuk
\ku̇mˌbu̇k\
Unknown
: trees

kunai
\küˌnī\
Guinean name
: grass

kunstlied
\ˈku̇nztˌlēt, -n(t)st-\
Middle Dutch>German
: art song

kupper
\kəpə(r)\
Sindhi
: viper

kurveyor
\kə(r)ˈvāə(r)\
Dutch+Afrikaans
: traveling trader

kusum
\kəˈsüm\
Sanskrit+Hindi
: Old World herb

kusimanse
\küsəˈman(t)sə\
Liberian name
: carnivorous mammal

kweek
\kwāk\
Dutch>Afrikaans
: grass

kyah
\kē'(y)ä\
Bengali
: partridge

kyanize
\kīəˌnīz\
English+English
: preserve wood

Kyloe
\'kīlō\
Unknown
: beef cattle

kynurenine
\ki|nyəˌrenēn\
ISV
: amino acid

Kyriale
\kirē'älā\
Middle Latin+New Latin
; liturgical book

laitance
\lātᵊn(t)s\
French
: concrete

lassu
\läshü\
Hungarian
: rhapsody

latah
\lätə\
Malay
: condition

Lazarus
\laz-rəs, 'la-zə-\
Middle Latin
: beggar

lespedeza
\lespə'dēzə\
New Latin
: shrubby plant

leucovorin
\lü'kävərən\
New Latin
: synthetic acid

lezginka
\lez'giŋkə\
Russian
: court dance

Liederkranz
\lēdə(r)ˌkran(t)s, -rän-\
Trademark
: cheese

lucivee
\lüsəˌvē\
Canadian French
: lynx

lwei
\lə'wā\
Angolan name
: monetary unit

macchia
\mäkēə\
Italian
: underbrush profuse

Macclesfield
\makəlzˌfēld, -lˌsf-\
English name
: silk

macheer
\mə'chi(ə)r\
Spanish
: knapsack

machicoulis
\mächē, kü-'lē\
French
: construction imitation

machin
\mə'chēn\
Spanish
: parrot

macigno
\mə'chēnyō\
Italian
: marine rocks

Macon
\mä'kōⁿ\
French
: burgundy wine

madhab
\mə'dab\
Arabic
: jurisprudence school

madoqua
\mə'dōkwə\
Amharic
: antelope

madrague
\mə'drag\
Provencal>French
: fish

madrepore
\madrəˌpō(ə)r\
Latin+French
: stony corals

magadis
\magədəs\
Greek
: twenty-stringed instrument

magot
\mə'gō, ma'-, mä'-\
French
: monkey

maguari
\mə'gwärē\
Tupi>Portuguese
: stork

mahant
\mə'hənt\
Sanskrit>Prakriti>Hindi
: elder

Mahdi
\mädē\
Arabic
: messianic guide

maholi
\mə'hōlē\
Tswana
: lemur

mahua
\mä(h)wə\
Hindi
: tree

mahuang
\mä-'(h)wäŋ\
Chinese
: plants

maidou
\mī'dü\
Burman name
: tree

maire
\mäē͵rä\
Maori
: tree

majid
\mäjəd, 'maj-\
New Latin
: crab

makar
\makər\
Middle English
: poet

makatea
\mäkə'täə\
Tuamotu
: coral reef

makhorka
\mə'k̭órkə\
Russian
: tobacco

makore
\mäkə'rä\
African name
: large tree

malbrouck
\mal͵brúk\
French
: monkey

malduck
\maldək\
Alteration
: bird

malguzar
\mälgə'zär\
Arabic>Hindi
: headman

Maliki
\maləkē\
Arabic
: orthodox school

malines
\mə'lēn\
Belgian name
: fine stiff net

Mallorquin
\ma(l)͵yò(r)¦kēn\
Spanish
: Balearic Island

malmsey
\mämzē\
Middle French
: aromatic wine

maloca
\mə'lōkə\
Portuguese
: dwelling

malvasia
\malvə¸zēə, -'sēə\
Italian
: grape

malvoisie
\malvəzē, malv͵wä¦zē\
French
: aromatic wine

mamani
\mämənē\
Hawaiian
: tree

mammoni
\mämə͵nē\
Italian
: autumn crop

mamoty
\mämətē\
Tamil
: hand tool

mampalon
\mampə͵län\
Indonesian name
: mammal

mamushi
\mə'müshē\
Japanese
: pit viper

mandilion
\man'dilyən\
Spanish>French
: outer garment

mandyas
\män'thēəs, -'dē-\
Greek>Late Latin
: outer garment

manoletina
\mə͵nōlə'tēnə\
Spanish
: bullfighting move

manomin
\mänəˌmin\
Ojibway
: tall aquatic grass

manuma
\mänəˈmä\
Samoan
: pigeon

manumea
\mänəˈmāə\
Samoan
: pigeon

mantelet
\mantᵊl, ȯt, *usually* -ȯt+V\
Middle French
: short cloak

mantellone
\mantᵊlˈōnē\
Italian
: cloak

manutagi
\maˌnüˈtägē, -täŋē\
Samoan
: pigeon

manusina
\mänəˈsēnə\
Samoan
: fern

manyatta
\mənˈyatə\
Kenyan name
: village

marabout
\marəˌbü(t)\
Arabic>Portuguese>French
: Muslim hermit

marae
\məˈrī\
Tahitian
: Polynesian temple

Maran
\məˈran\
French
: breed of fowls

marasca
\məˈraskə\
Italian
: cherry

maray
\məˈrā\
Australian name
: herring

marcel
\mär¦sel, mȧ¦s-\
French
: hair wave

Margate
\mär-ˌgāt\
English name
: fish

margay
\märgā\
Tupi>French
: wildcat

marguerite
\märg(y)ə¦rēt, ¦mȧg-\
French
: daisy

mariengroschen
\məˈrēənˌgrōshən\
German+German
: silver coin

markgraf
\märkˌgräf\
German
: German nobility member

marocain
\marə¦kän\
French
: dress crepe

marrubiin
\məˈrübēən\
ISV
: poisonous crystalline
lactone obtained from
horehound

martaban
\märtə¦bän, -ban\
Burman place
: pottery jar

martinoe
\märtᵊnˌō\
New Latin
: unicorn plant

mascagnite
\maˈskanˌyēt\
Alteration
: sulphate

Masham
\masəm\
English name
: crossbred mutton sheep

massasauga
\masə¦sȯgə\
Canadian river
: rattlesnake

matajuelo
\matəˈ(h)wālō\
American Spanish
: squirrelfish

matelassé
\mätᵊlä¦sā, ¦mätlä-\
French
: double cloth

matie
\matē\
Dutch+Dutch
: fat herring

matins
\matᵊnz\
Latin
: night office

mattamore
\matə¦mō(ə)r\
French
: storehouse

mattoid
\mat͵ȯid\
Italian
: psychopath

mattowacca
\matəˈwakə\
Algonquian
: herring

maubey
\mȯbē\
Unknown
: bitter drink

mauricio
\maüˈrēsē͵ō\
American Spanish
: magnolia

mavrodaphne
\mat͵ȯid\
Greek
: dessert wine

mayapis
\məˈyäpəs\
Tagalog
: timber tree

Mazdayasnian
\mazdəˈyäsnēən\
Russian
: Iranian religion

mazoplasia
\māzəˈplāzh(ē)ə, maz-\
New Latin
: degenerative condition

mebos
\mē͵bäs\
Japanese>Afrikaans
: confection

mechoacan
\mechəwə¦kän\
Spanish
: tuberous root

mediety
\məˈdīətē\
Latin>Middle English
: half of benefice

medrinaque
\medrənˈyäkē, -rəˈnä-\
Spanish
: fiber from palm

mehmandar
\məˈmän͵där\
Persian
: Indian official

melaxuma
\meləˈkümə, -ləkˈsü-, -ləˈzü-\
Greek+Greek
: plant disease

Melchizedek
\mel-ˈki-zə-͵dek\
Biblical name
: higher order priesthood

melengket
\meləŋ¦ket\
Philippine name
: resinous ooze

melocoton
\meləkə¦tōn, -tän\
Spanish
: peach grafted on a quenice rootstock

melosa
\məˈlōsə\
Latin+Spanish
: South American herb

Melusine
\mel(y)ə¦sēn\
Trademark
: silky long-haired felt

Menaion
\məˈnā͵ȯn\
Greek
: corpus of hymns

menarche
\məˈnärkē, meˈ-\
Greek+New Latin
: initiation

Menshevik
\menchə͵vik, -͵vēk\
Russian
: member of democracy

mephenesin
\məˈfenəsən\
Portmanteau
: crystalline compound

meraspis
\məˈraspəs\
New Latin+New Latin
: late larva

merawan
\məˈräwən\
Malay
: yellow durable wood

Mercersburg
\mərsərz͵bərg\
Pennsylvanian geo name
: American theology system

merels
\merəlz\
Middle French>Middle English
: ancient game

merengue
\məˈreŋgā\
Haitian Creole
: ballroom dance

meroxene
\məˈräk͵sēn\
New Latin
: mineral

mesityl
\mə'sit°l\
Greek+English
: radical

mesitylene
\mə'sit°l,ēn\
Portmanteau
: oily hydrocarbon

mesoveliid
\me|zō'vēlēəd, ,mē|, |sō-\
New Latin
: water treader

mesquital
\meskə|tal\
Spanish
: dominat plant area

metayer
\me'ta ¦yā\
French
: cultivater

meturgeman
\mə'tərgəmən\
Heb&Aramaic
: religious officiant

Metycaine
\metə,kān\
Trademark
: preparation of piperocaine

meute
\myüt\
Alteration
: cage for hawks

mezereon
\mə'zirēən, -zer-\
Persian>Arabic
: small shrub

Micarta
\mī'kärtə\
Trademark
: laminated products

Michtam
\mik,tam\
Hebrew
: Bible headings

midewiwin
\mə'dāwə,win\
Ojibwa
: powerful society

mignonne
\mēn'yōn\
French
: petite

migrantes
\mī'gran,tēz\
New Latin
: female aphid

Mimamsa
\mē'mänsə\
Sanskrit
: orthodox philosophy

minchiate
\mēn'kyätä\
Italian
: early form of card game

minhagim
\min,hägēm\
Hebrew
: Jewish religious custom

minivet
\minə,vet\
Unknown
: cuckoo shrikes

Minorca
\mə'nórkə, -nò(ə)kə\
Spanish
: domestic fowl breed

miriki
\mērē'kē\
Brazilian name
: lemur

mirliton
\mirlə¦tōn\
French
: kazoo

mishima
\mēshəmə\
Japanese
: pottery

mispickel
\mi,spikəl\
German
: arsenopyrite

misocainea
\misō'kīnēə, ,mīs-, -kän-\
Greek+New Latin
: hatred of new ideas

Mithraeum
\mi'thrēəm\
Greek>New Latin
: underground room

mitote
\mə'tōtē\
Nahuatl
: secular dance

mitsumata
\mitsə'mätə\
Japanese
: short shrub

moble
\mäbəl\
Alteration
: to wrap the head

modillion
\mō-'dil-yən\
Latin>Italian
: horizontal bracket

molave
\mō'lävä\
Tagalog
: timber tree

Molasse
\mə'läs\
Italian>French
: series of deposits

moldwarp
\mōl͜dwȯrp\
Middle Dutch
: European mole

molimina
\mə'limənə\
Latin
: discomfort

molluscum
\mə'ləskəm\
Latin
: skin disease

Molokan
\mälə'kän\
Russian
: religious member

momme
\mämē\
Japanese
: unit of weight

Monegasque
\mänə͜gask\
Provencal>French
: Monacan

moorpunky
\mȯ(r)'pəŋkē\
Hindi
: pleasure craft

mordore
\mȯ(r)də'rā\
Latin+French
: pencilwood

morillon
\mə'rilən\
French
: ducks

morlop
\mȯr͜läp\
Unknown
: jasper

morral
\mə'ral, -räl\
Spanish
: fiber bag

moschatel
\͜mäskə͜tel\
Late Latin+Italian
: shrub

moshava
\mōshə'vä\
New Hebrew
: settlement
(plural spelled moshavim)

moutan
\'mü͜tan\
Chinese
: pony

mujtahid
\müj'tä͜hid\
Arabic
: interpreter

mumruffin
\müm͜rüfin, 'məm͜rəf-\
Unknown
: long-tailed tit

muncheel
\mən'chē(ə)l\
Malayalam
: litter

mushaa
\müs'hä\
Arabic
: undivided property

musimon
\məsə͜män\
Latin
: wild sheep

musnud
\mə͜snəd\
Hindi
: cushioned seat

mydriasine
\mə'drīə͜sēn, mī'-, -sən\
Latin+ISV
: crystalline

mygale
\migəlē\
Latin>Greek
: shrewmouse

mynpacht
\mīn͜päkt\
Afrikaans
: mining concession

myophrisk
\mīə͜frisk\
Latin
: fibril

myrcene
\mər͜sēn, -sən\
ISV
: hydrocarbon

Myrrhophore
\mirə͜fō(ə)r\
Greek
: women bearing spices

mystax
\mi͜staks\
New Latin>Greek
: row of hairs

myxocoel
\miksə͜sēl\
Greek
: body cavity

nakuruitis
\nə͜kü͜rü'ītəs\
Kenyan name+New latin
: cobalt deficiency

nandubay
\nyändə¦bī\
Guarani>Spanish
: shrub

naras
\narəs\
Hottentot
: shrub

narsinga
\nərˈsiŋgə\
Sanskrit
: trumpet

navarho
\navəˌrō\
Portmanteau
: radio

navarin
\navᴀ̇raⁿ\
French
: mutton stew

nayaur
\nəˈyȯr\
Nepali
: wild sheep

nazir
\näˌzi(ə)r\
Hindi
: court official

negara
\nəˈgärə\
Indonesian
: federative state

neilah
\neēˈlä, neˈēlə\
Hebrew
: liturgy conclusion

neisserian
\nīˌsirēən\
New Latin+English
: caused by gonococcus

Nellore
\nəˈlō(ə)r\
Indian place
: cattle breed

nephthytis
\nefˈthītəs, ˈnefthət-\
Greek
: plant with arrow-shaped leaves

Nethinim
\netēˈnēm\
Hebrew
: temple servants

Nichiren
\nichə¦ren\
Japanese
: Buddhist sect

nigre
\nīgə(r), nig-\
Alteration
: water solution

ninon
\nē-nȯn\
French
: sheer fabric

nirles
\nirlz\
Unknown
: measles

nisnas
\ˈˈnisnəs\
Arabic
: monkey

nombril
\nämbrəl\
Middle French
: lower half of escutcheon

nomocanon
\nȯməˈkäˌnȯn\
Late Greek
: collection of laws

nopinene
\nōpəˌnēn\
ISV
: terpene

nordenskioldine
\nȯ(r)dᵊnˌshōldən\
Norwegian
: mineral

norie
\näri\
Unknown
: seabird

notan
\nōˈtän\
Japanese
: light combination

nsambya
\enˈsämbyə\
Ugandan name
: tree

nucule
\n(y)üˌkyül\
Latin>French
: nutlet

nuggar
\nəˈgär\
Arabic
: cargo boat

nullipore
\nələˌpō(ə)r\
ISV
: algae

nunnari
\nənərē\
Indian name
: sarsaparilla

nuzzer
\nəzə(r)\
Arabic>Hindi
: offering

Nyaya
\nyäyə\
Sanskrit
: orthodox system

nystatin
\nistətən\
New York State+English
: antibiotic

oakum
\ōkəm\
Middle English
: fiber

obrok
\ä'bräk, ə'brȯk\
Old English>Latin
: yearly tax

ocimene
\'äsə‚mēn\
Latin>ISV
: acrylic terpene

ocote
\ə'kōtā\
Nahuatl>Spanish
: woody pine

octavary
\äktə‚verē\
New Latin
: service book

octroi
\äk‚trȯi, äk¦trwä\
Middle French
: privilege

octylene
\äktə‚lēn\
ISV
: hydrocarbon

oflag
\ȯ‚fläg\
German
: prison camp

oikomonad
\ȯikə¦mō‚nad\
New Latin
: protozoan

oiticica
\‚ȯitə'sēkə\
Tupi>Portuguese
: tree

okvik
\äkvik\
Island in Bering Sea
: early phase of culture

oleoyl
\ō'lēə‚wil\
ISV
: radical of acid

olibanum
\ō'libənəm\
Arabic>Latin
: frankincense

olivet
\älə¦vet\
French
: floodlight

ololiuqui
\ōlə'l(y)ükē\
Nahuatl>Spanish
: woody vine

omadhaun
\ämə‚thȯn\
Irish Gaelic
: fool, idiot

Olynthian
\ō'lin(t)thēən\
Macedonian geographical
name
: native of a town in ancient
Macedonia

ommatin
\ämətən\
Greek
: pigment

omoideum
\ō'mȯidēəm\
Latin>New Latin
: pterygoid bone

omophorion
\ōmə'fōrēən,‚äm-\
Late Greek>Greek+Late
Greek
: vestment

omphacite
\äm(p)fə‚sīt\
Greek>German
: mineral

omphalos
\äm(p)fə‚läs, -ləs\
Greek
: focal point

omrah
\äm'rä\
Arabic>Hindi
: lord

onding
\än‚diŋ\
Scottish
: heavy fall

ondule
\ändə¦lā, -njə-\
New Latin>French
: wavy pattern

onkos
\äŋkəs\
Greek
: topknot

onyxis
\ō'niksəs\
Greek>New Latin
: ingrowing of nail

oocyesis
\ōəsī'ēsəs\
New Latin
: pregnancy

ooecium
\ō̦ēs(h)ēəm\
New Latin
: ovicell

oopuhue
\ō̦ōpə'hüē\
Hawaiian
: globefish

opepe
\ōpəpē\
Hawaiian
: forest

opopanax
\ə'päpə̦naks\
Greek>Latin
: gum resin

orarion
\ȯ'rärē̦ȯn\
Latin>Greek
: stole

orgue
\ȯ(ə)rg\
Latin>French
: timber

orihon
\ȯrē̦hän\
Japanese
: strip of paper

oropesa
\ȯrə'päsə\
British trawler
: float

orpheon
\ȯrfāȯⁿ\
French
: male chorus

orseille
\ȯr̦sā(ə)l, -sā, -sel\
French
: violet dye

orterde
\ȯrțerdə\
German
: soil horizon

orvietan
\ȯ(r)vē'ātᵊn\
Italian
: counterpoison

osmundine
\āz'mən̦dēn\
Old Swedish
: root material

osnaburg
\äznə̦bərg\
German place
: cotton fabric

osteria
\ästə'rēə, ̦ōs-\
Latin>Italian
: wayside inn

ouananiche
\wänə̦nēsh, -nish\
Canadian French
: landlocked salmon

ouricury
\ȯrəkə̦rē\ \̦är-\
Tupi
: palm

otaheitan
\ōtə̦hātᵊn\
Pacific island name
: Tahitian language

Otate
\ō'tätā\
Nahuatl>Spanish
: grass

outrecuidance
\ütə(r)'kwēdᵊn(t)s\
French
: self-conceit

ovolo
\ōvə̦lō, ȯv-\
Latin>Italian
: molding

owyheeite
\ō'wīē̦īt\
Idahoan name
: mineral

oxophenarsine
\äksəfə'när̦sēn, -ärsə̇n\
ISV elements
: hydrochloride

palohierro
\palō'yerō, ̦päl-\
Spanish
: tree

paepae
\pī̦pī\
Pacific native languages
: stone platform

pallall
\pa'lal\
Unknown
: hopscotch

pallone
\pə'lōnē\
Italian
: tennis-like game

palombino
\päləm'bēnō, pal-\
Latin>Italian
: marble

palpocil
\palpə̦sil\
New Latin+New Latin>ISV
: tactile process

pampelmoes
\pampəl̦müs\
Dutch>African
: butterfish

pampre
\pampə(r)\
Latin>French
: ornament

panathenaea
\pa͵nathə'nēə\
Greek
: festivities

pandour
\pan͵du̇(ə)r\
German>Croatian>Hungaria
n>French
: regiment member

panetiere
\panə'tye(ə)r\
French
: bread box

pangane
\päŋ'gänā\
East African geo name
: coarse plant

panglima
\pän'glēmə\
Malay
: highest noble

panuelo
\͵pänyə'wälō\
Latin>Spanish
: square cloth

pantetheine
\pantə'thē͵ēn, -thēən,
pan'teth-\
ISV
: growth factor

papelonne
\papələ¦nā\
Latin>French
: overlapping scales

papoula
\pə'pōlə\
Latin>Arabic>Portuguese
: kenaf

paramita
\pä'rəmə̇tə\
Sanskrit
: perfect virtues

parastas
\parə͵stas, pə'rastəs\
Greek
: vertical supports in Greek
temples

pardalote
\pärdᵊl͵ōt\
Greek>Latin
: bird

pardhan
\pär͵dän\
Sanskrit>Hindi
: ritual beggar

pareira
\pə'rerə, -rärə\
Portuguese
: vine root

pareoean
\parē'ēən\
Greek
: member of Mongolia

parentela
\parən'tēlə\
Late Latin
: line of blood relatives

pareja
\pə'rähä\
Latin>Spanish
: trawler

paries
\pa(a)rē͵ēz\
Latin>Slav
: cavity wall

parinari
\parənə¦rē\
Galibi
: tree rich in silica

paroli
\parə'lē\
Latin>Italian>French
: betting system

parr
\pär, på(r\
Unknown
: salmon

Parseval
\pärzə͵väl\
German name
: airship

parthenita
\pär'thenətə\
Greek>New Latin
: trematode worm

paryphodrome
\pə'rifə͵drōm\
Greek element
: marginal vein

pascola
\pä'skōlə\
Peru geo name
: fiesta dancer

patashte
\pə'täshtā\
American Spanish
: tropical tree

patayan
\pätə¦yän\
Walapai
: ancient Arizona culture

patera
\patərə\
Latin
: earthenware saucer

pedicel
\pedə͵sel\
Latin
: stalk

peeoy
\pēˈȯi\
prob. imit.
: fireworks gunpowder

pejerrey
\pähəˈrä\
Latin>Spanish
: silverside

pelok
\pe-lək\
Javanese
: scale

penates
\pə-ˈnā-tēz, -ˈnä-\
Latin
: Roman gods

penghulu
\peŋˈülü\
Malay
: village headman

penillion
\pəˈnilyən\
Welsh
: verses

penorcon
\pəˈnȯrkən\
New Latin
: obsolete guitar

pensionado
\pen(t)sēəˈnädō\
Latin>Spanish
: Philippine student

penthemimer
\pen(t)thəˈmimə(r)\
Greek>Late Latin
: ode

pepysian
\pēpsēən\
English name
: relating to Samuel's diary

peranakan
\perəˈnäkən\
Javanese
: immigrant

peregrina
\perəˈgrēnə\
American Spanish
: Cuban shrub

perichaetium
\perəˌkētē-əm\
Greek>New Latin
: sheath

pericon
\perəˈkȯn\
Spanish
: dance

perique
\pəˈrēk\
Latin>French
: tobacco

perruche
\pəˈrüsh\
French
: parrot of green

perseitol
\pərsēəˌtȯl,pərˈs-, -tōl\
New Latin>ISV
: alcohol

pestalozzian
\pestəˈlätsēən, -syən\
Swiss name
: educational system

peteca
\pəˈtēkə\
Italian
: disease

petronel
\petrənəl\
Latin>French
: firearm

Phalaecean
\faləˈsēən\
Greek name
: hendecasyllabic verse

phelonion
\fəˈlōnēən\
Latin>Greek
: vestment

phiale
\fīəlē\
Greek
: bowl

philantomba
\filənˈtämbə\
Unknown
: antelope

philiater
\filēˌātə(r)\
Greek
: doctor

phlobaphene
\fläbəˌfēn\
Greek>ISV
: reddish complex

phloretin
\flȯrətən, ˈflär-, fləˈrētən\
Greek+French
: ketone

photonosus
\fōˈtänəsəs\
Greek+New Latin
: snow blindness

phrenosin
\frenəsən\
ISV
: cerebroside

phthiocol
\thīəˌkȯl, -kōl\
Latin
: quinone

phulkari
\pül¸kärē\
Hindi
: flower pattern

phymatorhysin
\fīmə'tórəsən\
Greek>Latin
: melanin pigment

picarel
\pikə'rel\
French
: fish

picein
\pisēən, pīs-\
ISV+Latin
: glucoside

picot
\pēkō\
French
: loops

picqueter
\pikətə(r)\
French
: flower buncher

pieta
\pēā¦tä\
Latin>Italian
: sculpture

pikake
\pēkə¸kā\
Hawaiian
: Arabian jasmine

piligan
\pēlē¸gän\
New Latin
: club moss

pimelea
\pə'mēlyə *also* -lēə\
Greek
: pinkflower

pinnace
\pinəs\
Spanish>French
: sailing ship

pinole
\pə'nōlē\
Nahuatl>American Spanish
: corn

Pinzgau
\pin(t)s¸gaù\
German+Austrian
: horse

pionnotes
\pīə'nōtēz\
Greek>Latin
: gelatinous layer

pipsissewa
\pip'sisəwə\
Cree
: evergreen

piquia
\pēkē¦ä\
Tupi>Portuguese
: tree

piroot
\pī'rüt\
Alteration
: walk idly

piupiu
\pēü¸pēü\
Maori
: kilt

planaea
\plə'nēə\
Latin>New Latin
: organism

plastein
\pla¸stēn, -stēən\
Greek+Greek>ISV
: enzyme

plethysmothallus
\plə¸thizmə'thaləs, -ism-\
New Latin+Greek>New Latin
: dwarf brown algae

plumetis
\plümə¦tē\
Middle French>French
: dress fabric

pluries
\plùrē¸ēz\
Latin>Middle English
: writs

plygain
\pli¸gīn\
Latin>Welsh
: carol

poblacion
\pò¸bläsē'òn\
Spanish
: municipality

podeon
\pōdē¸än, 'päd-\
Greek>New Latin
: abdomen

Poligar
\pälə¸gär\
Marathi&Telegu
: feudal chief

polignac
\pōlēn'yak\
French
: card game

polos
\pä¸läs\
Greek
: crown

polverine
\pälvə¸rēn\
Latin>Italian
: pearl

polyene
\pälēˌ ēn\
ISV
: compound

pomarine
\pōməˌ rīn, -rən\
Greek>French
: roofed nostrils

pomfret
\päm-frət, pəm-\
Portuguese>French
: fish

poort
\pō(ə)rt, pu̇(ə)-\
Latin>Dutch>Afrikaans
: mountain pass

popeline
\päpə¦lēn\
English>French
: fabric

popliteus
\päp'litēəs, -itēəs, ˌpäplə'tēəs\
Latin>New Latin
: muscle

popoi
\pōˌ pȯi\
Marqueran
: food

porina
\pə'rīnə, -rēnə\
New Latin
: caterpillar

Porphyrio
\pȯ(r)'firēˌ ō\
New Latin
: purple bird

portugais
\pōrchə¦gā\
Portuguese>French
: angelfish

porwigle
\pȯrˌ wigəl\
Middle English
: tadpole

pospolite
\pȯ'spȯlyētə\
Polish
: militia

possentrie
\päsᵊntrē\
English>Dutch
: sandbox tree

postea
\pōstēə\
Latin
: judge's entry

poudreuse
\pü¦drərz, -drēz\
French
: dressing table

pounamu
\pō'nämü\
Maori
: nephrite

powan
\pōən\
Unknown
: whitefish

prakarana
\prə'kərənə\
Sanskrit
: drama

prasine
\prāˌ zēn, -zᵊn, -ˌ zīn\
Greek>Latin
: having a green color

prebendary
\prebənˌ derē\
Latin>Middle Latin
: member of church

preces
\prēˌ sēz\
Latin
: petitions

predikant
\prädē¦känt\
Middle French>Dutch
: preacher

pregnenolone
\preg'nēnᵊlˌ ōn\
ISV
: crystalline

preignac
\pren'yak\
French
: white wine

prele
\prel\
Latin>Old French
: horsetail

Premonstratensian
\prēˌ män(t)strə¦tenchən\
English+Latin
: member of canons

primaquine
\prēməˌ kwēn, prīm-, -kwən\
ISV elements
: antimalarial drug

primices
\priməsəz\
Latin>Old French>Middle
English
: first fruits

primocane
\prīməˌ kān\
Greek elements
: bramble fruits

printanier
\praⁿtányā\
French>Latin>French
: diced vegetables

procedendo
\prōsə'dendō\
Latin
: writ

procerus
\prō'sirəs\
Latin>New Latin
: muscle

prochooi
\prōkə,-wȯi, -räk-\
Greek
: jugs

profonde
\prō'fōⁿd\
Latin>French
: magician's pocket

prooemiac
\prō¦ēmē,ak\
Greek>Late Greek
: introductory

properispomenon
\prō,perə'spämə,nän, -spōm-,
-nən\
Greek
: circumflexed penult

propylparaben
\prōpəl'parə,ben\
ISV
: crystalline ester

proseuche
\prō's(y)ükē\
Latin&Greek
: ancient place

prostal
\präst°l\
Latin>New Latin
: spicule

prothonotary
\prə'thänə,terē, prō,thə'nätər
ē, -ri\
Late Latin>Middle English
: chief clerk

proveditor
\prō'vedətə(r)\
Latin>Italian
: functionary

provenance
\präv-nən(t)s, prä-və-nən(t)s,
-,nän(t)s\
French
: place of origin

proxenete
\präksə,nēt\
Greek>Latin>French
: marriage broker

prulaurasin
\prü'lȯrəsən\
ISV
: glucoside

prurigo
\prü'rīgō\
Latin>New Latin
: skin disease

prusiano
\prüsē'änō\
Prussian
: varied bunting

pryler
\prīlə(r)\
Unknown
: sweeper

psithyrus
\sithərəs\
New Latin
: bumblebee

psychopannychy
\sīkō¦pa¦nikē\
New Latin
: soul death

pteryla
\terələ\
Greek>New Latin
: feathery spot

ptilinum
\ti,li-nəm\\
Latin>New Latin
: vesicular organ

pukateine
\pükə'tā,ēn, -ən\
ISV
: alkaloid

Pulaski
\pə'laskē\
American name
: axe

pulperia
\pu̇lpə'rēə\
Latin>Spanish
: grocery

pulqueria
\pülkə'rēə ,pu̇l-\
Spanish+Mexican Spanish
: Mexican shop

pulwar
\pəl'wär\
Hindi
: riverboat

pungapung
\pəŋ'gä,pəŋ\
Tagalog
: aroid

pungi
\püŋgē\
Hindi
: reed pipe

punalua
\pünə'lüə\
Hawaiian
: marriage

purey
\pyu̇rē\
English
: marble

puriri
\pəˈrirē\
Maori
: ironwood

purvoe
\pə(r)ˈvō\
Sanskrit>Marathi
: writer caste

pyal
\pīˌäl\
Latin>Portuguese
: raised platform

pyknolepsy
\piknəˌlepsē\
Greek>ISV
: epilepsy form

pyrgeometer
\pī(ə)rjēˈämətə(r), ˌpi(-\
ISV
: radiation instrument

pyridoxine
\pirəˈdäkˌsēn, -sᶟn\
ISV
: alcohol

pyrryl
\pirᶟl\
ISV
: radicals

quadrans
\kwäˌdranz\
Latin
: bronze coin

rambong
\ramˈbäŋ\
Atjehnese
: rubber plant

Rambouillet
\ram-bə-ˌlā, -bü-ˌyā\
French
: breed of sheep

ramsch
\räm(p)sh\
French>German
: game

ramtil
\ramˌtil\
Sanskrit
: African herb

rangpur
\rəŋpür\
Pakistani town
: mandarin oranges

Raskolnik
\rəˈskȯlnik\
Russian
: dissenter

rasse
\rasə, ras\
Javanese
: civet

ravison
\ravəsən\
German+French
: seed

rechauffe
\rā-shō-ˈfā, -ˈshō-ˌfā\
French
: dish of food

recherché
\rə-ˌsher-ˌshā\
French
: sought out with care

recit
\rāˈsē\
French
: brief novel

redan
\rəˈdan\
French
: fortification

reeper
\rēpə(r)\
Marathi
: strip of wood

reflet
\rəˈflā, rēˈf-\
French
: metallic luster

regalia
\ri-ˈga-lyə, -lē-ə\
American Spanish
: cigar

renguera
\renˈgerə\
Spanish
: swayback

resaca
\rəˈsakə\
Latin+Spanish
: dry channel

retirade
\retəˈräd\
French
: retrenchment

retree
\rəˈtrē\
French
: imperfect paper

rhatany
\ratᵊnē\
Spanish&Portuguese
: dried root

rhigolene
\rigəˌlēn, -lᶟn\
Greek+English
: petroleum

rhyacolite
\rīˈakəˌlīt\
Greek>German
: orthoclase

Rhynsburger
\rīnz‚bərgə(r)\
German
: collegiant

ribityl
\ri-bi‚til\
ISV
: radical

ridley
\ridlē\
Name
: turtle

riempie
\rēmpē\
Afrikaans
: rawhide strip

rilawa
\rilə‚wä\
Sinhalese
: parrot

rincon
\riŋˈkōn\
Spanish
: valley

ripieno
\riˈpē-ānō\
Italian
: supplementary

ritenente
\rētəˈnentē, -entä\
Latin>Italian
: gradual slackening in tempo

rizzar
\rizər\
French
: currant

rodham
\rädˌham\
English+English
: patch of land

rollmops
\rōlˌmäps\
German
: salt herring

romal
\rəˈmal\
Spanish
: thong

Romeldale
\räməlˌdāl\
Blend
: breed of sheep

Romney
\rämnē-\
English geo name
: breed of sheep

rondavel
\rändəˌvel\
Afrikaans
: native hut

Roskopf
\räˌskäpf\
Swiss
: watch with barrel

russud
\rəˌsəd\
Hindi
: grain

ryania
\rīˈānēə\
New Latin
: insecticide

rytina
\ritᵊnə\
Latin
: aquatic mammal

sabzi
\səbˈzē\
Hindi
: green vegetable

saeta
\säˈätə\
New Latin>Spanish
: unaccompanied song

sagamite
\səˌgäməˈtā\
Canadian French
: hulled corn

sagapenum
\sagəˈpēnəm\
Greek>Latin
: gum resin

sagoweer
\sagə¦wi(ə)r\
Portuguese>Dutch
: feather palm

saguranes
\sägüˈräˌnäs\
Philippine name
: textile

Sahiwal
\sä(h)əˌväl\
Pakistani geo name
: cattle breed

sakkara
\səˈkärə\
Egyptian name
: mouse gray

salele
\səˈlälē\
Samoan
: percoid fish

salleeman
\salēmən\
Moroccan name+English
: pirate ship

Saluki
\səˈlükē\
Arabic
: dog breed

salvianin
\salvēənən, -ˌnin\
New Latin
: tea

samogon
\sämə¦gȯn\
Russian
: vodka

sampaloc
\sampəˌläk\
Tagalog
: tamarind

Samvat
\səmvət\
Sanskrit
: chronological era

sandan
\saŋdən\
Nepali
: East Indian tree

Sandia
\sanˈdēə, sän-\
Sanskrit>Spanish
: watermelon

sandunga
\sänˈdüŋgə\
Mexican Spanish
: couple dance

sangley
\säŋˈglā\
Chinese
: trader

Sanron
\sänˌrōn\
Japanese
: Buddhist school

sansevieria
\san(t)səˈvirēə\
New Latin
: sword-leaved plant

sapiao
\säpēˈau̇\
Philippine name
: haul net

sapit
\säˈpēt\
English>Moroccan
: sailboat

sarcina
\särsənə, -rkənə\
New Latin
: bacteria

sarkit
\särkət\
English
: provided with shirts

sarus
\särəs\
Sanskrit
: crane

sarwan
\sär¦wän\
Persian
: camel driver

sassenach
\sasᵊnˌa|k, -ᵊnə|, -ᵊnˌä|, |k̲\
Old English
: Englishman

satinay
\satᵊn¦ā\
French
: wood of tree

saucisson
\sōsē¦sōⁿ\
Latin>Italian>French
: paper tube

saulie
\sȯli\
Unknown
: hired mourner

sautille
\sōtēyā\
French
: rapid staccato

savelha
\səˈvelyə\
Portuguese
: fish

saveloy
\sav,ə-loi\
Middle French
: dry sausage

sawah
\säwə\
Malay
: wet rice

sawbwa
\sȯbwə\
Burmese
: hereditary rules

saxaul
\sakˌsȯl\
Turkistanian name
: xerophytic shrub

saynete
\sā¦net\
Spanish>French
: short comic

savoy
\səˈvȯi *also especially
attributively* saˌvȯi\
French
: cabbage

Sazerac
\sazəˌrak\
Trademark
: cocktail

scaevola
\sēvələ\
New Latin
: succulent fruit

scammony
\skamənē\
Greek>Latin
: twining plant

schaefferia
\shāˈfirēə\
New Latin+New Latin
: woody plant

schiedam
\skē-ˈdäm, sk̲ē-\
Netherlands geo name
: wine

schimmel
\skiməl\
Dutch
: gray horse

schlager
\shlāgə(r)\
German
: blunt sword

schradan
\shrā͵dan\
German+English
: viscous liquid

schrik
\skrik\
Dutch
: panic

Schwegel
\shfāgel, shvā-\
German
: wind instrument

Schwenkfelder
\shfeŋk͵feldə(r), shve-\
German
: advocate follower

sciniph
\sinəf\
Latin
: insect

sciara
\sīərə\
Greek>New Latin
: fungus gnat

scincoid
\s(k)iŋ͵kȯid\
New Latin
: lizard-like

scoggin
\skägənˈ
English name
: jester

scopperil
\skäpərəl\
Middle English
: spinning top

scorzonera
\skȯ(r)zəˈnirə\
Spanish>New Latin
: solitary headed plants

scruze
\skrüz\
Alteration
: crush

sealine
\sēˈlēn\
English+English
: rabbit

sebesten
\sə̇ˈbestən\
Arabic
: East Indian tree

Seccotine
\sek͵etēn\
Trademark
: adhesive cement

sedjadeh
\səˈjädə\
Turkish
: Oriental rug

semele
\semə͵lē\
New Latin
: mollusk

sementera
\sāmənˈtärə\
Latin>Spanish
: cultivated field

semul
\sēməl, sem-\
Hindi
: tree

sephirah
\sə̇ˈfērə\
Hebrew
: 49 days of Omer

septleva
\sept-levə\
French
: 7 times the amount

seraya
\səˈrīə\
Bornean name
: trees

sereh
\səˈrā\
Malay
: grass

serir
\səˈri(ə)r\
Moroccan
: desert

serpolet
\sərpəˈlet\
Latin>French
: wild thyme

seseli
\sesəlē\
Greek>Latin
: perennial herb

severy
\sev(ə)rē\
Middle French>Middle
English
: vaulted roof

Sevres
\sevrə\
French
: porcelain

sextur
\sek͵stu̇(ə)r\
Danish
: dance

shadrach
\sha͵drak *sometimes* shā͵d-\
Hebrew
: unfused material

shanachie
\shanə¦k̲ē\
Irish Gaelic
: taleteller

sharki
\sharkē\
Arabic
: wind

Shaysite
\shā͵zīt\
English+English
: sympathizer

shedder
\shedə(r)\
English+English
: female sheep

shedu
\shādü\
Assyrian-Babylon
: demon

shemittah
\shə'mētə\
Hebrew
: sabbatical year

sheyle
\shā(ə)l\
Middle German
: squint

shibuichi
\shē͵bu̇i͵chē\
Japanese
: silver alloy

shicer
\shīsə(r)\
German
: unproductive mine

shikargah
\shə'kärgä\
Hindi
: game preserve

shikii
\shikē\
Japanese
: cloth

shirakashi
\shirə'käshē\
Japanese
: white oak

Shirvan
\shə(r)'vän\
Russian
: rug

shisham
\shēshəm\
Hindi
: several trees

shkotzim
\shkȯtsəm\
Hebrew
: non-Jewish boy

shtetlach
\shtetläk̲, -lək̲\
Hebrew
: small towns

Sifflet
\sif͵flāt\
French>German
: woodpipe

Sinfonien
\sin-fə-'nyen\
German
: harmony of sounds

sinhasan
\sin'häsᵊn, -'həs-\
Sanskrit
: throne

siricid
\sə'risəd, 'sirəsəd\
New Latin
: wasp

siris
\sə'rēs\
Tamil>Hindi
: tree

siroc
\sī͵räk, sə'r-\
Italian>French
: oppressive wind

siruaballi
\s(h)irəwə'balē\
Arawak
: tree

sisalana
\sīsə'länə, ͵sīzə-, ͵sēs-, ͵sēz-,
-lanə, -länə\
Mexican Spanish+New Latin
: white fiber

siscowet
\siskə͵wet\
Ojibway
: lake trout

sitao
\sə'tau̇\
Tagalog
: cowpea

sitio
\sētēˌō\
Spanish
: village

sjambok
\shamǀbäk, -ǀbək\
Hindi>Afrikaans
: heavy leathered whip

skaffie
\skafi\
Latin>English
: fishing boat

skeigh
\skēk̲\
Swedish
: proudly spirited

skellat
\skelȧt\
Old French+Middle English
: small bell

skilligalee
\skiləgəǀlē\
Unknown
: broth

Skoptsy
\skäptǀsē\
Russian
: sect member

slainte
\slȯ(i)ntə\
Irish Gaelic
: toast

smoorich
\smōrȧk̲\
Imitative
: stolen kiss

snallygaster
\snälēˌgästə(r)\
Pennsylvanian German
: mythical creature

sodom
\sädəm\
Greek
: notorious place

soffione
\säfēˈōnē, ˌsōf-, -ōnā\
Italian
: jet of steam

sofkee
\säfkē\
Muskogee
: thin mush

sokhor
\sōǀkȯ(ə)r\
Unknown
: rodent

Solea
\sōlēə\
Middle Greek
: platform

sondeli
\sänˈdālē\
Kannada
: murkshrew

sopherim
\sōfərȧm, -ˌrēm\
Hebrew
: lawmen

sorge
\zȯrgə\
German
: concern

soroche
\səˈrōchē\
Quechua
: mountain sickness

sosie
\sōˈzē\
Latin>French
: twin

sotol
\sōtōl\
Nahuatl
: liqueur

sourdine
\sủ(ə)rˌdēn\
Latin>Italian>French
: musical instrument

sowens
\sōənz, süə-\
Scottish Gaelic
: porridge

sparteine
\spärtēˌēn, -tēᵊn\
ISV
: alkaloid

Sphacelaria
\sfasəˈla(a)rēə\
Greek
: gangrene

sphendone
\sfendəˌnē\
Greek
: headband

spilite
\spīˌlēt\
French+Greek>French
: dense rock

spleuchan
\splük̲ən\
Irish Gaelic
: pocket

squacco
\skwäkō *also* -wȯ(-\
Italian
: heron

squatina
\skwätᵊnə\
Latin
: shark

94

stackgarth
\stagə(r)th\
Middle English
: field of straw

Stakhanovite
\stəˈkänəˌvīt, -kan-\
Russian
: special privileged worker

stanhope
\stanəp, -nˌhōp\
English
: limo

startsy
\stärtsē\
Russian
: religious teacher

statice
\statəsē\
Latin
: plant

steinbock
\stīnˌbäk\
German
: ibex

sterrinck
\steriŋk\
New Latin
: crab eater seal

stokroos
\stäˌkrüs\
Dutch+Dutch
: reusable material

strappado
\strəˈpädō, -pä-\
Italian
: torturous punishment

strepsiceros
\strepˈsisərəs, -ˌräs\
Latin
: antelope

styca
\stīkə\
Old English
: copper

stylopized
\stīləˌpēzd\
New Latin+English
: parasitical alteration

suclat
\səˈklät\
Persian>Hindi
: woolen broad cloth

syllis
\siləs\
New Latin
: worm

synaptai
\sēˌnäpˈtā\
Middle Greek
: prayers

synechthran
\səˈnekthrən\
Greek
: insect

tabellion
\təˈbelyən\
Latin
: scrivener

tafia
\tafēə\
French
: rum

tagasaste
\tägəˈsästē\
Spanish
: shrub

taimen
\tīˌmen\
Finnish
: giant trout

takrouri
\təˈkrurē\
Unknown
: chopped tops

talbot
\tȯlbət, tal-\
English name
: white hound

talpacoti
\talpəˈkōtē\
American Indian
: ground dove

tamandua
\təˈman, düə\
Portuguese
: anteater

tamas
\təməs\
Sanskrit
: inertia

tamonea
\təˈmōnēə, ˌtaməˈnēə\
New Latin
: flower

tanacetin
\tanəˈsētᵊn\
ISV
: bitter principle

tanekaha
\tänəˈkähä\
Maori
: celery-topped pine

tangilin
\tanˈgilən\
Malay
: pangolin

taniko
\tänəkō\
Maori
: ornamental border

tanjong
\tän‚jȯŋ\
Malay
: cape, point

tarantass
\tärən¦täs\
Russian
: four-wheeled carriage

taraxacum
\təˈraksəkəm\
Arabic>New Latin
: dried rhizome

tasbih
\täz‚bē\
Arabic
: rosary

tazettine
\tazə‚tēn, -zətȯn\
New Latin+English
: alkaloid

Tazewell
\taz‚wel, -wəl\
Illinios county name
: glacial substance

tazia
\təˈzēə\
Arabic
: Muslim passion play

tebbad
\te‚bad\
Sanskrit+Persian
: sandstorm

tekiah
\təˈkēə\
Hebrew
: deep calls

temacha
\tämə‚chä, täˈmächə\
Persian
: farcical interlude

temene
\temə‚‚nē\
Greek
: sacred regions (pl.)

tenaille
\təˈnā(ə)l, -nī\
Middle French
: outwork

tendenzen
\tenˈdentsən\
German
: dominating point

tenio
\təˈnē‚ō\
Spanish
: timber tree

tepal
\tēpəl, ˈtep-\
French
: modified leaves

terramare
\terəˈmärē\
Italian
: dwelling

terrella
\təˈrelə\
New Latin
: spherical magnet

teruah
\təˈrüə, -üä\
Hebrew
: staccato blasts

terzina
\tertˈsēnə\
Italian
: triplet

tessarace
\tesərə‚sē\
Latin>Greek
: four-sided summit

testamur
\teˈstämə(r)\
Latin
: examination certificate

Tharparkar
\tär¦pärkər\
Pakistan district
: cattle breed

theetsee
\thētsē\
Burmese
: tree

thelaziasis
\theləˈzīəsəs\
New Latin
: infestation

theow
\thāō\
Old Norse>Old English
: slave

theriaca
\thəˈrīəkə\
New Latin
: antidote

thonzylamine
\thänˈzilə‚mēn, -mən\
Portmanteau
: antihistamine

thrymsa
\thrimzə, -msə\
Late Latin
: gold coin

Thucydidean
\th(y)ü¦sidə¦dēən\
Greek+English
: device of putting
appropriate speeches into
mouths of persons in history

thujaplicin
\th(y)üjəˈplīsᵊn\
New Latin+English
: crystalline

Thuringer
\th(y)ùrə̇njə(r), thərə̇-,thirə̇-
; tiriŋə-, ˈūēriŋə-\
German
: summer sausage

thymelici
\thī'melə̇ˌsī\
Greek
: chorus

thylakentrin
\thīlə'kentrə̇n\
Greek
: hormone

thyrse
\thərs, -ōs, -ə̇is\
New Latin
: inflorescence

thwaite
\thwāt\
Old Norse
: piece of land

tibey
\tə̇'bā\
American Spanish
: plant

tibourbou
\tə̇'bùrbü\
Galibi
: tropical tree

tifinagh
\tə̇'fēˌnak̲\
Tuareg
: Libyan alphabet

tikor
\tikər, tēk-, -ˌkò(ə)r\
Hindi
: arrowroot

tipiti
\tipətē, tipə̇ˌtē\
Portuguese
: plaited cylinder

tilyer
\tilyə(r)\
Hindi
: starling

tinea
\tinēə\
Latin
: fungus disease

Tiruchirapalli
\thirü-chirə, pəlē\
Indian place
: cigar

titar
\tētə(r)\
Hindi
: bird

tizeur
\tē¦zər(), tə̇'z-; tēzər\
French
: glass melting surface
operater

tocalote
\tōkə'lōtē\
Spanish
: weedy herb

tonjon
\tänˌjän\
Hindi
: chair

tordion
\tòrd¦yōⁿ\
French
: dance

tornote
\tòrˌnōt\
Greek
: sponge spicule

tosaphoth
\tōsəˌfõt\
Middle Hebrew
: glosses

tosca
\tōskə\
American Spanish
: calcium deposit

totara
\tōtəˌrä, tō'tärə\
Maori
: tall tree

tourill
\tù'ril\
French>German
: absorption vessel

toxicarol
\täk'sikəˌròl, -rōl\
New Latin
: greenish crystalline

toxotae
\täksəˌtē\
Greek
: slaves

tozee
\tōzē\
Dutch
: curling tee

trabuco
\trə'bükō\
Catalan
: machine gun

tragacanth
\trajəˌkan(t)th, -ˌkaa(ə)n-
also -kən- *sometimes* -
agək- *or* -aigə *or* -gəs-\
Greek>Middle French
: gum

transeuntes
\tran(t)sē'ùnˌtēz, -nzē'-\
Latin
: migratory lucusts phase

trapiche
\trə'pēchē\
Greek>Spanish
: sugar mill

Trappistine
\tra,pəstēn\
French
: nun

trekboer
\trek,bür\
Afrikaans
: cattle grazer

tremie
\tremē\
French
: concrete solidification

trental
\trentᵊl\
Middle Latin>Middle
English
: series of masses

tresette
\trāˈset-ē, trə-\
Italian
: card game

trews
\trüz\
Scottish Gaelic
: trousers

tristeza
\trəˈstāzə, -stēzə\
Portuguese
: disease

tronador
\trōnəˌdȯ(ə)r\
Spanish
: woody herb

trulli
\trülē\
Italian
: stone buildings

trussell
\trəsəl\
Middle English
: upper hand

tsatlee
\tsatˌlē\
Chinese
: raw silk

tucunare
\tüˌkünəˈrā\
Tupi>Portuguese
: freshwater fish

tufan
\tüˈfän\
Greek>Arabic
: violent storm

tuillette
\twēˈlet\
French
: hinged plates

tuinga
\tüˈiŋgə\
Samoan
: headdress

tukra
\tùkrə\
Hindi
: disorder

tulapai
\tüˈläˌpī\
Apache
: fermented beverage

tullibee
\tələˌbē\
Canadian French
: whitefish

tulnic
\tülnēk\
Romanian
: wooden trumpet

turlough
\tərˌläk\
Irish Gaelic
: winter lake

tutsan
\tətsən\
Latin
: St. Johns-wort

tylarus
\tilərəs, təˈla(a)rəs\
Greek
: birdtoe pad

tylion
\tilēˌän\
New Latin
: craniometric point

uintathere
\yüˈ(w)intəˌthi(ə)r\
New Latin
: mammal with small brain

ukase
\yü,kās\
French&Russian
: proclamation

uloborid
\yüˈläbərəd\
New Latin
: spider

Uniate
\yünēət, -ēˌāt\
Polish>Russian
: Christianite

unsonsy
\ənˈsän(t)sē\
British
: unlucky

urman
\ùrˌmän, -man\
Russian
: evergreen forest

usnea
\əsnēə\
Arabic>New Latin
: lichen

utas
\yü͵tas\
Middle Latin
: octave

Utraquist
\yütrə͵kwȯst\
New Latin
: member of a Hussite body

vaadim
\väˈädēm\
Late Hebrew
: representative body

vacoa
\vəˈkōə\
Mauritian name
: screw pine

Valdepenas
\väldəˈpānyəs\
Spanish
: table wine

Valenciennes
\vəˈlen(t)sēˈen(z) *sometimes* ¦
valənsēˈen(z) *or* ¦valənˈsēnz\
French
: bobbinlace

valeryl
\vəˈlirəl, valə͵ril\
ISV
: radical

Valpolicella
\¦väl͵pōləˈchelə\
Italian
: red table wine

vapourer
\vāpərə(r)\
British
: moth

vasicine
\vasə͵sēn, -azə-\
Sanskrit+ISV
: alkaloid

velella
\vəˈlelə\
Latin
: animal

veloute
\və͵lüˈtā\
French
: sauce

ventil
\ventᵊl\
Middle French>German
: valve

venturi
\venˈtu̇rē\
Italian
: short tube

vermorel
\vərməˈrel, verm-\
French
: spray nozzle

Vernunft
\ferˈnu̇nft, fər-, -u̇m(p)ft\
German
: reason

verstand
\ferˈshtänt, fər-\
German
: understanding

vertep
\vərˈtep\
Russian
: puppet show

verumontanum
\veryümän¦tanəm\
Latin+Latin
: floor elevation

verver
\vāˈvā, ve¦ve\
Haitian Creole
: ritualistic design

vervet
\vərvȯt\
French
: monkey

vibices
\vībə͵sēz\
Latin
: extravasation

vicilin
\visələn\
Latin+English
: globulin

vidicon
\vidə͵kän\
Portmanteau
: camera tube

vihuela
\vēˈwälə\
Spanish
: lute

villini
\viˈlēnē\
Italian
: detached houses

villote
\viˈlōtā\
Italian
: dances

vinyon
\vin͵yän\
Trademark
: fibers

vispered
\vēspə͵red\
Arabic
: ceremonial tents

vizard
\vizə(r)d\
Alteration
: mask of disguise

wabeno
\wȯˈbēnō\
Ojibwa
: shaman

wachna
\wäknə\
Russian
: cod of Alaska

waggel
\wagəl\
Unknown
: black-backed gull

waiata
\wīətə\
Maori
: memorative song

Waldenses
\wälˈden(t)ˌsēz, wȯl-\
Middle English
: Christians in France

wallaba
\wäləbə *also* wȯl-\
Arawak
: trees

wallago
\wäləˌgō\
Bengali native name
: catfish

wallaroo
\wäləˈrü *also* wȯl-\
Australian name
: euro

wandoo
\wänˌdü\
Australian name
: gum tree

warehou
\wärəˌhō, -haü\
Maori
: bream

warrandice
\wärəndəs\
Afrikaans
: obligation

warree
\wäˈrē, ˈwärē\
Miskito
: pig-like animal

wassie
\wäsē\
Unknown
: large cleavage in crystal

wawaskeesh
\wəˈwäˌskēsh\
Ojibwa
: North American deer

waterie
\wȯǀtərē, wäǀ, ǀtə-, -ri\
Portmanteau
: Old World birds

waterstead
\wätə(r)ˌsted, ˈwȯtə-\
English
: bed of a stream

Welsbach
\welzˌbak, -bäk\
Trademark
: burners for producing gasoline

whare
\(h)wärā, fä-\
Maori
: nut or house

whaup
\(h)wȯp\
Imitation
: curlew

whekau
\(h)weˌkaü, fe-\
Maori
: owl

whewl
\(h)wül\
Imitation
: cry complainingly

whirtle
\hwərtᵊl *also* wə-\
Middle English
: steel die

whitterick
\(h)witərik\
Imitation
: curlew

widdrim
\widrəm\
Old English
: mental excitement

winze
\winz\
Alteration
: vertical opening driven to connect mining places

wistaria
\wəˈstirēə, -tēr- *also* -ter- *or* -ta(a)r- *or* -tär-\
Alteration
: pale purple

wohlfahrtia
\vōlˈfärtēə\
German
: sarcophagoid fly

woilie
\wȯilē\
Australian name
: kangaroo

wonderboom
\vändə(r)ˌbüm\
Afrikaans
: fig

wongshy
\wäŋˈshē\
Chinese
: Asian tree

woolert
\wülə(r)t\
English
: barn owl

worrywart
\wər-ē, wȯ(ə)r|t\
English
: pessimist

wourali
\wüˈrälē\
Macushi
: arrow poison

wowser
\waùzə(r)\
Australian name
: amusement disliker

wrothful
\rȯth-fəl\
English+English
: angry

wurley
\wərlē\
Australian name
: hut

wyliecoat
\wīliˌkōt, wil-\
Scottish
: night gown

xanthorrhoea
\zan(t)thəˈrēə\
New Latin
: woody trunked tree

xanthydrol
\zanˈthīˌdrȯl, -rōl\
ISV
: alcohol

xenotime
\zenəˌtīm\
Greek>French
: mineral

xiphias
\zifēəs\
Greek>Latin
: swordfish

xylidine
\zīləˌdēn, ˈzil-, -dᵊn\
ISV
: crystalline

xylindein
\zīˈlindēə̇n\
French
: crystalline

yacata
\yäkətə\
Mexican Spanish
: mound of earth

yakamik
\yakəmik\
Tupi>Portuguese
: bird

yarran
\yarən\
Native name in New South Wales
: acacia

yertchuk
\yərˌchək\
Australian name
: medium-sized tree

yungan
\yəŋgən\
Australian name
: manatee

zabra
\zäbrə, sä-\
Arabic
: sailing vessel

zamandoque
\zämənˈdōkē,ˌsä-\
Mexican Spanish
: tree

Zanni
\(d)zänē\
Italian
: madcap

zanthoxylum
\zanˈthäkˌsiləm\
New Latin
: dried bark of ash

zapupe
\zəˈpüpē, pə-\
Mexican Spanish
: agaver

zarah
\zəˈrä\
Unknown
: kazoo

zebrula
\zēbrələ, zeb-\
Alteration
: horse and zebra hybrid

zecchini
\zeˈkēnē, tse-\
Italian
: sparkles

zedoary
\zedō, ārē\
Persian>Middle Latin
: fragrant drug

zemmi
\zemē\
Russian
: rat

zerda
\zərdə\
Persian>Arabic
: fox

zillah
\zilə\
Hindi
: district

zimarra
\zə'märə\
Italian
: black cassock

zimb
\zim(b)\
Amharic
: fly

Zimbel
\tsimbəl\
German
: cymbal

zimocca
\zə'mäkə\
New Latin
: sponge

zindiq
\zin'dēk\
Arabic
: heretic

zineb
\zi‚neb\
ISV
: agricultural fungicide

zingana
\ziŋgənə\
Italian
: trees with mottled wood

zingel
\tsiŋəl\
German
: freshwater perch

ziziphus
\zizəfəs\
Latin
: Asiatic shrubs

zoeaform
\zō‚ēə‚form\
Greek
: like an early larva

zokor
\zō‚kȯr\
Altai mountain
: rodent

zygadene
\zigə‚dēn, zīg-\
New Latin
: plant

zygion
\zigē‚än, zij-\
New Latin
: craniometrics point

zygocity
\zī'gäsətē, zə'-\
Greek
: pregnancy cond

Chapter 5: Jigsaw

aasvogel
\äs-ˌfȭ-gəl\
Afrikaans
: vulture

abacate
\a-bə-ˈkä-tē\
Portuguese
: avocado

aboideau
\ábwádō\
French
: tide gate

abozzi
\əˈbȯtsē\
Italian
: rough sketches

abwab
\əbˈwäb\
Hindi
: fine

acaciin
\əˈkās(h)ēən\
ISV
: glycoside

acana
\äkənə\
Spanish
: tree

accolle
\akəˌlā\
French
: collared

accoutrement
\əˈkü-trə-mənt\
French
: article of clothing

aceldama
\ə-ˈsel-də-mə\
Biblical name
: field of bloodshed

acenaphthylene
\asəˈnapˌthəlēn\
ISV
: hydrocarbon

achroodextrin
\a-krə-wō-ˈdek-strən\
ISV
: polysaccharide

acraein
\ə-ˈkrē-ən\
ISV
: substance

acroterion
\a-krə-ˈtir-ē-ˌän\
Greek
: pedestal

acuerdo
\ə-ˈkwer-dō\
Spanish
: resolution

adamantinomatous
\a-də-ˌman-tᵊn-¦ä-mə-təs\
Latin
: of jaw tumors

adhamant
\ad-¦hā-mənt\
Latin
: clinging as if by hooks

adjudicatio
\ə-ˌjü-di-ˈkä-tē-ˌō\
Latin
: court decree

admittatur
\ad-mə-ˈtā-tər\
Latin
: certificate

adytum
\a-də-təm\
Greek
: sanctum

aebleskiver
\e-blə-ˌski-vər\
Danish
: pastries

aedileship
\ē-ˌdī(-ə)l-ˌship\
Latin
: title of official

aegrotat
\ē-ˈgrō-ˌtat\
Latin
: medical certificate

aeneous
\ā-ˈē-nē-əs\
Latin
: greenish gold

aerugo
\ēˈ-rü-gō\
Latin
: rust

aestivate
\e-stə-ˌvāt\
Latin
: to pass the summer

afernan
\a-fər-ˌnan\
Arabic
: shrub

affricate
\a-fri-kət\
Latin
: phonetic stop

affronty
\ə-ˈfrən-tē\
French
: facing each other

aficionado
\ə-ˌfi-sh(ē-)ə-ˈnä-dō\
Spanish
: ardent follower

Agapemone
\a-gə-ˈpe-mə-nē\
Greek
: free-love institution

agata
\a-gə-də\
Italian
: glassware

aggag
\ä-ˌgäg\
Chamorro
: screw pine

agitpunkt
\a-jət-ˌpu̇ŋ(k)t\
Russian
: propaganda

agoge
\ə-ˈgō-jē\
Greek
: tempo

agrafe
\ə-ˈgraf\
French
: hook

agreation
\ä-grä-ä-ˈsyōⁿ\
French
: diplomatic procedure

ahuatle
\ä-ˌwät-lē\
Nahuatl
: insect eggs

aiel
\ā(-ə)l\
Middle English
: writ

aiguiere
\āg-ǀyer\
French
: pitcher

aikane
\ī-ˈkä-nē\
Hawaiian
: good friend

airampo
\ī-ˈräm-pō\
Spanish
: cactus

airig
\är-ik\
Irish Gaelic
: officials

ajowan
\a-jə-ˌwän\
Unknown
: fruit

akaakai
\ä-ˌkä-ä-ˈkī\
Hawaiian
: bulrush

akeake
\ä-kē-ˈä-kē\
Maori
: tree

akebi
\ä-kə-bē\
Japanese
: vine

akepiro
\ä-kə-ˈpir-ō\
Maori
: tree

akhrot
\ə-ˈkrōt\
Sanskrit
: walnut tree

alabarch
\a-lə-ˌbärk\
Latin
: chief magistrate

alalauwa
\ä-lə-ˈlau̇-ə\
Hawaiian
: food fish

alcaide
\al-ˈkī-dē\
Spanish
: castle commander

alcornoque
\al-kȯr-ˈnō-kē\
Portuguese
: tree

alegrias
\a-lə-ˈgrē-əs\
Spanish
: dance

Alencon
\ə-ˈlen-ˌsän\
French geographical name
: delicate lace

alesan
\a-lə-ˌsan\
French
: light brown

aliipoe
\ä-ˌlēē-ˈpō-ˌā\
Hawaiian
: plant

alisier
\ə'lēzē͵ā\
French
: shrub

aljamiado
\äl͵häme¦ät͟hō\
Spanish
: written in Spanish

alkekengi
\alkə'kenjē\
Arabic
: plant

Allasch
\ä͵läsh\
German
: sweet cake

allerion
\ə'lirēən\
French
: eagle

allocochick
\aləkə͵chik\
Yurok
: shell money

allonge
\a-'lōⁿzh\
French
: rider

almucantar
\almyü¦kantə(r)\
Arabic
: telescope

altilik
\altə͵lik\
Turkish
: coin

alular
\al-yə-lər\
Latin
: of scales

alveloz
\alvə¦lōz\
Portuguese
: milky sap

amalaka
\ä'mələkə\
Sanskrit
: ornament

amargoso
\ämər'gōsō\
Spanish
: bark

amati
\ä-'mä-tē\
Italian
: violin

ambalam
\əmbələm\
Sinhalese
: travel house

ambsace
\ām-͵zās\
English
: lowest throw at dice

amgarn
\am͵gärn\
Welsh
: ancient stone

ampelite
\ampə͵līt\
Latin
: coal

anadem
\a-nə-͵dem\
Greek
: garland

ananke
\ə'naŋkē\
Greek
: personification

anargyros
\ä'näryē͵rȯs\
Greek
: saint

anatta
\ənə'tä\
Sanskrit
: doctrine

ancile
\äŋ'kē͵lā\
Latin
: shield

andouille
\än-'dü-ē\
French
: sausage

anicca
\ə'nikə\
Sanskrit
: evanescence

ankole
\aŋ'kōlē\
Ugandan geographic name
: cattle

anonang
\ə'nō͵näŋ\
Tagalog
: tree

anoncillo
\änōn'sēl͵yō\
Spanish
: fiber

antigropelos
\antə'gräpələs\
Greek
: waterproof leggings

antoeci
\an'tē͵sī\
Latin
: those living on same meridian but opposite parallels

apeiron
\ə'pī͵rän\
Greek
: principle

apercu
\a-pər-¦sü\
French
: outline

apikores
\äpē'kȯrəs\
Hebrew
: atheist

apogalacteum
\apəgə'laktēəm\
Greek
: hypothetical orbit

apparentement
\ȧpȧräⁿtmäⁿ\
French
: alliance

appaume
\apō¦mā\
French
: opened out

apres
\ä-'prā\
French
: after

aquaehaustus
\a-kwə'hȯstəs\
Latin
: right to draw water

aracari
\ärə'särē\
Tupi
: toucan

araire
\ə're(ə)r\
French
: plow

archallaxis
\ärkə'laksəs\
Latin
: early deviation

archedictyon
\ärkə'diktē͵än\
Greek
: veinlike network

arcuale
\ärkyə'wālē\
Latin
: cartilage

ardennes
\är-¦den(z)\
French
: horse

arete
\a-rə-'tā\
Greek
: excellence

armitas
\är'mētəz\
Spanish
: aprons

armozeen
\ärmə¦zēn\
Persian geographic name
: silk

arrack
\a-rək\
Arabic
: alcoholic beverage

arriviste
\a-ri-¦vēst\
French
: upstart

arrondi
\a͵rōⁿ'dē\
French
: curved

arroyo
\ə-'rȯi-ō\
Spanish
: ravine

artel
\är'tel(ʸ)\
Russian
: labor union

Artenkreise
\ärtᵊn͵krīzə\
German
: species

aryballos
\arə'baləs\
Greek
: flask

ashraf
\a'shräf\
Arabic
: descendant of Muhammad

askarel
\askə¦rel\
Unknown
: liquid

assapanic
\asə͵panik\
Ojibwa
: flying squirrel

assegai
\a-si-͵gī\
Arabic
: javelin

ataraxy
\atə͵raksē\
Greek
: imperturbability

atemoya
\ä-tə-'mȯi-ə\
blend
: fruit

athanor
\athə͵nȯ(ə)r\
Latin
: furnace

attacco
\ə'täkō\
Italian
: short phrase

aubusson
\ō-bə-¦sōⁿ\
French
: dark red

auftaktigkeit
\aůf͵täktiḵ͵kīt\
German
: principle of music

aulos
\ȯ͵läs\
Greek
: flute

avion
\a̓vyōⁿ\
French
: airplane

avodire
\avədə¦rä\
French
: tree

ayuntamiento
\ī͵yùntämē'entō\
Spanish
: town hall

Azadirachta
\ə͵zadə'raktə\
Persian
: tree

babakoto
\bäbə'kōtō\
Malagasy
: lemur

babassu
\bä-bə-¦sü\
Portuguese
: palm

babbitt
\ba-bət\
English
: metal

babiche
\bə'bēsh\
French
: thread

bacubert
\bakyü¦be(ə)r\
French
: sword dance

badak
\bä͵däk\
Javanese name
: rhinoceros

baetyli
\bēdᵊlī\
Greek
: stones

bafaro
\bə'färō\
Afrikaans
: stonebass

baggala
\bəgə͵lä\
Marathi
: vessel

baggataway
\bə'gatə͵wä\
Algonquian
: game

bagtikan
\bäg'tēkən\
Filipino
: wood

bahuvrihi
\bähüv'rēhē\
Sanskrit
: compound

Bakshaish
\bäk¦shīsh\
Persian geographic name
: carpet

balaphon
\ba-lə-͵fōn\
French
: xylophone

balas
\ba-ləs\
English
: ruby

balatte
\bə'lat\
Unknown
: limestone

balche
\bäl¦chä\
Mayan
: fermented drink

balete
\bə'lētē\
Tagalog
: fig

ballam
\bə'läm\
Malayalam
: canoe

ballon
\ba-'lȯⁿ\
French
: buoyancy

balut
\bä'lüt\
Tagalog
: food

bamah
\bämä\
Hebrew
: high place

banlieue
\bän̄lyœ\
French
: environs

baratte
\bəˈrat\
French
: churn

barbone
\bärˈbōnē\
Italian
: pasteurellosis

barcarole
\bär-kə-ˌrōl\
French
: boat song

barege
\bəˈrezh\
French
: fabric

baris
\bärəs\
Balinese
: spear dance

barmecidal
\bär-mə-¦sī-dᵊl\
Persian name
: unreal

barnevelder
\bärnəˌveldər\
Dutch
: breed

bascine
\bəˈsēn\
French
: flush joint

bashlyk
\bash¦lik\
Russian
: protective hood

bastille
\ba-¦stēl\
French
: prison

bataan
\bəˈtan\
Philippine geographic name
: tree

batarde
\bə-ˈtärd\
French
: handwriting

bateleur
\ba-tᵊl-¦ər\
French
: eagle

battuta
\bə-ˈtü-tə\
Italian
: measure

bauno
\bä-ˈünō\
Philippine geographic name
: mango

bawley
\bȯ-lē\
Unknown
: boat

bawneen
\bä-ˌnēn\
Irish
: jacket

bearnaise
\bā-är-¦nāz\
French
: sauce

beauseant
\bō-sā-ˈäⁿ\
French
: banner

becasse
\bā-ˈkäs\
French
: shorebird

bechamel
\bā-shə-¦mel\
French
: white sauce

bedeguar
\be-də-ˌgär\
French
: moss

bejan
\bā-jən\
French
: freshman

bejuco
\bi-ˈhü-kō\
Spanish
: vine

belote
\bə-ˈlät\
French
: card game

belzebuth
\bel-zə-ˌbəth\
Latin
: spider monkey

bercy
\ber-¦sē\
French
: sauce

bergere
\ber-¦zher\
French
: armchair

berrugate
\ber-ə-ˈgä-tē\
Spanish
: fish

bersagliere
\ber-səl-ˈyer-ē\
Italian
: sharpshooter

besugo
\bi-ˈsü-gō\
Spanish
: food

betanin
\bē-tə-nən\
Latin
: anthocyanin

betise
\bā-ˈtēz\
French
: ignorance

bhikku
\bi-kü\
Pali
: monk

biajaiba
\bē-ə-ˈhī-bə\
Spanish
: snapper

bichir
\bi-chər\
French
: fish

biedermeier
\bē-dər-ˌmīr\
German
: bourgeois

biniou
\bē-ˈnyü\
French
: Breton bagpipe

bitanhol
\bē-ˌtäŋ-ˈhōl\
Tagalog
: tree

bliaut
\blēō\
French
: tunic

bloedpens
\blüt-ˌpen(t)s\
Afrikaans
: lambs

blouwildebeesoog
\blau-ˌvildə-ˌbā-ˌsȯk\
Afrikaans
: disease

bocor
\bō-ˈkȯ(ə)r\
Haitian Creole
: witch doctor

bodle
\bädᵊl\
English
: coin

boedelscheiding
\büdᵊl-ˌskādiŋ\
Dutch
: partition of estate

bohor
\bō-ˌhȯr\
Amharic
: reedbuck

bollix
\bä-liks\
English
: bungle

bombachas
\bəm-ˈbächəz\
Spanish
: trousers

bombazet
\bämbə¦zet\
English
: silk fabric

bombonne
\bäm-ˌbän\
French
: bottle

bonaght
\bänəkt\
Irish
: tax

boniato
\bō-nē-ˈä-tō\
Spanish
: potato

bonnaz
\bə-ˈnaz\
French
: embroidery

boreas
\bȯr-ē-əs\
Greek
: north wind

bostanji
\bȯ-ˈstanjē\
Turkish
: guard

bostryx
\bästriks\
Greek
: flower

bouginage
büzhē¦näzh
French
: dilation of cavity

boule
\bü-lē\
Greek
: council

bouzouki
\bü-'zü-kē\
Greek
: instrument

boxwallah
\bäk͜swälə\
Hindi
: peddler

bozzetto
\bət'setō\
Italian
: clay

braccae
\brä͜kī\
Gaulish
: trousers

braies
\brā\
French
: trousers

braireau
\brerō\
French
: badger

branle
\brä(ä)ⁿl\
French
: dance

breba
\brābə\
Spanish
: fig

bretesse
\bretə̖sā\
French
: embattled

brinjarry
\brin'järē\
Hindi
: traveling dealer

britska
\brichkə\
Polish
: carriage

brodequin
\brōdəkən\
French
: shoe

broigne
\bròin\
French
: medieval garment

brouillon
\brüyōⁿ\
French
: rough draft

brynza
\brinzə\
Slovak
: cheese

budgerow
\bəj(ə)͜rō\
Hindi
: boat

burnous
\bər-'nüs\
French
: cloak

bussu
\bə'sü\
Portuguese
: palm

bylina
\bə̇'lēnə\
Russian
: folk epic

caapi
\kä-pē\
Portuguese
: beverage

caatinga
\kä'tiŋgə\
Portuguese
: forest

cabecudo
\kabə'südō\
Portuguese
: palm

cabreuva
\kabrē'üvə\
Portuguese
: tree

cacaxte
\kə'kästē\
Spanish
: frame

cachexia
\kə-'kek-sē-ə\
Latin
: malnutrition

caciocavallo
\kächōkə'välō\
Italian
: cheese

cadastre
\kə-'da-stər\
French
: register

cadjan
\käjən\
Malay
: palm leaf

caerphilly
\kär-'fi-lē\
Welsh geographic name
: cheese

caesura
\si-'zyu̇r-ə\
Italian
: break

cafeneh
\kafəˌnā\
Turkish
: coffehouse

caixinha
\kīˈshēnyə\
Portuguese
: box rattle

cajeput
\ka-jə-pət\
Malay
: tree

calabrese
\kaləˈbrāzē\
Italian
: broccoli

calalu
\kaləˌlü\
Spanish
: plant

calamanco
\kaləˈmaŋkō\
Spanish
: fabric

calanque
\kəˈläŋk\
French
: inlet

calathos
\kaləˌthäs\
Greek
: basket

calcino
\kalˈchēnō\
Italian
: silkworm disease

calean
\kalēˌän\
Persian
: water pipe

caliche
\kə-ˈlē-chē\
Spanish
: rock

calin
\kàlaⁿ\
French
: alloy

caline
\kāˌlēn\
Unknown
: hormone

callais
\kalāə̇s\
Greek
: stone

callejon
\kàlʸeˈk̇òn\
Spanish
: passageway

calotte
\kə-ˈlät\
French
: skullcap

calpac
\kal-ˌpak\
Turkish
: cap

calusar
\kəˌlüˈshär\
Romanian
: dance

calymma
\kəˈlimə\
Greek
: chromosome

camachile
\käməˈchilē\
Spanish
: tree

cambiata
\kambēˈätə\
Italian
: nonharmonic note

camerlengo
\ka-mər-ˈleŋ-gō\
Italian
: cardinal

canao
\kənˈyau̇\
Spanish
: feast

canape
\ka-nə-pē\
French
: sofa

cancrizans
\kaŋkrə̇ˌzanz\
Latin
: musical retrograde

candomble
\kanˌdōmˈblā\
Portuguese
: religion

cangue
\kaŋ\
French
: rectangular device

canions
\kanyənz\
Spanish
: kneepieces

canistel
\kanəˌstel\
Spanish
: tree

cannabin
\kanəbə̇n\
Latin
: resin

111

cannelon
\kanᵊlˌän\
Italian
: hollow roll

canossa
\kəˈnäsə\
Italian geographic name
: place of penance

cantal
\kän-ˈtäl\
French geographic name
: cheese

cantil
\kanˈtēl\
Spanish
: snake

canzone
\kan-ˈzō-ne\
Italian
: lyric poem

capelin
\ka-p(ə-)lən\
French
: fish

capharnaum
\kəˈfärnēəm\
French
: confused jumble

capita
\käpəˌtä\
Latin
: university council

carabiniere
\ker-ə-bən-ˈyer-ā\
Italian
: police member

caramoussal
\karəməˈsal\
Turkish
: ship

carbamazepine
\kär-bə-ˈma-zə-ˌpēn\
ISV
: analgesic

carcer
\kärˌke(ə)r\
Latin
: race starting point

cardamom
\kär-də-məm\
Greek
: fruit

carignane
\kä-rə-ˈnyän\
French
: wine

carrageen
\ker-ə-ˈgēn\
Irish geographic name
: alga

cascaron
\kaskəˈrōn\
Spanish
: eggshell

casern
\kə-ˈzərn\
French
: barracks

cashel
\kashəl\
Irish Gaelic
: wall

casquetel
\kaskətel\
French
: helmet

cathexis
\kə-ˈthek-səs\
Greek
: investment

causse
\kōs\
French
: plateau

cavaquinho
\kavəˈkēnyü\
Portuguese
: ukulele

cecil
\sēsəl\
American geographic name
: soil

ceilidh
\kā-lē\
Irish
: visit

cendre
\sä(ä)ⁿdr(ᵊ)\
French
: blue

cenoby
\senəbē\
Latin
: religious community

cepe
\sēp\
French
: mushroom

ceras
\serəs\
Latin
: papilla

ceresin
\serəsȯn\
ISV
: wax

cermet
\sər-ˌmet\
Latin
: alloy

cervelases
\sər-və-ˌläz\
French
: sausage

cevine
\sev͟ˌēn\
ISV
: crystalline alkaloid

chacmool
\chäkˌmōl\
Mayan
: reclining figure

chador
\chə-dər\
Hindi
: cloth

chalone
\kā-ˌlōn\
Greek
: substance

chalumeau
\shaləˌmō\
French
: instrument

chamar
\chəmə(r)\
Hindi
: fan

chamiza
\shə-ˈmē-zə\
Spanish
: shrub

chantage
\shäⁿtààzh\
French
: blackmail

chantecler
\chantəˌkli(ə)r\
French
: fowl

charabanc
\sher-ə-ˌbaŋ\
French
: vehicle

charisticary
\kəˈristəˌkerē\
Greek
: official

chasse
\shäs\
French
: saint

chastushka
\chaˈstùshkə\
Russian
: folk verse

chaulmoogra
\chȯl-ˈmü-grə\
Bengali
: tree

chaussee
\shōˌsā\
French
: paved road

chebule
\kəˈb(y)ül\
French
: fruit

chechem
\chəˈchem\
Spanish
: tree

cheechako
\chē-ˈchä-kō\
Chinook
: tenderfoot

chelicere
\ke-lə-ˌsir\
French
: appendage

cheneau
\shāˈnō\
French
: cresting

chenier
\shinərē\
French
: ridge

chevee
\shəˈvā\
French
: gemstone

chevesaile
\shevəˌsāl\
French
: collar

chevrette
\shəvˈret\
French
: goatskin

chhatri
\chətrē\
Hindi
: resthouse

chiavette
\kyəˈvetē\
Italian
: clef

chibouk
\chə-ˈbük\
French
: tobacco pipe

chiffer
\shifə(r)\
French
: figure

chigetai
\chigəˌtī\
Mongolian
: donkey

113

chilicothe
\chilə'kōthē\
Spanish
: vine

chiltepin
\chil-tə-ˌpēn\
Spanish
: pepper

chinampa
\chə'nampə\
Spanish
: meadow

chinela
\chə'nālə\
Spanish
: slipper

chirata
\chə'rätə\
Hindi
: tissue

chitarrini
\kētə'rēnē\
Italian
: guitars

chitarrone
\kētə'rōnā\
Italian
: instrument

chlamys
\kla-məs\
Greek
: dress

choga
\chōgə\
Sindhi
: cloak

cholam
\chōləm\
Tamil
: sorghum

cholecystokinin
\kō-lə-ˌsi-stə-'kī-nən\
Greek
: hormone

choledoch
\kōləˌdäk\
Greek
: of bile ducts

chorizo
\chə-'rē-zō\
Spanish
: sausage

chotapeg
\chōtəˌpeg\
Hindi
: drink

chott
\shät\
Arabic
: lake

chouan
\shü än\
French
: insurgent

chowrie
\chaůrē\
Hindi
: whisk

chukka
\chə-kə\
Hindi
: boot

chunam
\chů'nam\
Tamil
: plaster

chupon
\chü'pōn\
Spanish
: tree

churel
\chù'rāl\
Hindi
: goblin

churinga
\chü'riŋgə\
Australian name
: wooden talisman

churrus
\chərəs\
Hindi
: well

cibol
\sibəl\
French
: onion

cicisbeo
\chē-chəz-'bā-ō\
Italian
: gallant

cidaris
\sidərəs\
Latin
: tiara

cienaga
\syānəgə\
Spanish
: swamp

cimbalom
\simbələm\
Hungarian
: dulcimer

cippus
\sipəs\
Latin
: pillar

cisele
\sēzəˌlā\
French
: chiseled

civilite
\sivələtā\
French
: cursive hand

clausewitz
\klau̇zəˌvits\
Prussian name
: military strategist

clechee
\klāˈshā\
French
: voided

clisere
\klīˌsi(ə)r\
blend
: ecological community

clivis
\klīvəs\
Latin
: note

cloisonne
\kloi̇-zə-ˌnā\
French
: decoration

clyssus
\klisəs\
Latin
: principle

cnidocil
\nīdəsil\
ISV
: minute process

cocarde
\kōˈkärd\
French
: distinguishing mark

coccagee
\käkəˈjē\
Irish
: apple

cockaigne
\kä-ˈkān\
French
: imaginary land

cockloche
\käˌklōch\
Unknown
: silly fellow

coemptio
\kōˈempshēō\
Latin
: ceremony

cogida
\kōˈhēthə\
Spanish
: tossing of bullfighter

cogon
\kō-ˈgōn\
Spanish
: grass

cohitre
\kōˈhētrā\
Spanish
: dayflower

cohune
\kōˈhün\
Spanish
: palm

colascione
\kōləˈshōnē\
Italian
: lute

colberteen
\kälbə(r)ˌtēn\
French
: lace

coleorhiza
\kō-lē-ə-ˈrī-zə\
Latin
: sheath

colichemarde
\kōlēshˈmärd\
French
: long sword

colicin
\kō-lə-sən\
Latin
: substance

colletin
\kälətⁿn\
French
: armor

collyba
\käləbə\
Greek
: sweet cake

colocynth
\kä-lə-ˌsin(t)th\
Latin
: fruit

colopexy
\käləˌpeksē\
Latin
: operation on abdomen

colorin
\kälərȧn\
Spanish
: tree

colpeo
\kälˈpāō\
Spanish
: dog

coltpixie
\kōltˌpiksē\
English
: hobgoblin

comble
\kōⁿbl(ᵊ)\
French
: acme

comitatus
\kämə'tätəs\
Latin
: county

commers
\kȯ'mers\
German
: social gathering

commis
\kə'mē\
French
: deputy

comoquer
\kōmō'ker\
Spanish
: card

compadrazgo
\kȯmpä'dräzgō\
Spanish
: relationship

condottiere
\kän-də-'tyer-ē\
Italian
: band leader

confiteor
\kən-'fē-tē-ˌȯr\
Latin
: liturgical form

conge
\kōⁿ-'zhā\
French
: dismissal

contrapas
\kōntrə'päs\
Catalan
: chain dance

contrayerva
\käntrə'yərvə\
Spanish
: herb

conveth
\känˌveth\
Latin
: burden upon land

conyrine
\känəˌrēn\
ISV
: oily base

corbeil
\kȯr-bəl\
French
: sculptured basket

cordonazo
\kȯ(r)dᵊn'äsō\
Spanish
: hurricane

cornichon
\kȯr-nē-'shōⁿ\
French
: gherkin

corody
\kȯr-ə-dē\
Latin
: allowance

corozo
\kə'rōsō\
Spanish
: palm

coryphaeus
\kȯr-ə-'fē-əs\
Greek
: leader of chorus

coryphee
\kȯr-i-¦fā\
French
: ballet girl

cotillion
\kō-'til-yən\
French
: ballroom dance

Coulommiers
\kəˌləmē'ā\
French
: cheese

courante
\ku̇-'ränt\
French
: piece of music

coutel
\kü¦tel\
French
: knife

coynye
\kȯin(y)ē\
Irish
: chieftain's food

cramponnee
\krampə¦nā\
French
: squared projection

crannog
\kra-nəg\
Scottish
: island

crapaudine
\krapədēn\
French
: ulcer

Crecy
\krāsē
French
: served with carrots

cremini
\kri-'mē-nē\
Italian
: mushroom

crevecoeur
\krevkər\
French
: domestic fowl

crokinole
\krōkə͵nōl\
French
: game

crotaphion
\krōˈtafē͵än\
Greek
: point at tip of wing

cuartelazo
\kwärtᵊlˈäsō\
Spanish
: military coup

cuiejo
\küˈyähō\
Spanish
: nighthawk

cultch
\kəlch\
French
: mollusk

cunjevoi
\kənjə͵vȯi\
Australian name
: fish

curacoa
\k(y)u̇r-ə-¦sō\
Dutch
: liqueur

cybotaxis
\sibəˈtaksəs\
Greek
: molecule orientation

cypsela
\sipsələ\
Greek
: fruit

dahabeah
\dä(h)əˈbēə\
Arabic
: boat

daimyo
\dī-mē-͵ō\
Japanese
: feudal baron

dakhma
\däkmə\
Farsi
: circular stone

dandizette
\dandē¦zet\
French
: woman

Decauville
\dəˈkō͵vil\
French
: of railroads

defassa
\dəˈfasə\
Latin
: antelope

dehnstufe
\dān͵shtüfə\
German
: lengthened grade

Deruta
\dāˈrütə\
Italian
: earthenware

dessus
\dəˈsūe\
French
: ballet move

dghaisa
\dīsə\
Maltese
: boat

dhawa
\dävə\
Hindi
: tree

dhikr
\dikər\
Arabic
: recitation

djebel
\jebəl\
Arabic
: mountain

domnei
\dämˈnā\
Provencal
: courtly love

douzaine
\dü¦zān\
French
: body of 12 officials

droitural
\drȯichərəl\
French
: of property

dutuburi
\dütəˈbu̇rē\
Spanish
: circle dance

duvetyne
\d(y)üvə͵tēn\
French
: fabric

dybbuk
\dibək\
Hebrew
: evil spirit

dzeren
\dzəˈren\
Russian
: gazelle

ecarte
\ā͵kär¦tā\
French
: card game

117

ecrevisse
\ākrəvēs\
French
: crayfish

effendi
\ə'fendē\
Turkish
: master

egalite
\āgȧlētā\
French
: political leveling

eglomise
\āgləmē¦zā\
French
: made of glass

ehuawa
\āhü'äwə\
Hawiian
: sedge

eisteddfod
\ī'steth̩vȯd\
Welsh
: festival

elepaio
\elə'pīō\
Hawaiian
: flycatcher

elinvar
\elȧn͟vär\
French
: alloy

emboite
\äⁿbwȧtā\
French
: interlocked

embonpoint
\äⁿbōⁿpwaⁿ\
French
: stoutness

emgalla
\em'galə\
African name
: wart hog

emoloa
\āmə'lōə\
Hawaiian
: grass

empeine
\em'pānā\
Spanish
: brown color

empyreuma
\empə'rümə\
Greek
: odor

encaenia
\en'sēnyə\
Latin
: graduation ceremony

enchiridion
\en¦ˌkī'ridēən\
Greek
: manual

encolpion
\eŋ'kȯlpˌyȯn\
Greek
: medallion

endecha
\en'dächə\
Spanish
: song

enfatico
\ām'fätēkō\
Italian
: emphatic

engoulee
\äⁿgülā\
French
: from mouths

entrefer
\äntrə¦fe(ə)r\
French
: air gap

entwicklungsroman
\ent¦vik(ə)lûŋ(k)srō'mään\
German
: autobiographical novel

envoutement
\äⁿvütmäⁿ\
French
: magical practice

epaulet
\e-pə-¦let\
French
: shoulder ornament

epazote
\epəˌzōt\
Spanish
: pungent leaves

ephyra
\efərə\
Latin
: larva

epieikeia
\epēˌī'kīə\
Greek
: interpretation of law

epimanikion
\epēməˈnēkˌyȯn\
Greek
: vestment

epulis
\ə'pyüləs\
Greek
: tumor

estampie
\e-ˌstäm-'pē\
French
: musical work

eulachon
\yülə͵kän\
Chinook
: candlefish

everett
\evə¦ret\
French
: slipper

evzone
\ev͵zōn\
Greek
: infantry corps member

exciple
\eksəpəl\
Latin
: vessel

eyra
\ārə\
Tupi
: wildcat

fabella
\fə'belə\
Latin
: cartilage

fabliau
\fablē͵ō\
French
: metrical tale

facon
\fä'kȯn\
Spanish
: knife

faham
\fä͵häm\
French
: plant

fahlerz
\fä͵lerts\
German
: mineral

fahlore
\fälō(ə)r\
German
: mineral

falanaka
\falə'näkə\
Malagasy
: mammal

faunizone
\fȯnə͵zōn\
Latin
: geological bed

faqih
\fä'kē\
Arabic
: theologian

farleu
\färlü\
Unknown
: slave money

farol
\fə'rōl\
Spanish
: bullfighting move

farruca
\fə'rükə\
Spanish
: gypsy dance

farsakh
\fär͵sak\
Persian
: unit of distance

fastnacht
\fäsh(t)͵näḵt\
German
: dough

fatiha
\fätē͵hä\
Arabic
: prayer

fauchard
\fō¦shär\
French
: weapon

faujdar
\faüj͵där\
Hindi
: criminal judge

fausen
\fȯsᵊn\
Unknown
: eel

fazendeiro
\fazᵊn'därō\
Portuguese
: Brazilian planter

fenouillet
\fenᵊl¦et\
French
: liqueur

feraghan
\ferə¦gän\
Persian geographic name
: carpet

fetii
\fə'tē͵ē\
Tahitian
: relation

fibulare
\fibyə'lärē\
Latin
: bone

fidejussionary
\fīdē'jəshənerē\
Latin
: of contracts

fidibus
\fidəbəs\
German
: paper spill

Fitzhugh
\fitshyü\
Chinese geographic name
: porcelain design

Fjall
\fē'el\
Swedish
: cattle breed

flacherie
\flashə'rē\
French
: silkworm disease

fliskmahoy
\fliskmə¦hȯi\
Scottish
: flighty woman

flurazepam
\flùr'azə‚pam\
ISV
: compound

foehn
\fərn\
German
: wind

foofaraw
\füfə‚rȯ'\
Unknown
: fuss

forlana
\fòr'länä\
Italian
: dance

fourchee
\fü(ə)r¦shā\
French
: divided near end

fravashi
\frə'väshē\
Avestan
: spiritual guardian

frizzen
\friz°n\
Unknown
: metal upright

frottola
\fròt°lə\
Italian
: song

Fugara
\fü'gärə\
Italian
: organ stop

fusilier
\fyüzə¦li(ə)r\
French
: soldier

gaine
\gān\
French
: support

galafate
\galə'fätā\
Spanish
: oldwife

galere
\gə'le(ə)r\
French
: group of people

galleass
\galēəs\
French
: ship

galyak
\gal‚yak\
Uzbek geographic name
: goat fur

gambeson
\gambəsən\
French
: medieval garment

Ganymede
\ga-ni-‚mēd\
Greek
: cupbearer

garbanzo
\gär-'bän-zō\
Spanish
: chickpea

garigue
\gə'rēg\
French
: grass

gattinara
\gätē'närə\
Italian
: wine

gaushala
\gaùshələ\
Sanskrit
: cattle shelter

gavotte
\gə'vät\
French
: dance

geelbec
\gēl‚bek\
Afrikaans
: duck

geeldikkop
\gēl'di‚käp\
Afrikaans
: serious sheep disease

Geheimrat
\gə'hīm‚rät\
German
: privy counselor

gemeinde
\gə'mīndə\
German
: local government

gerbe
\jərb\
French
: firework

gerefa
\yeˈrävä\
Old English
: administrative officer

gesellschaft
\gəˈzelˌshäft\
German
: relationship

ghawazee
\gəˈwäzē\
Arabic
: Egyptian dancing girls

ghazel
\gazəl\
Arabic
: lyric poem

gigas
\jīˌgas\
Greek
: having large stem

gigelira
\jēgəˈlirə\
Italian
: xylophone

gillaroo
\giləˌrü\
Irish Gaelic
: trout

gjetost
\y|ādˌōst\
Norwegian
: cheese

glaistig
\glashtig\
Gaelic
: sprite

grasseye
\grasəˌyā\
French
: pronounced as fricative

greylag
\grāˌlag\
blend
: goose

Guadagnini
\gwädəˈnēnē\
Italian
: violin

Guarnerius
\gwär|ˈnirēəs\
Italian
: violin

guaxima
\gwäˈshēmə\
Portuguese
: fiber

gwyniad
\gwinēˌad\
Welsh
: fish

gyassa
\gīˈasə\
Arabic
: ship

gyttja
\yichä\
Swedish
: lacustrine mud

habutai
\häbəˌtī\
Japanese
: sword

hacek
\haˌchek\
Czech
: diacritic

hadbot
\hädˌbōt\
English
: recompense

haecceity
\hekˈsēəˌdē\
Latin
: individuality

haematodocha
\hēmətōˈdōkə\
Greek
: sac

hagigah
\həˈgēgə\
Hebrew
: voluntary sacrifices

haikal
\hīˌkäl\
Hebrew
: main altar

halleflinta
\helə|flintə\
Swedish
: rock

halzoun
\hal|zün\
Arabic
: laryngeal infestation

hamantasch
\hämənˌtäsh\
Yiddish
: cake

hapkido
\häpˈkēdō\
Korean
: martial art

harakeke
\härəˌkäkē\
Maori
: flax

harquebus
\(h)ärk(w)əbəs\
French
: matchlock gun

harrateen
\harə͵tēn\
English
: fabric

hasenpfeffer
\häzᵊn͵(p)fefə(r)\
German
: stew

haulm
\hȯm\
English
: litter

hauriant
\hȯrēənt\
Latin
: being pale

Havaiki
\həˈvīkē\
Marquesan
: homeland

hazmat
\haz-͵mat\
blend
: dangerous substance

heiau
\hāˌau\ˈ
Hawaiian
: temple

heimin
\hāmən\
Japanese
: commoner

helepole
\he-lə-͵pōl\
Latin
: siege engine

hemippe
\hēˈmipē\
Greek
: donkey

hereenigeng
\həˈrēnəkiŋ\
Afrikaans
: South African coalition

hiccan
\hi¦kan\
blend
: tree nut

hinalea
\hēnəˈlāə\
Hawaiian
: fish

hirmos
\irˈmȯs\
Greek
: hymn

homelyn
\hōmlən\
Unknown
: ray

hoogaars
\hō͵gärs\
Dutch
: sloop

horme
\hȯrmē\
Greek
: vital energy

horokaka
\hȯrəˈkäkə\
Maori
: herb

hospodar
\häspə͵där\
Romanian
: governor

houvari
\(h)üvə¦rē\
Spanish
: thunderstorm

howdah
\hau̇də\
Hindi
: covered pavilion

hursinghar
\hərsiŋ¦gär\
Hindi
: tree

hyaenanche
\hīəˈnaŋkē\
Greek
: tree genus

hypothec
\həˈpäthik\
French
: obligation or right

idigbo
\əˈdig͵bō\
African name
: tree

igigi
\ēˈjējē\
Babylonian
: group of spirits

iiwi
\ēˈēwē\
Hawaiian
: honeycreeper

ikhwan
\ik̲ˈwän\
Arabic
: Muslim brethren

imbauba
\imbəˈübə\
Portuguese
: tree

immeubles
ēmœbl(ᵊ)
French
: class of property

immie
\imē\
imitation
: marble

indaba
\in'däbə\
Zulu
: conference

infula
\infyələ\
Latin
: white wool

ingerence
\injərən(t)s, aⁿzhärääⁿs\
French
: intrusion

inquilino
\ēŋkē'lēnō\
Spanish
: landed worker

interesse
\intə'resē\
Latin
: legal interest

intine
\in‚tēn\
Latin
: inner of two wall layers

intravitam
\intrə'vī‚tam, intrā'wē‚täm\
Latin
: performed on live subject

introitus
\ən'trōətəs\
Latin
: bodily orifice

inulin
\inyələn\
German
: polysaccharide

Ipiutak
\ipē'yü‚tak\
Alaskan geographic name
: Eskimo culture

irade
\ē'rädē\
Turkish
: Islamic decree

irbis
\ər'bēs\
Russian
: snow leopard

irofa
\ē'rōfä\
Japanese
: script

iruska
\ə'rüskə\
Pawnee
: fire dance

isba
\əz'bä\
Russian
: log hut

Ishmael
\ish-mā-əl\
biblical name
: outcast

istle
\is(t)lē\
Spanish
: fiber

itauba
\ētə'übə\
Tupi
: tree

ivermectin
\īvə(r)'mektən\
Latin
: drug mixture

izar
\ə'zär\
Hindi
: outer garment

izote
\ə'zōtē\
Spanish
: plant

jabiru
\jabə¦rü\
Portuguese
: stork

jacutinga
\jakyə'tiŋgə\
Tupi
: iron ore

Jahiliya
\jähə'lē(y)ə\
Arabic
: the pre-Islamic period of
Arabia and Middle East

jakhalsbessie
\ja‚kȯlẓ'besē\
Afrikaans
: ebony

jararaca
\zharə'räkə\
Portuguese
: pit viper

jataco
\hə'täkō\
Spanish
: amaranth

jazeran
\jazərən\
French
: armor

123

jinrikisha
\(jən)ˈriksho\'
Japanese
: vehicle

jizya
\jizyə\
Arabic
: capitation tax

jokul
\yō͜ˌkůl\
Icelandic
: mountain

jorobado
\hȯrə¦bau\'
Spanish
: moonfish

Jugendstil
\yügəntˌshtēl\
German
: art style

kaffeeklatsch
\käfəˌkläch\
German
: informal conversation

kaffiyeh
\kəˈfē(y)ə\
Arabic
: headdress

kaimakam
\kīməˌkäm\
Turkish
: Ottoman deputy

kalasie
\kälə¦sē\
Dayak
: monkey

kalkvis
\kälkˌfis\
Afrikaans
: frostfish

kamaaina
\käməˈīnə\
Hawaiian
: longtime resident

kaoliang
\kaůlē¦äŋ\
Chinese
: liquor

karakul
\karəkəl\
Uzbek geographic name
: breed of sheep

kasseri
\kəˈserē\
Greek
: cheese

Katharevusa
\käthəˈrevəsä\
Greek
: modern Greek

katipo
\kädəˌpō\
Maori
: spider

keddah
\kedə\
Hindi
: enclosure

kendyr
\ken¦di(ə)r\
Turkish
: fiber

keratto
\kəˈratō\
West Indies name
: fiber

kevazingo
\kevəˈziŋgō\
West African name
: tree

Kewasinga
\kewəˈsiŋgə\
West African name
: wood

khaddar
\kädə(r)\
Hindi
: homespun cloth

kiaat
\kēˈät\
Afrikaans
: tree

kiawe
\kēˈäwā\
Hawaiian
: mosquito

kibbeh
\kibə\
Arabic
: ground lamb cake

kibosh
\kī-¦bäsh\
Unknown
: stop

kieselguhr
\kēzəlˌgů(ə)r\
German
: diatomite

kimchi
\kimchē\
Korean
: pickled dish

kinkhab
\kinˌkäb\
Hindi
: silk fabric

kipfel
\kipfəl\
German
: cookie

124

klepht
\kleft\
Greek
: Greek under Turkish rule

kludge
\klüj\
Unknown
: computer system

kopje
\käpē\
Afrikaans
: hill

kordax
\kȯ(ə)r͵daks\
Greek
: dance

krewe
\krü\
Alteration
: private organization

Krummholz
\krům͵hōlts\
German
: stunted forest

kukeri
\kůk(ə)rē\
Hindi
: sword

Kuvasz
\ků͵väs\
Hungarian
: dog

kwatuma
\kwäˈtümə\
African name
: eel

kwazoku
\kwäzō͵kü\
Japanese
: class of nobility

kylie
\kīlē\
Australian name
: boomerang

kylikes
\kilə͵kēz\
Greek
: drinking cups

kyrielle
\kirēˌel\
French
: verses

Labouchere
\labüˈsher\
French
: betting system

lachsschinken
\läks(h)͵shiŋkən\
German
: loin of pork

langaha
\läŋˈgähä\
Unknown
: snake

Laodicean
\lā-ˌä-də-ˌsē-ən\
Greek geographic name
: lukewarm or indifferent

lasya
\läsyə\
Sanskrit
: feminine dance

lazaretto
\lazəˈretō\
Italian
: hospital

lazzarone
\lazəˈrōnē\
Italian
: homeless idler

lechoza
\lāˈchōzə\
Spanish
: papaya

lechwe
\lēchwē\
Bantu
: antelope

lekach
\lekəḵ\
Hebrew
: honey cake

lokelani
\lōkāˈlänē\
Hawaiian
: pink rose

lorimer
\lȯrəmə(r)\
English
: metal mounting maker

loutrophoros
\lüˈträfə͵räs\
Greek
: vase

lytta
\litə\
Greek
: cartilaginous rod

machancha
\məˈchänchə\
Spanish
: snake

mahaleb
\mä(h)ə͵leb\
Arabic
: cherry

mahseer
\mä͵si(ə)r\
Hindi
: food fish

maidan
\mīˈdän\
Hindi
: parade ground

maigre
\māgrə\
French
: of food with no flesh

majlis
\majˈlis\
Persian
: parliament

makroskelic
\makrəˌskelik\
Greek
: having long legs

malanders
\maləndə(r)z\
English
: chronic eczema

malinche
\məˈlinchē\
Spanish
: Mexican dancer

Malinois
\malənˌwä\
French
: dog

Malmaison
\malməˌzōⁿ\
French geographic name
: greenhouse carnation

mameliere
\maməlˈye(ə)r\
French
: steel plate

mameluco
\maməˈlükō\
Portuguese
: mestizo

manak
\maˌnak\
Eskimo
: wooden implement

mandruka
\manˈdrükə\
Libyan geographic name
: sponge

manege
\maˈnezh\
French
: riding academy

Manetti
\məˈnetē\
Italian name
: rose

maniu
\mänēˈü\
Spanish
: tree

manul
\mänəl\
Mongolian
: wildcat

maquillage
\makēˌ(y)äzh\
French
: cosmetics

marchen
\me(ə)rk̲ən\
German
: folktale

marinheiro
\märəˈnyārō\
Portuguese
: tree

maskilic
\mäˌskēlik\
Hebrew
: of one versed in Yiddish

massicot
\masəˌkät\
French
: lead monoxide

matamata
\madəməˈtä\
Portuguese
: turtle

matzoon
\mätˌsün\
Armenian
: fermented milk

mazdoor
\mazˈdu̇(ə)r\
Hindi
: laborer

mazurka
\məˈzərˌkə\
Russian
: dance

mbira
\emˈbirə\
Shona
: music

mecate
\məˈkädē\
Spanish
: rope

Mechlin
\meklən\
Belgian geographic name
: lace

melada
\məˈlädə\
Spanish
: sugar

melena
\məˈlēnə\
Greek
: passage of dark stool

meranti
\mə'rantē\
Malay
: tree

meshuggaas
\məshu̇'gäs\
Yiddish
: nonsense

metis
\mā'tē(s)\
French
: crossbred animal

mirgil
\mi(ə)rgəl\
Hindi
: fish

mishpachah
\məsh'päk̲ə\
Hebrew
: family unit

mizpah
\mizpə\
Biblical name
: worn to signify
remembrance

modinha
\mō'dēnyə\
Portuguese
: art song

moellon
\mwe¦lōⁿ\
French
: fatty substance

mokihana
\mōkē'hänə\
Hawaiian
: tree

mokum
\mōkəm\
Japanese
: alloy

mondaine
\mōn'dān\
French
: woman of world

monteith
\män¦tēth\
Scottish name
: punch bowl

montre
\mōⁿtrə\
French
: organ stop

morwong
\mȯr͵wäŋ\
Australian name
: food fish

moucharaby
\mü'sharəbē\
French & Arabic
: oriel window

mouflon
\müflən\
French
: sheep

movingui
\mō'viŋgē\
African name
: tree

mozzetta
\mōt'setə\
Italian
: cape

msasa
\əm'säsə\
African name
: tree

muffuletta
\məfə'letə\
Italian
: sandwich

mukluk
\mə͵klək\
Eskimo
: boot

muladi
\mülə'th̲ē\
Spanish
: Spanish Muslim

munjistin
\mən'jistən\
Latin
: compound

muscovado
\məskə'vädō\
Spanish
: sugar

mussurana
\mu̇sə'ränə\
Portuguese
: snake

mutawalli
\mu̇təwə¦lē\
Arabic
: trustee

muyusa
\mü'yüsə\
Spanish
: fruit

mysost
\mī͵säst\
Norwegian
: cheese

naartje
\närchə\
Afrikaans
: fruit

nagaika
\nə'gīkə\
Russian
: whip

nagelfluh
\nägəl͵flü\
German
: massive sedimentary rock

nakhoda
\näkə͵dä\
Persian
: master of Indian vessel

namaqua
\nəˈmäkwə\
African geographic name
: dove

nanduti
\nyändə¦tē\
Spanish
: lace

nangca
\näŋˈkä\
Tagalog
: jackfruit tree

narghile
\närgəlē\
Persian
: pipe

nataka
\nätəkə\
Sanskrit
: dance

nauplius
\nȯplēəs\
Greek
: larva

naveta
\nəˈvätə\
Catalan
: barrow

nebenkern
\nābən͵kərn\
German
: organized body

nektonic
\nek¦tänik\
German
: of swimming animals

ngaio
\nīō\
Maori
: tree

nigun
\nēˈgün\
Hebrew
: melody

nixtamal
\nēshtəˈmäl\
Nahuatl
: corn kernels

nizam
\nəˈzäm\
Hindi
: soldier

njave
\nyävə\
African name
: tree

nockerl
\näkər(ə)l\
German
: dumpling

nodiak
\nōdē͵ak\
Guinean name
: echidna

noekkelost
\nākə͵lōst\
Norwegian
: dark cheese

notaulix
\nōˈtȯliks\
Latin
: furrow

nuraghe
\nüˈrägā\
Italian
: stone structure

nymss
\nim(p)s\
Egyptian name
: mongoose

obbligato
\äbləˈgätō\
Italian
: not to be omitted

ochidore
\äkə͵dō(ə)r\
Unknown
: crab

ocote
\əˈkōtā\
Nahuatl
: pine

oeillade
\ə(r)ˈyäd\
French
: glance

Oerlikon
\ərlə͵kän\
Swiss geographic name
: aircraft

okoume
\ōkəˈmä\
French
: wood

oorali
\üˈrälē\
Carib
: poison

opelu
\ōpə͵lü\
Hawaiian
: mackerel

orcein
\ȯ(r)sēən\
French
: dye

orfgild
\ȯrf͟gild\
English
: fine

oribi
\ȯrəbē\
Afrikaans
: antelope

orichalc
\ȯrə͟kalk\
Greek
: metallic substance

Orloff
\ȯrläf\
Russian name
: horse breed

orphrey
\ȯrfrē\
English
: gold embroidery

ouricury
\u̇rəkə¦rē\
Portuguese
: palm

ovale
\ō'vālē\
Latin
: of parasites

oxymel
\äksə͟mel\
Greek
: honey mixture

oyapock
\ȯiə͟päk\
Brazilian geographic name
: opossum

ozena
\ō'zēnə\
Greek
: chronic disease

pactiones
\päktē'ō͟nās\
Latin
: informal agreement

pagne
\pȧnʸ\
French
: costume

pairle
\pa(a)r(ə)l\
French
: heraldic ordinary

paixtle
\pīchtlē\
Spanish
: fiesta dance

palaestra
\pə'lestrə\
Greek
: wrestling

palafitti
\paləfētē\
Italian
: lake dwellings

paldao
\päl'däō\
Tagalog
: tree

pampootie
\pam'püdē\
Alteration
: cowhide

panatela
\panə'telə\
Spanish
: cigar

panisc
\panisk\
Greek
: forest godling

papaloi
\päpəl'wä\
Haitian Creole
: voodoo priest

parandja
\pə'ranjə\
Uzbek
: veil

pareu
\pärā͟ü\
Tahitian
: loincloth

pareve
\pärə¦vä\
Yiddish
: made without milk

paristhmion
\pa'rismēən\
Greek
: tonsil

parmentier
\pȧrmäⁿtyā\
French
: made with potatoes

pashm
\pəshəm\
Persian
: fleece

pastitsio
\pä'stētsēō\
Greek
: baked dish

patesi
\pə'tāzē\
Sumerian
: ruler of city-state

pattu
\pətü\
Hindi
: fabric

paxiuba
\päshē'übə\
Tupi
: palm

paxwax
\pak͵swaks\
English
: ligament

pebrine
\pā¦brēn\
French
: silkworm disease

pelamyd
\peləməd\
Greek
: tuna

pelike
\peləkē\
Greek
: jug

pelog
\pe-ləg\
Javanese
: tuning

pensee
\pänⁿsā\
French
: thought in literary form

penuche
\pə'nüchē\
Spanish
: fudge

periaktos
\perē'aktəs\
Greek
: apparatus

peripeteia
\perəpə'tē(y)ə\
Greek
: unexpected reversal

perleche
\per¦lesh\
French
: inflammatory condition

perron
\perən\
French
: platform

pervenche
\pər͵vänch\
French
: purplish blue

pessulus
\peshyələs\
Greek
: bar

petuntse
\pə'tüntsə, bī'dəndzə\
Chinese
: granite

phagedena
\fajə'dēnə\
Greek
: ulceration

phulkari
\pül͵kärē\
Hindi
: flower pattern

phyllade
\fi͵lād\
Greek
: leaf

pichiciago
\pichēsē'¦ägō\
Allentiac
: armadillo

pichurim
\pishərəm\
Portuguese
: bean

pickadil
\pikə͵dil\
French
: cutwork

piepoudre
\pī͵paùdə(r)\
English
: traveler

pilon
\pē'lōn\
Spanish
: bonus

pinabete
\pēnə'bādē\
Spanish
: fir

piscina
\pə's(h)ēnə\
Latin
: reservoir

pissaladiere
\pēsälä'dyer\
French
: pastry

piyyutim
\pē͵yü'tēm\
Hebrew
: religious poems

plakat
\plə'kat, 'pla͵kat\
Siamese
: fish

platteland
\plädə͵länt\
Afrikaans
: isolated rural section

pocosin
\pəˈkōsᵊn, ˈpōkəsən\
Delaware
: swamp

poecilocyttarous
\pēsəlōˌsidərəs\
Greek
: of social wasps

polacre
\pōˈläkə(r)\
French
: ship

poleyn
\pōˌlān\
French
: armor

polynee
\pälənā\
Swedish
: tart

pommettee
\pämətē\
French
: adorned with small balls

pororoca
\pùrəˈrōkə\
Portuguese
: tidal bore

poulaine
\püˌlān\
French
: pointed toe

praecipuum
\prēˈsipyəwəm\
Latin
: bonus

praemunire
\prēmyəˈnīrē\
Latin
: legal writ

praetexta
\prēˈtekstə\
Latin
: white robe

precieux
\prāsyə̄\
French
: affected

presa
\prā-sə\
Italian
: musical symbol

presidio
\prəˈsidēˌō\
Spanish
: garrisoned place

pretil
\prāˈtēl\
Spanish
: adobe wall

prevenance
\prävəˈnäⁿs\
French
: attentiveness

printanier
\praⁿtȧnyā\
French
: made with vegetables

prisiadka
\prisˈyädkə\
Russian
: male dance

prokeimenon
\prōˈkīməˌnän\
Greek
: short anthem

provand
\prävənd\
English
: supply of food

provolette
\prōvəˌlet\
Italian
: cheese

proxenet
\präksəˌnet\
Latin
: marriage broker

psykter
\siktə(r)\
Greek
: jar

ptisan
\tə̇ˈzan, ˈtizᵊn\
English
: tea

puszta
\pùˌsto\
Hungarian
: steppe

putelee
\pətəlē\
Hindi
: boat

pwe
\pwā\
Burmese
: festival

pykrete
\pīˌkrēt\
English name
: frozen mixture

qasida
\kəˈsēdə\
Arabic
: poem

qiyas
\kēˈyäs\
Arabic
: analogy

quaalude
\kwā͵lüd\
Trademark
: tablet

quaesitum
\kwē'sīdəm\
Latin
: end, objective

quaestio
\kwīstē͵ō\
Latin
: criminal acquisition

quahog
\kwȯ͵hȯg\
Narraganset
: clam

quale
\kwālē\
Latin
: object

quete
\ket\
French
: collection of money

quipu
\kēpü\
Quechua
: cord

raadzaal
\räd͵zäl\
Dutch
: assembly hall

rabat
\rabē, rə'bat\
French
: breast piece

rafraichissoir
\rə͵freshə'swär\
French
: small table

rahdar
\räd͵är\
Hindi
: tollkeeper

raion
\rī'ōn\
Russian
: district

rakija
\räkē(y)ə\
Serbo-Croatian
: brandy

ramekin
\ram-kən\
French
: cheese preparation

rapakivi
\räpə'kēvē\
Finnish
: granite

raphe
\rā-fē\
Greek
: seamlike union

rastik
\rastək\
Turkish
: dye

razzia
\razēə\
French
: raid

razzmatazz
\raz-mə-¦taz\
Alteration
: state of confusion

rebec
\rē-͵bek\
French
: instrument

regur
\regər\
Hindi
: black loam

Reiki
\rā͵kē\
Japanese
: system of touching

remanie
\rə͵män'yā\
French
: residual

remate
\rā'mätā\
Spanish
: bullfighting move

Rephaim
\refēə̇m\
Hebrew
: ancient giants

requin
\rə'kan\
French
: shark

resak
\rə̇'sak\
Malaysian name
: heavy wood

rezai
\rə̇'zäē\
Hindi
: mattress

rhupunt
\rē͵pint\
Welsh
: verse

ricercar
\rē͵cher'kär\
Italian
: instrumental composition

riegel
\rēgəl\
German
: rock formation

rillett
\rə̇ˈlet\
French
: potted pork

risotto
\rə̇ˈs|ȯtō\
Italian
: cooked rice

romaika
\rōˈmäə̇kə\
Greek
: folk dance

rooigras
\rüē͕gras\
Afrikaans
: grass

rounceval
\rauṅ(t)səvəl\
Spanish geographic name
: pea

rutuburi
\rütəˈbu̇r\
Spanish
: dance

ryotwar
\rīə̇¦twär\
Hindi
: rent-collecting system

saeculum
\sekyələm\
Latin
: age

saengerbund
\zeŋə(r)͕bu̇nt\
German
: choral society

sagaie
\sə̇ˈgī\
French
: javelin point

sagene
\sä͕zhen\
Russian
: unit of length

saibling
\zīpliŋ\
Gerrman
: trout

sainfoin
\sān͕fȯin\
French
: herb

sakaki
\sə̇ˈkäkē\
Japanese
: herb

sakieh
\sakē͕e\
Arabic
: waterwheel

Salicet
\saləˈset\
German
: organ stop

Salmanazar
\salməˈnazə(r)\
Assyrian name
: wine bottle

salomonica
\saləˈmänə̇kə\
Spanish
: architectural column

saltarello
\saltəˈrelō\
Italian
: dance

saltierra
\saltēˈerə\
Spanish
: salt left by evaporation

samarkand
\sa-mər-͕kand\
Uzbek geographic name
: rug

samel
\saməl\
Old English
: soft and crumbling

samiel
\səmˈyel\
Turkish
: dry wind

samisen
\samə͕sen\
Japanese
: instrument

samshu
\samˈshü\
Chinese
: liquor

sancho
\saŋkō\
Ewe (African origin)
: guitar

sangh
\saŋ, ˈsəŋ\
Hindi
: association

sangrado
\säŋˈgrädō\
French literary name
: quack

sanies
\sānē͕ēz\
Latin
: wound discharge

sapeque
\sə'pek\
French
: coin

sapsago
\sap'sā͵gō\
German
: cheese

sarin
\zä'rēn\
German
: ester

sarod
\sə'rōd\
Hindi
: stringed instrument

Sarouk
\sə'rük\
Persian geographic name
: carpet

sasanqua
\sə'säŋkwə\
Japanese
: shrub

sashoon
\sa¦shün\
French
: pad

sawah
\säwə\
Malay
: wet rice field

sbrinz
\sprints\
Swiss geographic name
: cheese

schaapsteker
\skäp͵stikə(r)\
Afrikaans
: snake

schapska
\shäpskə\
Polish
: helmet

scheltopusik
\sheltō¦p(y)üzik\
Russian
: lizard

schiffli
\shiflē\
German
: power machine

schlager
\shlägə(r)\
German
: sword

schlepp
\shlep\
Yiddish
: steal

schouw
\skaủ\
Dutch
: pleasure boat

scungilli
\skün'jēlē\
Italian
: alimentary paste

scytale
\sitᵊlē\
Latin
: message

sedile
\sə'dīlē\
Latin
: church seat

sekos
\sē͵käs\
Greek
: sacred enclosure

Septieme
\se¦tyem\
French
: mutation stop

serac
\sə'rak\
French
: jagged pinnacle

Sercial
\sersē¦al\
French
: dry wine

serif
\serə̇f\
Dutch
: short line

seringueiro
\serə̇n'gārü\
Portuguese
: rubber gatherer

seroon
\sə̇'rün, sə̇'rōn\
Spanish
: package

seudah
\südə\
Hebrew
: meal

seviche
\sə'vēchā\
Spanish
: raw fish dish

shadoof
\shə'dủf\
Arabic
: sweep

shallu
\sha͵lü\
Marathi
: sorghum

shamianah
\shämē'änə\
Hindi
: cloth canopy

sheheheyanu
\she(he)k̲ə'yänü\
Hebrew
: blessing

sheitel
\shāt°l\
Yiddish
: wig

shenzi
\shenzē\
Swahili
: tribesman

shikken
\shi¦ken\
Japanese
: executive officer

shikra
\shikrə\
Hindi
: hawk

shimose
\shə'mōsə\
Japanese
: explosive

shtadlan
\shtädlän\
Yiddish
: Jewish appointee

siafu
\sēäfü\
Swahili
: ant

sierozem
\sē¦erə¦zem\
Russian
: soil

sifac
\sē͵fak\
Malagasy
: lemur

sigatoka
\sigə'tōkə\
Fijian geographic name
: leaf spot disease

sikinnis
\sə'kinəs\
Greek
: dance

simoom
\sə'müm, sī'müm\
Arabic
: wind

sinhasan
\sin'häs°n\
Sanskrit
: throne

sipapu
\sē͵päpü\
Hopi
: hole in floor

sirkeer
\sər͵ki(ə)r\
Hindi
: cuckoo

sirtaki
\sir'täkē\
Greek
: circle dance

sissonne
\sə'sän\
French
: ballet step

sittringee
\sə'trinjē\
Persian
: carpet

sixain
\sə'zän, sik¦sän\
French
: stanza of six lines

sixte
\sikst\
French
: fencing parry

sizar
\sī-zər\
Alteration
: student

skaamoog
\skä͵mōg\
Afrikaans
: cat shark

slepez
\slə'pets\
Russian
: mole rat

slivovitz
\slivə͵vits\
Serbo-Croatian
: plum brandy

sloyd
\slȯid\
Swedish
: manual tracking

societaire
\sō͵syä'ta(a)(ə)r\
French
: actor

solonchak
\sälən¦chak\
Russian
: soil

soukous
\sü͵küs\
French
: dance music

sphaeraphis
\sfirəfəs\
Greek
: aggregation

spreeuw
\spriü\
Afrikaans
: starling

squeteague
\skwə'tēg\
Narraganset
: trout

squetee
\skwə'tē\
Narraganset
: weak fish

stacte
\staktē\
Greek
: sweet spice

stalace
\staləs\
Greek
: central mass of cells

stephane
\stefənē\
Greek
: headdress

sternalis
\stər'nāləs\
Latin
: muscle

Stradivarius
\stradə'va(a)rēəs\
Italian
: stringed instrument

suasoria
\swə'sōrēə\
Latin
: orations

superius
\sə'pirēəs\
Latin
: treble voice

surma
\sùrmə\
Persian
: antimony sulfide

surnape
\sər͵nap\
English
: cloth

svarga
\sʃärgə\
Sanskrit
: heaven

svelte
\svelt\
Italian
: slim

swanimote
\swänə͵mōt\
English
: court

swiple
\swipəl\
English
: part of flail

sycee
\sī'sē\
Chinese
: silver money

syllabub
\silə͵bəb\
Unknown
: drink

synaloepha
\sinə'lēfə\
Greek
: blending

synaxarion
\sēnäksäryȯ(n)͵sinaksarēən\
Greek
: narrative

synizesis
\sinə'zēsəs\
Greek
: contraction

Szczecin
\shche-͵chēn\
Polish
: city

tabasheer
\tabə'shi(ə)r\
Hindi
: concretion

Tabulatur
\täbələ'tù(ə)r\
German
: system of rules

taharah
\tä'härä\
Hebrew
: religious ceremony

takhaar
\tak͵här, 'ta͵kär\
Afrikaans
: backveld Boer

talaje
\tə'lähä\
Spanish
: tick

Talavera
\talə'verə\
Spanish geographic name
: earthenware

talayot
\tə'lä͵yōt\
Catalan
: stone tower

tallegalane
\taləgə͵lān\
Australian name
: fish

tamis
\tamē, taməs\
French
: strainer

tangile
\täŋəlē\
Tagalog
: mahogany

tantieme
\täⁿtyem\
French
: bonus

tarente
\tə˙ränt\
French
: gecko

Tarpeian
\tär¦pē(y)ən\
Roman geographic name
: of cliffs

Tartuffe
\tär¦túf\
French
: hypocrite

tatajuba
\tätə˙zhübə\
Portuguese
: wood

taupou
\taú˙pō\
Samoan
: hostess

teiglach
\tāglə̱k\
Yiddish
: small pieces of dough

telpher
\telfə(r)\
Greek
: light car

tenaillon
\tənäyōⁿ\
French
: work

terai
\tə˙rī\
Indian geographic name
: sun hat

terek
\terək\
Russian
: sandpiper

terfez
\tə(r)˙fez\
French
: fruit

Thakur
\tä͵kù(ə)r\
Hindi
: member of warrior caste

thyiad
\thī͵(y)ad\
Greek
: worship group

tikug
\tə˙küg\
Philippine name
: sedge

tiple
\tēplä\
Spanish
: guitar

tjanting
\chäntiŋ\
Javanese
: instrument

tomalley
\tə˙mal-ē, ˈtäm͵al-ē\
Cariban
: lobster liver

torchere
\tȯr¦she(ə)r\
French
: floor lamp

toxcatl
\tō͵skätᵊl\
Nahuatl
: new year festival

trehala
\trə˙hälə\
Turkish
: edible substance

tremissis
\trə˙misəs\
Latin
: small coin

tulafale
\tülə˙fälā\
Samoan
: chief

tulisan
\tülə˙sän\
Tagalog
: bandit

turnhalle
\tùrn͵hälə\
German
: gymnastics building

twibil
\twī͵bil, -bəl\
English
: battle-ax

tylotoxea
\tīlə˙täksēə\
Latin
: sponge

137

tzimmes
\tsiməs\
Yiddish
: combination of vegetables

uayeb
\wī͵eb\
Mayan
: time period

ullucu
\ü'yükü\
Spanish
: plant

umfaan
\əm͵fän\
Afrikaans
: general worker

umiak
\ümē͵ak\
Eskimo
: boat

umquhile
\əm͵(h)wīl\
English
: old

urachus
\yùrəkəs\
Greek
: fibrous tissue

urazine
\yùrə͵zēn\
ISV
: compound

urdee
\ərdē, ər¦dā\
Unknown
: each arm expanding

urheen
\ər'hē(ə)n\
Chinese
: fiddle

urunday
\ùrən¦dī\
Guarani
: tree

urutu
\ùrə¦tü\
Portuguese
: viper

Uskok
\ù͵skäk\
Slavic
: Dalmatian

vadose
\vā͵dōs\
Latin
: of water solutions

vaivode
\vī͵vōd\
Hungarian
: military commander

vakass
\vä͵käs\
Armenian
: priest garmnet

vakeel
\və'kē(ə)l\
Hindi
: representative

varec
\va͵rek\
French
: seaweed

verek
\fe͵rek\
Berber
: acacia

viejitos
\vyā'hē͵tōs\
Spanish
: dance

vivax
\vī͵vaks\
Latin
: parasite

vizsla
\vizhlə\
Hungarian geographic name
: dog breed

Volapuk
\vōlə¦pūek\
German
: international language

vraic
\vrāk\
French
: seaweed

vrouw
\vr|au'\
Dutch
: mistress

wabur
\wäbə(r)\
Arabic
: hyrax

waiata
\wīətə\
Maori
: song

wamara
\wämərə\
Arawak
: tree

waqf
\wəkf\
Arabic
: endowment

warabi
\wòrəbē\
Japanese
: brake

watap
\waˈtäp\
French
: thread

Wehrmacht
\verˌmä|kt\
German
: armed forces

werowance
\werəˌwan(t)s\
Delaware
: chief

whapuku
\h(w)äˌpükə\
Maori
: fish

whipparee
\hwipəˈrē\
Alteration
: stingray

whydah
\hwidə\
Alteration
: weaverbird

winze
\winz\
Alteration
: passageway

wistit
\wistət\
French
: marmoset

witteboom
\vitəˌbüm\
Afrikaans
: silver tree

wommera
\wämərə\
Australian name
: throwing stick

wysiwyg
\wizēˌwig\
Acronym
: word-processing display

wyvern
\wīvə(r)n\
English
: animal

Xantippe
\zanˈtipē\
Greek name
: shrew

xarque
\shärkē\
Portuguese
: jerked meat

xiphopagus
\zəˈfäpəgəs\
Latin
: conjoined twin

yarmulke
\yärməlkə\
Yiddish
: skull cap

yataghan
\yatəˌgan\
Turkish
: knife

yohimbihi
\yəˈhimbəhē\
Bantu
: tree

zamindar
\zə¦mēn¦där\
Hindi
: revenue collector

zampogna
\(t)sämˈpōnyə\
Italian
: bagpipe

zemmi
\zemē\
Russian
: mole rat

zeppole
\zepōlē\
Italian
: doughnut

ziamet
\zēˈäˌmet\
Turkish
: fief

zibeline
\zibəˌlēn\
French
: fabric

Zoilus
\zōələs\
Greek name
: bitter critic

zoril
\zȯrəl\
French
: weasel

zortzico
\zȯ(r)ˈsēkō\
Basque
: dance

zufolo
\tsüfəˌlō\
Italian
: little flut

139

Chapter 6: Stallion

abashev
\əbäshəf\
Russian
: belonging to the Bronze Age culture

abderite
\abdərīt\
Greek>Latin
: simpleton, scoffer

abeigh
\əbēḵ\
Norse>Scottish
: cautiously aloof

abele
\əbēl, əbāl, ābəl\
Dutch
: Eurasian tree

abelian
\ə¦bēlyən\
Norwegian
: concept where order does not matter in mathematics

abgesang
\äpgəzäng\
German
: concluding section of the medieval bar

abies
\ābē͵ēz\
Latin
: balsam fir

abietene
\abēətēn\
ISV
: salt or ester acid; resinate

abilla
\ə'bē(y)ə\
Peruvian
: oily seed of plant

abiuret
\ā¦bīyə͵ret\
ISV
: not treated with alkaline solution of proteins

ablaut
\äplau̇t\
German
: vowel variation of Indo-European root (sing, sang)

abraum
\äprau̇m\
German
: red iron ore used to darken tree woods

abrazo
\əbräsō, äbräsō\
Latin>Spanish
: salutation or embrace

abusua
\abəsüə\
Ashanti
: exogamous clan

abutilon
\əbyütəlän, abyətīlən\
Arabic>Latin
: tropical plant with flowers

acanthor
\ə'kan͵thȯ(ə)r\
Latin
: mature embryo

acceptilation
\ak͵septə'lāshən\
Latin
: verbal acknowledgmnent of payment by mortgagor

accroides
\ə'krȯidēz\
Latin
: ink resin

aceraceous
\asə¦rāshəs\
Latin
: of small clustered flowers

acerola
\a-sə-'rō-lə\
Latin
: large shrub

Achaemenidian
\akəmə|nidēən\
Greek
: relating to members of the Persian ruling society

achariaceous
\ə-¦ka-rē-¦ā-shəs\
Latin
: resembling monoecious flowers

achatinella
\akətənelə\
Latin
: any snail peculiar to Hawaii

achimenes
\ə-'ki-mə-nēz\
Latin
: commonly cultivated herbs

140

achroacyte
\ākrōəsīt\
Greek
: colorless cell; lymphocyte

achyranthes
\a-kə-ˈran-thēz\
Greek>Latin
: herbs with white flowers

acinarious
\a-sə-¦na-rē-əs\
French
: covered with grape-like
seeds

acipenserine
\a-sə-¦pen(t)-sə-ˌrīn\
Latin
: relating to sturgeons

acmonital
\ak-ˈmä-nə-ˌtal\
Italian
: stainless steel alloy

aconitase
\ə-ˈkä-nə-ˌtās\
ISV
: enzyme in animal and plant
tissues converting acids

acousmatic
\a-ˌküz-ˈma-tik\
Greek
: receiving exoteric teachings
of Pythagoras

acritarch
\a-kri-ˌtärk\
Greek
: planktonic organism

acroamata
\a-krō-ˈa-mədə, a-krō-ˈä-
mədə\
Greek
: oral teachings or doctrines

acrolein
\ə-ˈkrō-lē-ən\
Latin
: toxic poisonous liquid

actinophrys
\ak-tə-ˈnä-frəs, ak-ˈti-nə-frəs\
Latin
: protozoans in stagnant water

acyclovir
\ā-ˈsī-klō-ˌvir\
Greek
: cyclic nucleoside

acyloin
\əsiləwən, əsiləwēn
a-sə-ˌlȯin, ˌa-sə-ˈlō-ən\
ISV
: ketone of a general formula

adiaphonon
\a-dē-ˈa-fə-ˌnän\
Greek
: keyboard instrument

adinidan
\ə-ˈdi-nə-dən\
Latin
: flagellate protozoan

adjudicataire
\ə-¦jü-di-kə-¦ter\
French
: purchaser at sale

aedicular
\ē-ˈdi-kyə-lər\
Latin
: relating to shrines or niches

aegeriid
\ē-ˈjir-ē-əd\
Latin
: scaly moth

aeolight
\ē-ə-ˌlīt\
Greek+English
: gas-discharge glow lamp

aequorin
\ē-ˈkwȯrən\
Latin
: bioluminescent protein

aerenchyma
\er-ˈeŋ-kə-mə\
Latin
: spongy tissue of plants

aeroscepsis
\er-ō-ˈskep-səs\
Latin
: sensibility to air in animals

aeschynanthus
\e-skə-ˈnan(t)-thəs\
Greek
: woody flowery plant

aethalioid
\ē-ˈthā-lē-ˌȯid\
Greek
: resembling a fruity body

aethrioscope
\ēthrē-ə-ˌskōp, ethrē-ə-ˌskōp\
Greek + English
: thermometer used in
differing sky conditions

affeiring
\ə-ˈfir-iŋ\
Scottish
: pertaining, relating

afikomen
\ä-fē-ˈkō-mən\
Hebrew
: bread eaten after ceremony

aflatoxin
\a-flə-¦täk-sən\
Latin
: poisonous fungus substance

afwillite
\af-wə-ˌlīt\
American name
: hydrous mineral

Agapemone
\a-gə-ˈpe-mə-nē\
English name
: free-loving institution

agaricin
\ə-ˈger-ə-sən\
Greek
: impure form of acid

agilmente
\a-jəl-ˈmen-tē\
Italian
: with quickness and
dexterity- used in music

aglipayan
\a-glə-ˈpī-ən\
Filipino
: member of dependent
church in Philippines

agoniada
\ə-ˌgō-nē-ˈä-də\
Portuguese
: bark of tropical trees

agrégés
\ä-grā-ˈzhā, ä -gre-ˈzhā\
French
: academic ranks (pl.)
(singular spelled agrégé)

agrypniai
\ə-ˈgrip-nē-ˌī,\
Latin>Greek
: vigils before Easter

ahuula
\ä-hə-ˈü-lə, ˌä-ˌhü-ˈü-lə\
Hawaiian
: feather cloak

aizoaceous
\ā-ˌī-zə-ˌwā-shəs\
Latin
: of capsular fruit

ajourise
\ä-ˌzhur̀-ə-ˌzā\
French
: open-worked

akaroa
\ä-kə-ˈrō-ə\
Maori
: ribbon tree

akermanite
\ō-kər-mə-ˌnīt\
Swedish
: mineral consisting of
calcium

Akhissar
\äk-hi-ˌsär\
Turkish geographical name
: heavy modern carpet

akrochordite
\a-krō-ˈkòr-ˌdīt\
Greek
: mineral with manganese

albigensian
\albəjen(t)shən, albəjen(t)sē-
ən\
Latin
: members of a Christian sect

alborada
\al-bə-ˈrä-də\
Spanish
: instrumental serenade

alcaligenes
\al-kə-ˈli-jə-ˌnēz\
Latin
: organisms with
carbohydrates

alcheringa
\al-chə-ˈriŋ-gə\
Australian
: time of creation, dreamtime

alchornea
\al-ˈkòr-nē-ə\
Latin
: white showy plant

alcyonacean
\al-sē-ə-ˈnā-shən\
Latin
: relating to corals

aldimine
\al-də-ˌmēn\
ISV
: control of Schiff base

alectryomancy
\ə-ˈlek-trē-ō-ˌman(t)-sē\
Latin
: divination through corn
grain

Alembert
\aləm|be(ə)r\
French
: system of betting in
gambling

alembroth
\ə-ˈlem-ˌbròth\
Arabic
: ammonium mercury

alexipharmic
\ə-ˌlek-si-ˈfär-mik\
Greek
: antidote against infection

aleyrodid
\ə-ˈler-ə-dəd\
Latin
: whitefly

algarrobin
\al-gə-ˈrō-bən\
Spanish
: brown dyestuff

algodoncillo
\al-gə-ˌdän-ˈsē-ō\
Spanish
: erect forest tree

aliesterase
alē¦estə͜ˌrās
ISV
: enzyme that promotes
chemical reaction

Aligote
\älēgō'tā\
French
: white grape wine

aligreek
\alə̇ˌgrēk\
Italian
: ornamental network

alinota
\ālə'nōtə\
Latin
:dorsal skeleton

alipata
\aləpə¦tä\
Spanish
: poison tree

alkanet
\al-kə-ˌnet\
English
: red European dyestuff

alkannin
\al'kanə̇n\
ISV
: coloring matter

alkaptonuric
\al-ˌkap-tə-'n(y)ùr-ik\
Latin
: recessive metabolic
anomaly

alkavervir
\alkə'vərˌvi(ə)r\
ISV
: agent reducing hypertension

allanitic
\alə¦nitik\
Latin
: concerning black minerals

alkermes
\alkərmēz,
alkərmə̇s; alkə̇rmes\
Arabic>French
: Italian liqueur with leaves

allassotonic
\ə¦lasə¦tänik\
Greek>ISV
: temporarily induced
by   stimulus

allicin
\a-lə-sən\
ISV
: liquid compound

alliin
\alēə̇n\
ISV
: amino acid

allivalite
\alə̇vəˌlīt\
Scottish
: mineral found in the
foothills

allochroous
\ə'läkrəwəs\
Latin
: changing color

alloiobiogenesis
\ə¦lȯiōbī-ō-¦je-nə-səs\
Latin
: alternation of generations

allothimorphic
\ə'läthəˌmȯrfik\
ISV
: pertaining to rocks which
possess crystals

alluaudite
\alyə'wōˌdīt\
German
: rare mineral

allylthiourea
\¦alə̇lthīōyə¦rēə\
ISV>Latin
: white crystalline ammonia

almique
\almə¦kē\
Spanish
: red-wooded tree

alocasia
\alə'kāzh(ē)ə\
Latin
: plant with showy leaves

alpargata
\alpə(r)'gätə\
Spanish
: strapless sandal

alphametic
\alfə¦metik\
Latin
: mathematical puzzle

alphitomorphous
\al¦fitə¦mȯfəs\
French
: resembling barley meal

alphonsine
\al¦fän(t)sə̇n, alf-änzə̇n\
Latin
: of astronomical tables

alraun
\alraủn\
German
: purple-flowered herb

alsinaceous
\alsə¦nāshəs\
Latin
: relating to chickweed plants

alsophila
\al'säfələ\
Greek + Latin
: any fern near mountains

alstonine
\ȯlztə͵nēn\
German>ISV
: alkaloid found in bark

altingiaceous
\al͵tinjēˈāshəs\
Latin
: of clustered flowers

alutaceous
\alyə¦tāshəs\
Latin
: qualities of tawny leather

amalekite
\a-mə-͵le-͵kīt, ə-ˈma-ləkīt\
Hebrew
: member of Canaan during
the time of Exodus

amanitin
\a-mə-ˈnī-tᵊn\
ISV
: highly poisonous peptide

amaryllideous
\aməri¦lidēəs\
Latin
: of a tropical plant

ambatoarinite
\ambətōˈarə͵nīt\
French geographical name
: mineral containing cerium

amitriptyline
\a-mə-ˈtrip-tə-͵lēn\
ISV
: antidepressant drug

ammiaceous
\amēˌ¦āshəs\
Latin
: relating to plants

amoraim
\ämōˈrä͵im\
Hebrew
: group of rabbis in law

amortisseur
\ə¦mȯrtə¦sər\
French
: short-circuited squirrel cage

ampalaya
\ampələ¦yä\
Filipino
: balsam apple

ampelitic
\ampə͵litik\
Greek>Latin
: of carbonaceous schist

ampherotokous
\amfə¦rätəkəs\
Greek
: fertilization of female and
male offsprings

amphibali
\amˈfibəlī, amˈfibəlē\
Greek
: church vestments

amphicytulae
\amfəˈsichəlē\
Latin
: pairs of circular depressions

amphithyra
\amˈfithə͵rə\
Greek
: veils before curtains

amplexicaul
\amˈpleksə͵kȯl\
Latin
: leaf with stipules

ampongue
\amˌpȯŋ\
Madagascar name
: woolly lemur

anaclases
\əˈnakləsēz\
Latin
: exchanges in short syllables

anacruses
\a-nə-ˈkrü-͵sēz\
Greek
: poetry syllables

anagallis
\anəˈgaləs\
Latin
: herb with circular flowers

analabos
\äˈnälə͵bȯs\
Greek
: church vestment

alloxuric
\a͵läk¦sürik, a͵läks¦yu̇ rik\
ISV
: relating to crystalline
compounds

auriscope
\ȯrə͵skōp\
Latin
: otoscope; something to look
at the ear with

ascarides
\a-ˈska-rə-͵dēz\
Greek>Latin
: nematode worms (plural)

allulose
\ˈalyə͵lōs\
ISV
: sugar found in

Anaxagorean
\a͵nak͵sagə¦rēən\
Greek
: homogeneous particle world

anchieutectic
\aŋkēyü¦tektik\
Greek
: having proportionate
mineral

ancilia
\äŋˈkilēə, anˈsilēə\
Latin
: sacred shields of preservation

ancree
\aŋˌkrā\
French
: having the end of each arm shaped like an anchor

anemobiagraph
\anəmōˈbīəˌgraf\
Greek
: pressure-tube measuring wind speed

angoni
\aŋˈgōnē\
African geographical name
: animal resembling zebu cattle

anidian
\a¦nidēən\
Greek
: formless, lacking change

aniliid
\anᵊlˈīəd\
Latin
: a nonvenomous snake

animatronics
\a-nə-mə-ˈträ-niks\
Latin
: technology dealing with applying zest to cartoons

animikite
\əˈniməˌkīt\
Ojibwe
: mineral containing silver granular masses

anisocoria
\a-ˌnī-ˌsəkōrēə\
Latin + Greek
: inequality of pupil size

ankaratrite
\aŋkəˈräˌtrīt\
French
: mineral in Madagascar

annerodite
\anəˈrōˌdīt\
Norwegian>Swedish
: rare velvet luster

annonaceous
\anə¦nāshəs\
Latin
: resembling custard apples

anopheline
\ə-ˈnä-fə-ˌlīn\
Latin + English
: pertaining to malaria-spreading mosquitoes

antara
\antarə\
Quechua
: Peruvian panpipe

anthocerotean
\anˈthäsəˌrōtēən\
Latin
: relating to liverworts

anthracycline
\an(t)thrəˈsīˌklēn\
ISV
: class of drugs

anthraxylon
\anthraksəˌlän\
Latin + Greek
: glossy black constituent

antiarin
\antēərən\
ISV
: crystalline glycosides

anticor
\antē-kȯ(ə)r\
Latin
: inflammatory swelling of the horse's chest due to harnesses

antiparabemata
\antē parə¦bēmədə\
Latin
: either of two chapels in the Byzantine Empire

antirrhinum
\antə́ˈrīnəm\
Latin
: plant of the Northern hemisphere with flowers

Antrycide
\antrəˌsīd\
Trademark
: white crystalline compound

apabhramsa
\əpəˈbrəmshə\
Sanskrit
: non-linguistic forms

apheresis
\a-fə-ˈrē-səs\
Latin
: withdrawal of blood

aphthartodocetae
\afthärtōdōsēte, afthartodō-sētē\
Greek
: monk sect of 6th century

apitong
\əˈpēˌtȯŋ\
Tagalog
: Philippine timber tree

aplustre
\əˈpləstrē\
Greek
: ornamented stern of a ship

apolytikia
\ä͵pȯlēˈtē͵kyä\
Greek
: concluding hymns in church

aponogeton
\apənōˈjē͵tän\
Latin
: aquatic herbs

aporrhaoid
\apəˈrāȯid\
Greek
: of small snails

Aproscopiny
\ā͵präskäpənē\
Latin
: lacking supraorbital ridges

aquaflorium
\akwəˈflōrēəm\
Latin
: inverted glass bowl

aquamanilia
\akwəməˈnīlēə\
Latin
: water vessels used by priests

aquilian
\əˈkwilēən\
Latin
: arisen from the government

aracanga
\arəˈkaŋgə\
Portuguese>Tupi
: scarlet parrot

arachidonate
\arəˈkidᵊn͵āt\
ISV
: salty acid

aralkoxy
\arəl¦käksē\
ISV
: univalent radical

aramina
\arəˈmēnə\
Portuguese
: fiber of Caesar weed

arariba
\arərē¦bä\
Portuguese
: Brazilian tree

araucarioxylon
\arȯka(a)rēˈäksə͵län\
Latin
: fossil redwood

archaecraniate
\ärkēkrā-nē-ət\
Latin
: primitive type of skull

archallaxes
\ärkəˈlaksēs\
Greek
: early deviation from development in ancestors

archetista
\ärkəˈtistə\
Latin
: assemblage of viruses

archiater
\är-kēä¦tə(r)\
Latin
: chief physician

arcifinious
\ärsə¦finēəs\
Latin
: having a natural boundary

ardealite
\ärdēˈä͵līt\
German
: mineral containing clalcium

arduinite
\ärdəˈwē͵nīt, ärˈdüə͵nīt\
Italian name
: mineral in minute crystals

areolet
\əˈrēələt, ˈa(a)rēə͵let\
Latin
: small area

arfvedsonite
\ävədsə͵nīt\
Swedish
: mineral with igneous rocks

argemone
\arjemənē\
Latin
: herb with showy white flowers and prickly leaves

ariegite
\arēˈä͵zhīt\
French
: rock with dark green grains

arnaut
\ärnau̇t\
Turkish
: Albanian living in mountains

arquerite
\ärˈke͵rīt\
French
: soft soldering mineral

arrhenite
\əˈrā͵nīt\
Swedish
: variety of brown mineral

arrish
\arish\
English
: stubbled wheat or grass

arrojadite
\arəˈjä͵dīt\
Portuguese
: Brazilian mineral with salt

arsacid
\är¦sasəd, 'ärsəsəd\
Latin
: relating to the Persian
Empire

arsphenamine
\ärs-'fe-nə-ˌmēn\
ISV
: yellow toxic powder

artemones
\är'teməˌnēz\
Greek
: masts in sailing ships

arthrodeses
\är-'thrä-də-sēs\
Latin
: surgical operations on
cartilaginous surfaces

artiad
\ärtēˌad, -ärshēad\
Greek
: element with even valence

artotyrite
\ärtə'tīˌrīt\
Latin>Greek
: one who reenacts the Lord's
Supper with bread and cheese

aruhe
\ä-rü-ˌhā\
Maori
: starchy rhizome of the brake
in New Zealand

arundinaceous
\ə¦rəndə¦nāshəs\
Latin
: resembling reed or cane

ascariases
\a-skə-'rī-ə-ˌsēz\
Latin
: infestation of human
intestine caused by
roundworms

asclepias
\ə'sklēpēəs\
Latin
: dried root of herb

ascyphous
\ā¦sīfəs\
Latin
: relating to lichen having no
stalks to walk with

aselli
\ə'selē, ə'selī\
Latin
: freshwater isopods

ashre
\ä'shrä\
Hebrew
: recital in Jewish liturgy

ashura
\ə'shùrə\
Arabic (1) Japanese (2)
1: Muslim voluntary fast day
2: breed of water fowl

aspidinol
\a'spidᵊnˌòl\
German>ISV
: yellow crystalline
compound

aspiratae
\aspə'rätē, aspə'rätī, aspə'r
ātē\
Latin
: voiceless stops in languages

assacu
\asə¦kü\
Portuguese>Tupi
: tropical American tree

assoilziing
\ə'sòil(y)ē-ing\
French>Scottish
: freeing by sentence of court

astarte
\ə-'stär-tē\
Greek
: bivalve mollusk

astrex
\astreks\
English blend
: rabbit with wavy hair

atabal
\adəbal\
Spanish
: Arabian kettledrum

ataxiagram
\ə'taksēəˌgram\
Latin + English
: record measured by
involuntary unsteadiness

atenolol
\ə-'te-nə-ˌlòl\
ISV
: beta-blocker

atheteses
\athə'tēsēs\
Greek
: marking of poems as false

atragene
\ə'trajəˌnē\
Latin
: plant with perennial vines

attapulgite
\atə'pəlˌjīt\
English
: fibrous clay mineral

aufklarung
\aùf-ˌkler-əŋ\
German
: philosophic movement

augelite
\òjəˌlīt\
German>ISV
: mineral with aluminum

aumildar
\ȯməl¦där\
Hindi
: revenue collector, manager

auncel
\ȯnsəl\
English
: medieval balance of weight

aurantiaceous
\ȯˈranch(ē)āshəs\
Latin
: resembling the sour orange

aurignacian
\ȯr-ēn-¦yā-shən\
French
: relating to the culture of
bone and cave paintings

auriphrygiate
\ȯrə¦frijēət\
Latin
: adorned with gold
embroider

ausformed
\ȯs͵fȯ(ə)rmd\
Latin>ISV
: subject to increase strength

austenitic
\ȯ-stə-¦ni-tik\
French
: composed primarily of iron

austringer
\ästrinjər\
French>English
keeper of hawks

ausubo
\aùˈsübō\
Spanish
: dark heavy wood

autoschediastic
\odōskēdē͵aztik\
Greek
: extemporaneously, offhand

autostrada
\aù-tō-ˈsträ-də\
Italian
: multiline highway

autunite
\ō-ˈtə-͵nīt, ˈȯ-tə-͵nīt\
French
: radioactive yellow mineral

auxanometer
\ȯgzəˈnämətə(r)\
ISV
: instrument determining
growth of plants

auximone
\ȯksə͵mōn\
Greek
: certain substance

averroism
\əˈverə͵wizəm\
Latin
: diverse doctrines

axillant
\aksələnt, ak¦silənt\
Latin
: growing in between leaves

axinomancy
\aksənə͵mansē\
Greek
: divination of posts

axonolipous
\aksəˈnäləpəs\
Latin
: relating to extinct animals

aylesbury
\ālzbərē\
English name
: breed of white ducks

ayllu
\īlü\
Quechua
: clan of Incan society

azedarach
\əˈzedə͵rak\
French>Persian
: rapid-growing Asian tree

azathioprine
\a-zə-ˈthī-ə-͵prēn\
ISV
: suppression of natural
immune responses

azilian
\əˈzēlyən, ə-zillēən\
French
: characterized by bone tools

azinphosmethyl
\ā-zⁿ-fäs-ˈme-thəl\
ISV
: pesticide against mites

azoturia
\ā-zō-ˈtur-ē-ə\
Latin
: excess of nitrogenous
substances in the urine

azulejo
\ä-sü-ˈlā-hō\
Spanish
: glazed ceramic tile

babala
\bäbə͵lä\
Afrikaans
: tall cereal grass

babbitting
\ba-bəting\
American name
: furnishing with alloys

bacalao
\bäkə¦laù\
Spanish
: marine food fish

bacsonian
\bak¦sōnēən\
Vietnamese
: relating to East Asian polished stone implements

badan
\bəˈdän, bəd-an\
Russian
: Siberian plant with roots used as tanning materials

baddeleyite
\bad(ə)lēˌīt\
English name
: mineral containing zirconium

badenite
\badᵊnˌīt, bəˈdenīt\
French
: mineral with cobalt & nickel

baguio
\bägēˈō, bägˈyō\
Spanish>Tagalog
: tropical cyclone

bahut
\bäˌhut, bəˈhut, -üt, F báūe\
French
: chest or cabinet

baikerinite
\bīkərəˌnīt
German
: hydrocarbon

bailliage
\bäˈyäzh\
French
: medieval agent's jurisdiction

Bairam
\bī¦räm\
Arabic
: Muslim festivals

bajonado
\bäkəˈnädō\
Spanish
: yellow food fish

Bakshaish
\bäk¦shīsh\
Iranian name
: antique Persian carpet

balaghat
\bälə¦got\
Hindi
: mesa above mountain passes

balatong
\bäləˌtoŋ\
Tagalog
: brushy mung sprout

balinger
\balȯnjə(r)\
French
: outgoing ship

ballonne
\balə¦nä\
French
: wide circular jump in ballet

ballottine
\ba-lətēn\
French
: boned meat

Balzacian
\bȯl¦-zā-shən, bal-za-kē-ən\
French
: large and comprehensive

bamoth
\bəmōth, -bəmōt, -bəmōs\
Hebrew
: high places, sanctuaries

bandurria
\banˈdu̇ryə\
Spanish
: stringed instrument

banjaxing
\ban-ˌjaksing\
Unknown
: damaging, ruining

banovine
\bänəˌvēnä\
Serbo-Croatian
: former divisions of Yugoslavia (pl.)

baraboo
\berəbü\
American geographical name
: dug-up hill

baraka
\bəˈräkə\
Arabic
: blessings recognized by saints, and natural objects

Bararite
\bəˈräˌrīt\
Bengal + English
: mineral containing crystals

barbotine
\bärbə¦tēn\
French
: mixture of fine clay

barkevikitic
\bärkəvikidik\
Norwegian
: relating to a velvet mineral

baroto
\bəˈrōtō\
Filipino
: dugout canoe

barrera
\bəˈrerə\
Spanish
: red wooden fence

bartholinites
\bärtələnīdēz\
German + Latin
: inflammation of the glands
which secrete mucus

Bartokian
\bär'täkyən\
Hungarian
: of musical compositions

barysilite
\bə'risə‚līt, ‚barə'si‚līt\
Swedish
: rare lead silicate

basanite
\basə‚nīt\
Latin
: extrusive igneous rock

basileus
\bäsə'leüs\
Greek
: ruler of Roman Empire

basommatophorous
\bə‚sämə'täf(ə)rəs\
Latin
: of snails with tentacles

bassetite
\basət‚īt\
French
: mineral of yellow phosphate

bassorin
\basərən, bəsərən\
ISV
: substance obtained from
gum

batonnier
\bätȯ'nyā\
French
: chief of lawyers in court

batuque
\bə'tükə\
Portuguese
: impassioned Brazilian
dance

bauhinia
\bō-'i-nē-ə\
Latin + Swiss
: plant with fibrous bark

baumier
\bōm'yā\
French
: any of several plants

bayldonite
\bāldə‚nīt\
English
: mineral containing lead
copper arsenate found in
large green masses

bayott
\bī¦ät\
Unknown
: tall tree with resinous oil

bdellium
\de-lē-əm\
Latin
: gum resin found in trees

bebization
\bābəzāshən\
German
: old doremifasolatido scale

becassine
\bākasēn\
French
: game bird

beccafico
\bekə'fēkō\
Italian
: European songbirds

becquerelite
\be'kre‚līt\
French
: mineral with yellow crystals

bediasite
\bē'dī‚zīt\
American geographical name
: glassy body of meteorite

beegerite
\bēgə‚rīt\
English
: mineral with massive lead

beggiatoaceous
\bə¦jatə¦wāshəs, bejə‚tō¦āshəs\
Italian
: relating to bacteria

belleek
\bə-'lēk\
Trademark
: pale orange yellow color

belleric
\bə'lerik\
Persian>Arabic>French
: of the fruit of the Eastern
tree

belonoid
\belənȯd\
Greek
: relating to shape of needles

bemegride
\bemə‚grīd\
ISV
: counteracting drug

benitier
\bānētyā\
French
: holy water glass

bennettitalean
\bə‚netə'tālēən\
Latin
: relating to fossils

bentinck
\benti(ŋ)k\
English
: triangular storm sail

benzonitrile
\benzō¦nītrəl\
German
: toxic oily compound

beraunite
\bāˈraủˌnīt\
German geographical name
: hydrous basic iron

berberis
\bər-bər-əs\
Latin
: dried rhizome of berries

berengelite
\berənˈgāˌlīt\
Peruvian name
: brown resinous substance

bergerette
\berzhə¦ret\
French
: pastoral song used in dances

berghaan
\berk̲ˌhän\
Afrikaans
: any of various eagles

berginization
\bergənəˈzāshən\
German
: hydrogenation of coal

bertillonage
\bərtᵊlə¦näzh, bertēyȯnàzh\
French
: system of human
identification by description

berzelianite
\bərˈzēlyəˌnīt\
Swedish
: mineral containing copper

bethanechol
\bəˈthānəˌkȯl\
ISV
: chloride agent

betony
\be-tə-nē\
Latin>English
: any of several woundworts

betulinol
\bechələnȯl\
ISV
: crystalline alcohol

beudantite
\byüdᵊnˌtīt\
French
: mineral containing ferric
lead

bhikshu
\bikshə\
Sanskrit
: Hindu or Buddhist monk

bhokra
\bōkrə\
Hindi name
: four-horned antelope

bhutatathata
\büdədətätä\
Sanskrit
: suchness in Buddhism

bidonville
\bē-ˌdōⁿ-ˈvēl\
French
: settlement of badly built
buildings in the outskirts

bikkurim
\biˌküˈrēm\
Hebrew
: first ripe fruits

bilinite
\biləˌnīt\
Czech
: hydrous mineral

billbergia
\bilˈbərjēə\
Latin
: plant with showy flowers

billietite
\bil(ē)əˌtīt\
French
: mineral with uranium oxide

bindheimite
\bintˌhīˌmīt\
German
: mineral with hydrous lead

bisabolene
\bisəbəlēn\
ISV
: colorless oily substance

bischofite
\bishəˌfīt\
German
: mineral with magnesium

bobierrite
\bōbēəˌrīt\
French
: mineral with magnesium

bockwurst
\bäkwủ(ə)rst\
German
: seasoned sausage

boedelscheiding
\büdᵊlˌskādiŋ\
Dutch
: partition of an estate

Boethusian
\bōəˈthüzh(ē)ən\
Hebrew
: member of a Jewish sect

bohor
\bōˌhȯr\
Amharic
: small red antelope

boigid
\bō'ijəd\
Latin
: nonvenomous snake

Borgesian
\bòr'hāzhēən\
Argentine
: suggestive of writings

borickite
\bòrə͵kīt, bòrzhət͵skīt\
Czech name + English
: mineral with reddish
compact

botallackite
\bō'talə͵kīt\
English
: blackish-green basic
chloride of copper

bougie
\bü-͵zhē\
French
: wax candle

bouquetiere
\bùk(ə)'tye(ə)r\
French
: garnished with vegetables

bourree
\bù-'rā\
French
: lively dance in duple time

boustrophedonic
\büstrəfēdänik, bü¦strä-fə dä-
nik\
Greek
: relating to writing in
alternate lines of opposite
directions (left-right>right-
left)

boxwallah
\bäk͵swälə\
Hindi
: peddler

brackebuschite
\brakəbùshīt\
German
: hydrous manganese and
lead

bradykinin
\brā-di-¦kī-nən\
ISV
: hormone formed locally in
damaged tissue

bragozzi
\brə'gòtsē\
Italian
: 2-masted trawlers of Venice

brancardier
\bräⁿkàrdyā\
French
: stretcher-bearer

brandade
\bräⁿdàd\
Provencal
: seasoned puree of fish

brayerin
\brə'yerən\
Latin
: brownish powder

brazilette
\brazə¦let, ͵brazə'letē\
Spanish
: wood of tropical America

brecham
\brekəm\
Scottish
: horse collar

brehon
\brē͵hän, bi'rehùv\
Irish
: class of lawyers

bremsstrahlung
\brem(p)-͵shträ-ləŋ\
German
: electromagnetic radiation
produced by electron particle

brevicipitid
\brevə'sipətəd\
Latin
: frog or toad

brilliandeer
\brilyən¦di(ə)r\
Dutch
: cutter of diamonds

brochan
\bräk̲ən\
Gaelic
: porridge or gruel

broggerite
\brəgə͵rīt\
Swedish
: 8-sided crystals

brugnatellite
\brünyə'te͵līt\
Italian
: carbonate of iron

Buchmanism
\bùkmə͵nizəm\
Egnlsih
: life- changing movement

buckshee
\bək¦shē\
Hindi>Persian
: windfall, extra rations

budgeree
\bəjərē\
Australian name
: good, fine, pretty

burele
\bùrə¦lā\
French
having a network pattern

burkundaz
\bərkən¦däz\
Persian>Hindi
: armed guard of India

burseraceous
\bərsə¦rāshəs\
Latin
: relating to aromatic shrubs

Butazolidin
\byütəˈzäləˌdēn\
ISV
: preparation of yellow
powder

buttgenbachite
\bətgənˌbaˌkīt\
French
: mineral of hydrous copper

caballine
\kabəˌlīn, kabəˌl-ən\
English
: imparting poetic inspiration

cabasset
\kabə¦sā\
French
: helmet of small size

caber
\kā-bər, ˈkä bər\
Scottish
: young tree trunk

caboceer
\kabə¦si(ə)r\
Portuguese
: West African native chief

cabook
\kəˈbu̇k\
Portuguese>Latin
: rock decay used as building
material of Sri Lanka

cabouca
\kəˈbükə\
American French
: lazy crab

cachaca
\kəˈshäsə\
Portuguese
: Brazilian sugarcane liquor

cachalot
\ka-shə-ˌlät, ka-shə -ˌlō\
French
: sperm whale

caenostyly
\sēnəstīlē\
Greek>Latin
: gills attached to the brain

caesalpiniaceous
\sezalpinēˈāshəs\
Latin
: relating to tropical shrubs

cagoulards
\kagü¦lär(z)\
French
: members of secret
revolution
(singular spelled cagoulard)

cahot
\kà(h)ō\
French
: bump or depression in road

caiarara
\kīəˈrärə\
Portuguese
: megalocephalic monkey

calalu
\kalə¦lü\
Spanish
: plant with vegetables

calandria
\kəˈlandrēə\
Spanish
1: heating element of
vacuums
2: black-headed mockingbird

calathea
\kaləˈthēə\
Latin
: plant with short stems

calciovolborthite
\kalsēōˈvȯlˌbȯrˌthīt\
German>ISV
: mineral of calcium

calembour
\kaləm¦bu̇(ə)r\
French
: humorous use of word

calicivirus
\kəlisəvīrəs, kəlēchēvīrəs\
ISV
: RNA disease germ

calinut
\kalēˌnət\
Bambara>Mende
: African flattened brown
seed

callaides
\kəˈlāəˌdēz\
Greek>Latin
: dark green stones
(singular spelled callais)

callimico
\kaləˈmēkō\
Portuguese + Spanish
: spider monkey

callithricid
\kaləˈthrisəd\
Latin
: beautiful monkey

calmodulin
\kalmä-jə-lin, kalmädyu̇-lin\
ISV
: milk-binding protein

caloneurodean
\kalōn(y)üˈrōdēən\
Latin
: relating to winged insects

calool
\kəˈlül\
Australian
: fibrous shrub

caloyer
\kəˈlȯiə(r), kaləyə(r)\
Italian + French
: monk of Eastern church

calycozoan
\kāləkəzōən\
Latin
: jellyfish with stalks

camagon
\kaməˌgän\
Tagalog>Spanish
: timber tree

camaieux
\kámàyœ̄\
Italian>French
: painting in a single color

camail
\kəˈmāl\
French
: hood or neck guard

camalig
\kəˈmälig\
Tagalog
: storehouse, hut

camboge
\kambō¦zhā\
Unknown
: pierced concrete block for building in architecture

camogie
\kəˈmōgē\
Scottish
: team sport similar to hurling in Ireland

campagnol
\kampə¦nyȯl, kampə¦nyōl\
French
: European field vole

campignian
\kam¦pēnyən\
French
: relating to pottery culture

campoody
\kamˈpüdē\
Latin>Spanish>Paiute
: American Indian village

canaline
\kanᵊlˌēn, kanᵊl-ən\
Latin
: crystalline amino acid

cancion
\kȧnˈsyən, kanˈthyȯn\
Spanish
: popular song

candiru
\kandə¦rü\
Portuguese>Tupi
: bloodsucking catfish

candollea
\kanˈdälēə\
Latin
: plant with showy flowers

cangia
\kanj(ē)ə\
Arabic>Italian
: light sailboat on Nile

cannetille
\kanə¦tē(l), kántēēy\
Spanish>French
: gold or silver thread

canotier
\kanə¦tyā\
French
: man's hat with low brim

canthaxanthin
\kan(t)-thə-ˈzan-ˌthin\
ISV
: color additive for food

canutillo
\kan(y)əˈtēō\
Spanish
: drink made form plant

Caodaism
\kaủ¦dī̠ˌizəm\
Vietnamese
: religion believing in supernatural forces mixed with Confucianism and Buddhism

capeline
\kapəˌlēn\
Provencal
: small skullcap

capitania
\kapətəˈnēə\
Spanish
: territorial division of Brazil

capotasto
\käpōˈtästō\
Italian
: bar or fingering on guitar

cappelenite
\kap(ə)ləˌnīt\
Swedish
: greenish crystals

capsaicin
\kap-ˈsā-ə-sən\
Latin
: colorless amide

capsumin
\kapsəmȧn\
German>ISV
: pigment in Guinean pepper

caraibe
\karə¦ēb, kəˈrīb\
French
: moderate yellowish brown

caraunda
\kəˈrau̇ndə, kəˈrau̇n-ˌdä\
Hindi
: East Asian evergreen shrub

carbocer
\kärbəsər\
Latin
: mineral with substances containing rare-earth elements

carbodiimide
\kärbōˈdīəˌmīd\
French>ISV
: form of acidic compound

carbonara
\kärˈbōnärə\
Italian
: dish of pasta

carcoon
\kärˌkün\
Persian>Marathi
: salesclerk

cardamine
\kärˈdamənē\
Greek>Latin
: plant with perennial herbs

carisoprodol
\kəˌrīsəˈprōˌdȯl\
ISV
: drug to relieve pain

carmoisin
\kärmˌwäˌzēn, kärˌmȯizᵊn\
Arabic>Italian>German
: blue acid dye

carnifex
\kärnəˌfeks\
Latin
: executioner of ancient Rome

carosella
\karəˈselə\
Italian
: fennel grown for salads

caroubier
\kəˈrübēˌā\
French
: moderate chestnut brown

carreta
\kəˈretə\
Spanish
: two-wheeled wagon

carronade
\ker-ə-ˌnād\
Scottish
: obsolete cannon

caryinite
\karēəˌnīt, kəˈrīənīt\
Greek
: mineral with calcium

castrensian
\kasˌtrenchən\
Latin
: relating to a camp

catalinite
\katᵊlˈēˌnīt\
American geographical name
: beach pebble used as a gem

catananche
\katəˈnaŋkē\
Latin
: herbs with yellow flowers

catapleiite
\katəˈplīˌīt\
German
: rare mineral

catarrhinian
\katəˈrinēən\
Latin
: relating to the nostrils of the higher end of the evolution cycle

cateran
\ka-tə-rən, ˈka-trən\
Scottish
: military of the Highlands

cathedratica
\kathədradəkə\
Latin
: annual sums paid to bishops

Catilinarian
\katᵊləˌnerēən\
Latin
: conspirator

catoctin
\kəˈtäktən\
American geographical name
: hill or ridge

cattierite
\kəˈtiˌrīt\
African geographical name
: mineral of the pyrite group

cattleya
\kat-lē-ə; katˈlā-ə\
Latin
: moderate purplish color

caulerpaceous
\kȯlərˌpāshəs\
Latin
: relating to algae

cavascope
\kavəˌskōp\
Latin
: instrument for lighting up dark cavities in the body

cebollite
\sēˌbȯi(y)īt, ˈsebəˌlīt\
American geographical name
: mineral with calcium

cecidogenous
\sesəˌdäjənəs\
Greek
: producing galls on plants

155

celastraceous
\seləstrāshəs\
Latin
: belonging to shrubs with colorful fruits

cellocut
\selō͵kət\
Latin
: artist's print on plates

cenobian
\sə̇'nōbēən\
Latin
: monkish, monastic

cenosite
\senə͵sīt\
Greek>Swedish
: yellowish mineral

censitaires
\säⁿsēteer(z)\
French
: those who paid their dues

centrallasite
\sen'tralə͵sīt\
English>Greek
: mineral composed of calcium

cephaeline
\se'fāə͵lēn\
ISV
: colorless crystalline alkaloid of the ipecac root

cephaloridine
\se-fə-'lȯr-ə-͵dēn\
ISV
: semisynthetic antibiotic

cepharanthine
\sefə'ran͵thīn\
Latin
: alkaloid of tuberous roots

cephenomyia
\sə̇͵fēnə'mī(y)ə\
Greek>Latin
: blood-sucking deer ticks

cerambycid
\sə̇'rambəsəd\
Latin
: long-horned beetle

ceratodus
\sə̇'ratədəs\
Latin
: fish or fossil with pelvic fins

cercariaea
\sər͵karē'ēə\
Latin
: tailless tadpole larvae (pl.)

cercles
\serkl(ᵊ)\
French
: administrative districts

cerniture
\sərnə͵chu̇(ə)r\
Latin + English
: formal acceptance of inheritance (as in wills)

cerolite
\sirə͵līt\
German
: magnesium silicate

certosina
\chertə'sēnə\
Italian
: Renaissance style of ivory

cerveliere
\servəl¦ye(ə)r\
Latin>French
: close-fitting steel cap

cesarevich
\sə̇'zarə͵vich\
Latin>Russian
: heir to throne

cesarolite
\chāzə'rō͵līt\
Belgian>French
: spongy gray-massed mineral

cestraciont
\se'strāshē͵änt\
Latin
: shark

Cevian
\chāvēən\
Italian
: straight line of vertex in triangle for intersection of face

ceyssatite
\sāsə͵tīt\
French
: earthy form of opal

chaetetid
\kē'tētəd\
Greek>Latin
: fossil coral

chaitya
\chītyə, chīchə\
Hindi
: sacred place, monument

chakravartin
\chəkrə'värtᵊn\
Sanskrit
: sovereign leader, ideal ruler

chalan
\chələn\
Hindi
: bill, record of transaction

chalazoidite
\kaləzȯidīt\
Greek
: spherical body in volcanoes

chalchuite
\chälchəˈwētē\
Nahuatl
: blue or green turquoise

chalcocite
\kal-kə-ˌsīt\
French + English
: dark gray mineral

chalybeate
\kə-ˈlē-bē-ət\
Latin
: having a taste like iron

chamaecephalies
\kaməsefəlēz\
ISV
: conditions of flattened head

chamaeliria
\kaməˈlirēə\
Greek
: dried rhizome roots

chamaerrhiny
\kaməˌrīnē\
ISV
: having a short broad nose

chamoline
\shaməlēn\
French
: strong yellow brown color

chantiers
\shäⁿtyā(z)\
French
: huts in lumber camps

chappaul
\chəˈpȯl\
Unknown
: dull-green fish

chaptalize
\shaptəˌlīz\
French
: normalize wine by stirring

charneco
\shärˈnäkü\
Portuguese
: sweet popular wine

chartophylax
\kärˈtäphəˌlaks\
Latin
: chancellor or bishop of
Orthodox Church

chassignite
\shasᵊnˌyīt, shaˈsēnyīt\
German>French
: greenish meteorite

Chatelperronian
\shaˌtelpə¦rōnēən\
French
: flint-chipping technique

chaulmoograte
\chälmügrāt\
Bengali
: salt of crystalline acid

cheirogaleus
\kīrōˈgälēəs\
Latin
: arboreal lemur

cheiropompholyx
\kīrōˈpämfəˌliks\
Latin
: skin disease on hands

Chekhovian
\cheˈkōvēən\
Russian
: suggestive of the
atmosphere of plays which
Chekhov wrote

chenevixite
\shenə¦vikˌsīt\
French
: hydrous copper mineral

chevkinite
\chefkəˌnīt\
Russian>German
: mineral of rare-earth
element

chiasmatypy
\kīˈazməˌtipē\
Latin>French
: chromosomal pairings

chicaric
\chikərik\
Imitative
: migratory shorebirds

chichipe
\chəˈchēpē\
Spanish
: tall cactus with fruits

chickell
\chikəl\
Imitative
: small bird of Alaska

chicot
\shēˈkō\
French
: tall tree with seeds

chillagite
\chiləˌgīt\
Australian geographical name
: mineral full of tungsten

chillumchee
\chi-ləmchē\
Persian>Hindi
: metal wash basin

chimarrogale
\kiməˈrägəlē\
Greek
: Asian water shrew

Chincoteague
\shiŋkə¦tēg\
American geographical name
: Chesapeake Bay oyster

chipolata
\chipə'lätə\
French
: small spicy sausage

chirivita
\chirə'vētə\
Spanish
: black angelfish

chkalovite
\chə'kälə‚vīt\
Russian
: mineral with sodium

chlorcyclizine
\klȯr'sīklə‚zēn\
Latin>ISV
: antihistaminic agent

chlormerodrin
\klȯr'merədrən\
ISV
: mercurial drug

chlorpyrifoses
\klȯr-'pir-ə-fäs‚əz\
ISV
: toxic crystalline pesticides

chlorochrous
\klō'räkrəwəs\
Latin
: color close to green

chloroxiphite
\klō'räksə‚fīt\
Greek
: mineral of lead and copper

chobdar
\chōb‚där\
Persian>Hindi
: usher, attendant

chobie
\chōbē\
Unknown
: large marine fish

cholecalciferol
\kō-lə-kal-'si-fə-‚rȯl\
ISV
: vitamin in liver oils

choledochi
\kə'ledəkē\
Latin
: common bile ducts

chondroitin
\kän-'drȯi-tᵊn\
German>ISV
: gummy nitrogenous acid

chorises
\kōrəsēs\
Greek
: separation of floral organs

choultry
\chaültrē\
Hindi
: inn, hall of temple

choumoellier
\shə'mälyə(r)\
French
: hybrid of cabbage and kale

chronaximeter
\krō‚nak'simətə(r)\
Latin
: device to measure minimum time of electrical current

chrysarobin
\kri-sə-'rō-bən\
Greek>ISV
: yellow crystalline powder

chymosin
\kīməsən\
Latin>French
: gastric enzyme

Cibacron
\sēbə‚krän\
Trademark
: fiber- reactive dye

cibolero
\sibə'le‚rō\
Spanish
: buffalo hunter

cicely
\si-s(ə-)lē\
folk etymology
: any of several herbs

cichoriaceous
\sə‚kōrē'āsh‚əs\
Latin
: relating to flower heads with milky juices inside

cimelia
\sə'mēlēə\
Latin
: church treasures

cincholoipon
\siŋkə'lȯi‚pän\
ISV
: yellow crystalline acid

cinnamein
\sə'namēən\
French>ISV
: mixture of compounds

ciprofloxacin
\si-prə-'fläk-sə-sən\
ISV
: derivative of bacteria

cirogrille
\sirə‚gril\
Greek>Latin
: Syrian goat

cissing
\sisiŋ\
Unknown
: gathering of wet film

Cistercian
\si-¦stər-shən\
French>Latin
: austere order

citrullin
\sə'trələn\
Latin
: yellow resinous preparation

cixiid
\siksēəd\
Latin
: elongated insects

clausthalite
\klaůstə‿līt\
German>French
: mineral full of lead

clavicytheria
\klavə‿sī'thirēə\
Latin
: early upright keyboards

cleidoic
\klī-¦dō-ik\
Greek
: relating to eggs isolated
from the environment

clogwyn
\klȯgwēn\
Welsh
: cliff, precipice

cobbra
\käbrə\
Australian geographical name
: head, skull

cocash
\kə'kash\
Algonquian
: North American herb

cochliodont
\kōklēə‿dänt\
Latin
: fish

cocorico
\kōkə'rēkō, kə‿kōrē'kō\
French Imitative
: game bird of Trinidad

Coelicolist
\sə'likələst\
Latin
: Jewish and Christian
doctrines follower

coelogyne
\sə'läjənē\
Greek
: plant with white orchids

coenoecia
\sə'nēs(h)ēə\
Greek>Latin
: horny aquatic animals

colane
\kə'lān\
Unknown
: subacid fruit like nectarines

colleter
\kə'lētə(r), kälətə(r)\
Greek>German
1: gelatin secreting substance
2: wheel worker

collyridian
\kälə'ridēən\
Latin
: priestess

coloquintida
\kälə'kwintədə\
Latin
: herbaceous vine

comacine
\kōmə‿chēn\
Latin>Italian
: medieval skilled workman

comitatensian
\kämətə¦tenchən\
Latin
: relating to a body of men
serving the king

connexiva
\känək'sēvə\
Latin
: flattened abdomen of insects

convallamarin
\kənvalə'marən, känvəlamərən\
Latin
: bitter poisonous glycoside

coonjine
\kün‿jīn\
Unknown
: walk with a shuffle

copellidine
\kō'pelə‿dēn\
ISV
: several liquid bases

copihue
\kə'pēwā\
Spanish
: showy twining vine

cordonnet
\kȯr-dᵊn ā\
French
: thread or small cord

cordycepin
\kȯ(r)də'sepən\
ISV
: antibiotic activity

corposant
\kȯr-pə-‿sant\
Portuguese
: flaming phenomenon
occurring in stormy weather

corycium
\kə'ris(h)ēəm\
Latin
: globular rock object

corydalis
\kə-'ri-də-ləs\
Latin
: dried roots of alkaline

coryphaei
\kȯr-ə-'fē-ˌī\
Greek>Latin
: leaders of school

cotunnite
\kə'tə͝ˌnīt\
Italian>German
: mineral of yellow lead

coulibiac
\külē'byäk\
Russian>French
: fish rolled in pastry dough

coumaphos
\küməˌfäs\
ISV
: insecticide used on cattle

creashaks
\krēshaks\
Unknown
: glossy red berries (pl.)
(singular spelled same way)

crenelet
\krenᵊlət\
French
: small opening in a fort

crocidolite
\krō-'si-də-ˌlīt\
Greek>German
: lavender-blue mineral

cronstedtite
\kränˌstetˌīt\
Swedish>German
: mineral of black hydrous
iron

crostarie
\krästerē\
Gaelic
: burning cross of wood

crystoleum
\kri'stōlēəm\
Latin
: obsolete photography
process

ctenizid
\tenəzəd\
Latin
: large burrowing spider

cundeamor
\kündāə'mȯ(ə)r\
Spanish
: tropical American plant

curucucu
\sù̇rəkə¦kü, ¦kúrəkü¦kü\
Tupi>Portuguese
: New World pit viper

cyaphenine
\sī'afəˌnēn\
ISV
: white crystalline compound

cyclandelate
\sī'klandᵊlˌāt\
ISV
: drug to treat arterial
diseases

cyclorrhaphous
\sī¦klȯrəfəs\
Latin
: resembling fly larvae

cylicostome
\siləkōˌstōm\
Greek>Latin
: nematode worm

Cymric
\kəm-rik\
Welsh
: long-haired cat

cynanchum
\sə̇'naŋkəm\
Greek
: roots of several plants

cynipid
\sinəpə̇d\
Latin
: gall wasp

cyphellae
\sə̇'felē\
Latin
: small pits on lichen

cypripedia
\si-prə-'pē-dē-ə\
Greek
: leafy-stemmed orchids

cypseline
\sipsəˌlīn\
Greek
: resembling swifts

cysticerci
\si-stə-¦sər-ˌsī\
Latin
: tapeworm larvae

cytisi
\sidəzī\
Latin
: plants with stiff shiny
shrubs and showy flowers

dachiardite
\däkē'ärˌdīt\
Italian
: mineral of hydrous silicate

dahllite
\däˌlīt\
German
: calcium carbonate

daikering
\dākəring\
French>Scottish
: putting into order

damkjernite
\damkyə(r)ˌnīt\
Norwegian>German
: dike rock

160

dannemorite
\danəˈmōrˌīt\
Swedish
: mineral of fibrous iron

daubreelite
\dȯbrēˌlīt, dōˈbrālīt\
French
: black chromium sulfuric acid

daunorubicin
\dȯnərübisən\
ISV
: antibiotic to treat leukemia

dediticiancy
\dedəˈtishənsē\
Latin
: full citizenship rights

deeses
\dēˈēsēs\
Greek
: tripartite icons

defterdar
\deftərˈdär\
Persian>Turkish
: government officer

deguelin
\dəˈgelən\
Latin
: crystalline ketone

dehrnite
\derˌnīt\
German
: basic calcium

delesseriaceous
\deləˈsirēˌāshəs\
Latin
: pertaining to algal leaves

demeton
\deməˌtän\
ISV
: insecticide of plants

dennstaedtioid
\denˈstetēˌȯid\
Latin
: tropical fern

derrengadera
\deˌreŋgəˈderə\
Spanish
: infectious horse disease

desaparecido
\dāsəpärəˈsētō\
Spanish
: citizen abducted by terrorists

descloizite
\dāˈklȯiˌzīt\
French
: mineral of lead and zinc

desipramine
\dəˈziprəˌmēn\
ISV
: antidepressant for bipolars

desmarestiaceous
\deməˈrestēˌāshəs\
French
: relating to brown algae

detraque
\dāˌträˈkā\
French
: mental, psychopathic

dewindtite
\dəˈwintˌīt\
French
: basic phosphate

dhimmi
\dimē\
Arabic
: resident of land conquered by Muslims to retain faith

diallagic
\dīəˈlajik\
Greek>French
: of bronze igneous rocks

dialleli
\dīəˈlēˌlī\
Greek
: reasoning of circles

diapedetic
\dīəpəˈdedək\
Latin
: characterizing the loss of blood in capillary walls

dicyemid
\dīˌsīˈēməd\
Latin
: one of the minute parasites

didymolite
\didəməˌlīt\
Latin
: calcium silicate

dietzeite
\dētsəˌīt\
German
: yellow mineral

diffarreation
\difarēˈāshən\
Latin
: Roman ceremony

difflugia
\dəflüjēə\
Latin
: protozoan

dinanderie
\dəˈnandərē, ˌdēˌnanˈdrē\
French
: decorative bronze

Diodorean
\dīəˈdōrēən\
Greek
: of a philosopher who contributed much logical skills

dioscorea
\dīəˈskōrēə\
Greek>Latin
: dried rhizome roots

doitrified
\dȯitrəˌfēt\
Scottish
: dazed, stunned

domeykite
\dōˈmāˌkīt\
German
: mineral of steel color

donnees
\dȯ¦nā(z)\
French
: main assumptions of works

doodskop
\dütˌskäp\
Afrikaans
: shallow water fish

doornboom
\dȯrnˌbüm\
Afrikaans
: thorny shrub

dossennuses
\dəˈsenəsəz\
Latin
: Roman stock characters

dothideaceous
\dō¦thidēˈāshəs\
Greek>Latin
: of parasitic fungi

doucepere
\düs(ə)ˌpi(ə)r\
French
: illustrious noble

dragee
\dra¦zhā\
French
: sugar-coated confection

dreddour
\dredər\
Scottish
: terror, danger

drosera
\dräsərə\
Latin
: air dried-flowering plant

dryinid
\drīənəd\
Latin
: parasitic wasp

dufrenoysite
\d(y)üfrəˈnȯiˌzīt\
French
: lead-gray mineral

dukhn
\dükən\
Arabic
: tall cereal grass

dumortierite
\d(y)üˈmȯrtēəˌrīt,
d(y)ümȯrtirīt\
French
: blue mineral

durchkomponiert
\dúrk̲ˌkȯmpō¦ni(ə)rt\
German
: individual music setting

Durkheimian
\d(y)úr¦kemēən\
French
: of a sociological theory

dussertite
\dəsə(r)ˌtīt\
French
: mineral of iron

Dynel
\dī¦nel\
Trademark
: yarn or fiber fabric

dynorphin
\dīˈnȯrfən\
Greek
: group of potent peptides

dyschezic
\dəskēzik\
Latin
: associated with constipation

dysodile
\disəˌdīl\
Greek>French
: hydrocarbon mineral

dyvour
\dīvər\
English
: man in debt, bankrupt

ebauchoir
\ābōsh¦wär\
French
: chisel used for sculpting

ebenaceous
\ebəˈnāshəs\
Latin
: comprising of shrubs

eccrinid
\ekrənəd\
Latin
: fungus

echeneid
\ekəˈnāəd\
Latin
: broad fish

echimyine
\əˈkimēˌīn\
Latin
: relating to rodents

ecorche
\āˌkȯr¦shā\
French
: anatomical figure showing muscles and bones

Ediacaran
\ēdē'ak(ə)rən\
Latin
: of marine cellular organisms

edriophthalmian
\edrē͵äf'thalmēən\
Latin
: crustacean with large eyes

egeran
\āgərən\
German
: brown calcium deposit

ehretia
\e'rēsh(ē)ə\
Latin
: subtropical shrub with white
flowers and fleshy fruits

eide
\ī͵dē, 'ā͵dā\
Greek
: things which have been seen

eikonometer
\īkə'nämətə(r)\
Greek
: instrument for measuring
optical conjunction

ekhimi
\e'kēmē\
African name
: hardened wood

ektexine
\ektek͵sēn\
Latin>German
: outer layer of spore wall

elaeagnaceous
\elē¦ag¦nāshəs\
Latin
: relating to trees with silver
foliage and fruits

elaeoblastic
\ə'lēə͵blastik\
Latin
: of outgrowths in embryos

elaeodochon
\elē'ädə͵kän\
Latin
: oil gland

elaioplast
\ə'līə͵plast\
Greek
: colorless plant tissue
secreting oil

elaphurine
\elə¦fyù͵rīn\
Greek
: relating to large deer

eledoisin
\elə'dòisᵊn\
Latin
: small salivary protein

elegit
\ə'lējət, ā'lāgət\
Latin
: judicial writ

eleidin
\ə'lēədən\
French
: substance resembling
keratin

eleotrid
\elē¦ōtrəd\
Latin
: large fish

eleusine
\elyü'sīnē\
Latin
: grasses with spikes

Elkesaite
\elkə͵sīt; ͵elkə'sā͵īt\
fictional name
: member of sect with magic

elleck
\elik\
Unknown
: Australian fish

Elzevir
\elzə͵vi(ə)r\
Dutch
: relating to Testament books

emberizine
\embə'rēzən, embə'rīzīn\
German
: of numerous typical finches

embiotocid
\embē'ätəsəd; emb-ēə'täsəd\
Latin
: a fish laying live eggs

emboitement
\äⁿbwàtmäⁿ\
French
: enclosure of a living germ

emeute
\āmœœt\
French
: outbreak of violence

encastre
\äⁿkàstrā\
French
: built in at the supports

encephalocoele
\ensefələsēl\
Latin
: ventricles of brain

endellionite
\en'delyə͵nīt\
German
: lead mineral

ensete
\en(t)sət\
Amharic
: perennial plant with fruits

entomophthorous
\entəmäfthərəs\
Latin
: caused by fungi

eolation
\ēəˈlāshən\
Greek
: action of wind on surfaces

eolienne
\āˌōlēˈen\
French
: lightweight dress

eosuchian
\ēōˈsükēən\
Greek
: relating to primitive extinct snakes and lizards

epacridaceous
\epəkrəˈdāshəs\
Latin
: of small trees and woody vines with scales

epeirogeneses
\əˌpīrōjenəsēs\
Latin + Greek
: deformations in Earth's crust like oceans and mountains

eperythrozoonosis
\eperithrəzōəˈnōsəs\
Latin
: infectious parasitic disease

epimeletae
\epəˈməˈlēˌtē\
Greek
: civil or religious officials

epingle
\āˈpaŋˌglā\
French
: silk, rayon, or fabric

episcotister
\epəskōˈtistə(r)\
Greek
: device measuring intensity

equisetaceous
\ekwəsəˈtāsēˌē əs\
Latin
: relating to existing flora

erechtites
\erəkˈtītēz\
Greek>Latin
: herb with silky flowers

erigeron
\əˈrijərən\
Latin
: plant used as a diuretic

erzahler
\ertˈsälər\
German
: organ pipe

escallonia
\eskəˈlōnēə\
Latin
: plant with glossy leaves

eschscholtzia
\eˈshōltsēə\
German
: yellow-flowered plant

espiegle
\espyegl(ə)\
German>French
: playful, sportive

esplees
\əˈsplēz\
French
: profits of land

essenhout
\esᵊnˌhaùt, esᵊn-hōt\
Afrikaans
: South African tree

étagère
\āˌtäˈzhe(ə)r\
French
: cabinet of shelves

ethamivan
\eˈthaməˌvan, ˌethəˈmīvən\
ISV
: nervous system stimulant

ethosuximide
\ethōˈseksəˌmīd\
ISV
: anticonvulsant drug

etidronate
\ētəˈdrōˌnāt\
ISV
: disodium salt

etouffee
\ātüˈfā\
French
: Cajun stew cooked over rice

euchologia
\efk̲ȯˈlȯyä\
Greek
: principal service books

eudalene
\yüdᵊlˌēn\
ISV
: liquid hydrocarbon

euphroe
\yüˌfrō\
Dutch
: black slat of wood

Eupolidean
\yüˌpäləˌdēən\
Greek
: characteristic rhyming meter used in poetry

Euroclydon
\yəˈräkləˌdän\
Greek
: cold Mediterranean wind

Eutychian
\yüˌtikēən\
Greek
: believer that Christ is within the human body

exequatur
\eksəˈkwātə(r)\
Latin
: written official recognition of an honor or deed

exereses
\ekˈserəsēs\
Greek
: surgical removals of organs

exomologeses
\eksəˌmäləˈjēsēz\
Latin
: public confessions of sins

exuviae
\igˈzüvēˌē\
Latin
: natural coverings of animals

Fabrikoid
\fabrəˌkȯid\
Trademark
: imitation leather

Factice
\faktəs\
Trademark
: rubber substitute

fahlunite
\fäləˌnīt\
Swedish
: altered mineral

famatinite
\faməˈtēˌnīt\
German
: grayish copper

Fammenian
\fəˈmēnēən\
Belgian geographical name
: relating to the European Devonian time period

fardel
\färdᵊl\
Arabic>French
: bundle of silk

farnesol
\färnəˌs|ȯl\
ISV
: liquid alcohol

fascioloid
\fəˈsēəlȯid\
Latin
: resembling worms

faubourg
\fōbüür, fōˌbu̇rg\
French
: suburb of a city

faujasite
\fōzhəˌsīt\
French
: colorless mineral of calcium

fauxbourdon
\fōbə(r)dōⁿ\
French
: 15th century harmonic progressions of chords

Faverolle
\favərōl\
French
: breed of purpose fowls

fedayeen
\fədayēn\
Arabic
: member of commando group

felibres
\fāˈlēbrə(z)\
French
: member of literary association of Provencal authors

fellagha
\fəˈlägə\
Arabic
: Muslim guerrilla band

ferredoxin
\ferəˈdäksən\
Latin
: group of plant proteins

ferrocene
\ferəˌsēn\
ISV
: crystalline compound

Fescennine
\fesᵊnˌīn\
Latin
: read at a rural festival (adj.)

Feuerbachian
\fȯiə(r)ˌbäk̲ēən\
German
: of a sensational theory

Feulgen
\fȯilgən\
German
: uitilizing the Schiff agent

ficary
\fikərē\
Latin
: herb

fiedlerite
\fēdləˌrīt\
German
: hydroxychloride mineral

165

filicin
\filəsən\
Latin>ISV
: mixture of active principles obtained from fern chemicals

filipins
\filəpənz\
Latin
: antifungal antibiotics

filixmas
\fīlik'smas, ¦fīlik'smäs\
Latin
: male fern

fiorin
\fīərən\
IrishGaelic
: various lawn grass

fioriture
\fē͵ōrə'túrā\
Italian
: embellishing notes in a musical composition

fizelyite
\fə'zālē͵īt\
Hungarian
: mineral of lead silver

flacourtiaceous
\flə'kúrtē āshəs\
Latin
: of tropical trees and flowers

flajolotite
\flajə'lō͵tīt\
French
: mineral of iron

flanken
\flaŋkən, fläŋkən\
Yiddish
: steak boiled with vegetables

flauchtbred
\flak̲tbred\
Scottish
: with limbs outstretched

flavianate
\flāvēə͵nāt\
ISV
: salty acid

Flaxedil
\flaksə͵dil\
Trademark
: mixture of ammonium salts

fleurdelise
\flərdᵊl¦ēz ā\
French
: ornamented with royal emblems in the time of the king's reign

florencee
\flòrən¦sā, flə'ren(t)sē\
French
: with seeded or flowered stem

fluellite
\flüə͵līt\
ISV
: mineral of aluminum

flyting
\flītiŋ\
Scottish
: dispute among poets

foehnlike
\fœœnlīk, fərnlīk\
German
: having the characteristics of a warm dry wind

Folsom
\fōlsəm\
American geographical name
: of the prehistoric culture in the Rocky Mountains

forritsome
\fòrətsəm\
Scottish
: bold, impudent

foscarnet
\fäs'kärnət\
ISV
: hydrated salt

Foucauldian
\fü'kōdēən\
Frenhc
: characteristic of philosophy

fourmarierite
\für'marēə͵rīt\
French
: mineral of hydrous oxide

frailejones
\fräēlā'hōn ās\
Spanish
: desert-growing plants

fraischeur
\frāshər\
French
: coolness, freshness

frankenthal
\fraŋkən͵thòl, 'fräŋkən͵täl\
German
: porcelain

Fraticelli
\fratə'chelē\
Italian
: band of seceders

fraxetin
\fraksətən\
ISV
: yellow crystalline compound

Fregean
\frāgēən\
German
: of the foundations in math

freirinite
\frā'rē͵nīt\
Chilean geographical name
: mineral of sodium and copper

friedelin
\frē'delən\
German
: crystalline ketone

Froebelian
\frā¦bēlēən\
German
: derived from the system of education for kindergarten

frohbergite
\frō͵bər͵gīt\
German
: mineral containing iron

frottage
\frȯ'täzh\
French
: artistic process of drawing

frottole
\frȯtᵊlā , frȯttōlā\
Italian
: secular part-songs (pl.)

fubsy
\fübsi\
English
: chubby and somewhat bent

fucalean
\fyü¦kālēən\
Latin
: of brown algae

fuidhir
\fwi͵thi(ə)r\
Irish
: stranger or refugee

fumagillin
\fyümə'jilən\
Latin>ISV
: crystalline antibiotic

furazolidine
\fyu̇rə'zälə͵dōn\
ISV
: antimicrobial drug

furfurylidene
\fərf(y)ə'rilə͵dēn\
ISV
: bivalent radical

furison
\fyu̇rəsən\
German
: iron for striking flint

furphies
\fərfēz\
Australian geographical name
: false reports, rumors (pl.)

furzechat
\fərzchat\
English
: small European bird

fusarole
\fyüzə͵rōl\
French
: rounded frieze of a column

fustet
\fə¦stet\
French
: smoke tree, shrubby plant

fusulinid
\fyüzə'līnəd\
Latin
: index fossil

Gabar
\gäbər\
Persian
: Zoroastrian of Iran

gaberlunzie
\gabər'lənzi\
Scottish
: beggar, mendicant

gaedown
\gädün\
Scottish
: drinking bout

Gaeltacht
\gā(ə)ltək̲t\
Irish
: the state of being Gaelic

galatea
\galə'tēə\
English
: striped-cotton cloth

galegine
\gə'lējən\
ISV
: crystalline base

galesaur
\galə͵sȯ(ə)r\
Latin
: reptile

galet
\gālət\
Greek
: small carnivorous mammal

galinsoga
\galən'sōgə\
Latin
: small tropical herb

galiongee
\galyənjē\
Turkish
: sailor

gamelote
\gamə'lōtē\
Spanish
: any of several grasses

gammelost
\gamə͵lȯst\
Norwegian
: blue-mold cheese

ganciclovir
\gan'sīkləvir\
ISV
: antiviral drug for treatment
of kidney inflammation

ganomalite
\gə'nämə‚līt\
Swedish
: tetragonal mineral

Gantrisin
\gantrəsən\
Trademark
: drug derivative

gardinol
\gärdᵊn‚ȯl\
Trademark
: laundry detergent

gargouillade
\gärgü¦yäd\
French
: catlike forward leap in
ballet

garrots
\garō(z)\
French (pl.)
: swift-flying diving ducks

garsil
\gärsəl\
Scandinavian origin
: shrubs growing under the
larger trees of the forest

gastraeal
\ga¦strēəl\
Latin
: relating to eukaryotic-celled
organisms in an ecosystem

gauffrage
\gȯfrij, gȯ¦fräzh\
French
: ornamentation with frilly
patterns and designs

gaultherin
\gȯlthərən\
ISV
: crystalline glycoside

gawney
\gȯni\
Unknown
: simpleton, imbecile

gaylussite
\gālə‚sīt\
French
: hydrous carbonate

gazania
\gə'zānēə\
Latin
: plant with brilliant red and
yellow flower heads

gearksutite
\jē'ärksə‚tīt\
Greenland name
: hydrous calcium

gedecktwork
\gə'dektwərk\
German
: stops in a pipe organ
covered with tubes

geebung
\jē‚bəŋ\
Australian name
: shrubs and small trees

gegenstandstheorie
\gāgənshtäntstāōrē\
German
: theory of existing objects

geikielite
\gēkē‚līt\
Scottish
: sedimentary black rock

geilsiekte
\gāl‚sēktə\
Afrikaans
: sheep poisoning

geison
\gā‚sän\
Greek
: typical mold of crown

gelechiid
\jə'lekēəd\
Latin
: moth with slender wings

gemara
\gə'märə\
Aramaic
: rabbinic commentary on the
Holy Scriptures

gemauve
\gə'mōv\
French
: tropical herb with flowers

gemeinden
\gə'mīndən\
German (pl.)
: units of police departments

gemfibrozil
\jem'fībrəzil\
Unknown
: drug that regulates blood
serum lipids to lower levels
of triglycerides in the body

gender
\jende(ə)r\
Javanese
: xylopohone-like instrument

geocronite
\jē'äkrə‚nīt\
Greek
: mineral of gray lead

gephyrocercies
\jefərō¦sərsēz\
Greek (pl.)
: states of having dorsal fins

gerhardtite
\ger͵härt͵īt\
French
: emerald mineral

gerrhonotine
\jerə͵nō͵tīn\
Latin
: of slow-moving lizards

gersdorffite
\gerz͵dȯr͵fīt\
German
: mineral of gray nickel

gerzean
\gerzēən\
Egyptian geographical name
: of the culture stressing
importance on technology

Gesamtkunstwerk
\gəˈzämt͵kúnst͵verk\
German
: art work produced in many
forms such as music or drama

gesithcundmen
\yeˈsēthkúndmən\
German>English
: men serving for the Anglo-
Saxon king

geylies
\gəilēz\
Scottish
: tolerably well, very much

gezerah
\gə͵zāˈrä, gzā͵rä\
Hebrew
: temporary rabbinical decree

ghaffir
\gaˈfi(ə)r\
Arabic
: native guard or watchmen

Ghassulian
\gaˈsülēən\
Jordanian geographical name
: of the Palestinian culture

ghorkhar
\gȯr͵kär\
Persian
: donkey of Northwestern
India

gillar
\gə̇ˈlär\
Indian name
: disease of Eastern sheep

gilgulim
\gilˈgúləm\
Hebrew
: evil spirits of the dead

ginkgoaceous
\giŋkōāshəs\
Latin
: of certain extinct pink plants

Giorgionesque
\jȯrjōˈnesk\
Italian
: resembling the paintings

glycureses
\glikyəˈrēsēs\
Latin
: excretions of large amounts
of sugar in urine

glycyrrhizin
\glisəˈrīzᵊn\
ISV
: crystalline acid

glyphosate
\glifə͵sāt\
ISV
: nonselective herbicide

gmelinite
\gəˈmelənīt\
German
: colorless mineral

gnetalean
\nətālēən\
Latin
: relating to woody
dicotyledonous plants

gobiesocid
\gōˈbīəˈsäsəd\
Latin
: marine fish with dorsal fins

gobonated
\gäbə͵nātəd\
French
: divided into segments
depending on the curve

Gomorrah
\gəˈmȯrə\
Biblical name
: place known for corruption

gonocoxite
\gänəˈkäk͵sīt\
Latin
: inner segment of an organ

gorceixite
\gȯ(r)sə̇k͵sīt\
German
: mineral of hydrous
aluminum

Gorsedd
\gȯr͵se<u>th</u>\
Welsh
: mock institution

grasseyement
\gra͵säˈmäⁿ\
French
: voiceless pronunciation

grattage
\graˈtäzh, grətäzh\
French
: removal by scraping

graysbies
\grāzbēz\
Unknown
: tropical Atlantic fish (pl.)

greenalite
\grēnᵊlˌīt\
ISV
: ferrous silicate

greenwithe
\grēnwith\
English
: climbing orchid

grieshoch
\grēshək̲\
ScottishGaelic
: bed of the smoldering ashes
in a fire

grihastha
\gərˈhəstə\
Sanskrit
: second stage of ascetic's life

grimmiaceous
\grimēⵌāshəs\
Latin
: relating to mosses with
stalks

gringolee
\griŋgəⵌlā\
French
: pair of serpent heads at the
end of both arms outstretched

gristbite
\grizbət\
English
: to gnash with the teeth

Groenendael
\grünənˌdäl\
Belgian name
: black-coated sheepdog

grognard
\grōⵌnyär\
French
: old soldier

gruenlingite
\grünliŋˌīt\
German
: mineral of bismuth

gruppetti
\grüˈpetē\
Italian
: musical ornamentations (pl.)

gryphaeoid
\grifēˌȯid\
Latin
: pertaining to fossil mollusks

guachipilin
\gwächəpəⵌlēn\
Spanish
: Central American timber
tree

guadalcazarite
\gwädᵊlˈkazəˌrīt\
German
: mineral consisting of zinc

guaiacum
\g(w)īəkəm\
Spanish
: hard green brown wood
resin

guanajuatite
\gwänəˈ(h)uäˌtīt\
Mexican geographical name
: mineral of blue gray crystals

guanethidine
\gwäˈnethəˌdēn\
ISV
: synthetic derivative

Guesdism
\geˌdizəm\
French
: Marxian socialism

guidwillie
\gœˈdwili\
Scottish
: generous, cheering

gurdwara
\gùrˈdwärə\
Sanskrit + Panjabi
: Sikh shrine

gymnolaematous
\jimnəlēmətəs\
Latin
: of extinct aquatic animals

gympies
\gimpēz\
Australian geographical name
: nettle trees with silver
foliage

gynaeconitis
\jȧnəkōnīdəs\
Greek
: nave of Orthodox church

gyroceran
\jīˈräsərən\
Latin
: of fossil nautiloids

haboob
\həˈbüb\
Arabic
: violent dust storm

haematoxylon
\hēməˈtäksəˌlän\
Latin
: wood or dye of log

haemodoraceous
\hēmōdəˈräsēˌēəs\
Greek
: of tropical plants

haeremai
\hääˌräˈmäē, ˈhäərəˌmī\
Maori
: used to express welcome

Haiathalah
\hīə'tälə\
Hebrew
: a White Hun

haloperidol
\halō'perə͵dȯl\
ISV
: depressant of nervous
system

hashkabah
\häsh'käbə\
Hebrew
: recital of memorial prayer

hauberget
\hȯbə(r)¦jet\
Latin
: early woolen cloth

Haviland
\havələnd\
French
: porcelain ware

havlagah
\hävlə'gä\
Hebrew
: self-control

Hearstling
\hərstliŋ\
English
: reactionary journalist

heemraden
\hām͵räd°n\
Afrikaans (pl.)
: councils of South Africa
(singular spelled heemraad)

hegari
\hə'garē, hegərē\
Arabic
: any of grain sorghums

Heian
\heē'än\
Japanese
: rf the period of history
from 8ᵗʰ to 12ᵗʰ centuries

Heideggerian
\hī͵de¦girēən\
German
: of the existential philosophy

helenalin
\helə'nalən\
Latin
: poisonous compound

helichrysum
\helə'krīsəm\
Greek
: plant with flower heads

helonias
\hə'lōnēəs\
Latin
: dried rhizome roots

hemiepe
\hemēepē\
Greek
: meter of third foot

Hennebique
\henə¦bēk\
Frenhc
: of or relating to concrete
reinforced with steel or iron

hercynite
\hərs°n͵īt\
German
: black iron mineral

Heroult
\ā¦rü\
Trademark
: radiated arc furnace

herschelite
\hərshə͵līt\
German
: glassy crystal

hesperinos
\hespərə¦näs\
Greek
: Eastern Church office

hetaerolite
\hə'tirə͵līt\
Greek
: zincky mineral

heterozeteses
\hetərōzē'tēs ēz\
Greek
: logical fallacies

hexenbesen
\heksən͵bāz°n\
German
: witch's broom

Hillelite
\hi͵le͵līt\
Hebrew
: follower of a rabbi

hiortdahlite
\yȯ(r)t͵dä͵līt\
Norwegian
: rare mineral

Hjelmslevian
\hyelmz¦levēən,
hyeúmz¦levēən\
Danish
: of linguistic methods

hoernesite
\hərnə͵sīt\
German
: hydrous mineral

Hohenzollern
\hōənzälərn\
German
: princely family sovereign

Holmquistite
\hōm͵kwi͵stīt\
Persian>Swedish
: alkaline mineral

homoeomerous
\hōmē¦ämərəs\
Latin
: relating to algal cells

homoiousian
\hō͵mȯi¦üzēən\
Greek
: similar but not identical

homoscedasticity
\hōmōs(k)ə¦dastisidē\
Latin
: equality in standard
deviations or averages

Honiton
\hänət°n\
English
: various laces

hooley
\hülē\
Unknown
: Irish drinking party

hoolock
\hü͵läk\
Burmese name
: small gibbon

hordeola
\hȯ(r)ˈdēələ\
Latin
: inflamed swellings

hortonolite
\hȯ(r)ˈtän°l͵īt\
American name
: silicate mineral

houppelande
\hüpländ\
French
: loose belted gown

hubbellite
\həbə͵līt\
Trademark
: copper cement

huhnerkobelite
\h(y)ünə(r)¦kōbə͵līt\
German
: sodium mineral

huiscoyol
\wēskə¦yȯl\
Nahuatl
: shrubby palm

Hyblaean
\hī¦blēən\
Greek
: mellifluous, honeyed

hydatidocele
\hīdəˈtidə͵sēl\
Latin
: tumorous condition

hydroxylysine
\hī¦dräksəlī͵sēn\
ISV
: amino acid

hyoscyamus
\hīəsīəməs\
Latin
: dried leaves

hyporhined
\hīpərīnd\
Latin
: having small nostrils

iambelegus
\ī͵amˈbeləgəs\
Greek
: classical prosody verse

ibogaine
\əˈbōgə͵ēn\
ISV
: crystalline alkaloid

ichthammol
\ikˈtha͵mȯl\
ISV
: black viscous liquid

idiozome
\idēə͵zōm\
Greek>ISV
: cap-like prolongation

idrialite
\ˈidrēə͵līt\
French
: hydrocarbon mineral

ihleite
\ēlə͵īt\
German
: basic iron mineral

illuminagraphic
\əˈlümə͵nəgrafik\
Latin
: designed for photography

ilmenorutile
\ilmənōrü͵tēl\
German
: black trimorphous mineral

ilsemannite
\il(t)səmə͵nīt\
German
: black-blue mineral

imaret
\əˈmärət\
Arabic>Turkish
: inn or hospice

imerinite
\iməˈrē͵nīt\
French
: blue crystal

indinavir
\inˈdinəvir\
ISV
: protease inhibitor

indophenin
\indəˈfēnən, ənˈdäfənən\
ISV
: blue crystalline compound

inesite
\īnəˌsīt\
Greek>German
: pale red mineral

ingerences
\injərən(t)səz, aⁿzhārääⁿs\
French
: intrusions, invasions (pl.)

iniomous
\inēˈōˌm əs\
Latin
: of fish lacking spines

injera
\inˈjerə\
Amharic
: flat spongy bread

inspeximus
\ənzˈpeksəməs\
Latin
: letter patent

intercolline
\intə(r)ˌkälən\
Latin
: situated between hills

iproniazid
\īprəˈnīəzəd\
Latin
: derivative of oxide

iresine
\īrəˈsīnē\
Greek>Latin
: tropical leaved herb

ischiocerite
\iskēˈäsəˌrīt\
Greek
: antenna of a crustacean

isotretinoin
\īsōˈtretəˌnȯin\
ISV
: synthetic derivative of
vitamin A in fatty glands

ithagine
\ithəˌjīn\
Latin
: remarkable red-colored
pheasant of the Himalayas

jacinthe
\jāsən(t)th\
French
: moderate orange color

jaguey
\häˈgwā\
Spanish
: East Indian tree

jarool
\jəˈrül\
Hindi
: deciduous tree

jaulingite
\yaùliŋˌīt\
German
: fossil resin

jelerang
\jeləˌraŋ\
Unknown
: giant squirrel

jelick
\yelik\
Turkish
: vest of a dress

jezail
\jəˈzī(ə)l\
Persian
: heavy Afghan rifle

jindyworobak
\jindēˈwȯrəˌbak\
Australian name
: idea promoters

juamave
\(h)wəˈmävē\
Mexican geographical name
: high-grade fiber

Jugurthine
\jüˈgərthən\
Latin
: pertaining to the king of
Numidia or their reign

Jumnapari
\jəmnəˈpärē\
Hindi
: breed of milking goats

juramentado
\hùrəmənˈtädō\
Spanish
: Muslim who swore by oath
to kill Christians

juvabione
\jüvəˈbīˌōn\
Latin
: substance isolated from firs

jyngine
\jinˌjīn, jinjən\
Latin
: relating to woodpeckers

kabbalah
\kəˈbälə\
Hebrew
: rabbinic written certificate

Kabirpanthi
\kəˌbirˈpənˌtē\
Hindi
: member of a reform sect

kabukalli
\kabəˈkalē\
British Guianese name
: tropical tree

kainosite
\kīnəˌsīt\
Swedish
: hydrous silicate

kalimba
\kəˈlimbə\
Bantu
: African thumb piano

kaliophilite
\kalē'äfə͟ˌlīt\
German
: colorless mineral

kallikrein
\kalə'krēən\
Greek>German
: protease from blood plasma

kamacite
\kamə͟ˌsīt\
Greek>German
: ferrous mineral

kammererite
\kemərə͟ˌrīt\
Swedish
: iron mineral

karatas
\karə͟ˌtas\
Latin
: tropical plant

katonkel
\kə'täŋkəl\
Afrikaans
: large game fish

Khaksar
\käk¦sär\
Persian>Hindi
: member of militant Muslim
nationalist movement

kharif
\kə'rēf\
Hindi
: of the autumn season

Kharijite
\kärə͟ˌjīt\
Arabic
: member of secessionist sect
(plural spelled Khawarij)

kiaugh
\kyȧk̲\
ScottishGaelic
: trouble, anxiety

Kidderminster
\kidə(r)͟ˌminztə(r)\
English
: Scotch carpet

kiddushin
\kidu̇shə͟n\
Aramaic
: betrothal ceremony

kikumon
\kikə͟ˌmän\
Japanese
: chrysanthemum flower

Kirsebaer
\kirsə͟ˌba(a)(ə)r\
Danish
: cherry liqueur

kiskadee
\kiskədē\
Imitative
: large insectivorous bird

klebelsbergite
\klabəlz͟ˌbər͟ˌgīt\
Hungarian name
: sulfate mineral

klebsiella
\klebzē'elə\
German
: rod-shaped bacteria

kleeneboc
\klīn(ə)͟ˌbäk, klān(ə)͟ˌbäk\
Afrikaans
: tiny western antelope

kliphaas
\klip͟ˌhäs\
Afrikaans
: small reddish hare

klismos
\kliz͟ˌmäs\
Greek
: chair with curved legs

klockmannite
\kläkmə͟ˌnīt\
German
: copper mineral

Klydonograph
\klī'dänə͟ˌgraf\
Trademark
: photographic record

knebelite
\nābə͟ˌlīt\
German
: variously colored mineral

knemidokoptic
\nēmədō'käptik\
Greek
: relating to itch mites

knez
\kə'nez\
Slavic
: prince or duke

kniphofia
\nip'hōfēə\
German>Latin
: showy African herb

koechlinite
\keklə͟ˌnīt\
Austrian
: bismuth mineral

koelreuteria
\kel͟ˌrȯi'tirēə\
German
: Asiatic tree with fruits

kokanee
\kō'kanē\
British Columbian name
: small salmon

kolkhoznik
\kəl'kȯznik\
Russian
: member of collective farm

kolkwitzia
\kōl'kwitsēə\
German
: Chinese shrub

kollergang
\kälə(r)ˌgaŋ\
German
: heavy machine

krameriaceous
\krə'mirē āshəs\
German
: of the dried roots of plants

kraseis
\kräsēs\
Greek
: chalices of wine

kromogram
\krōməˌgram\
Latin
: photographic positives

kuphar
\küfə(r)\
Arabic
: round boat

kurtorachic
\kərtəˌrakik\
Greek
: having or relating to a
concave lumbar region

Kutani
\kü'tänē\
Japanese
: highly decorated and
colored porcelain on Honshu

Kuvaszok
\kùväˌsók\
Hungarian
: white dog breed

laagte
\läk̲tə\
Afrikaans
: low-lying valley

laboulbeniaceous
\ləˌbül'bēnēāshəs\
Latin
: relating to minute fungi

lachenalia
\lashə'nālēə\
Latin
: plant with yellow flowers

lacroixite
\lə'krwäˌzīt\
French
: phosphate mineral

laetrile
\lāəˌtril\
ISV
: drug derived from apiroct
pits to treat cancer

laitance
\lātᵊn(t)s\
French
: accumulation of fine
particles

lamantin
\lə'mantᵊn\
French
: sea cow

landsmanshaften
\läntsmənˌshäftən\
German
: Jewish charity associations

landvogt
\läntˌfōkt\
German
: governor of royal province

langooty
\ləŋ'gütē\
Hindi
: piece of hanging cloth

Laplacian
\lə'pläsēən\
French
: differential operator

lardizabalaceous
\lärdəˌzabə'lāshəs\
Latin
: relating to woody vines

larvaevorid
\lär'vēvərəd\
Latin
: 2-winged fly

latakia
\latə'kēə\
Syrian geographical name
: superior aromatic tobacco

Lauegram
\laùəˌgram\
German
: photographic record

launeddas
\laù'nedəs\
Italian
: Sardinian triple clarinet

laurinoxylon
\lòrə'näksəˌlän\
Latin
: fossil wood

laurustine
\lòrəˌstīn\
Latin
: European shrub

lavaret
\lavəret\
French
: European whitefish

lechatelierite
\ləˌshätᵊl'iˌrīt\
French
: vitreous mineral

lechriodont
\lekrēōˌdänt\
Greek
: having palatial teeth

lelwel
\lel‚wel\
Unknown
: Sudanese antelope

leodicid
\lē'ädəsid\
Latin
: large worm

lernaeiform
\lər'nēəfȯ(ə)rm\
Latin
: relating to the shape of
parasitic crustaceans

leskeaceous
\leskē'āshəs\
Latin
: of tree-growing mosses

letovicite
\letə'vi‚sīt\
German
: acid mineral

leuconostoc
\lükənä‚stäk\
Latin
: flesh-dwelling bacteria

leucosticte
\lükəstiktē\
Latin
: rosy finch

leucoxene
\lü'käk‚sēn\
German
: rocky mineral

leukocytolysin
\lükə‚sī¦tæləsən, lükə‚sīt°līs°n\
ISV
: special antibody

leukoplakia
\lükō'plākēə\
Latin
: condition of thickened
sclera

levallorphan
\levə'lȯr‚fan\
ISV
: morphine poisoning

liatris
\lī'atrəs\
Latin
: purple herb

licareol
\lə'ka(a)rē‚ȯl\
ISV
: fragrant liquid

limacon
\lēmə'sōⁿ, 'limə‚sän\
French
: plane curve

limnephilid
\lim¦nefələd\
Latin
: pond-dwelling insect

lioncel
\līən‚sel\
French
: heraldic representation

liskeardite
\li'skär‚dīt\
English geographical name
: basic hydrous mineral

litholapaxy
\li'thälə‚paksē\
Greek
: operation of removing
kidney stones in the bladder

livraison
\lēvrā¦zōⁿ\
French
: division of a book

llautu
\laůtü\
Quechua
: cord of vicuna wool

loasaceous
\lōə'sāshəs\
Latin
: of bristly haired plants

longifolene
\länjə'fō‚lēn\
ISV
: liquid hydrocarbon

lophosteon
\lə'fästē‚än\
Latin
: bird's sternum
(plural spelled lophostea)

lophophorate
\lōfə'fō(ə)rət\
Latin
: invertebrate animal

loriot
\lȯrēət, lȯr-ē‚ō\
French
: golden bird of Europe

loutrophoroi
\lü'träfə‚rȯi\
Greek
: drinking vessels

lovozerite
\lō'väzə‚rīt\
Russian
: mineral of zirconium

loxodograph
\läk'sädə‚graf\
Greek
: apparatus for measuring
ship's magnetism

lupetidine
\lü'petə‚dēn\
ISV
: dimethyl derivative

lycaenid
\lī'sēnəd\
Greek>Latin
: slender butterfly

lymantriid
\līˈmantrēəd\
Latin
: typical moth

lynnhaven
\linˈhāvən\
American geographical name
: large oyster

lysigenous
\līˌsijənəs\
Greek
: made by cells wearing down

lyssacine
\lisəˈsīn\
Latin
: relating to aquatic sponges

lyxoflavin
\liksəflāvən\
Latin
: yellow crystalline
compound

maarad
\mäˌrad\
Unknown
: long-staple cotton

maclurin
\məˈklùrən\
ISV
: crystalline pigment

macrozamia
\makrōˈzämēə\
Greek
: tree with large cones

magainin
\məˈgā(ə)nən\
Hebrew
: poisonous substance in
frogs

maggidim
\mäˈgēdəm\
Hebrew
: itinerant preachers

manchineel
\manchəˈnē(ə)l\
French
: poisonous tropical tree

mangeao
\män(g)āˈaù\
Maori
: timber tree

marcgraviaceous
\märkˈgrāvēāshəs\
Latin
: relating to tropical shrubs

Marshalsea
\märshəlsē\
English
: former court

martagon
\märtəgən\
Turkish
: widely cultivated lily

maskelynite
\maskələˌnīt\
German
: white meteorite

masoola
\məˈsülə\
Unknown
: boat made of planks

mazaedia
\məˈzēdēə\
Latin
: fruiting bodies

meclizine
\mekləˌzēn\
ISV
: drug to treat nausea

melassigenic
\məˌlasəˌjenik\
Latin
: of sugar crystallization

melilot
\meləˌlät\
Greek
: sweet clover

mellotron
\meləˌträn\
Trademark
: electronic keyboard

melolonthine
\meləˈlän(t)thən\
Latin
: of stout- bodied beetles

melologue
\meləˌlòg\
Latin
: vocal declamaiton

menaccanitic
\məˈnakəˌnitik\
Latin
: black mineral

menologion
\mēnəˈlòyòn\
Greek
: ecclesiastical calendar

mesalliances
\māˌzalˌyänsəz,
māzəˈlīən(t)səz\
French
: inferior marriages (pl.)

mesymnions
\məˈsimnēˌänz\
Greek
: short rhythmic series (pl.)

metaraminol
\metəˈraməˌnòl\
ISV
: drug to maintain or reduce
blood pressure

methapyrilene
\methəˈpirəˌlēn\
ISV
: sedative drug

methaqualone
\methə'kwālōn,
me'thakwəlōn\
ISV
: hypnotic drug

methylenimine
\methə̇¦lēnə‚mēn\
ISV
: hypothetical compound

metoclopramide
\metə'klōprə‚mīd\
ISV
: drug administered as a
chemical compound

meturgemans
\mə'tərgəmənz\
Hebrew + Aramaic
: synagogue officiants (pl.)

metyrapone
\mə'tirə‚pōn\
ISV
: hormone to test normality in
the pituitary gland

midrash
\mi‚dräsh\
Hebrew
: ancient Jewish narrative

mifepristone
\mifə'pris‚tōn\
ISV
: drug used during pregnancy

migniardise
\minyə(r)də̇s\
French
: delicate fondling

millefleurs
\mēl¦flər\
French
: flower extract perfume

minoxidil
\mi'näksə̇‚dil\
ISV
: peripheral widening of
white cells for treating
hypertension

mizzonite
\miz°n‚īt\
Greek>German
: silicate mineral

mlechchha
\mə'lechə\
Sanskrit
: foreigner, outcast

modioli
\mə'dīəlī\
Latin
: bony columns

mollienisia
\mälēə'nisēə\
Latin
: brightly colored fish

mollisol
\mälə‚säl\
Latin
: permanently frozen ground

montebrasite
\mäntē'brä‚zīt\
French
: phosphate alulminum

montmorillonitic
\mäntmə'rilə‚nitik\
French
: like a soft clayey mineral

moriche
\mə'rēchä\
Spanish
: palm tree

morphactin
\mȯr'faktə̇n\
ISV
: synthetic compound

morrhuate
\mȯ rə‚wāt\
Latin
: salty acid

moskeneering
\mäskə'niəing\
Yiddish
: overpaying

mottramite
\mätrə‚mīt\
English
: basic mineral

moutonnee
\müt°n¦ā\
French
: ice-sculptured hill

muhajirun
\mu̇‚häj ə'rün\
Arabic
: immigrants who left with
Muhammad the Prophet

mulloway
\mələ‚wā\
Unknown
: silvery fish

muraenoid
\myü'rēn ȯid\
Latin
: voracious eel

muscardine
\məskə(r)də̇n\
French
: fungus disease

mutsuddy
\müt¦sədi\
Hindi
: salesclerk

myelocoele
\miəlō‚sēl\
ISV
: central canal of spinal cord

myosotis
\mīəˈsōtəs\
Latin
: flowery plant

Nabal
\nābəl\
Biblical name
: churlish man, miser

naegelia
\nāˈgēlēə\
German
: perennial herb

nafcillin
\nafˌsilən\
ISV
: semisynthetic penicillin

nagmaal
\näk̲ˌmäl\
Afrikaans
: evening meal

nagor
\nāˌgȯ(ə)r\
French
: reddish brown antelope

nanninose
\nanəˌnōs\
Algonquian
: soft-shell clam

Naugahyde
\nȯgəˌhīd\
Trademark
: of vilnyl-coated fabrics

naujakasite
\naůyəkäsīt\
Greenland geographical name
: hydrous sodium and iron

navarins
\návȧraⁿ\
French
: stews with vegetables (pl.)
(singular spelled navarin)

neftgil
\neftˌgil\
German
: waxy mineral

nemestrinid
\neməˌstrīnəd\
Latin
: parasitic insect

neotocite
\nēˈätəˌsīt\
Greek>Swedish
: hydrous silicate

Nephilim
\nefəˌlim\
Hebrew
: biblical race of giants

nesquehonite
\neskwəˈhōˌnīt\
Pennsylvanian name
: prismatic crystal

nevyanskite
\nevˈyan(t)ˌskīt\
German
: iridium in white scales

niaouli
\nēˈaůlē\
New Caledonian name
: evergreen shrub

nickey
\nikē\
English
: fishing boat

nienock
\nēnək\
Unknown
: American lotus

nifedipine
\nīˈfedəˌpēn\
ISV
: calcium channel blocker

niggliite
\niglēˌīt\
Swiss
: platinum mineral

nigraniline
\nīˈgranᵊlən\
ISV
: basic compound

nispero
\nēspəˌrō\
Spanish
: American plant

nitinol
\nītᵊnˌȯl\
ISV
: alloy of titanium

nitriary
\nītrēˌerē\
French
: artificial bed

Njoroan
\nyəˈrōən\
Kenyan geographical name
: relating to polished stone

nocifensor
\nōsēfen(t)sə(r)\
Latin
: system of nerve fibers

nockerln
\näkər(ə)ln\
German
: light dumplings (pl.)
(singular spelled nockerl)

noematachograph
\nōˌēməˈtakəˌgraf\
Greek
: instrument measuring fast
reaction time

nontronite
\näntrəˌnīt\
French
: clay mineral

179

norethynodrel
\nȯrə'thīnō͵drel\
ISV
: progesterone derivative

noria
\nōrēə\
Arabic
: bucket wheel

norimon
\närə͵män\
Japanese
: covered litter

noselite
\nōzə͵līt\
German
: brownish mineral

notaulices
\nō'tȯlisēz\
Latin
: furrows of insects (pl.)
(singular spelled notaulix)

notoryctid
\nōtə'rik͵tid\
Latin
: marsupial mole

novobiocin
\nōvō'bīəsən\
Acronym
: acid antibiotic

nritta
\en'ritə\
Sanksrit
: abstract dance

nyctaginaceous
\niktəjə'nāshəs\
Latin
: of herbs with flowers

nycteribiid
\niktə¦ribēəd\
Latin
: bat fly

nymphaeaceous
\nim(p)fē'āshəs\
Latin
: of aquatic plants with fruit
and numerous petals

Nynorsk
\n(y)ü'nu̇(ə)rsk\
Norwegian
: literary form of grammar

Obbenite
\äbə͵nīt\
Dutch name
: member of Protestant sect

ochnaceous
\äk'nāshəs\
Latin
: relating to rare plants with
shiny leaves

ochratoxin
\ōkrətäksən\
Latin
: fungal poisoning

ocreate
\äkrēət\
Latin
: provided with stem sheaths

odylism
\äd°l͵izəm\
Latin
: theory believed that a
supernatural force resides in
human soul

oedemerid
\ēdə'mirəd\
Latin
: soft-bodied beetle

oestriases
\e'strīəsēs\
Greek
: botfly diseases (pl.)

oestroscope
\estrə͵skōp\
Latin
: device for gathering mucus

Ogdoad
\ägdō͵ad\
Greek
: seat of rule of 8 divine
beings

oikoplast
\ȯikə͵plast\
Greek
: cell secreting gelatinous
layers on the skin

Oklabar
\ōklə͵bär\
American geographical name
: tall domestic fowl

olethreutid
\ōlə¦thrütəd\
Latin
: small moth

onagraceous
\änə'grāshəs\
Latin
: of simple plants

oostegopod
\ō'ästəgō͵päd\
Latin
: modified thoracic leg

opilionine
\ō͵pilē'ōnīn\
Latin
: of harvesting arachnids

opisthorchiid
\äpəs¦thȯ(r)kēəd\
Latin
: parasitic trematode

oprichnik
\ä'prichnik\
Russian
: police official

opticoel
\äptə‚sēl\
Greek
: cavity of ocular vesicle

opuntioid
\ō'pənch(ē) öid\
Latin
: resembling a prickly pear

oquassa
\ō'kwäsə\
American geographical name
: lake trout

orabassu
\ōrə'bä‚sü\
Tupi
: South American monkey

orcinol
\örsənöl\
ISV
: crystalline phenol

oribatid
\ō'ribətəd, ōrə¦batid\
Latin
: eyeless mite

orpheons
\örfāōⁿz\
French
: male choral societies (pl.)

oryzenin
\örizənən\
Greek
: protein found in rice

ostariophysan
\ä‚sta(a)rēō'fīsᵊn\
Latin
: small-boned fish

ottavino
\ōtə'vēnō\
Italian
: small shrill flute

ottrelite
\ätrə‚līt\
Belgian
: black scaly mineral

outarde
\ü'tärd\
French
: Canada goose

overden
\ōvə(r)‚den\
German
: place where hay is kept

ovicystic
\ōvə‚sistik\
Latin
: pertaining to the pouch in
which eggs develop

oxalylurea
\äksə‚lilyü'rēə\
Latin
: nitrogenous acid

oxyntic
\äk¦sintik\
Greek
: secreting acid

paclitaxel
\pakli'taksəl\
ISV
: agent in Pacific yew tree

paedotribe
\pēdə‚trīb\
Greek
: gymnastics trainer

pajaroello
\pähərə'welō\
Unknown
: venomous tick

palaeoniscid
\pālēōnisəd, ¦palēōnisəd\
Latin
: extinct fish or fossil

palaetiological
\pə¦lētēə¦läjəkəl\
Latin
: relating to the explanation
of past events

paleencephalon
\pālē ən'sefə‚län\
Greek
: oldest part of brain

palissandre
\pal əsandər\
French
: handy fragrant shrub

Pallottine
\palə‚tīn\
Italian
: member to aid mission work
among young immigrants

palmary
\palmərē, pämərē\
Latin
: worthy of praise,
outstanding

palygorskite
\palə'gör‚skīt\
German
: hydrous silicate

Panathenaean
\pa‚nathə'nēən\
Greek
: of the festive activities
occurring in the Acropolis

Panionia
\panē¦ōnēə\
Greek
: matters discussed openly
(pl.)
(singular spelled Panionium)

Paraiyan
\pə'rī(y)ən\
Tamil
: relating to the lower caste

181

parareka
\parəˈrākə\
Maori
: potato fern

parashah
\pärəˌshä\
Hebrew
: weekly portions of lessons

parietes
\pəˈrīəˌtēz\
Slavic>Latin
: cavities in human organs

paroophoron
\parōˈäfəˌrän\
Latin
: broad ligament

parsettensite
\pärˈsetᵊnˌzīt\
German
: hydrous manganese

Parshall
\pärshəl\
American geographical name
: device for measuring flow

passewa
\pəˈsāwə\
Hindi
: viscous poppy extract

paukpan
\pȯkˌpan\
Burmese
: strong woody fiber

paulownia
\pȯˈlōnēə\
Latin
: tropical deciduous tree

paxillose
\paksəˌlōs\
Latin
: resembling a little stake

paysage
\pāsij, ˌpāēˈzäzh\
French
: landscape

pearceite
\pirˌsīt\
English
: silver mineral

pebrinous
\pebrənəs\
Provencal
: relating to a contagious
silkworm disease

pedocal
\pedəˌkal\
Latin
: hardened soil

pelecypodous
\peləˈsipədəs\
Latin
: relating to oysters and clams

pellitory
\peləˌtōrē\
Latin>French
: southern European shrub

penaeaceous
\penēˈāshəs\
Latin
: like small evergreen shrubs

pendill
\pendᵊl\
French
: vertical ornamental pillar

pennatulacean
\pəˌnachəˈlāshēən\
Latin
: like sea feathers

peperek
\peperək\
Indonesian name
: slimy fish

periaktoi
\perēˈaktȯi\
Greek
: revolving apparatus (pl.)
(singular spelled periaktos)

periegeses
\perēəˈjēsēs\
Greek
: descriptions of regions (pl.)

perillaldehyde
\perəlal-də-ˌhīd\
ISV
: liquid compound

peronosporaceous
\perənōspəˈrāshəs\
Latin
: relating to parasitic fungi

peroxisome
\pəˈräksəˌsōm\
ISV
: of gooey plasmatic cell
membranes in chromosomes

perseulose
\pərsēyəˌlōs\
ISV
: bacterial sugar

petaurine
\pȧˈtȯˌrīn\
Latin
: resembling a flying
marsupial

petrogale
\pəˈträgəˌlē\
Greek
: medium-sized kangaroo

pfleiderer
\flīdərə(r)\
German name
: machine for ripping
cellulose

phainopepla
\fā͵īnə'peplə\
Greek>Latin
: uniform black bird

phellandral
\fə'lan͵dral\
Latin
: liquid oil

phenelzine
\fenᵊl͵zēn\
ISV
: oxidase inhibitor

pheophorbide
\fēə'fòr͵bēd\
ISV
: crystalline acid

pherentasin
\fə'rentəzən\
Greek
: pressor amine used to lower
blood pressure

philipstadite
\filəp͵stä͵dīt\
Swedish
: calcium mineral

philine
\fə'līnē\
Latin
: bubble shell

philonium
\fə'lōnēəm\
Latin
: ancient remedy

phleboedesis
\flebē'dēsəs\
Greek>Latin
: large vascular system

phlyctenule
\fliktənyül\
Greek
: small sac in cornea

phorminx
\fòr͵miŋks\
Greek
: ancient sounding board

photeolic
\fōtē¦älik\
Sanskrit>Greek
: exhibiting sleep movement

phreaking
\frēking\
English
: gaining illegal access to the
telephone system

phrenemphraxes
\fre͵nem'fraksēs\
Greek>Latin
: incisions in nerves for
therapeutic reasons (pl.)

phrynoderma
\frīnə'dərmə\
Latin
: rough skin eruption

phylactolaematous
\fə'laktəlēmədəs\
Latin
: of freshwater mosses

phylloxeric
\fi͵läk¦serik\
Greek
: resembling plant lice

physcioid
\fish(ē)òid\
Greek>Latin
: relating to grayish lichens

physeteroid
\fī'sētə͵ròid\
Latin
: beaked whale

physoclist
\fīsə͵klist\
Latin
: canal fish

piacevole
\pyä'chāvə͵lā\
Italian
: pleasantly, soothing

pilikia
\pēlē'kēə\
Hawaiian
: trouble

pilliwinks
\pilə͵wiŋks\
English
: instrument of torture

pinakiolite
\pə'nakēə͵līt\
Greek
: black crystal

piperocaine
\pī'perə͵kān\
ISV
: basic liquid

pirssonite
\pirsᵊn͵īt\
American name
: hydrous calcium

Pisistratean
\pīsistrətēən\
Greek
: of the Homeric poems

piskun
\piskən\
Blackfoot
: steep cliff

plagiochila
\plājēō'kīlə\
Latin + Greek
: leafy liverwort

Plantagenet
\plan'tajənət\
English
: member of royal family

platyctenean
\platiktēnēən\
Greek
: of flattened dorsal fins

plectenchymatous
\plek͵teŋ¦kimətəs\
Latin
: of amassed tissues

pleochroous
\plēäəkrəwəs\
Greek
: spectral as in crystals

pneumatocele
\n(y)ümətō͵sēl\
Latin
: gas-filled cavity in lungs

pneumocystises
\n(y)ümə'sistəsəs\
Latin
: lung diseases caused by
fungi

poblaciones
\pȯ͵bläsē'ȯnās\
Spanish
: seats of government (pl.)

poephagous
\pōefəgəs\
Greek
: eating plants, herbivorous

pohutukawa
\pō͵hütə'käwə\
Maori
: crimson tree

pondokkie
\pän͵däkē\
Afrikaans
: crude hut

poplitei
\päp'litēī\
Latin
: flat muscles (pl.)
(singular spelled popliteus)

porokaiwhiria
\pōrō͵kī'(h)wirēə\
Maori
: small shrubby tree

powsowdy
\pōsōdi, paủsaủdi\
Unknown
: sheep dish

predelle
\prə'delē, prə'delā\
Italian
: raised steps for altars (pl.)

preghiera
\prəg'yerə\
Italian
: musical composition, prayer

primeverin
\prīmə'virən\
French>ISV
: crystalline glucoside

probenecid
\prō'benəsəd\
ISV
: drug to incrase
concentration on other drugs

proceleusmatic
\prōsə͵lüz'matik\
Greek>Latin
: metrical foot

procoelia
\prōsēlēə\
Latin
: lateral ventricle

prokeimena
\prō'kīmə͵nə\
Greek
: short church anthems (pl.)

promyshlenniki
\prämə'shlenəkē\
Russian
: fur trappers and traders (pl.)

propoxyphene
\prō'päksə͵fēn\
ISV
: pain reliever

propylaea
\präpə'lēə\
Greek>Latin
: entrances to buildings (pl.)
(singular spelled propylaeum)

proviant
\prävēənt\
Italian>German
: food, provisions

pruinescence
\prüə'nesᵊn(t)s\
Latin
: dusty or blooming condition

psettodid
\setədəd\
Latin
: tropical flatfish

pseudomonades
\südə'mänə͵dēz\
Latin
: fluorescent bacteria

pseudopelletierine
\südəpelə'ti͵rēn\
ISV
: crystalline alkaloid

psilocybin
\sīlə'sībən\
Greek
: hallucinogenic crystalline

psoralen
\sōrələn\
ISV
: substance that sensitizes the
skins of plants

psydracious
\sī¦drāshəs\
Greek
: resembling pimples

pukras
\pəkrəs\
Indian name
: Himalayan pheasant

pumpellyite
\pəmˈpelē‚īt\
American geographical name
: hydrous calcium

Purkinjean
\pərˌkinjēən, ˌpůrkən‚yāan\
Czech
: discovered by a physiologist

purwannah
\pə(r)ˈwänə\
Persian>Hindi
: order, royal grant

pylagore
\pilə‚gō(ə)r\
Greek
: deputy or councilman

pyrimethamine
\pirəˈmethə‚mēn\
ISV
: crystalline vitamin

pyrocoll
\pīrō‚käl\
ISV
: crystalline glue

pyrrhocorid
\pəˈräkərəd\
Latin
: brightly colored bug

pyrrhuloxia
\pir(y)əläksēə\
Latin
: showy finch

quadrigae
\kwäˈdrīgē\
Latin
: ancient Roman chariots (pl.)

quadrual
\kwädrəwəl\
Latin
: of four pronouns

quadruplane
\kwädrə‚plān\
Latin
: four supporting surfaces

quamoclit
\kwamə‚klit\
Latin>Nahuatl
: twining vine

quantasome
\kwäntə‚sōm\
ISV
: coloring material in plants

quaresma
\kwäˈrezmə\
Portuguese
: Brazilian purple shrub

quaruba
\kwəˈrübə\
Portuguese
: tropical fragrant shrub

quaskies
\kwäskēz\
American geographical name
: small slender trout (pl.)

quatuor
\kwädə‚wȯr\
French
: musical composition
performed by four people

quellung
\kweləŋ\
German
: swelling of capsule

quenstedtite
\kwen‚ste‚tīt\
German
: hydrous silicate

quercetagitrin
\kwərsəˈtajətrən\
ISV
: crystalline glucoside

querelae
\kwəˈrēlē\
Latin
: actions in court

querflote
\kwerˌflœtə\
German
: organ stop

quica
\kēkə\
Tupi>Portuguese
: four-eyed opossum

quickhatch
\kwik‚hach\
Algonquian
: carnivorous mammal

quidditates
\kwidə‚tā‚dēz\
Latin
: trifling points (pl.)

quimper
\kaⁿˌpe(ə)r\
Trademark
: grayish chinaware

quinalizarin
\kwinə-ˈli-zə-rən\
ISV
: red crystalline compound

quinicine
\kwinə‚sēn\
ISV
: bitter alkaloid

quinyie
\kwin(y)ē\
English
: small cupboard

quominus
\kwōmənəs\
Latin
: former writ

Quonset
\kwän(t)sət\
Trademark
: prefabricated shelter

raadzalen
\räd͵zälən\
Dutch
: assembly halls

rabinet
\rabə͵net\
English
: small century piece

rabirubia
\räbəˈrübēə\
Spanish
: common snapper

rafflesiaceous
\rə͵flēz(h)ēˈāshəs\
Latin
: resembling parasitic plants

railleur
\raˈyər\
French
: one given to mockery

rajpramukh
\räjprə͵mùk\
Hindi
: constitutional head

ramdohrite
\räm͵dōˌrīt\
German
: rare mineral

ramontchi
\rəˈmänchē\
Unknown
: small shrubby tree

raoulia
\räˈülēə\
French
: cushion plant

rapateaceous
\rə͵pātēˈāshəs\
Latin
: resembling flowered herbs

raschel
\räˈshel\
French
: fabric made by warp
knitting with openwork
patterns

rauschpfeife
\raùsh͵(p)fīfə\
German
: organ stop

recercelee
\rəˈsərsəˈlā\
French
: having arms curved back

recollet
\rekəˈlet, räkòlā\
French
: showy bird

Recuay
\räˈkwī\
Peruvian geographical name
: of stone-carved pottery

reduncine
\rəˈdəŋsīn\
Latin
: resembling African
antelopes

reduviid
\ri-ˈd(y)ü-vē-əd\
Latin
: bloodsucking insect

Reihengraber
\rīən͵grābə(r)\
German
: long hills

reineckate
\rīnə͵kāt\
ISV
: salt of ammonium

reizianum
\rītsēˈanəm\
Latin + German
: diacritical marking

rendzina
\renˈjēnə\
Polish
: dark humid soil

resedaceous
\resəˈdāshəs\
Latin
: of irregular herbs

ressentiment
\rə͵sänᵗtēˈmänⁿ\
German>French
: deep-seated frustration

rezbanyite
\rezˈban͵yīt\
German
: lead mineral

rhabdocoele
\rabdə͵sēl\
Latin
: flatworm

rhagionid
\rajēə͵nid\
Latin
: 2-winged fly

rhizonctoniose
\rī͵zäkˈtōnēōs\
Latin
: fungus disease

rhodanthe
\rōˈdan(t)thē\
Latin
: annual flower

rhodophyceous
\rōdəˈfīshəs\
Latin
: relating to marine algae

rhodymeniaceous
\rōdəˌmēnēˈāshəs\
Latin
: resembling red algae

rhusiopathia
\rüzēōˈpathēə\
Greek>Latin
: destructive mammal disease

rhytina
\rəˈtīnə, rə-tēnə\
Latin
: sea cow (NOTICE! "rytina"
has same definition yet
pronounced ritᵊnə)

ricinoleate
\risᵊnə ē-ə-lət\
ISV
: salty acid

ridotto
\rəˈdätō\
Italian
: public entertainment

ringelnatter
\riŋəlˌnätə(r)\
German
: harmless snake

riroriro
\rirəˈrērō\
Maori
: gray singing bird

rissoid
\risəwə́d\
Latin
: freshwater snail

Ritschlian
\richlēən\
German
: among theological
principles

ristocetin
\ristəˌsētᵊn\
ISV
: antibiotic mixture

Robigalia
\rōbəˈgālēə\
Latin
: ancient festival procession

roccelline
\rōˈchelən\
Latin
: relating to maritime lichens

rohrflote
\rōrˌflœtə\
German
: organ stop

roitelets
\ròitᵊlˌets, rwätlā\
French
: petty kings (pl.)

roncet
\ränˈsā\
French
: grape disease

rondeletia
\rändəˈlēshēə\
Latin
: fragrant flower

rosickyite
\rōˈzitskēˌīt\
Czech
: crystal mineral

roystonea
\ròiˈstōnēə\
Latin
: West Indian palm tree

Rydberg
\ridˌbərg\
Swedish
: energy constant

rynchosporous
\riŋˈkäspərəs\
Latin
: having a beaked fruit or
seed

Saanen
\sänən, zänən\
Swiss
1: short-haired goat
2: long-lasting cheese

Saadian
\sädēən\
Moroccan
: relating to Arab dynasty

sabadinine
\səˈbadᵊnˌēn\
ISV
: crystalline alkaloid

sabbeka
\sabəkə\
Amharic
: ancient triangular harp

sabellariid
\sabəˈla(a)rēəd\
Latin
: tailless worm

sabia
\səbˈyä\
Tupi>Portuguese
: one of Brazilian thrushes

sabicu
\sabəˌkü\
Spanish
: dark wood

saburral
\səˈbərəl\
Latin
: of foul matter

sabutan
\säbə¦tän\
Tagalog
: coarse fiber or straw

sadducee
\sajəsē\
Greek
: one who denies immortality

saebeins
\sā¦bēə̇nz\
Scottish
: provided that

saimiri
\sī'mirē\
Portuguese
: squirrel monkey

saleeite
\sə'lā͵īt\
French
: hydrous phosphate

sallenders
\salə̇ndə(r)z\
Unknown
: eczematous eruption on hind legs of horses

salpiglossis
\salpə'gläsə̇s\
Greek
: Chilean herb

sandkruiper
\san(d)͵krȯipə(r)\
Dutch
: small ray

Sangiovese
\sänjō'vāzā\
Italian
: dry red wine

Saoshyant
\saȯshyənt\
Avestan
: deliverer of Zoroastrianism

sapiutan
\säpē'ütᵊn\
Malay
: wild ox

sapucainha
\sapəkīnyə\
Portuguese
: tall central tree

sarinda
\särən¦dä\
Hindi
: bow-stringed instrument

sarmatier
\zärmə¦ti(ə)r\
German
: tiger weasel

sarraceniaceous
\sarə'sēnēāshəs\
Latin
: resembling bog herbs

Sarvastivadin
\sə(r)͵västə'vädᵊn\
Hindi
: student in Buddhist school

saururaceous
\sȯrə'rāsēhəs\
Latin
: of perennial herbs

scamillus
\skə'miləs\
Latin
: Corinthian column

scammoniate
\skə'mōnēə̇t\
Latin
: made with twining vines

scawtite
\skȯ͵tīt\
Irish
: hydrous silicate

sceloporus
\sə'läpərəs\
Latin
: large lizard

sceuophylax
\skyü'äfəlaks, ͵skevȯ'fē͵läks\
Greek>Latin
: holiest place in Eastern Orthodox Church

schafarzikite
\shäfə(r)͵zi͵kīt\
Hungarian
: iron oxide

scheelite
\shā͵līt\
German
: calcium tungsten

scheteligite
\shə'telə̇͵gīt\
Norwegian
: oxide of calcium

schizaeaceous
\skizē¦āshəs\
Latin
: of tropical ferns

schmierkase
\shmi(ə)r͵kāzə\
German
: cottage cheese

schoepite
\ske͵pīt\
Belgian
: uranium oxide

schonfelsite
\shōn͵fel͵zīt\
German
: dense brown glass

schroeckingerite
\shrekiŋə͵rīt\
German
: hydrous carbonate of calcium

schrother
\shrōtə(r), shräthə(r)\
German
: machine for flaking metals
to make powders

scilliroside
\skilərō͵sīd\
Latin>ISV
: cardio steroid

scirenga
\sə̇'reŋgə\
Unknown
: Mediterranean bird

scitamineous
\sitəmə̇'nē əs\
Latin
: relating to tropical plants

sclareol
\sklə(a)rē͵ōl\
Latin
: liquid alcohol

scleretinite
\sklə̇'retᵊn͵īt\
Greek
: mineral resin

scyliorhinid
\silēō¦rīnə̇d\
Latin
: cat shark

sdrucciola
\zdrüchə͵lä\
Italian
: rhyme where stress is put on
antepenultimate syllables

seacunny
\sē͵kənē\
Persian
: quartermaster, second-in-
line

searlesite
\sərl͵zīt\
American geographical name
: hydrous calcium

selaginellaceous
\sə̇͵lajə'nelāshəs\
Latin
: of tropical terrestrial plants

semaeostome
\sə͵mēə'stōm\
Greek>Latin
: large jellyfish

senecioses
\sə̇'nēs(h)ēōsēs\
Latin
: livestock intoxications (pl.)

seringal
\serə̇n¦gäl\
Portuguese
: collection of trees

serioline
\sə̇'rīələn\
Latin
: resembling typical fish

sewellel
\sə̇'weləl\
Chinook
: nocturnal rodent

seymouriamorph
\sē'mōrēə͵mȯrf\
Latin
: amphibian or fossil

shergottite
\shərgə͵tīt\
Indian geographical name
: geological meteorite

sheristadar
\shə̇'ristə͵där\
Persian + Hindi
: recorder, secretary

shoreyer
\shō͵rī(ə)r\
English
: large North Sea duck

sibucao
\sēbə¦kau̇\
Tagalog
: red soluble wood

sifflot
\sif͵flət\
German
: small organ stop with a
whistling tune

sildenafil
\sil'denə͵fil\
ISV
: enzyme or hormone to
initiate vascular changes

simaroubaceous
\simə'rübāshəs\
Latin
: of pale light soft wood

sinsring
\sins͵riŋ\
Javanese
: arboreal mammal

sisyrinchium
\sisə'riŋkēəm\
Greek>Latin
: blue-flowered herb

skutterudite
\skətə͵rə͵dīt\
German
: cobalt nickel

smorrebrod
\smœrə͵brœ͟th\
Danish
: slice of buttered bread
served as an appetizer

soffioni
\säfē'ōnē\
Italian
: jets of steam (pl.)
(singular pronounced same)

solasodine
\sə'lasəˌdēn\
ISV
: crystalline steroid

sooterkin
\sùtə(r)kən\
Dutch
: mishap, flaw

soroban
\sòrəˌbän\
Japanese
: ancient abacus

souari
\sü'ärē\
Galibi>French
: fine-grain wood

soukouses
\süˌküsəz\
Congolese geographical
name
: popular guitar-driven dance

souterliedeken
\saùtə(r)ˌlēdəkən\
German
: collection of psalms

spagyric
\spə'jirik\
Latin
: alchemic, of metal fusion

sparaxis
\spə'raksəs\
Greek>Latin
: small bulbous plant

sphacelial
\sfa'sēlēəl\
Latin
: relating to fungus spores

sphaeraphides
\sfə'rafəˌdēz\
Latin>Greek
: aggregation of crystals in
plant cell membranes

sphaerococcaceous
\sfə'rəkäkāshəs\
Latin
: resembling red algae

spirillicidal
\spī'riləsīdəl\
Latin
: destroying bacteria

spodosol
\spädəˌsòl\
Latin
: group of humid soils

spodumene
\späjəˌmēn\
Greek
: lithium aluminum

sporadin
\spōrədən\
Greek>Latin
: algal protozoan

sporidesm
\spōrəˌdezəm\
Greek
: multicellular bonding of
reproductive bodies

sprauchle
\spräk̲əl\
Scandinavian
: scramble, sprawl

spreath
\sprēk̲\
Gaelic
: raid, foray

sprechstimme
\shprek̲ˌshtimə\
German
: vocal passage or
performance

spruiker
\sprükə(r)\
Australian
: one who uses loud voice to
gain attention

spulziing
\spū͞el(y)ing\
French>English
: stealing, ransacking

squadrol
\skwä¦drōl\
English
: police automobile

squarrulose
\skwer(y)əˌlōs\
Latin
: with rough scales

squarson
\skwärsᵊn\
English
: proprietor, clergyman

squinancy
\skwinənsi\
French
: European perennial herb

sramana
\s(h)rəmənə\
Sanskrit
: religious ascetic

sravaka
\s(h)rävəkə\
Sanskrit
: direct disciple

stachydrine
\stakəˌdrēn\
ISV
: crystalline alkaloid

Stahlian
\stälēən\
German
: of the doctrine of animism

stainierite
\stīnēə͵rīt\
Dutch
: rare mineral

staminodies
\stamə͵nōdēz\
Latin
: metamorphoses into floral organs of seed plants (pl.)

stanhopea
\stan'hōpēə\
Latin
: tropical orchid

stapedii
\stə'pēdēī\
Latin
: small ear muscles (pl.)

staphisagrias
\stafə'sāgrēəz\
Latin
: seeds to kill head lice (pl.)

staphyleaceous
\stafəlē'āshəs\
Latin
: of temperate plant zones

stauropegia
\stäurȯ'pē͵yä\
Greek
: territorial churches (pl.)

steenstrupine
\stēnstrə͵pēn\
Danish
: complex silicate

stegomyia
\stə́'gōmīə\
Latin
: yellow-fever mosquito

Stendahlian
\stan¦dälēən\
French pseudonym
: of the works of Stendahl

stepney
\stepnē\
Welsh
: automobile wheel

stercovorous
\stər¦kävərəs\
Latin
: eating dung

sterraster
\stə́'rastə(r)\
Latin
: small sponge

sterrettite
\sterə͵tīt\
English
: hydrous basic phosphate

stevioside
\stēvēə͵sīd\
Latin
: hydrous glucoside

sticharia
\stə́'kär͵yä\
Greek>Latin
: ecclesiastical vestment

stillicide
\stilə͵sīd\
Latin
: water falling from house

stipites
\stipə͵tēz\
Latin
: second stalks of plants (pl.)

stockinette
\stäkə¦net\
French
: knitting pattern

stokrooses
\stä͵krüs\
Afrikaans
: valuable fiber plants (pl.)

stramoniums
\strə'mōnēəmz\
Latin
: dried leaves of apples (pl.)

strappadoed
\strə'pādōd\
Dutch>German
: tortured by beating whips

strepsitene
\strepsə͵tēn\
ISV
: tied threads

Strepyan
\strāpēən\
Belgian geographical name
: of worked flint stones

strigillose
\strijə́lōs\
Latin + English
: with fine hairs

strobilae
\strə'bīlē\
Latin
: linear series

stromateoid
\strə'matē͵ȯid\
Latin
: of marine feeble fish

stromming
\strœmiŋ\
Swedish
: small Baltic herring

strophanthidin
\strə'fan(t)thədə́n\
ISV
: toxic glycoside

struthioniform
\strüthēänəfȯ(ə)rm\
Latin
: resembling an ostrich

stylidiaceous
\stī͵lidēˈāshəs\
Latin
: of seed-bearing flowers

styracaceous
\stīrəˈkāshəs\
Latin
: of widely distributed shrubs

subdolous
\səbdələs\
Latin
: cunning, artful, sly

subsellia
\səbˈselēə\
Latin
: low seats or benches (pl.)
(singular spelled subsellium)

subtilin
\səbtələn\
Latin
: antibiotic mixture

subtilisin
\səbˈtiləsən\
Latin
: extracellular protein

subtilizing
\sətᵊl͵īzing, ˈsə(b)tᵊl͵īzing\
Latin
: clarify or sharpen the senses

subulicorn
\sübyələ͵kȯrn\
Latin
: having linear antennae

succinimide
\səkˈsinə͵mīd; ͵səksəˈni͵mīd\
Latin
: crystalline ammonium

sucupira
\sükəˈpirə\
Tupi
: timber tree

suffragan
\səfrə|gən\
Latin
: church bishop

suggillation
\sə(g)jəˈlāshən\
Latin
: bruise, scab

sulfanilyl
\səlˈfanə͵lil\
ISV
: acidic radical

sulforaphane
\səlfȯˈraf͵ān\
ISV
: cancer-treating compound
found in vegetables

Sulpician
\səlˈpishən\
French
: relating to Catholic priests

sunyata
\shu̇nyə͵tä\
Sanskrit
: nonexistence of objects

supersedere
\süpə(r)səˈdārē\
Latin
: judicial order

suramin
\su̇rəmən\
ISV
: sodium drug

surturbrand
\sərtər͵brand\
Icelandic
: variety of volcanic rock

svedberg
\sfed͵bərg\
Swedish
: minute unit of time

svetambara
\s(h)wäˈtämbərə\
Sanskrit
: sacred image

Swaledale
\swā(ə)l͵dā(ə)l\
English
: breed of hill sheep

swissing
\swisiŋ, swisēŋ\
Unknown
: process of pressing cotton
cloth to smooth it

syconoid
\sīkə͵nȯid\
Latin
: resembling hard sponges

sylloge
\siləjē\
Greek
: collection, composition

Sylvaner
\silˈvänər\
German
: white grape wine

sylvilagus
\silˈviləgəs\
Latin + Greek
: cottontail rabbit

sympharicarpos
\sim(p)fərəˈkär͵päs\
Greek>Latin
: small bell-shaped flower

symphynote
\sim(p)fə͵nōt\
Greek
: having cemented valves

symplesite
\simplə͵sīt\
German + Greek
: hydrous iron mineral

synaesthesises
\sinəsˈthēsəsəs\
Greek
: having different impulses

syncelli
\sənˈselī\
Greek
: church officials

synchisite
\siŋkə͵sīt\
Greek
: carbonate calcium

synechiae
\səˈnekēē\
Latin>Greek
: adhesion of parts (pl.)

syrettes
\səˈrets\
Trademark
: small collapsible tubes (pl.)

szaibelyite
\sāˈbel͵yīt\
Hungarian
: magnesium crystal

taaffeite
\tä͵fīt\
German
: rare mineral

taeniosomous
\tēnēə͵sōmǝs\
Latin
: of delicate fish

taffetized
\tafə͵tīzd\
Italian
: having a crisp finish

tagetes
\tajə͵tēz, təˈjetēz\
Latin
: tropical herb

taglioni
\talˈyōnē\
Italian
: early overcoat

tahsildar
\täsēl¦där\
Arabic + Persian>Hindi
: revenue officer

takahe
\təˈkī\
Maori
: flightless bird

takosis
\təˈkōsəs\
Greek>Latin
: bacterial waste

taliera
\talēerə\
Sanskrit>Kannada
: palm tree

talisay
\təlēsī\
Tagalog
: white-flowered tree

tamanoir
\tamənwär\
Galibi>French
: large anteater

tamaricaceous
\tamərəkāshəs\
Latin
: resembling desert shrubs

tamarugite
\tamərügīt\
Chilean geographical name
: hydrous sulfate

tamoxifen
\taˈmäksi͵fen\
ISV
: estrogen to treat breast cancer

tanghinin
\tanginən\
ISV
: poisonous crystalline

tanist
\tanəst, thȯnəst\
Irish Gaelic
: landowner, proprietor

tanylobous
\tanəlōbəs\
Latin
: having an elongated mouth in worms

taoiseachs
\thēshəks\
Irish Gaelic
: prime ministers, teachers (pl.)

tapete
\təpēdē\
Latin
: layer of nutritive cells which heal broken tissue

taphrinaceous
\tafrənāshəs\
Latin
: resembling fungi which have thin walls

taqlid
\təˈklēd\
Arabic
: unqualified acceptance

taramosalata
\tärəmōsəˈlä¦tə, ¦tə\
Greek
: dip or spread with potatoes

tarbuttite
\tärbətīt\
Australian name
: basic zinc phosphate

tarbagan
\tärbə¦gan\
Russian
: reddish rodent

tartarin
\tärtərən\
French
: venerated monkey in Egypt

tastevin
\tastə¦va^n\
French
: silver wine-tasting cup

tataupa
\tətȯpə\
Tupi
: South Americna bird

tathagatagarbha
\tə͵tägə͵tə'gərbə\
Sanskrit
: matrix of all reality

taubada
\taú'bädə\
Papuan
: master, tutor

tauriscite
\tȯrə͵sīt\
German
: hydrous iron

taurokathapsia
\tȯrəkə'thapsēə\
Greek
: ancient sport where fighters
somersault over bulls

taxaspidean
\taksa¦spidēən\
Latin
: relating to scaly bird feet

taxeopodous
\taksē'äpədəs\
Greek + English
: having bones in a certain
way

taxifolin
\taksə'fōlən\
Latin
: yellow crystalline

tayassuid
\təyasəwəd\
Latin
: wild swine

teaette
\tē¦et\
English
: perforated spoon

teallite
\tē͵līt\
English
: black tin

tebeldi
\tə'beldē\
Berber>Arabic
: fruit-bearing tree

tectrices
\tekrə͵sēz, tek'trī͵sēz\
Latin
: tail feathers on birds

teepleite
\tēpə͵līt\
English
: hydrous sodium

telakucha
\tə'läkə͵chä\
Bengali
: tropical fruit vine

telega
\tə'legə, təl'yegə\
Russian
: 4-wheeled wagon

teleodesmacean
\telēōdezmāshən\
Latin
: of bivalve mollusks

teleutosori
\tə¦lütəsōrī\
Latin
: stalked fungi

temadau
\temə'daú\
Borneo name
: wild ox

teocalli
\tēə'kalē, ͵tāə'kälē\
Nahuatl
: ancient temple

teraglin
\terəglən\
Australian name
: large fish

teredinid
\terə¦dinəd, tə'red°nəd\
Latin
: mollusk, marine clam

tettigoniid
\tetə¦gōnēəd\
Latin
: grasshopper with long
antennae, green insect

thalictrum
\thə'liktrəm\
Greek
: meadow flower

thamakau
\thämə¦kaú\
Fijian Hindi
: large canoe

theotokia
\theȯ'tȯ͵kyä\
Greek
: church hymns (pl.)
(singular spelled theotokion)

theraphose
\therə‚fōs\
Latin
: rare spider

thingstead
\thiŋz‚ted\
English
: Scandinavian assembly hall

tholeiitic
\t(h)ōlēitik\
German
: relatin to basaltic rock

thomsenolite
\täm(p)sənə‚līt\
Danish
: hydrous fluoride

thortveitite
\tȯ(r)t¦vī‚tīt\
German
: silicate mineral

threitol
\thrēə‚tȯl\
ISV
: sweet crystalline

thwaites
\thwāts\
Scandinavian
: pieces of meadows (pl.)

thylakoid
\thīlə‚kȯid\
ISV
: membranous plant

thymele
\thiməlē\
Greek
: ancient altar

tibouchina
\tibə'kīnə, tibəkēnə\
Latin
: purple flower

tiemannite
\tēmə‚nīt\
German
: mercuric mineral

tierceron
\tirsərən\
French
: Gothic vault

tikkun
\tikùn\
Hebrew
: recital of prayers

tilbury
\til‚berē, tilb(ə)rē\
English
: 2-wheeled carriage

tilletiaceous
\tə'lēsh(ē) āshəs\
Latin
: of fungal spores

tilleyite
\tilē‚īt\
English
: carbon mineral

timariot
\tə'märēət\
Turkish>French
: one holding a feudal estate
under military service

tincalconite
\tin'kalkə‚nīt\
Greek
: mineral with boron

tindals
\tindᵊlz\
Hindi
: petty officers (pl.)

tineine
\tinē'īn, tinēēn\
Latin
: resembling small moths

tineola
\tə'nēələ, ‚tinē'ōlə\
Latin
: larval moth

tinikling
\tinə¦kliŋ\
Tagalog
: popular dance

tirasse
\tə'ras, tərás\
French
: pipe organ mechanism

tirodite
\tirə‚dīt\
Indian geographical name
: silicate mineral

tithymal
\tithəməl, tə'thīməl\
Latin>Greek
: fleshy cactus

titrimetrically
\tītrə¦metrik (ə)lē\
Latin
: measured by reactive
capacity in solution

tlachtli
\tlächtlē\
Nahuatl
: ball game

tobira
\tə'bīrə\
Japanese
: commonly cultivated herb

todlowrie
\todlaùri\
Scottish
: fox, wolf

toggenburgs
\tägən‚bərgz\
Swiss geographical name
: dairy goats (pl.)

toheroa
\tōə'rōə\
Maori
: bivalve mollusk

tolazoline
\tō'lazə͵lēn\
ISV
: weak blocking agent

tolsester
\tōlsestər\
English
: feudal toll

tolypeutine
\tälə'pyütīn\
Latin>Greek
: of yellow armadillos

tonalpohualli
\tō'nälpō͵wälē\
Nahuatl
: Aztec calendar

tongkang
\täŋ'kaŋ\
Malay
: large junk boat

tophaceous
\tə'fāshəs\
Latin
: gritty, sandy

torcular
\tȯ(r)kyələ(r)\
Latin
: point at which four cranial
sinuses meet

tournasin
\tùrnəsən\
French
: tool for smoothing pottery

toxaphene
\täksə͵fēn\
Trademark
: waxy insecticide

trachyspermous
\trakē¦spərməs\
Latin
: rough-seeded

traditores
\tradə'tōrēz\
Latin
: disciples giving up
Scriptures

tragelaphine
\trə'jelə͵fīn\
Latin
: belonging to typical
antelopes

tranylcypromine
\tranºl'sīprə͵mēn\
ISV
: antidepressant drug

Trebbiano
\tre'byänō\
Italian
: white grape wine

trechmannite
\trekmə͵nīt\
English
: silver arsenic

trehalase
\trēhə͵lās, trə'hälās\
ISV
: yeast enzyme

trentepohliaceous
\trentə'pōlēāshəs\
Latin
: resembling terrestrial algae

triaenophorid
\trī͵ē'͵näf(ə)rəd\
Latin
: parasitic tapeworm

triazinyl
\trī'azºn͵il\
ISV
: univalent radical

trichothecene
\trikə'thē͵sēn, tri'käthə͵sēn\
ISV
: fungal poison

tricinium
\trī'sinēəm\
Latin
: 3-part vocal composition

tricrotism
\trīkrə͵tizəm\
Latin
: condition of arterial pulse
where there is triple beat

trieteric
\trīə¦terik\
Latin
: occurring in alternate years

trigonelline
\trigəne͵lēn\
ISV
: crystalline alkaloid

triodion
\trē'ȯthyȯn\
Greek
: liturgical book

trippkeite
\tripkē͵īt\
Polish
: copper mineral

tripuhyite
\tripə'wē͵īt\
Brazilian geographical name
: antimony and iron

trisagia
\trē'sȧya\
Greek
: invocations, hymns (pl.)

triteleia
\trītºl'īə, trītºlē(y)ə\
Greek>Latin
: grass-like leaf

trochalopodous
\trōkə'läpədəs\
Latin
: relating to ball-and-socket
joints in insects

troegerite
\trēgə͵rīt\
German
: hydrous uranium mineral

troolie
\trülē\
Galibi
: immense banana leaf

tropaeolaceous
\trōpēō'lāshəs\
Latin
: resembling showy leaves

Trubetzkoyan
\trübət¦skóiən\
Russian
: of linguistic methods

truxilline
\trü'hē(y)ȯn\
ISV
: isomeric compound

tscheffkinite
\chefkə͵nīt\
German
: iron calcium

tsine
\(t)sīn\
Burmese
: wild ox

tsugaresinol
\(t)sügərezᵊn͵ȯl\
Latin + English
: crystalline liquor

tsukupin
\(t)sükəpȯn\
Micronesian name
: large canoe

tsumebite
\(t)sümə͵bīt\
African geographical name
: hydrous copper

tuath
\tüə\
Gaelic
: governor of territory

tuchun
\dü'jūēn\
Pekingese
: Chinese warlord

tuladi
\tülədē\
French
: lake trout

turacin
\t(y)ùrəsən\
Latin
: red pigment

turcopolier
\tərkə͵pōlyər\
English
: high official

turriliticone
\tərə'litə͵kōn\
ISV
: sea fossil

Twaddell
\twädel\
Trademark
: relating to the process of
measuring water

tylotoxeae
\tīlə'täksēē\
Latin
: of rodlike sponges

tyrolienne
\tə¦rōlē¦en\
French
: peasant song

tyuyamunite
\tyü(y)ə'mü͵nīt\
Turkmen
: calcium mineral

tzolkin
\(t)sȯl͵kēn\
Mayan
: period of time

uintatheria
\yü'(w)intəthirēə\
Latin
: large herbivorous mammals

ullmannite
\əlmə͵nīt\
German
: sulfide mineral

ultroneous
\əl'trōnēəs\
Latin
: voluntarily offering a
testimony in court

umbilroot
\əmbəlrü|t\
English
: beautiful orchid

umbonulate
\əm¦bänyələt\
Latin
: having a sharp spike

umbratile
\əmbrə͵tīl\
Latin
: carried on in seclusion

umohoite
\yümə͵hō͵īt\
ISV
: radioactive mineral

unesthetic
\ənesthetik\
English
: uncomely, grotesue

unfeued
\ənfyüd\
Scottish
: free of fees

ungetatable
\əngetˌatəbəl\
Latin
: hard to reach

ungyved
\ənjīvd\
English
: unfettered, unchained

unjelled
\ənjeld\
English
: undecided, not stabilized

unprelatical
\ənprelatəkəl\
Latin
: not adhering to the bishop

upaithric
\yüˌpīthrik\
Greek
: roofless

uppertendom
\əpə(r)ˌtendəm\
English
: highest social class

uppowoc
\əˈpōˌwäk\
Algonquian
: tobacco, snuff

uredinous
\yəˈredᵊnəs\
Latin
: of fruity fungi

ureylene
\yəˈrēəˌlēn\
ISV
: bivalent radical

urginea
\ərˈjinēə\
Latin
: young bulb of plant

usneaceous
\əsnēˈāshəs\
Latin
: resembling fruity lichens

Ussherian
\əˌshirēən\
Irish
: of the world's creation

ustilaginaceous
\əstəˌlajəˈnāshəs\
Latin
: relating to fungi

utilidor
\yüˈtiləˌdȯ(ə)r\
Latin
: above ground conduit

utrubi
\ətrəˌbī\
Latin
: Roman civil law

uzarigenin
\üˌzärəˈjenᵊn\
ISV
: crystalline steroid

vaalhaais
\välˌhīz\
Afrikaans
: small sharks

vadimonium
\vadəˈmōnēəm\
Latin
: contract

vaesite
\väˌsīt\
Belgian
: sulfide nickel

Vaibhasika
\vīˈbäs(h)əkə\
Sanskrit
: philosophical school

Vajrayana
\vəjrəˈyänə\
Sanskrit
: religious mystical writing

valerianaceous
\vəˌlirēəˈnāshəs\
Latin
: of temperate herbs

Valkyrian
\valˌkirēən\
Norse
: relating to battle

vallisneriaceous
\valəˈsnirēāshəs\
Latin
: resembling aquatic herbs

vanilloyl
\vəˈniləˌwil\
ISV
: univalent radical

Varangian
\vəˈranjēən\
Greek
: Byzantine bodyguard

varulite
\värəˌlīt\
Swedish
: sodium mineral

vashegyite
\väshˌheˌjīt\
Hungarian
: basic aluminum

Vaudois
\vōˌdwä\
French
: those who suffered from
severe persecution

vauquelinite
\vōk(ə)lə͵nīt\
Swedish
: brown lead copper

veatchite
\vē͵chīt\
English
: hydrous calcium

veldschoen
\velt͵skün\
Afrikaans
: rawhide shoe

velellidous
\və॑leledəs\
Latin
: relating to oceanic animals

velloziaceous
\və͵lōzē॑āshəs\
Latin
: of woody-stemmed plants

velociman
\və॑läsəmən\
French
: hand-driven vehicle

velutina
\velə॑tīnə\
Latin
: marine gastropod

vendace
\vendəs\
Latin
: fish

ventilagin
\ven॑tiləjə̇n; ͵vent²l॑ājən\
ISV
: brown resinous tree bark

verapamil
\ve॑rapə͵mil\
ISV
: calcium channel blocker

veratrylidene
\verətrilədēn\
ISV
: oxygen derivative

verbesina
\vərbə॑sīnə\
Latin
: with yellow-headed flowers

veretillum
\verə॑tiləm\
Latin
: zooid animal

Verstehen
\fer॑shtāən\
German
: intuitive doctrine

verticillaster
\vərtəsə॑lastə(r)\
Latin
: arrangement of flowers

vetkousie
\fet͵kōsē\
Afrikaans
: small fig

vetturini
\vetə॑rēnē\
Italian
: people who drives a carriage

vicianin
\visēənə̇n\
ISV
: crystalline glucoside

vigoureux
\vēgə¦rā\
French
: painting fabric

villiaumite
\vē॑yō͵mīt\
French
: sodium chloride

vincristine
\vin॑kri͵stēn\
ISV
: chemical alkaloid to treat human tumor diseases

vinhatico
\vēn॑yätə͵kō\
Portuguese
: timber trees

violotta
\vēə॑lätə\
Italian
: instrument extending until fourth octave

virilescent
\virə॑les²n(t)\
Latin
: acquiring male characteristics

virustatic
\vīrə¦statik\
Latin
: check growth of bacteria

Visitandine
\vizə॑tandə̇n\
French
: religious nun

vizcachera
\vi͵skä॑cherə\
Spanish
: group of burrows

vochysiaceous
\vō॑kizh(ē) āshəs\
Latin
: of irregular flowers

voetganger
\füt͵gäŋər\
Afrikaans
: wingless locust

volapie
\vōləpē'ä\
Spanish
: method of killing bulls

Volksraad
\fōlks‚rät\
Afrikaans
: parliament, legislature

Volsteadian
\väl¦stedēən\
Latin
; relating to prohibition

vraicking
\vrākiŋ\
Chinese:
gathering of seaweed

vrbaite
\vərbə‚īt\
German
: black mineral

vriesia
\vrēzh(ē)ə\
Latin
: epiphytic herb

vulsella
\vəl'selə\
Latin
: tweezers, forceps

walpurgite
\wäl'pər‚jīt\
German
: hydrous uranium

wankapin
\wäŋkə‚pin\
Ojibwa
: American lotus

waringin
\wə'riŋən\
Javan
: common fig

wattevilleite
\wätvi‚līt\
German
: calcium mineral

weibullite
\wī‚bủ‚līt\
Swedish
: sulfide of lead

weigelia
\wī'jēlēə\
Latin
: moderate red yellow color

weinschenkite
\vīn‚sheŋ‚kīt\
German
: hydrous phosphate

Wertherism
\vertə‚rizəm\
German
: morbidly sentimental

wharfedale
\(h)wȯ(r)f‚dāl\
English
: cylinder press

whewellite
\hyüə‚līt\
English
: colorless calcium

whittret
\(h)witrət\
Scottish
: weasel

wilger
\wilgə(r)\
English
: furniture twigs

wittichenite
\witəkə‚nīt\
German
: steel copper

wobbegong
\wäbē‚gäŋg\
Australian
: large shark

wolfachite
\vōl‚fȧk̠‚īt\
German
: silver-white mineral

wollastonite
\wu̇ləstənīt\
English
: triclinic mineral

woollenizing
\wu̇lə‚nīzing\
Latin
: giving appearance by
chemical treatment

woubit
\wü‚bit\
English
: hungry caterpillar

wulfenite
\wu̇lfə‚nīt\
German
: tetragonal mineral

Wundtian
\vu̇ntēən\
German
: of theories and
investigations

wurtzilite
\wərtsə‚līt\
English
: similar asphalt

Wyandotte
\wīəndät\
American geographical name
: domestic fowl

Wykehamist
\wikəməst\
English
: graduate from
the Winchester college

wynkernel
\wiŋkə(r)ˌnel\
English
: female hazel hen

xanthelasma
\zanthəlazmə\
Latin
: irregular yellow patches on
the eyelid

xanthochroous
\zanthäkrəwəs\
Greek
: having yellowish skin

xanthomonad
\zanthämənad\
Latin
: necrotic bacterium

xanthoxyletin
\zanthäksəlētˀn\
Greek
: compound of prickly ash

xenacanthine
\zenəkanthən\
Latin
: fish, fossil

xenodocheionology
\zenədəkīənäləjē\
Greek
: learning about inns or hotels

xenodochium
\zenədəkīəm\
Latin
: medieval house for care of
the poor and sick

Xenophanean
\zənäfənēən\
Greek
: of emphatic doctrines

xeriscape
\zirəˌskāp\
ISV
: landscaping method

xerosere
\zirəsir\
Greek
: dry land

xonotlite
\zōnətlīt\
Mexican geographical name
: hydrous calcium

Xylocaine
\zīlōˌkān\
Trademark
: preparation of crystalline

xylotile
\zīlətīl\
German + Greek
: hydrous iron

xyridaceous
\zirədāshəs\
Latin
: resembling basal leaves

yabbies
\yabēz\
Australian name
: Tasmanian wolves (pl.)
(singular spelled yabbi)

yaguaza
\yəgwäzə\
Spanish
: tree duck

yangtao
\yäŋtaȯ\
Pekingese
: subtropical twining vine

yanacona
\yänəˈkōnə\
Quechua
: serf, servant

yaray
\yərī\
Spanish
: slender fan palm

yarphas
\yärfəz\
Scandinavian
: peat bog

yaruru
\yərürü\
name from Guiana
: tree wood

yaxche
\yäshchā\
Mayan
: tree producing sily cotton

yeara
\yäärə\
Unknown
: bushy poison ivy of Pacific

yeibichai
\yābəchī\
Navaho
: supernatural force

yetapa
\yetəpə\
American Indian
: bird

yetzer
\yātsər\
Hebrew
: impulse inclination

ynambu
\ēnämbü\
Portuguese
: very large bird in the
Brazilian and Argentine areas

yponomeutid
\ēpänəmyüdəd\
Latin
: black-spotted moth

yuloh
\yülō\
Chinese
: sculling oar

yungas
\yüngəs\
Unknown
: rat living in swampy regions

zacaton
\zakətōn\
Spanish
: wiry stem grass

zalambdodont
\zəlamdədänt\
Latin
: golden mole

zalcitabine
\zalˈsitəˌbēn\
ISV
: synthetic virus treatment

zamarra
\zəˈmärə\
Spanish
: sheepskin coat

zamzummim
\zamzəmə̇m\
Hebrew
: aboriginal giants

zaphrentoid
\zəfrent ȯid\
Latin
: resembling corals

zauberflote
\tsau̇bə(r)flādə\
German
: flute organ stop

zauschneria
\zȯshnirēə\
Bohemian name
: perennial herb

zemiism
\zemēizm\
Spanish
: belief of supernatural beings

zenaida
\zənāədə\
Latin
: tropical pigeon

zeolitize
\zēˈäləˌtīz\
Latin
: treat with hydrous silicate

zeophyllite
\zēäfəlīt\
German
: basic silicate

zidovudine
\zəˈdōvyüˌdēn\
ISV
: antiviral drug

zietrisikite
\zētrəsikīt\
Moldovan name
: waxy mineral

zingiberene
\zinjəbərēn\
ISV
: liquid hydrocarbon

zinnwaldite
\tsinvältīt\
German
: pale mineral

zippeite
\tsipəīt\
German
: hydrous sulfate

ziricote
\zirəkōtā\
Spanish
: dark wood tree

zoisitization
\zȯisədəzāshən\
German
: conversion of purple minerals into aluminum

zoopraxiscope
\zōəpraxəskōp\
Latin
: motion-picture projector

zubrowkas
\zübrəfkəs\
Polish
: dry herbs (pl.)

zuisin
\zȯisən\
Algonquian
: small duck

zuurveldt
\zürvelt\
Afrikaans
: land covered with perennial grasses and affords grazing

zwitterionic
\tsfidərīänək\
German
: resembling dipolar particles

zygaenid
\zīˈjēnəd\
Latin
: of bright-colored moths

zygnemataceous
\zignēmətāshəs\
Latin
: relating to slimy masses of freshwater algae

zygophyceous
\zīgəfishəs\
Latin
: resembling greenish algae

zymosterol
\zīmästəròl\
ISV
: unsaturated crystalline alkaloid chemical

Chapter 7: Galaxy

actinophryan
\ak-tə-¦nä-frē-ən\
Latin
: resembling protozoans

actinopterygious
\ak-tə-ˌnäp-tə-ˈri-jē-əs\
Latin
: relating to teleost fishes

actinospectacin
\aktinōspektəsən\
ISV
: compound

acyloxy
\a-sə-¦läk-sē\
ISV
: containing any radical

adderspits
\a-dər-ˌspits\
English
: common ferns

adelite
\a-də-ˌlīt\
Latin
: mineral

adelocodonic
\ədēləkədänik, adəlōkədä-nik\
Latin
: developing no umbrella

adenosylmethionine
\ədenəsilmethīənēn\
ISV
: compound

adrenoleukodystrophy
\ədrēnəlükədistrəfē\
Latin
: demyelinating disease

advowsons
\əd-ˈvaù-zənz\
English
: right of presenting nominees

aecidiospore
\ē-ˈsi-dē-ə-ˌspȯr\
Latin
: spores of fruiting bodies

aeciosporic
\ē-ˈshē-ə-ˌspȯrik\
Latin
: of spores of fruiting bodies

aedilitian
\ē-də-li-shən, ē-ˌdīli-shən\
Latin
: relating to Roman city officials

aegagri
\ē-ˈga-ˌgrī\
Greek>Latin
: wild goats

aegagropilous
\ē-gə-¦grä-pə-ləs\
Latin
: resembling ball shaped masses

Aeginetan
\ē-jə-¦nē-tən\
Greek
: relating to the island

aegyptianelloses
\ē-ˌjip-shə-ne-ˈlō-ˌsēz\
Latin
: fowl diseases

aegyptillas
ē-jəp-ˈti-ləz
Latin
: gems

aeluropodous
\ēl-(y)ə-¦rä-pə-dəs\
Latin
: having feet with retractile claws

aeolianly
\ē-ˈō-lē-ən-lē\
Greek
: in a soughing manner

aeolinas
\ē-ə-ˈlī-nəz, ē-ə-ˈlē-nəz\
Latin
: mouth harmonicas

aeolodicon
\ē-ə-ˈlä-də-kən\
Greek
: keyboard

aeolodions
\ē-ə-ˈlō-dēənz\
Greek
: keyboard

aepyornis
\ē-pē-ˈȯr-nəs\
Greek
: gigantic bird

Aequiculi
\ē-ˈkwi-kyə-ˌlī\
Latin
: people of ancient Rome

aeroides
\er-ˈȯi-dēz\
Greek
: pale blue beryl

aerugos
\ēˈ-rü-gōz\
Latin
: rusts of metal

ailettes
\ā-ˈlets\
French
: plates of forged armor

aiseweed
\āz-ˌwēd\
French
: course plant

Aitutakian
\ī-tə-ˈtä-kē-ən\
Maori
: relating to Cook Islands

aiwains
\ī-ˌwīnz\
Hindi
: Indian herbs

akekis
\ä-kə-kēz\
Japanese
: large evergreens

Akeldamas
\ə-ˈkel-də-məz\
Hebrew
: places of highly disagreeable associations

albumblatter
\äl-bəm-ˌble-tər\
German
: instrumental compositions

Alcmanians
\alk-ˈmā-nē-ənz\
Greek
: metrical line

alcyoniform
\al-sē-ˈä-nə-ˌform\
Latin
: resembling soft corals

alfereces
\al-fə-ˈrā-sēz\
Spanish
: military titles

alforjas
\al-ˈför-häz\
Spanish
: saddlebags

alkalitrophic
\alkələˈträfik\
Latin
: growing in a base

alkylphenol
\alkəlfēnöl\
ISV
: compound

Allentiacan
\alənˈtīəkən\
Argentine geographical name
: relating to San Juan province

allocochicks
\aləkəˌchiks\
Yurok
: Indian shell money

allosaur
\aləsör\
Latin
: dinosaur

allotriophagies
\əˌlätrēˈäfəjēz\
Latin
: eating anything in sight

allylating
\aləˌlāting\
Greek
: introducing radicals into

almemar
\alˈmēˌmär\
Hebrew
: platform in synagogue

almemors
\alˈmēmörz\
Hebrew
: platforms in synagogue

almeriite
\alməˈrēˌīt\
Spanish
: basic sulfate mineral

alumblooms
\aləmˌblümz\
English
: several herbs

amatrice
\əˈmātrəs\
English
: cut gem

ambalams
\əmbələmz\
Sinhalese
: resthouse

ambarella
\ambərelə\
Sinhalese
: tropical tree

ambitty
\amˈbitē\
French
: devitrified- of glass

amblystegite
\amˈblistəˌjīt\
ISV
: variety of hypersthene

ambystomid
\amˈbistəməd\
Latin
: salamander

amiloride
\əmilərīd\
ISV
: compound

amitrole
\amətröl\
ISV
: compound

Amoreuxia
\amə'rüksēə\
French
: genus of undershrubs

ampangabeite
\äm͵pän'gäbē͵īt\
Malagasy name
: brown mineral

amphibalus
\am'fibələs\
Latin
: church vestment

amphibolous
\am'fibələs\
Latin
: manifesting ambiguity in language
(Note: This word has a homonym)

amphigouris
\amfəgü'rēz\
French
: nonsensical verses

amphilinid
\am'filənəd\
Latin
: flatworm

amphirhine
\amfə'rīn\
Latin
: of double nasal chambers

amphotericin
\amfəterəsin\
ISV
: compound

Amsinckia
\am'siŋkēə\
German
: genus of annual herbs

amynodont
\ə'minə͵dänt\
Latin
: rhinoceros

Amyraldism
\amə'ral͵dizəm\
English name
: liberal form of salvation

anapestically
\a-nə-¦pe-sti-k(ə-)lē\
Greek
: consisting of metrical feet

anargyroi
\ä'näryē͵rē\
Greek
: one of thirteen saints

anbury
\anbərē\
English
: disease of cabbage

ancistrosyrinx
\ansistrōsiriŋks\
Latin
: mollusk

andromonoecisms
\andrōmənē͵sizəmz\
Latin
: having perfect organs

androstenedione
\andrōstēndīōn\
ISV
: compound

anomodont
\anəmō͵dänt\
Latin
: concave-clawed reptile

anonymae
\ə'nänəmē\
Latin
: unnamed arteries

antimins
\antəminz\
Greek
: consecrated piece of silk

antipolos
\äntē'pōlōz\
Tagalog
: tropical fruits

anusvara
\anəs'värə\
Sanskrit
: sound after accent

aortographic
\ā-òr-də-'gra-fik\
Latin
: through visualization of heart wall

apagoge
\apəgōjē\
Latin
: syllogistic argument

aparaphysate
\āpərafəsət\
Latin
: lacking gametogenous organs

aperitive
\ə'perətiv\
French
: stimulating appetite

apharyngent
\āfə¦rinjənt\
Greek>Latin
: lacking the alimentary canal

aphelinid
\afə'līnəd\
Latin
: insect

206

aphetically
\ə-ˈfe-ti-k(ə-)lē\
Latin
: formed by loss of beginning letters

aphetohyoidean
\afə͵tō͵hīˈȯidēən\
Greek+Latin
: fish fossil

aphthitalite
\afˈthitəl͵īt\
Greek
: mineral of potassium

aporhyolite
\apərīə͵līt\
Greek
: rock mineral

apogaeic
\apəˌjēik\
Latin
: of the point farthest from Earth

aposoros
\apəˈsōrōz\
Akan
: flying lemurs

apotome
\əˈpätəmē\
Greek
: interval of tone

appestat
\apəˌstat\
Greek
: neural center in brain

appinite
\apəˌnīt\
Scottish
: rock mineral

appressorial
\aprəsōrēəl\
Latin
: of tuftlike branches

aproterodont
\āprädərəˌdänt, āprō¦terədänt\
Latin
: toothless

aptychus
\aptəkəs\
Latin
: shelly plate

aquaeducti
\akwəˈdəktē\
Latin
: right in law to lead water

aquafortises
\ä-kwə-ˈfȯr-təsəs\
Latin
: etching in nitrous acids

aquametries
\əˈkwämətrēz\
Latin
: determinations of amount of water

aquatinta
\a-kwə-ˌtintə\
Latin
: in engraving processes

aquilege
\a-kwə-ˈlē-j\
Latin
: red-flowered plant

aquotizing
\akwəˌtīzing\
Latin
: undergoing water molecule replacement

arachnactis
\a͵rakˈnaktəs\
Latin
: free-swimming larva

araeosystyle
\ərēəsiˌstīl\
Latin
: interwoven columns

araminas
\arəˈmēnəz\
Portuguese
: fibers

araponga
\arəˈpäŋgə\
Portuguese
: loud bird

archaebacterial
\ärkēbaktirēəl\
Latin
: of the animal kingdom

archaeocete
\ärkēəsēt\
Latin
: slender whale

archaizing
\är-kē-ˌīzing\
Latin
: making antique

archecentric
\ärkəsentrik\
Latin
: designating an original model

archilochian
\ärkəlōkēən\
Latin
: sarcastic or bitter

archioligochaetes
\är-kēäləgō͵kēts\
Latin
: aquatic worms

archontate
\ärkəntāt\
Greek
: office of magistrate

archosaur
\ärkəsȯr\
Latin
: reptile

arendalite
\ə'rendəl͵īt\
German
: red mineral

arere
\ə'rerē\
African name
: large tree

aretaics
\arə'tāiks\
Greek
: science of virtue

Aretinian
\arə'tinēən\
Italian
: relating to theories of
movable hexachords

arghans
\ärgənz\
Unknown
: fiber-yielding plants

arilloid
\arə͵lȯid\
Latin
: resembling appendages

arkosic
\är-'kō-sik\
Latin
: of sandstone

arret
\a're, arā\
French
: sovereign decision

arrha
\arə\
Latin
: earnest money

arrhae
\arē\
Latin
: earnest money

arrhal
\arəl\
Latin
: relating to earnest money

arrhenokaryotic
\arə͵nō͵karē¦atik\
Greek
: of paternal chromosomes

artels
\är'tel(ʸ)s\
French
: cooperative craft society

artiodactyl
\är-tē-ō-¦dak-təl\
Greek
: even-toed

ascaris
\a-skə-rəs\
Latin
: nematode

asclepiadean
\ə'sklēpēədēən\
Latin
: Greek lyrics verses

Astburyware
\as(t)b(ə)rēwer\
English name
: 18th century pottery

Atabrine
\a-tə-brən\
Trademark
: preparation of drug

atocha
\ə'tōchə\
Spanish
: basket grass

Ausonian
\ȯ¦sōnyən\
Latin
: the Italian language

autolysate
\ȯ-'tä-lə-͵sāt\
ISV
: product of self-digestion

awabi
\ə'wäbē\
Japanese
: mollusk

azelate
\azəl͵āt\
Latin
: salt or ester

azidothymidine
\azədōthīmidēn\
ISV
: drug

azym
\azȯm\
Latin
: unleavened bread

babingtonite
\babiŋtə͵nīt\
English name
: iron silicate

bacchiac
\bə'kīək\
Greek
: composed of metrical feet

balaenoidean
\balə¦nȯidēən\
Latin
: whale

balibago
\bälē'bägō\
Tagalog & Bisayan
: tree

ballate
\bəlä͵tā\
Italian
: medieval songs

banghies
\baŋgēz\
Hindi
: shoulder yokes

bankskoites
\baŋk͵skȯitəz\
Swedish
: bank fisheries

bardane
\bär¦dän\
French
: any flowerhead

barklyite
\bärklē͵īt\
English name
: opaque mineral

Barmecide
\bär-mə-͵sīd\
Arabic
: unreal, illusory

baria
\bəˈrēə\
Spanish
: timber tree

barrulets
\bar(y)ələ̇ts\
French
: fourth of a bar

bateaux
\ba-ˈtōz\
French
: small crafts

bathybius
\bathibēəs\
Greek
: gelatinous substance

baumhauerite
\bau̇¦mau̇ə͵rīt\
Swiss
: lead mineral

bavians
\bāvēənz\
German
: black monkey

beckelite
\bekə͵līt\
Austrian
: mineral

beekite
\bē͵kīt\
English
: pseudomorph of coral

Benzedrine
\ben-zə-͵drēn\
Trademark
: preparation of amphetamine

benzpyrinium
\benzpəˈrinēəm\
ISV
: substituted ion

Berengarian
\berə̇nˈga(a)rēən\
French
: denying wine

berkovets
\berkə͵vets\
Russian
: pound measurement

berrettino
\berəˈtēnō\
Italian
: skullcap

berettinas
\berəˈtēnəz\
Italian
: cardinal's caps

berthollide
\bərthə͵līd, bərˈthä͵līd\
Latin
: solid chemical compound

berzeliite
\bərˈzēlē͵īt\
German
: yellow arsenate

bethylid
\bethələd\
Latin
: resembling wasps

bettong
\be͵tȯŋ\
Australian name
: kangaroo

beylerbey
\bālə(r)͵bā\
Turkish
: governor of Ottoman Empire

beylical
\bālikəl\
Turkish
: relating to governor's jurisdiction

bezantee
\bə̇ˈzantē\
French
: flat disk

bharti
\bärtē\
Hindi
: barnyard grass

bibitory
\bibə̇͵tōrē\
Latin
: absorbing moisture

bigelowia
\bigəˈlōēə\
Latin
: alternately-leaved plant

bijasal
\bējə͵säl\
Sanskrit
: tree yielding dried juice

209

bilcock
\bil͵käk\
Unknown
: wading bird

bildar
\bilˈdär\
Hindi
: excavator, digger

bilifuscin
\biləfəsən\
Latin
: brown pigment in gallstones

billian
\bilēən\
Malay
: timber tree

bilsted
\bil͵sted\
Unknown
: sweet gum tree

binit
\bīnət\
English
: either 1 or 0

biopyribole
\bīōˈpirə͵bōl\
Latin
: composed of igneous rocks

birling
\bərliŋ\
English
: sport of logrolling

bizet
\bəˈzet\
English
: oblique side of gem

Boasian
\bō͵asēən\
German
: relating to anthropological theories

bocconia
\bəˈkōnēə\
Latin
: garden plant

bodegon
\bōdäˈgōn\
Spanish
: genre of still-life painting

Bodleian
\bädⱡlēən\
English
: relating to Oxford University

Boehmeria
\bāˈmirēə\
German
: genus of trees

bohea
\bō-ˈhē\
Pekingese
: black tea

Boerhaavia
\bùrˈhāvēə\
German
: tropical herb genus

Bokhara
\bō-ˈkär-ə\
Turkish
: purplish red

bombacopsis
\bämbəˈkäpsəs\
Latin
: tree with capsular fruits

bonailie
\bäˈnäli\
Scottish
: parting drink

bonavist
\bänəvəst\
Italian
: twining vine

bonze
\bän(d)z\
Portuguese>French
: Buddhist monk

borele
\bórə͵lā\
Tswana
: black rhinoceros

Borotuke
\bōr͵ōtəⱡkā\
Paraguayan
: language stock

borrelia
\bəˈrelēə\
Latin
: bacteria

bostrychid
\bästrəkəd\
Latin
: beetle

borunduk
\bórənⱡdük\
Russian
: fur of chipmunk

boschveld
\bäs(h)͵felt\
Afrikaans
: south African land

botryllid
\bōˈtriləd\
Latin
: animal

boucle
\bü-ⱡklā\
French
: yarn

bouget
\büjət\
French
: leather bag

brachyskelous
\bra'kiskələs\
Greek
: having short legs

braees
\braz, brāz\
Norwegian
: glacier, ice cap

brattishing
\bratəshiŋ\
English
: form of screen paneling

braula
\brȯlə\
Latin
: wingless fly

breitschwantz
\brīt͜shfän(t)s\
German
: fish

breunnerite
\brȯinə͜rīt\
German
: ferritic mineral

brevier
\brə'vi(ə)r\
Dutch
: size of type

briscola
\brēskōlä\
Italian
: card game

brochidodromous
\bräkə¦dädrəməs\
Latin
: forming in loops

brocho
\brȯk̲o̲\
Yiddish
: benediction, blessing

broderer
\brōdərə(r)\
French
: guild of embroiderers

brodiaea
\brōdē'ēə\
Latin
: various flower

bromvogel
\bräm͜fügəl\
Afrikaans
: wading bird

Broussonetia
\brüsə'nēsh(ē)ə\
Latin
: genus of trees

Brunfelsia
\brὺn'felzēə\
Latin
: genus of shrubs

Brunnichia
\brə'nikēə\
Danish
: genus of herbs

bruyere
\brū͞eyeer\
French
: heath of Europe

bryonia
\brī'ōnēə\
Latin
: dried root

bufotalin
\byüfə'talən\
ISV
: crystalline

bufotenine
\byüfə'te͜nēn\
ISV
: crystalline alkaloid

bugara
\bü'garə\
Unknown
: rainbow perch

bulli
\bὺ͜lī\
Australian name
: black soil

buloke
\bὺ͜lōk\
Australian name
: tree

bultow
\bὺltō\
Unknown
: rope line

bunsenite
\bənsənīt\
English
: oxide mineral

burgall
\bər͜gȯl\
Unknown
: fish

burra
\bərä\
Hindi
: great

burrawang
\bərə͜waŋ\
Australian
: plant

burroweed
\bərōwēd\
English
: sage bush

byerite
\bī(ə)͜rīt\
English
: coal

byrlawmen
\bir͵lȯmən\
English
: local officers

bystromite
\bistrə͵mīt\
English
: magnesium mineral

caama
\kämə\
Afrikaans
: fox

cabas
\kəbäz\
French
: women's handbags

cabalassou
\kabə'lasü\
Portuguese
: giant armadillo

Cabralea
\kə'brälēə\
Latin
: genus of trees

cachimilla
\kächə'mē(y)ə\
Spanish
: shrub

Caddoan
\ka-də-wən\
Ojibwa
: language family

cadinene
\kadən͵ēn\
ISV
: oily hydrocarbon

caimitillo
\kīmə'tē(y)ō\
Spanish
: timber tree

cailcedra
\kīl'sēdrə\
Unknown
: tree

caiquejee
\kä'ēkjē\
Turkish
: sailor

caji
\kə'hē\
Spanish
: brown fish

cala
\kə'lä\
African
: fried rice cake

calathi
\kaləthī\
Greek
: fruit baskets

Calchaquian
\kalchə¦kēən\
Spanish
: relating to language family

calclacite
\kalklə͵sīt\
ISV
: chloride acetate

calin
\kȧlaⁿ\
French
: alloy of tin

calliphorine
\kə'lif(ə)rīn\
Latin
: relating to bottleflies

calthrops
\kalthrəps\
Latin
: sponges

calycoideous
\kālə͵kȯidēəs\
Latin
: resembling floral leaves

Camaldolese
\kə¦maldə¦lēz\
Latin
: member of barefooted
soldiers

camanay
\kamə¦nī\
Spanish
: Pacific coast bird

caman
\kə'mȯn\
Gaelic
: stick

camarilla
\ka-mə-'ri-lə\
Spanish
: group of advisers

camatina
\kamə'tēnə\
Italian
: unripe acorns

cameralistics
\ka-mə-rəlistiks\
Latin
: public finance

camerostome
\kam(ə)rə͵stōm\
Latin
: marginal depression

camote
\kə'mōtē\
Spanish
: sweet potato

camphoroyl
\kam'fȯrə͵wil\
ISV
: bivalent radical

Campidanese
\kämpədəˈnāsē\
Italian
: Sicilian language

camus
\kaməs\
French
: short and flat nose

canalete
\kanəlˈetē\
Spanish
: timber tree

candicidin
\kandəˌsīdən\
Latin
: antibiotic

cannabidiol
\kanəbəˈdīˌȯl\
Latin
: crystalline

cantoris
\kanˌtōrəs\
Latin
: ecclesiastical east side of church

canzonet
\kan-zə-ˌnet\
Italian
: light song

caoines
\kēnz\
Irish
: lamentations of dead

capocollo
\kapəˈkōlə\
Italian
: smoked pork

capataces
\kapəˈtäˌsäs\
Spanish
: bosses, overseers

cappae
\käpā\
Latin
: academic garb

capparidaceous
\kapərədāshəs\
Latin
: resembling herbs

caprylin
\kaprələn\
ISV
: sugar

Capuan
\kapyəwən\
Italian
: luxurious

capuchin
\ka-pyə-shən\
French
: pigeon

capuchiness
\ka-pyə-shənes\
French
: nun of austere order

carabeen
\karəˌbēn\
Welsh
: tree

carabidan
\kəˈrabədən\
Latin
: resembling large beetles

caraco
\karəˌkō\
French
: women's short coat

caracara
\ka-rə-ˈka-rə\
Spanish
: hawk

carbanion
\kär-ˈba-ˌnī-ən\
ISV
: organic compound

Carbitol
\kärbəˌtȯl\
Trademark
: high boiling

carbolfuchsin
\kärˌbälˈfyüksən\
ISV
: alcohol solution

cardines
\kärdənˌēz\
Latin
: proximal parts of shell

cariniform
\kəˈrinəˌfȯ(ə)rm\
Latin
: shaped like a keel

Carlisle
\kärˌlīl\
French
: fish hook

Carlylese
\kärˌlīˌlēz\
French
: relating to style of writing

Carmelite
\kär-mə-ˌlīt\
Latin
: mendicant order

Carnegiea
\kärˈnegēə\
Latin
: genus of cacti

carnet
\kärˌnā\
French
: credit card

carpellary
\kär-pə-ˌler-ē\
Latin
: containing seed plants

carriwitchet
\kərəwichət\
Unknown
: riddling question

carromata
\karəˈmätə\
Philippine
: boxlike carriage

cartulary
\kär-chə-ˌler-ē\
Latin
: collection of deeds

carvacryl
\kärvəkril\
ISV
: radical

caryophyllaceous
\karēōfəlāshəs\
Latin
: resembling trees

casabe
\kəsäbē\
Spanish
: fish

Casasia
\kəˈsäzh(ē)ə\
Latin
: genus of trees

cascabel
\kaskəbel\
Spanish
: breach of cannon

cascara
\ka-ˈsker-ə\
Spanish
: tree bark

Casimiroa
\kazəməˈrōə\
Latin
: genus of trees

Castilloa
\kastəˈlōə, kaˈstiləwə\
Latin
: genus of trees

castorette
\kastəˌret\
French
: beaver fur

catapan
\katəˌpan\
Latin
: Byzantine governor

cataphyllary
\katəfilərē\
Latin
: rudimentary leaf

cathay
\kəˈthā\
French
: yellow

catjang
\käˌchäŋ\
Dutch
: tropical herb

catocalid
\kəˈtäkələd\
Latin
: dull-winged moth

Caughnawaga
\kägnəˈwägə\
Mohawk
: native of Montreal

Caytonia
\kāˈtōnēə\
Latin
: genus of plants

caza
\kəˈzä\
Turkish
: subdivision of district

cecidomyiid
\sesədōmīəd\
Latin
: two-winged fly

celandine
\se-lən-ˌdīn\
French
: perennial herb

cenobitically
\se-nə-ˌbi-ti-k(ə-)lē\
French
: in the manner of monks

censive
\säⁿsēēv\
French
: relating to orderly payments

cephalob
\sefəˌlōb\
Latin
: nematode worm

cetotherean
\sētəˌthi(ə)rēən\
Latin
: diurnal beetle

Chabakano
\chäbəˈkänō\
Philippine
: language

Chabertia
\shəˈbertēə\
French
: genus of nematode worms

chacate
\chəˈkätē\
Spanish
: small shrub

214

chaetigerous
\kēˈtij(ə)rəs\
Latin
: bearing bristles

chaetophorous
\kēˈtäf(ə)rəs\
Latin
: bearing bristles

chaetotaxy
\kēˈtətaxē\
Latin
: arrangement of bristles

chakdar
\chəkdär\
Hindi
: land tenant

chalcidic
\kalˈsidək\
Latin
: large building

chalicothere
\kaləkōˌthi(ə)r\
Latin
: mammal

chamaeconchy
\kaməkäŋkē\
Latin
: low orbital index

chamisal
\shaməsal\
Spanish
: jungle of shrubs

chamotte
\chəˈmät\
French
: fined material

charadrine
\karəˌdrīn\
Latin
: resembling plovers

Charmeuse
\shär-ˌm(y)üz\
Trademark
: fine fabric

chartularies
\kär-chə-ˌler-ēz\
Latin
: keepers of records

chassezes
\shaˈsā(zə̇)z\
French
: dance steps

chatellanies
\shatəlˌanēz\
French
: jurisdiction of castle owner

chavender
\chavəndə(r)\
English
: fish

chaverim
\ḵäˈvärim\
Hebrew
: associates

chavicine
\chavəˌsēn\
ISV
: alkaloid

chebec
\chēˈbek\
Imitative
: small bird

chebog
\chəbäg\
Natick
: fish

cheddite
\shedīt\
French
: blasting explosive

cheecha
\chēchə\
Ceylonese
: lizard

cheirolin
\kīrələn\
ISV
: alkaloid

chekker
\chekə(r)\
Unknown
: stringed instrument

chelerythrine
\keləˈriˌthrēn\
ISV
: alkaloid

chelicerate
\kəˈlisəˌrāt\
Latin
: provided with pincers

chelodine
\keləˈdīn\
Latin
: relating to a genus of turtles

chelonethid
\keləˈnēthəd\
Latin
: scorpion

chelydroid
\kelədròid\
Latin
: snapping turtle

chemigraph
\kemə̇ˌgraf\
ISV
: engraving

Chemnitz
\kemˌnits\
German
: from the city

cheneaus
\shā'nōz\
French
: crestings

chenet
\shənā\
French
: metal support

chengal
\cheŋgəl\
Malay
: durable wood

Cheremissian
\cherə¦misēən\
Finnish
: farmer

Cherethite
\kerə͵thīt\
Hebrew
: Philistine

Chernovtsy
\cher'nȯftsē\
Ukrainian
: from the city

Chettyar
\chetē͵är\
Tamil
: merchant

cheyletus
\kīlētəs\
Latin
: mite

Chhattisgarhi
\chətēs'gärē\
Hindi
: dialect of India

Chibchan
\chibchən\
Spanish
: relating to language stock

chicalote
\chikə'lōtē\
Spanish
: prickly poppy

chiastolite
\kī'astə͵līt\
German
: mineral

chibigouazou
\shēbē͵gü'äzü\
Portuguese
: ocelot

chicharro
\chēchärō\
Spanish
: big-eyed fish

Chichimecan
\chēchə͵mekən\
Spanish
: relating to Aztec Empire

chichipate
\chichə'pätē\
Spanish
: timber tree

chichituna
\chēchə'tünə\
Spanish
: fruit

chidra
\chēdrə\
Spanish
: young fiber

chiliarch
\kilē͵ärk\
Greek
: commander of thousand men

Chimarikan
\chimə'rēkən\
Spanish
: language family

Chinantecan
\chinən͵tekən\
Spanish
: language family

chingma
\chinmä\
Pekingese
: jute fiber

chinin
\chə'nēn\
Spanish
: avocado

chionodoxa
\kī-ə-nō-'däk-sə\
Latin
: plant

chiquero
\chə'kerō\
Spanish
: cell in bullring

Chiquitoan
\chə'kētəwən\
Spanish
: language family

chiripa
\chirə¦pä\
Spanish
: woolen garment

chirographary
\kī'rägrə͵ferē, kīrə¦grafərē\
Latin
: evidenced by arguments

chishti
\chishtē\
Arabic
: Islam brotherhood

Chitimachan
\chitə'mäshən\
Spanish
: language family

chiveys
\shivēz\
Natick
: whitefish

chladnite
\klad‚nīt\
English
: mineral

chlamydeous
\klə'midēəs\
Latin
: floral envelope

chlamydozoon
\klamədəzōən\
Latin
: microorganism

chlamyphore
\klamə‚fō(ə)r\
Latin
: armadillo

chloragocyte
\klōrəgə‚sīt\
Latin
: cell

chloralosane
\klōrə'lō‚sān\
French
: crystalline

chlorarsen
\klōr'ärsən\
ISV
: hydrochloride

chloritize
\klōrə‚tīz\
ISV
: to alter a mineral

chloroxylenol
\klōrəzīlə‚nȯl\
ISV
: derivative

chokidar
\chōkē¦där\
Hindi
: watchman

cholelith
\kōlə‚lith\
ISV
: gallstone

cholepoieses
\kōlə‚pȯi'ēsēz\
Greek
: productions of bile

cholestene
\kə'le‚stēn\
ISV
: hydrocarbon

cholis
\chōlēz\
Hindi
: tunics

chondriocont
\kändrēō‚känt\
ISV
: rod-shaped bacterium

chondrosin
\kändrəsən\
German
: acid

chondrule
\kän-drül\
Latin
: rounded granule

chordacentrum
\kȯrdəsentrəm\
Latin
: vertebral bones

choreoathetotic
\kōrēōathə¦tätik\
Latin
: resembling nervous
distances

choristate
\kə'ristət\
Greek
: exhibiting leaf separation

Chorotegan
\chōrə'tāgən\
Spanish
: language family

chouans
\shüänz\
French
: Western insurgents

Choukoutien
\jō‚kō¦tyen\
Pekingese
: chopper tools

chowk
\chau̇k\
Hindi
: main street

christendie
\krisən¦dē\
English
: portion of world following
Christ

christophine
\kri-stə-‚fēn\
French
: pear

chromascope
\krō-məskōp\
Greek
: instrument

chromatophorous
\krō-mə-¦tä-f(ə-)rəs\
Greek
: of pigment-based cells

chrysoeriol
\krīsōerēəl\
ISV
: compound

217

chuckwalla
\chək-ˌwä-lə\
Spanish
: lizard

chukars
\chə-ˈkärz\
Hindi
: partridges

chultunes
\chülˈtüˌnās\
Maya
: boats

Chumashan
\chüˌmashən\
Spanish
: language family

churingas
\chüˈriŋgəz\
Australian
: wooden object

chytridiosis
\kəˌtrīdēˈōsəs\
Latin
: disease caused by fungi

cicuta
\səˈkyütə\
Latin
: poisonous herb

cidarid
\sidərəd\
Latin
: sea urchin

ciliola
\səˈlīələ\
Latin
: minute hair

cimborio
\simˈbōrēˌō\
Spanish
: raised dome

cimices
\siməˌsēz\
Latin
: bedbug

cimicifugin
\siməˈsifyəjən\
Latin
: resin

ciminite
\chiməˌnīt\
Italian
: extrusive rock

cinchocaine
\siŋkəˌkān\
Latin
: anesthetic

cinchophen
\siŋkəfen\
ISV
: compound

cinerolone
\sinərōˌlōn\
ISV
: alcohol

cinnoline
\sinəˌlēn\
German
: crystalline

cionid
\sīənəd\
Latin
: bacteria

cipo
\sēˈpō\
Spanish
: climbing vines

cippi
\sipī\
Latin
: small pillars

Circean
\sərsēən\
Latin
: dangerously misleading

cirio
\sirēˌō\
Spanish
: candlewood

cirratulid
\səˈrachələd\
Latin
: of marine worms

cirriform
\sirəˌform\
Latin
: slender and prolonged

citharoedic
\sithəˌrēdik\
Latin
: relating to zithers

citoler
\səˈtōlə(r)\
Italian
: lute player

citrangedin
\səˈtranjədən\
ISV
: flavor of lime

citrylidene
\səˈtriləˌdēn\
ISV
: bivalent radical

cladocerous
\klə-ˈdä-sə-rəs\
Latin
: relating to insects

cladoselachian
\kladōsəˌlākēən\
Latin
: sharkfish

claes
\klāz\
English
: vestments

clairon
\klārōⁿ\
French
: organ stop

clarin
\klə'rēn\
Spanish
: wind instrument

clathrarian
\klə'thra(a)rēən\
Latin
: plant

clausilia
\klȯ'zilēə\
Latin
: rodlike closures

clavellated
\klavə‿lātəd\
Latin
: made of dried matter

cleading
\klēdiŋ\
English
: lining of boards

cleistothecia
\klīstə'thēs(h)ēə\
Latin
: spore-bearing structure

cleome
\klē'ōmē\
Latin
: plant

clerestoried
\klirstōrēd\
English
: having a roof

cleruchial
\klə'rükēəl\
Greek
: relating to citizens

cleveite
\klē‿vīt, klävə‿īt\
Swedish
: mineral

clinoenstatite
\klīnōenztətīt\
Latin
: mineral

clitellate
\klə'telət\
Latin
: having a thick section

cloacinal
\klōə¦sīnəl\
Latin
: having a bird's neck

clootie
\klü-tē\
Scottish
: devil

clubstart
\klùb‿stärt\
Scottish
: weasel

clyers
\klī(ə)rz\
Dutch
: cattle tuberculosis

clymenid
\klimənəd\
Latin
: worm

clyssi
\klisī\
Latin
: efficacious principles

cnidophorous
\nī¦däfərəs\
Latin
: structure bearing sacs

Coahuiltecan
\kōəwēltekən\
Spanish
: language family

coakum
\kōkəm\
Unknown
: pokeweed

coalport
\kōl‿pōrt\
English
: porcelain

coble
\kō-bəl\
English
: boat

Cocceian
\käk'sēyən\
English
: adherent of beliefs

coccostean
\kə'kästēən\
Latin
: fish

coccydynia
\käksə'dinēə\
Latin
: pain in the acetabulum

cocle
\kō¦klā\
geographical name
: Panamanian culture

codicillary
\kä-də-¦si-lə-rē\
French
: belonging to appendices

coelolepid
\sēlə‚lepəd\
Latin
: insect

coendou
\kōˈendü\
Latin
: porcupine

coenenchym
\səˈneŋ‚kəm\
Latin
: complex amoeba

coenesthesia
\sēnesˈthēzh(ē)ə\
Latin
: totality of sensations

coenobioid
\səˈnōbēoid\
Latin
: colonies of cells

coenostea
\səˈnästēə\
Latin
: skeletons

coenuri
\senyurī\
Latin
: worms

coeruleolactite
\sə‚rülēōˈlak‚tīt\
Latin
: mineral

cohenite
\kōə‚nīt\
German
: mineral

Cohonina
\kō(h)əˈnēnə\
Spanish
: culture

coigue
\kȯigā\
Spanish
: tree

coihues
\kȯiwāz\
Spanish
: evergreens

coixes
\kōəksəz\
Latin
: plants

cokernut
\kōkə(r)‚nət\
English
: edible seed

colacobioses
\kälə‚kōbīˈōsēs\
Latin
: social parasitisms

colasciones
\kōləˈshōnēz\
Italian
: lute

colature
\käləchə(r)\
Latin
: straining

colchicinize
\kälˈchisənīz\
ISV
: induce mitosis

colemanite
\kōl-mə-‚nīt\
English
: mineral

coleochaetaceous
\kōlē‚ōkēˈtāshəs\
Latin
: resembling algae

coleuses
\kō-lē-əsəs\
Latin
: plants

coliphage
\kō-lə-‚fāj\
Latin
: bacteria

colk
\kōk\
Gaelic
: duck

collembolous
\kə-ˈlem-bə-ləs\
Latin
: of arthropods

collibert
\kälə‚bərt\
French
: peasant tenant

colliculi
\kəlikyəlī\
Latin
: prominences

collinsonia
\kälənˈsōnēə\
Latin
: plant

colloform
\kälə‚förm\
Latin
: shaped like substances

collomia
\kəˈlōmēə\
Latin
: plant

colluctation
\käləkˈtāshən\
Latin
: struggle

colmatage
\kälmətij\
French
: impounding of water

colobomatous
\kälə'bōmətəs\
Latin
: relating to eye fissures

colocolic
\kälə¦kälik\
Latin
: relating to two parts of colon

colpindach
\kōlpə̇ndək\
English
: young cow

coluber
\käləbə(r)\
Latin
: snake

columnea
\kə'ləmnēə\
Latin
: plant

colure
\kə'lù(ə)r\
Latin
: circle on sphere

coly
\kōlē\
Latin
: bird

colytic
\kə'litik\
Greek
: inhibitory

combretum
\kəm'brētəm\
Latin
: plant

comburimetry
\kämbyə'rimətrē\
ISV
: combustion apparatus

comedones
\kä-mə-'dō-nēz\
Latin
: collection of dead cells

comfit
\kəm(p)-fət\
English
: sweet confection

comitat
\kōmə¦tät\
German
: administrative decision in Hungary

commelinaceous
\kämə'lənāshəs\
Latin
: like plants

commiscuum
\kə'miskyəwəm\
Latin
: subdivision of organisms

commissurotomy
\kämə͜shu̇'rätəmē\
ISV
: operation of cutting fibers

commorient
\kə'mōrēənt\
Latin
: dying together

compages
\kəm'pā͜jēz, 'käm͜pājə̇z\
Latin
: combined parts of structure

compere
\käm-͜per\
French
: emcee

composograph
\kəm'pōzə͜graf\
ISV
: synthetic picture

comtist
\käm(p)-tist\
French
: adherent to confidence

concanavalin
\känkanəvalən\
ISV
: bean

conciliabule
\känsilēə͜byül\
French
: secret meeting

concitato
\känchə'tätō\
Italian
: in agitated state

condulet
\kändəlet\
Trademark
: pipe box

condurangin
\kändə'raŋ(g)ə̇n\
ISV
: compound

condylarth
\kändə͜lärth\
Latin
: fossil

confitent
\känfətənt\
Latin
: one who removes sins

congee
\kän-jē\
French (1), Tamil (2)
: (1) bow ceremoniously
: (2) soaked rice water

congii
\känjēī\
English
: gallons

coniceine
\kəˈnisēən\
German
: poisonous base

conichalcite
\känəˈkalˌsīt\
German
: mineral

conidiophorous
\kə-ˈni-dē-ä-f(ə-)rəs\
ISV
: structure in fungi

coniine
\kō-nē-ˌēn\
ISV
: liquid alkaloid

connach
\känək\
Gaelic
: spoil, waste

connaraceous
\känəˈrāshəs\
Latin
: resembling shrubs

conopid
\kōnəˌpid\
Latin
: fly

conquinine
\käŋkwəˌnēn\
ISV
: alkaloid

consertal
\kənˈsərtəl\
Latin
: sutured

consol
\känˌsäl\
Latin
: bond issue

consuetudinary
\kän(t)-swi-ˈt(y)ü-də-ˌner-ē\
Latin
: manual

contabescent
\käntəˈbesən(t)\
ISV
: resembling anthers

contorniate
\kənˈtȯ(r)nēət\
Italian
: encircled by grooves

contrahent
\käntrəhənt\
Latin
: entering agreement

contrapletal
\käntrəplētəl\
Latin
: polar and complementary

contraponend
\käntrəpəˌnend\
Latin
: proposition

convolvulaceous
\kənˌvälv(y)əˈlāshəs\
Latin
: resembling vines

cookeite
\kůˌkīt\
English
: mineral

copalm
\kōˌpäm\
French
: tree

Copehan
\kōˈpā(h)ən\
Spanish
: language family

copei
\kōˈpāē\
Spanish
: apple

copepodan
\kōˈpepədən\
Latin
: minute organisms

copiapite
\kōpēəˌpīt\
German
: mineral

copperas
\kä-p(ə-)rəs\
Latin
: green sulfate

coprostanol
\kəˈprästəˌnȯl\
ISV
: crystalline sterol

coqueiro
\küˈkärü, kəˈka(a)rü\
Portuguese
: palm tree

coqui
\kō-kwē\
Sechuana
: partridge

coraciiform
\kəˈrāsēəˌfȯrm\
Latin
: resembling birds

cordeliere
\kȯ(r)dəlˈye(ə)r\
French
: knotted cord

cordelle
\kȯrdel\
French
: keel towline

cordyline
\kȯ(r)dəlˈīnē\
Latin
: tree

coregonine
\kȯrəˈgōnīn\
Latin
: of freshwater fish

coreid
\kȯrēəd\
Latin
: bug

coremia
\kōˈrēmēə\
Latin
: fruiting body

corixid
\kəˈriksəd\
Latin
: resembling aquatic bugs

coromandel
\kȯr-ə-ˈman-dəl\
Hindi
: moderate reddish brown

coronene
\kȯr-ə-ˌnēn\
Latin
: hydrocarbon

coronillin
\korənilən\
ISV
: glucoside

coronis
\kəˈrōnəs\
Latin
: mark over vowel

correa
\kəˈrēə\
Latin
: plant

correlogram
\kəˈreləˌgram\
ISV
: plotted curve

cortinae
\kȯrˈtīnē\
Latin
: cobwebby remnants

corvusite
\kȯrvəˌsīt\
Latin
: mineral

corydine
\kȯrəˌdēn\
ISV
: crystalline alkaloid

corylaceous
\kȯrə⎮lāshəs\
Latin
: resembling shrubs

coryphaenoid
\kȯrəˈfēnoid\
Latin
: percoid fish

coryphodont
\kəˈrifəˌdänt\
Latin
: fossil

cosalite
\kōzəˌlīt\
geographical name
: mineral

cosaque
\kōˈzäk\
French
: party favor

coscoroba
\käskəˈrōbə\
Spanish
: bird

cosmatesque
\käzmətesk\
Italian
: of geometric patterns

Cosmoline
\käz-mə-ˌlēn\
Trademark
: used for petrolatum

cossid
\käsəd\
(1) Hindi (2) Latin
(1): mounted messenger
(2): moth

costiasis
\käˈstīəsəs\
Latin
: fatal fish disease

coterell
\kätər(ə)l\
English
: peasant class

cothurnus
\kō-ˈthər-nəs\
Latin
: boot

cotoin
\kōtəwȯn\
ISV
: crystalline ketone

cotoneaster
\kətō-nēastər\
Latin
: shrub

cotonier
\kətō-nēā\
Latin
: tree

cotswold
\kätswōld\
English
: sheep

cotyligerous
\kätəl¦ijərəs\
Latin
: having cuplike cavities

coude
\küdā\
French
: telescope

coueism
\küāizm\
French
: psychotherapy

coulier
\külyər\
French
: knitting machine

coulsonite
\kōlsəˌnīt\
English
: magnet

coulterneb
\kōltə(r)ˌneb\
English
: bird

coumaran
\k(y)üməˌran\
ISV
: colorless oil

counterriposte
\kaùn-tərrə'pōst\
French
: parry in fencing

courida
\kü'rēdə\
geographical name
: plant

couronne
\kü'rȯn\
French
: loop in pattern

couxia
\küshēə\
Tupi
: monkey

cowanyoung
\kaùənˌyəŋ\
Australian
: fish

cowdie
\kaùdē\
Maori
: tree

coween
\kə'wēn\
Algonquian
: duck

cowroid
\kaùrȯid\
English
: resembling an Egyptian seal

cowthwort
\küˌthwərt\
Unknown
: plant

coxswain
\käk-sən, käkswān\
English
: steer a ship

craggan
\kragən\
English
: earthenware vessel

craichy
\krāchi\
Unknown
: dilapidated

crapette
\kra'pet\
French
: card game

crassulaceous
\kras(y)əlāshəs\
Latin
: resembling herbs

creat
\krē¦at\
Hindi
: herb

creedalism
\krēdəlˌizəm\
English
: undue insistence

cresylite
\kresəˌlīt\
ISV
: explosive rock

criniere
\krēn'ya(a)(ə)r\
French
: articulated armor

crispin
\krispən\
biblical name
: shoemaker, cobbler

crithidiform
\krithidəˌfȯrm\
Latin
: shaped like flagellates

crithmene
\krithˌmēn\
ISV
: radical

crocidura
\kräsə'd(y)ùrə\
Latin
: musk shrew

croppy
\kräpē\
Irish
: rebel

croquill
\krō͜ˌkwil\
English
: artist's pen

crossosomataceous
\kräsə'sōmətāshəs\
Latin
: resembling shrubs

crotal
(1) \krō͜ˌtäl\ (2) \krätəl\
(1) Greek (2) Gaelic
(1): spherical rattle
(2): brownish red

crotonoyl
\krō͜ˌtänəwil\
ISV
: univalent radical

croze
\krōz\
French
: machine

crutter
\krədər\
English
: mine driller

cryosel
\krīō͜ˌsel\
French
: crystalline solid

cryptocoryne
\kriptə'kȯrə͜ˌnē\
Latin
: plant

ctenidial
\tə̇'nidēəl\
Latin
: relating to mollusks

cuaguayote
\kwägwə'yōtē\
Spanish
: tree

cuapinole
\kwäpə͜ˌnōl\
Spanish
: locust tree

cuartel
\kwär'tel\
Spanish
: barracks

Cubalaya
\kyübə'läə\
geographical name
: fowl

cucujid
\kə'küyə̇d, kə'k(y)üjə̇d\
Latin
: beetle

cucullaris
\kyükə'la(a)rə̇s\
Latin
: muscle

cucullately
\kyü-kəlātlē\
Latin
: shaped like a hood

cuittling
\kütəling\
Unknown
: coax, wheedle

cultellation
\kəltə'lāshən\
French
: transferral to higher
elevation

cumacean
\kyü'māshēən\
Latin
: resembling crustaceans

cumbly
\kəmlē\
Sanskrit
: blanket

cumbu
\kəmbü\
Hindi
: tall grass

cumenyl
\kyümə͜ˌnil\
ISV
: radical

cuorin
\kyü(ə)rən\
ISV
: heart muscle compound

cupellation
\kyü-pə-'lāshən\
Latin
: refinement of gold

curculio
\kər-'kyü-lē-͜ˌō\
Latin
: weevil

curtal
\kər-təl\
English
: tenor instrument

cururo
\kə'rürō\
Spanish
: rodent

custodiam
\kə'stōdēəm\
Latin
: grant of land

Cuvierian
\k(y)ü¦virēən\
French
: relating to classification of
animals

225

cyanuret
\sī'anyə͵ret\
ISV
: compound

cycadeoid
\sī-'ka-dē-͵ȯid\
Latin
: any of fossils

cycloidian
\sī͵klȯidēən\
Latin
: of fish

cyclophyllidean
\sīkləfəlidēən\
Latin
: of worms

cydippid
\sədipəd\
Latin
: resembling larvae

cydonium
\sīdōnēəm\
Latin
: seed

cymbidia
\sim-'bi-dē-əm\
Latin
: plant

cynthiid
\sinthēəd\
Latin
: resembling worms

cyphonautae
\sifənotā\
Latin
: free-swimming larvae

cyrillaceous
\sirəlāshəs\
Latin
: resembling herbs

cytolyzate
\sī'tälə͵zāt\
Latin
: product

dalag
\däläg\
Filipino
: snake

daman
\damən\
French
: Syrian lion

darak
\də'räk\
Tagaog
: rice product

darbha
\därbə\
Sanskrit
: tuft of grass

dartmoor
\därt͵mu̇(ə)r\
English
: sheep breed

dashkesanite
\dashkə'sa͵nīt\
Russian
: sodium mineral

dasycladacean
\dasə̇klə'dāshən\
Latin
: resembling algae

dauws
\dau̇z\
Afrikaans
: zebras

davaineid
\də'vānēəd\
Latin
: tapeworm

debiteuse
\debə¦tüz\
French
: clay block

decury
\dekyərē\
Latin
: Roman division of ten

deforceor
\dəforsər\
Latin
: one who withholds wrongfully

dekanal
\dekənəl\
Greek
: relating to astronomy

delphinidin
\del'fīnədə̇n\
ISV
: glycoside

deptford
\detfərd\
Unknown
: Georgian culture

dermanyssid
\dərmə¦nisə̇d\
Latin
: of parasitic mites

descort
\de'skȯ(ə)r\
French
: medieval lyric

desthiobiotin
\dez͵thīəbī-ə-tən\
ISV
: alkaloid

determa
\də̇'tərmə\
geographical name
: tree

detur
\dē̱ˌtər\
Latin
: bound book

devillite
\dəˈvē̱ˌlīt\
French
: mineral

dewan
\dəˈwän\
Hindi
: chief officer

dewar
\d(y)üə(r)\
Latin
: glass container

deweylite
\d(y)üēlīt\
English
: mineral

dharana
\därənə\
Sanskrit
: fixed attention

dhaura
\därə\
Hindi
: tree

dhauri
\därē\
Hindi
: shrub

dhoon
\dün\
Hindi
: valley

diablotin
\dēäblōtan\
French
: bird

diaboleite
\dīəbōˈlāˌīt\
French
: mineral

Diabolo
\dīabəlō\
Trademark
: hourglass game

diachylum
\dīˈakəˌləm\
Latin
: plaster

diacle
\dīəˈkəl\
Scottish
: pocket compass

diacodium
\dīəˈkōdēəm\
Latin
: narcotic syrup

diadochokinetic
\dīadəkōkȧnetik\
Latin
: muscle power

diaglyph
\dīəˌglif\
Latin
: marble

diallyl
\dīaləl\
ISV
: containing two groups

diapause
\dīəˌpȯz\
Greek
: environmental conditions

diapente
\dīəˈpentē\
English
: interval in music

diascordia
\dīəˈskȯrdēə\
Latin
: stomachic confection

diastimeter
\dīəˈstimətə(r)\
ISV
: distance measurer

diathermanous
\dīəthərmənəs\
French
: transmitting infrared
radiation

diazomata
\dīəˈzōmədə\
Greek
: passages in auditorium

dichasium
\dīˈkāzh(ē)əm\
Latin
: inflorescence

dicksonioid
\dikˈsōnēəȯid\
Latin
: tropical fern

dicrocoelid
\dīkrəsēləd\
Latin
: worm

dictyostely
\diktēəstēlē\
Latin
: vascular cylinder

diddledees
\didəldēz\
English
: fallen pine needles

didot
\dȩ̄dō\
French
: typographical point system

227

didric
\didrik\
Afrikaans
: cuckoo bird

dietine
\dīətēn\
French
: nobleman

digeneous
\dījēnēəs\
Latin
: relating to parasites

digenite
\dijənīt\
Latin
: mineral

digilanide
\dijəˈlaˌnīd\
Trademark
: poisonous crystalline

digoxigenin
\dīˌgäksəˈjenən\
ISV
: crystalline lactone

dikegrave
\dīkˌgrāv\
Dutch
: officer in Holland

Dilaudid
\dīˈlódəd\
Trademark
: crystalline ketone

dilleniaceous
\dəˌlēnēˈāshəs\
Latin
: resembling trees

dillue
\dəˈlü\
Corn
: separate by washing

Diodoquin
\dīˈōdəkwən\
Trademark
: medicinal compound

Diogenean
\dīˌäjəˌnēən\
Greek
: of philosophers

dioxolane
\dīˈäksəˌlān\
ISV
: derivative

diphenan
\dīˈfenən\
ISV
: crystalline ester

diploidion
\diplōˈidēˌän\
Greek
: ancient garment

diplotegia
\diplōtējēə\
Greek
: capsule in body

discinoid
\dis(k)əˌnoid\
Latin
: pertaining to reptiles

discodrilid
\diskōˈdrīləd\
Latin
: worm

discophorous
\dəˈskäf(ə)rəs\
Latin
: bearing disklike structures

diskographies
\dəskägrəfēz\
Latin
: radiogram of invertebrates

dissava
\dəsävə\
Sinhalese
: governor of state

dististyle
\distəstīl\
Latin
: accessory parts

distoclusion
\distəklüzhən\
Latin
: malposition of lower tooth

distringas
\distringəs\
Latin
: writ

disulfiram
\dīsəlfəram\
Trademark
: drug

dital
\dēdəl\
Italian
: key fingering

dithizone
\dīˈthīˌzōn\
ISV
: crystalline compound

ditrochean
\dītrōkēən\
Latin
: relating to metrical feet

dittander
\dətandər\
Latin
: herb

divoto
\dəˈvōtō\
Italian
: with religious emotion

djati
\jätē\
Malay
: tree

dochmii
\däkmēī\
Latin
: five-syllable poems

docoglossate
\däkə'gläsət\
Latin
: gastropod

dodrantes
\dō'dranˌtēz\
Latin
: unit of six syllables

dogana
\dō'gänə\
Persian>Italian
: customhouse

dogaressa
\dōgə'resə\
Italian
: wife of magistrate

doina
\dȯinə\
Romanian
: folk song

dolerophane
\dälərəˌfän\
Latin
: mineral

dolichos
\dälə'käs\
Latin
: plant

dolichurus
\dälə'kyu̇rəs\
Latin
: redundant syllables

dollardee
\dälə(r)ˌdē\
Unknown
: fish

Domitian
\də'mishən\
Latin
: of the Roman emperor

domra
\dämrə\
Russian
: lute

domsiekte
\dämˌsēktə\
Afrikaans
: sheep disease

donum
\dänəm\
Turkish
: land measure

doodiae
\düdēē\
Latin
: plants

dopatta
\dō'pətə\
Hindi
: scarf

doppio
\däpēō\
Italian
: twice

doria
\dōrēə\
Hindi
: fabric

dorippid
\dəripəd\
Latin
: crab

dormidera
\dȯrmə'derə\
Spanish
: plant

dorr
\dȯr\
English
: glacial trough

dorset
\dȯrsət\
English
: blue flower

dorsiflexor
\dȯrsəfleksər\
Latin
: muscle

dosimetric
\dōsəmetrik\
ISV
: relating to x-rays

dottore
\dōtōrē\
Italian
: stock character

douar
\dü'är, də'wär\
Arabic
: village

doubleton
\dəbəltən\
English
: two card game

doublette
\düblet\
French
: organ stop

douc
\dük\
French
: monkey

dozenten
\dōt'senten\
German
: university teachers

drabi
\dräbē\
Hindi
: driver

draegermen
\drāgə(r)mən\
German
: crew of miners

dragoman
\dragəmən\
Turkish
: interpreter

driases
\drīəsəz\
English
: carrots

duan
\düən\
Scottish
: poem, song

duce
\düchā\
Italian
: supreme ruler

dufrenite
\d(y)üˈfrāˌnīt\
French
: mineral

duhat
\düˌhät\
Tagalog
: plum

dulia
\dülīə\
Latin
: paid respect

dumky
\du̇mkē\
Czech
: slow movements

dundasite
\dəndəˌsīt\
geographical name
: mineral

dungon
\düŋˌȯn\
Tagalog
: timber tree

duply
\düˈplī\
Latin
: defendant's answer

duppy
\dəpē\
Bube
: haunting spirit

durham
\dərəm\
English
: cattle breed

duricrust
\d(y)u̇rəˌkrəst\
Latin
: surficial crust

dwaible
\dwābəl\
Unknown
: feeble and shaky

Dyassic
\dīasik\
Latin
: division of era

dysluite
\dislüīt\
Greek
: brown variety

dysyntribite
\dəˈsintrəˌbīt\
Greek
: mineral

earlandite
\irlənˌdīt\
English
: mineral

earock
\irək\
Scottish
: young hen

Eastlake
\ēstˌlāk\
English
: machine-made furniture

ebano
\äbəˌnō\
Spanish
: tree

ecalcarate
\ēkalkəˌrāt\
Latin
: without growths

ecanda
\ēkandə\
Mbundu
: vine

eccle
\ekəl\
Unknown
: woodpecker

echinite
\ekənīt\
Latin
: sea urchin

eckermanite
\ekərmənīt\
English
: mineral

ecthymatous
\ekthimətəs\
Latin
: of skin eruptions

edestin
\ədestən\
ISV
: crystalline

edingtonite
\ediŋtə͵nīt\
English
: mineral

edreobenthos
\edrēōben-͵thäs\
Greek
: sedentary organisms

eglestonite
\egəlstənīt\
English
: mineral

ejoo
\ējü\
Javan
: fiber

ekka
\ekä, ˈekə\
Hindi
: light carriage

elaenia
\əˈlēnēə\
Latin
: bird

elaidin
\əˈlāədən\
ISV
: ester of acid

elaphure
\eləͺfyu̇(ə)r\
Latin
: deer

elecampane
\eləkampān\
Latin
: perennial herb

electrocautery
\əˈlektrōkȯ-tə-rē\
Latin
: burning

elemicin
\əleməsən\
ISV
: liquid ether

eleocyte
\əˈlēə͵sīt\
Latin
: fatty cell

eliasite
\əˈlēə͵sīt\
German
: mineral

ellagitannin
\əˈlajətanən\
Latin
: compound

ellestadite
\eləstadīt\
German
: mineral

elotillo
\elōˈtē(y)ō\
Spanish
: scaly herb

elpidite
\elpədīt\
Latin
: mineral

emagram
\eməgram\
ISV
: thermodynamic chart

embolo
\embəlō\
Afrikaans
: fruit

embraceor
\embrāsər\
Latin
: one who bribes

embusque
\ämbü¦skā, änbū̄eskā\
French
: slacker of military service

emeraude
\emə͵rōd\
French
: green

emetine
\emətēn\
French
: compound

emmonsite
\emən͵zīt\
English
: mineral

empedoclean
\empedəclēən\
Greek
: of philosophers

emprosthotonos
\em͵präsˈthätənəs\
Latin
: tetanic spasm

empyreumata
\empəˈrümətə\
Greek
: incense

emydosaurian
\emədōsorēən\
Latin
: crocodilian

231

enalite
\enəlˌīt\
Japanese
: mineral

enchylema
\enkīlēmə\
Latin
: ground substance

encina
\ənˈsēnə\
Spanish
: oak tree

encinillo
\en(t)səˈnē(y)ō\
Spanish
: shrub

encrinite
\eŋkrəˌnīt\
Latin
: fossil

endosepsis
\endəsepsəs\
Latin
: fungal decay

enediol
\ēndīäl\
ISV
: organic compound

enfeoff
\enfef\
Latin
: pay fees

englynion
\eŋˈlinˌyòn\
Welsh
: poems

engobe
\ängōb\
French
: silk pattern

enoplion
\enäplēˌän\
Greek
: syllable poem

entellus
\enteləs\
Greek
: common monkey

entypy
\entəpē\
Latin
: method formation

eoan
\ēōən\
Latin
: relating to dawn

eozoonal
\ēəzōənəl\
Latin
: of banded arrangements

ephebeum
\efəbēəm\
Greek
: exercise court

ephippium
\efipēəm\
Latin
: pouch

ephorate
\efərāt\
Greek
: office of magistrate

epicrisis
\epikrəsəs\
Greek
: medical case history

epigonation
\epēgòˈnätyòn\
Greek
: rhombic vestment

epimenidean
\epəˌmenəˈdēən\
Greek
: of philosophers

epinine
\epənēn\
ISV
: compound

epiploon
\əˈpipləˌwän\
Latin
: fat body

episcia
\əˈpishə\
Latin
: plant

epistates
\əˈpistətēz\
Greek
: administrative official

epistropheus
\epistrōfēəs\
Greek
: vertebra

epithumetic
\epith(y)ümedik\
Greek
: pertaining to appetite

epitrachelion
\epētrəˈk̲ēlyòn\
Greek
: church vestment

epthianura
\epthēənùrə\
Latin
: plant

equilin
\ekwələn\
Latin
: hormone

equitant
\ekwədənt\
Latin
: overlapping leaves

eranthemum
\əranthəməm\
Latin
: grass

erven
\ervən\
Afrikaans
: plots of land

ergodicity
\ərgədisədē\
Latin
: involving the recurrence

ergothioneine
\ərgəthīōnēēn\
Latin
: compound

eriophyid
\erēäfēid\
Latin
: mite

erminois
\ərmənoiz\
French
: rabbit fur

eruc
\ə̇ˈrük\
Tagalog
: palm fiber

eryngo
\əringō\
Latin
: candied root

erythredema
\ərithrədēmə\
Latin
: disease of unknown cause

escambron
\e͜skäm¦bròn\
Spanish
: shrub

escharoid
\e͜skəròid\
Latin
: bryozoan

eseroline
\esərəlēn\
Latin
: nitrogenous base

esodic
\e͜sädik\
Latin
: afferent nerves

espagnolette
\espanyəlet\
French
: fastening in doors

estafiata
\estəfēädə\
Spanish
: sage tree

estofado
\estəfädō\
Spanish
: sculpting

estrade
\esträd\
French
: platform, dais

etaac
\āˈtäts\
Unknown
: antelope

ethel
\ethəl\
Latin
: ancestral land

ethylhexoate
\ethəlhexəāt\
ISV
: compound

ethylidene
\ethilədēn\
ISV
: compound

ettringite
\etriŋˌīt\
German
: mineral

eucaine
\(y)ükān\
ISV
: anesthetic

eumolpique
\œmȯlpēk\
French
: poetic measure

euphausiid
\(y)üfȯzēəd\
Latin
: crustacean

eupyrion
\(y)üpirēən\
Greek
: match

eurhodol
\ürōdȯl\
ISV
: compound

Euroaquilo
\(y)ürōakwəlō\
Greek
: wind

euthyneuran
\(y)üthənürən\
Latin
: gastropod

excipuliform
\ek'sipyələˌfȯrm\
Latin
: shaped like a rim

exheredation
\eksˌherəˈdāshən\
Latin
: disinheritance

exocortis
\eksəkȯrdəs\
Latin
: orange disease

exordial
\egzȯrdēˈəl\
Latin
: introductory

exorhason
\ekˈsȯräsȯn\
Greek
: long cloak

exsectile
\eksectəl\
Latin
: capable of being cut

extincteur
ekstanktər
French
: chemical extinguisher

eyre
\ār\
French
: circuit court

facellite
\fəˈseˌlīt\
Italian
: mineral

fado
\fäthü\
Portuguese
: folk song

fagopyrismus
\fagōˈpīˌrizəməs\
German
: swine photosensitization

fagine
\fāˌjēn\
Latin
: narcotic principle

fahlband
\fälbänt\
German
: crystalline rock

falanouc
\falənük\
Malagasy
: mammal

Falernum
\fələrnəm\
Trademark
: syrup

faltboat
\fältbōt\
English
: collapsible canoe

Falstaffian
\fȯlzˌtafēən\
English
: of humorous character

faon
\fäⁿ\
French
: variable shade of brown

farfara
\färfərə\
Latin
: dried leaves

farinogram
\fərēnəgram\
Latin
: dough quality instrument

favellidium
\favəˈlidēəm\
Latin
: algal frond

favonian
\fəvōnēən\
Greek
: of the western wind

Favrile
\fəvrēl\
Trademark
: glassware

fecit
\fākət\
Latin
: writ

feddan
\fədän\
Egyptian
: acre

feijoa
\fāyōə\
Spanish
: fruit

fenestelloid
\fenestelȯid\
Latin
: resembling moss

fermail
\fərˌmāl\
French
: clasp for clothing

ferreiro
\fererō\
Portuguese
: tree frog

ferroequinologist
\ferōēkwənäləjəst\
Latin
: one who enjoys railroads

ferruccite
\fəˈrüˌchīt\
Latin
: mineral

feverfew
\fēvə(r)ˌfyü\
French
: herb

Fichtean
\fiktēən\
German
: of ideal philosophy

fidia
\fidēə\
Latin
: beetle

filariform
\filerəfȯrm\
Latin
: shaped like esophagus

fili
\fil(y)ə\
Irish
: poet

fillowite
\filəwīt\
Latin
: mineral

filoplume
\filəplüm\
Latin
: feather

finnemanite
\finəmənīt\
Latin
: mineral

fique
\fēkā\
Spanish
: durable fiber

firca
\fi(ə)rkə\
Hindi
: community

firlot
\fi(ə)rlət\
Scottish
: bushel

firmisternal
\fərməstərnəl\
Latin
: vertebra in neutral line

fissury
\fishərē\
Latin
: abounding in cracks

flabellinerved
\fləbelənərvd\
Latin
: nerves shaped like fans

flamant
\flamənt\
Latin
: heraldry

flambeed
\fläm¦bād\
French
: served or dressed with fire

flamborough
\flambərə\
English
: sword dance

flamingant
\flaməⁿgaⁿ\
French
: reformer

Flaminian
\fləminēən\
Latin
: relating to Roman Emperor

flammule
\flam(y)ül\
Latin
: small flame as depicted to gods

flandan
\flanˌdan\
English
: woman cap

Flaubertian
\flōbərshən\
French
: of realistic novels

flebile
\flebəl\
Latin
: tearful

fleerish
\flērəsh\
Scottish
: piece of steel

fleuret
\flu̇ret\
French
: light fencing foil

fleury
\flu̇rē\
French
: decorated with floral patterns

flic
\flēk\
French
: policeman

flicflac
\flikflak\
French
: ballet step

florican
\flōrəkən\
Unknown
: bustard

floripondio
\flōrəpändēō\
Spanish
: tree

flotant
\flōtənt\
French
: in air

fluorothene
\flü(ə)rəthēn\
ISV
: resin

foederati
\fedəˈrātī\
Latin
: soldiers

folioliferous
\fōlēəlifərəs\
Latin
: bearing leaflets

forcat
\försa\
French
: convict

forfar
\förfər\
English
: coarse linen cloth

forgettery
\fərgetərē\
Latin
: poor memory

Fortisan
\fö(r)təˌsan\
Trademark
: yarn

fothergilla
\fäthə(r)ˈgilə\
Latin
: plant

fourgon
\fürgōⁿ\
French
: wagon

foyaitic
\föi(y)əitik\
Portuguese
: of rock

franckeite
\fräŋkəˌīt\
German
: mineral

frijolillo
\frē(h)əˈlē(y)ō\
Spanish
: leguminous herb

frisure
\frizhər, frəˈzhù(ə)r\
French
: hairdressing

frondelite
\frändelīt\
German
: mineral

frondent
\frändənt\
Latin
: having leaves

fucoidin
\fyüˈkȯidən\
ISV
: sulfuric ester

fulgorid
\fəlgərəd\
Latin
: insect

fundi
\fəndē\
Limba
: grass

funkia
\fənkēə\
Latin
: plant

fuqaha
\fükähä\
Arabic
: Muslim theologians

furcellate
\fərsəˌlāt, ˌfərˈselət\
Latin
: minutely forked

gageite
\gājīt\
English
: mineral

galanga
\gəˈlaŋgə\
Latin
: root

galipine
\galəpēn\
ISV
: compound

gallowglass
\galōˌglas\
Irish
: soldier

gamari
\gəˈmärē\
Sanskrit
: tree

gambet
\gambət\
Latin
: bird

gambo
\gambō\
Welsh
: cart

236

gammarid
\gamərəd\
Latin
: arthropod

gammagraph
\gaməgraf\
Latin
: x-ray measurer

gangava
\gangavə\
Latin
: seawater basin

gangwa
\gangwə\
Unknown
: plant

gansey
\ganzi\
English
: sweater

gardebras
\gärdə¦brä\
French
: piece of armor

garni
\gárnē\
French
: embellished

garoo
\gärü\
Malay
: tree

garrupa
\gərüpə\
Portuguese
: bird

garrapata
\garəpädə\
Spanish
: tick

garrick
\gerik\
Unknown
: fish

garvey
\gärvi\
English
: boat

gaspereau
\gaspərō\
French
: fish

gatch
\gach\
Persian
: plaster

gayal
\gəyäl\
Sanskrit
: ox

geatish
\ya(ə)¦dish\
Swedish
: of Scandinavians

gebanga
\gəbangə\
Malay
: palm tree

gedanite
\gedənīt\
German
: fossil resin in Tibet

Gedinnian
\jədinēən\
Latin
: subdivision

geest
\gāst\
German
: alluvial matter

gelidium
\jəlidēəm\
Latin
: alga

gelong
\gālong\
Tibetan
: monk

genappe
\jənap\
French
: sew

geneserine
\jə́nesərēn\
ISV
: acid

genestrole
\jə́nestrōl\
Latin
: compound

gentiopicrin
\jenchēə́picrən\
Latin
: compound

georama
\jēəramə\
French
: hollow globe

geonoma
\jēänəmə\
Latin
: plant

gephyrean
\jefīrēən\
Latin
: of marine worms

gerrhosaurid
\jerōsorid\
Latin
: lizard

gersum
\gərsəm\
Norse
: fine

Gervais
\zhervā\
Trademark
: cheese and milk

Ghiordes
\gēˈȯrdəs\
Turkish
: rug

ghol
\ghäl\
Hindi
: fish

gibbsite
\gibzīt\
Latin
: mineral

gibel
\gēbəl\
German
: fish

gigeria
\jəjirēə\
Latin
: alimentary canals

gilet
\zhəlā\
Turkish
: waistcoat

gilly
\gilē\
English
: wagon

gillespite
\gəlespīt\
Latin
: mineral

ginglyform
\jiŋglə͵fȯrm\
ISV
: shaped like elbow bones

giocoso
\jōkōsō\
Italian
: lively in music

Giottesque
\jȯtesk\
Italian
: resembling painters

ginorite
\jinərīt\
Latin
: mineral

gitalin
\jətalən\
ISV
: soluble solution

glacieret
\glāshəret\
Latin
: small ice shelf

glagolitsa
\gləˈgȯlyētsə\
Croatian
: Slavic alphabet

glaur
\glȯr\
English
: slimy mud

gliriform
\glirəfȯrm\
Latin
: resembling rodents

glissile
\glisəl\
Latin
: capable of gliding

glochidiate
\glōkidēət\
Latin
: having barbed tips

glossiphoniid
\gläsəfōnēəd\
Latin
: leech

glucityl
\glüsətil\
Latin
: radical

glucuronide
\glüˈkyu̇rə͵nīd\
ISV
: compound

glutamate
\glüdəmāt\
ISV
: salt ester

glycinin
\glīsənən\
ISV
: soybean compound

glyoxime
\glīäxēm\
ISV
: compound

gobbe
\gäb\
Unknown
: nut

gobernadora
\gōbə(r)nəˈdōrə\
Spanish
: bush

Gobinism
\gōbənizəm\
Latin
: superior theory

goel
\gōel\
Hebrew
: redeemer

golah
\gōlä\
Hebrew
: exodus

goldschmidtine
\gōlshmitēn\
ISV
: compound

goliard
\gōlyərd\
Latin
: wandering student

golilla
\gəlēyə\
Spanish
: white collar

gonimolobe
\gänəməlōb\
Latin
: terminal cell

gonnardite
\gänərdīt\
French
: mineral

gonyaulax
\gōnē'ȯ͵laks\
Greek
: jellyfish

goongarrite
\gün'ga͵rīt\
Australian
: mineral

gooranut
\gu̇rənət\
Hausa
: caffeine seed

gootee
\gütē\
Hindi
: air layering

gosport
\gäspȯrt\
English
: speaking tube

gossypol
\gäsəpäl\
ISV
: compound

goumier
\güm¦yā\
French
: soldier

goutte
\güt\
French
: pear-shaped figure

goyazite
\gȯi(y)ə͵zīt\
French
: mineral

granatum
\grənātəm\
French
: bark of fruit

granita
\grənēdə\
Italian
: sherbet

graphometric
\grafəmetrik\
Latin
: handwriting

grasset
\grasā\
French
: songbird

gratonite
\gratən͵īt\
English
: mineral

gravemente
\grävə'mentā\
Italian
: serious in music

gravette
\grəvet\
French
: prehistoric flint

gravitater
\gravətādər\
Latin
: tend in direction

greaves
\grēvz\
Scottish
: crisp residue

greenovite
\grēnəvīt\
Latin
: mineral

greking
\grēking\
English
: dawn

gremio
\grämē͵ō\
Spanish
: union

grenatite
\grenətīt\
Latin
: mineral

greycing
\grāsing\
English
: dog racing

griphite
\grifīt\
Greek
: mineral

grouze
\graúz\
English
: chew munching

Grundtvigian
\grúntvigēən\
Norse
: adherent of religion

guacacoa
\gwäkəˈkōə\
Spanish
: tree

guacharo
\gwächərō\
Spanish
: bird

guango
\gwängō\
Spanish
: tree

guanophore
\gwänəfōr\
Latin
: skin color changer

guatambu
\gwädəmbü\
Spanish
: tree

guignol
\gēnˈyòl\
French
: puppet

guimbard
\gimbärd\
French
: small instrument

guitermanite
\gidərmənīt\
English
: mineral

Guittonian
\gwə́ˈtōnēən\
Italian
: of the sonnet-inventing poet

gulmohur
\gúlməˌhùr\
Hindi
: royal flower

gumhar
\gəmhär\
Sanskrit
: tree

gunite
\gəˌnīt\
Trademark
: to apply mixture to

gunnera
\gənirə\
Latin
: plant

Gunzian
\güntsēən\
German
: four epochs of glacial ages

gurdy
\gərdē\
Unknown
: drum

gurmukhi
\gúrmükē\
Sanskrit
: alphabet

guzerat
\güzərät\
Hindi
: cattle breed

gynecophore
\jīnēkəfōr\
Latin
: canal
(adjective spelled
gynaecophoric)

gynetype
\jīnətīp\
Latin
: female specimen

gyrovague
\jīrōˌvāg\
French
: wandering monk

haastia
\hästēə\
Latin
: plant

habrobracon
\habrōˈbrakən\
Latin
: insect

hadada
\hadədə\
Afrikaans
: bird

haematinum
\hēmatənəm\
Latin
: red glass

hagdon
\hagdən\
Unknown
: bird

haitsai
\hītsī\
Chinese
: transparent alga

haldu
\häldü\
Hindi
: tree

halfmens
\hälfmentz\
Afrikaans
: plant

hallan
\halən\
Unknown
: cottage

hallel
\hälāl\
Hebrew
: praise

hammarite
\hamərīt\
Latin
: mineral

hanbali
\hanbəlē\
Arabic
: orthodox school

hanif
\hənēf\
Arabic
: hermit

hanusite
\hänəˌs(h)īt\
Czech
: mineral

haole
\haůlē\
Hawaiian
: tribesperson

hapalonychia
\hapəlōˈnikēə\
Latin
: softness of fingernails

hardim
\härdim\
Arabic
: starred lizard

harmaline
\härməlēn\
ISV
: compound

harmost
\härmäst\
Greek
: Spartan leader

harstigite
\härstəgīt\
Latin
: mineral

haskalah
\haskəlä\
Hebrew
: intellectual enlightenment

hassar
\hasər\
Arawak
: catfish

hati
\hadē\
Egyptian
: physical heart

haustellum
\hästelləm\
Latin
: proboscis

havildar
\havəldär\
Hindi
: noncommissioned officer

hawok
\häwäk\
Maidu
: money

heatronic
\hētränik\
ISV
: utilizing warmth

heautophany
\hēätäfənē\
Latin
: manifestation of self

heazlewoodite
\hēzəl, wůˌdīt\
geographical name
: mineral

hectocotylize
\hektəkätəlˌīz\
Latin
: impregnate with arthropods

hedenbergite
\hedənbərgīt\
Swedish
: mineral

hedeoma
\hedēˈōmə\
Latin
: plant

heilsgeschichte
\hīəlzgəshiktə\
German
: interpretation of history

helbeh
\helbə\
Arabic
: seed

hellandite
\heləndīt\
German
: mineral

helvellic
\helvelik\
Latin
: of fungus

hemafibrite
\hēməˈfīˌbrīt\
ISV
: mineral

hematein
\hēmətēən\
ISV
: compound

hemelytral
\həmelətrləl\
Latin
: of anterior wings

hemoptoe
\hēˈmäptəwē\
Latin
: bleeding in lungs

heneicosane
\henīkəˌsān\
ISV
: hydrocarbon

heptachlor
\heptəˌklō(ə)r\
ISV
: insecticide

heptitol
\heptətäl\
ISV
: alcohol

herapathite
\herəpathīt\
Latin
: mineral

herderite
\hərdərīt\
Latin
: mineral

heriot
\herēət\
Latin
: feudal tenant

Hermaean
\hərmēən\
Greek
: of the god's feet

hermeneut
\hərmənüt\
Greek
: church interpreter

Herodian
\hərōdēən\
Latin
: of the Bible

Herrnhuter
\hernhüdər\
German
: evangelical movement

hesiodic
\hesēädik\
Greek
: of theology

hetmanate
\hetməˌnāt\
Polish
: administration of cossack

Hetrazan
\hetrəzan\
Trademark
: drug

hexachlorophene
\heksəˈklōrəˌfēn\
ISV
: antibacterial agent

hexaxon
\heksaksän\
Greek
: sponge

hidability
\hīdəˈbilətē\
Latin
: ability to obscure

hibbertia
\hibərtēə\
Latin
: plant

hieracia
\hīərāshēə\
Latin
: plants

hieracosphinx
\hīərākəsfinks\
Latin
: hawk-headed lion's body
with wings

hieratite
\hīərətīt\
geographical name
: mineral

hierosolymitan
\hīərəsäləmītən\
Latin
: pertaining to Jerusalem

highbelia
\hībēlēə\
Latin
: tall plant

hikuli
\hiˈkülē\
Huichol
: cactus

hilarymas
\hilərēməs\
Latin
: festival

hilgardite
\hilgärdīt\
Latin
: mineral

hinau
\hēˌnau̇\
Maori
: timber tree

hinoki
\hȧnōkē\
Japanese
: cypress

242

hinsdalite
\hinz͵dā͵līt\
geographical name
: mineral

hippeastrum
\hipēastrəm\
Latin
: plant

hippolytid
\hipälətəd\
Latin
: of prawns

hipponactean
\hipənaktēən\
Latin
: verse

hiragana
\hirəgänə\
Japanese
: cursive script

hisingerite
\hisingərīt\
Latin
: mineral

hislopite
\hizləpīt\
Latin
: mineral

histiocyte
\histēəsīt\
Latin
: cell tissue

histolyzate
\histäləzāt\
Latin
: cell tissue

hoc
\häk\
French
: card game

hodgkinsonite
\häjkənsənīt\
Latin
: mineral

hodograph
\hädəgraf\
Latin
: path of extremity

hoegbomite
\hōgbəmīt\
German
: mineral

hogsteer
\hägstēr\
English
: wild boar

hohenstaufen
\hōənshtaufən\
German
: of princely family

hohlflote
\hōlflātə\
German
: flute stop

hohmannite
\hōmənīt\
Latin
: mineral

hoja
\ōhä\
Spanish
: dried meat

Hokaltecan
\hō͵kalˈtekən\
Spanish
: language family

holectypoid
\hōlektəpoid\
Latin
: sea urchin

holluschickie
\häləschikē\
Russian
: young fur seal

hollong
\häläng\
Assamese
: tree

holocoenotic
\häləsēnädik\
Latin
: acting in concert

holoside
\häləsīd\
ISV
: glucoside

homeology
\hōmēäləjē\
Latin
: similarity

homoeotopy
\hōmēädəpē\
Latin
: occurrence in writing

homoiomeria
\hōməyōmərīə\
Latin
: theory of particles

homoosis
\hōmōōsəs\
Latin
: development of organism

homoousion
\hōmōüzēän\
Latin
: theory of doctrine

homurai
\hōmərī\
Nepali
: bird

243

hookupu
\hōōkəpü\
Hawaiian
: gift ceremony

hoolaulea
\hōōlaulāə\
Hawaiian
: festival

hootamaganzy
\hüdəməganzē\
English
: bird

Hopcalite
\häpkəlīt\
Trademark
: granular mixture

hoplite
\häplīt\
Greek
: armed soldier

hordenine
\hordəˌnēn\
ISV
: crystalline alkaloid

hormogon
\horməgän\
Latin
: filament

horopito
\horəpētō\
Maori
: tree

houbara
\hüˈbärə\
Arabic
: bird

houdan
\hüdan\
French
: fowl

hougher
\häk̲ər\
Scottish
: lawbreaker

Housatonic
\hüsəˈtänik\
geographical name
: band member

houtou
\hütü\
French
: bird

howkit
\həúkət\
Scottish
: dug up

huebnerite
\hēbnərīt\
German
: mineral

huehuetl
\wā(h)wātəl\
Spanish
: drum

hukuma
\həkəmä\
Arabic
: physicians

humboldtine
\həmbōltēn\
ISV
: compound

humettee
\hümətā\
French
: couped at extremities

humetty
\hümətē\
French
: couped at extremities

humulene
\hümyəlēn\
ISV
: compound

hureaulite
\hyürōlīt\
French
: mineral

huskanaw
\həskənä\
Virginian
: initiate rite

huttonweed
\hətənwēd\
English
: plant

hyaenodont
\hīēnədänt\
Latin
: mammal

hydracarian
\hīdrəkarēən\
Latin
: freshwater fish

hydrazinium
\hīdrəzinēəm\
Latin
: univalent ion

hydroxycitronellal
\hīdräksēsitrənelal\
ISV
: liquid aldehyde

hymeneal
\hīmēnēəl\
Latin
: pertaining to marriage

hyolithid
\hīäləthid\
Latin
: of mollusks

hypericin
\hīperəsən\
Latin
: pigment

hyperlepteny
\hīpərleptənē\
Latin
: very narrow forehead

hyperpietic
\hīpərpīedik\
Latin
: high blood pressure

hyphaeresis
\hīferəsəs\
Latin
: omission of vowel

hyphomycete
\hīfəmīsēt\
Latin
: fungus

hypoiodite
\hīpəīədīt\
Latin
: mineral

hypophloeous
\hīpəflēəs\
Latin
: below bark

hyporchematic
\hīporkēmadik\
Greek
: of chorus

hyppish
\hipish\
English
: blue

hypsicephal
\hipsəsefəl\
Latin
: high forehead

hypsiloid
\hipsəloid\
Latin
: resembling upsilon

hypsistarian
\hipsəsterēən\
Latin
: member of sect

hystericky
\histerəkē\
Latin
: funny

hysterioid
\histerēoid\
Latin
: boat-shaped

hythergraph
\hīthərgraf\
Latin
: climograph measuring
temperature

ianthinite
\īēanthənīt\
ISV
: mineral

ichthyophthirius
\ikthēäfthirēəs\
Latin
: fish

icosasphere
\īkōsəsfēr\
Latin
: spherical tank

ictidosaur
\iktədəsȯr\
Latin
: reptile

iddingsite
\idingzīt\
Latin
: mineral

identacode
\īdentəkōd\
Latin
: means of classification

ideophobia
\īdēəfōbēə\
Latin
: fear of reason

idiorrhythmism
\idēərithmizəm\
Latin
: self-regulation

ieroe
\ēərȯi\
Scottish
: great-grandchild

ihram
\ēräm\
Arabic
: pilgrimage

ilesite
\īəlzīt\
Latin
: mineral

illapse
\əlaps\
Latin
: influx, accession

illation
\əlāshən\
Latin
: inference

ilvaite
\ilvəīt\
Latin
: mineral

imbrices
\imbrəsēz\
Latin
: curved roofs

imidazolyl
\imidazəlil\
ISV
: amine

imidogen
\əmidəjen\
Latin
: compound

imonium
\imōnēəm\
ISV
: element

impedor
\impēdər\
Latin
: electrical circuit component

imphee
\imfē\
Afrikaans
: sorghum

impostrous
\impästrəs\
Latin
: fraudulent

impressable
impresəbəl
Latin
: capable of be imprinted

impudicity
\impyədisədē̆\
Latin
: shamelessness

incanestrato
\ēnkänəsträdō\
Italian
: cheese

incanous
\inkānəs\
Latin
: hoary

inceptor
\inseptər\
Latin
: one who introduces

incitory
\insīdərē\
Latin
: serving to excite

Inconel
\inkənel\
Trademark
: alloy

indaconitine
\indəkänətēn\
ISV
: compound

indican
\indəkan\
ISV
: compound

indolyl
\indəlil\
ISV
: compound

inductothermy
\indəktdəthərmē\
Latin>ISV+Ecf
: fever therapy

induline
\indyəlēn\
ISV
: violet dye

indumentum
\indyəmentəm\
Latin
: feathery covering

indusium
\indüzhēəm\
Latin
: outgrowth

infangthief
\infəngthēf\
English
: medieval franchise

infusoriform
\infyüzōrəfòrm\
Latin
: minute organism

inositol
\inōsətäl\
ISV
: compound

insupposable
\insəpōzəbəl\
Latin
: unbelievable

intarsiature
\intärsēətůrā\
Italian
: mosaics

intercreedal
\intərkrēdəl\
Latin
: occurring between races

interferograph
\intərfirəgraf\
Latin
: apparatus measuring phenomena

interloculus
\intərläküləs\
Latin
: small chamber

intermicellar
\intərmīselər\
Latin
: between molecules

intervallic
\intərvalik\
Latin
: pertaining to pauses

interzooecial
\intərzōēshəl\
Latin
: among cells

Intoximeter
\intäximədər\
Trademark
: chemical test

introital
\intrōədəl\
Latin
: body cavities

Inugsuk
\ēnəgsük\
Eskimo
: culture

involucellate
\invälyüselət\
Latin
: secondary flowers

iodobehenate
\īədōbəhenāt\
Latin
: salt

iodoform
\īədəfòrm\
Latin
: volatile compound

ionophoresis
\īänəfərēsəs\
Latin
: movement of particles

ipiti
\ipədē\
Xhosa
: antelope

ipsilaterally
\ipsəladərəlē\
Latin
: affecting the same side

iridodonesis
\irədōdənēsis\
Latin
: twitching of iris

iridophore
\īridəfōr\
ISV
: cell

isatogen
\īsadəjen\
ISV
: compound

isethionate
\īsethīənāt\
ISV
: compound

irrisor
\ərīzər\
Latin
: bird

isidiiferous
\īsidēifərəs\
Latin
: having outgrowths

isnad
\iznäd\
Arabic
: chain of authorities

isodiaphere
\īsōdīəfir\
Latin
: nuclear species

isodomon
\īsädəmän\
Greek
: masonry

isoflurophate
\īsəflürəfāt\
ISV
: compound

isonipecaine
\īsənipəkān\
ISV
: drug

itabirite
\ēdəbirīt\
German
: mineral

iynx
\īinks\
Latin
: bird

jabarite
\jabərīt\
Arabic
: educated Muslim

jacare
\häkərä\
Spanish
: alligator

jagla
\jäglə\
Sanskrit
: antelope

Jajman
\jəjmän\
Hindi
: fixed circle

jako
\jakō\
Unknown
: gray color

jambolan
\jambəlan\
Javan
: plum

jampan
\jam‚pan\
Bengali
: covered vehicle

jarbot
\järbət\
Unknown
: dilation of esophagus

jaspachate
\jaspəkāt\
Latin
: quartz

jawab
\jəwäb\
Hindi
: shrine

jefferisite
\jefərəsīt\
Latin
: mineral

jenoar
\jenəwär\
Arabic
: rodent

jessur
\jesər\
Unknown
: viper

jetteau
\jetō\
French
: forceful rush of water

jezebelish
\jezəbelish\
Hebrew
: of casually dressed people

jezekite
\jezhəkīt\
Czech
: mineral

jharal
\järəl\
Nepali
: mountain goat

jhukar
\jəkär\
Hindi
: culture

joseite
\zhəsāīt\
German
: mineral

judicia
\yüdikēə\
Latin
: judgments

jura
\yùrə\
Latin
: rights

jurupaite
\hərüpəīt\
Spanish
: mineral

jurat
\jùrat\
Hindi
: municipal officer

kaama
\kämə\
Afrikaans
: antelope

kadsura
\kädsərə\
Japanese
: tree

kaferita
\kafərēdə\
Arabic
: grain sorghum

kaffa
\käfə\
Egyptian
: gray color

kaid
\kīd\
Arabic
: tribal chief

kaikara
\kīkärə\
Arabic
: young lady

kailyard
\kālyärd\
Arabic
: Muslim school

kalicinite
\kəlisənīt\
German
: mineral

kalsilite
\kalsəlīt\
German
: mineral

kamarezite
\kamerəzīt\
German
: mineral

kapellmeister
\kəpelmīstər\
German
: directors of choir

karadagh
\kärədä\
Persian
: rug

karinghota
karəngōdə
Unknown
: tree

karren
\kärən\
German
: unused land

karrusel
\kerəsel\
German
: revolving escapement

karyorrhectic
\kerēərektik\
Latin
: pertaining to nucleus
disintegration

kashim
\kashəm\
Eskimo
: meeting house

kasolite
\kasəlīt\
geographical name
: mineral

kehoeite
\kēhōīt\
Latin
: mineral

kellupweed
\keləpwēd\
Latin
: plant

ketazine
\kēdəzēn\
ISV
: compound

kibitka
\kəbitkə\
Afrikaans
: tent

kieserite
\kēzərīt\
German
: mineral

kisan
\kēsän\
Hindi
: peasant

knapweed
\napwēd\
Unknown
: grass

knopite
\näpīt\
German
: mineral

knut
\kənət\
Unknown
: dandy

koenenite
\kānənīt\
German
: mineral

koilonychia
\koilōnikēə\
Latin
: thinness of nails

kolbeckite
\kōlbekīt\
German
: mineral

kolelim
\kōlāləm\
Hebrew
: congregations of devotees

koniocortex
\kōnēəkȯrteks\
Latin
: part of brain

koombar
\kümbər\
Tamilian
: tree

kornelite
\kornəlīt\
Latin
: mineral

Koroseal
\korəsēl\
Trademark
: plastic composition

kraurotic
\krorädik\
Greek
: hardening of skin

kribergite
\kribərgīt\
German
: mineral

Kulanapan
\külənäpən\
Spanish
: language family

kugelhof
\kügəlhōf\
German
: sweet cake

kupfferite
\ku̇pfərīt\
German
: mineral

labarum
\labərəm\
Latin
: imperial standard

labba
\labə\
Arawakan
: rodent

lablab
\laˌblab\
Arabic
: vine

labradorescence
\labrədoresənts\
Latin
: show of colors

Lacedaemonian
\lasədəmōnēən\
Latin
: fortuitous person

lacinia
\ləsinēə\
Latin
: network segment

lacrimale
\lakrəmalē\
Latin
: posterior tear duct

lacrimoid
\lakrəmoid\
Latin
: shaped like a teardrop

lactucarium
\laktəkerēəm\
Latin
: milky juice

ladik
\lädēk\
Turkish
: rug

laet
\lat\
English
: cultivator

lagen
\lāgən\
Latin
: unit of volume

lagopous
\ləgōpəs\
Latin
: having hairy roots

Lamarckian
\ləmärkēən\
Latin
: theory of evolution

lampadite
\lampədīt\
Latin
: mineral

lampas
\lampəs\
French
: silk fabric

lampatia
\lampadēə\
French
: timber tree

lanarkite
\lanərkīt\
Latin
: mineral

lanas
\lanəs\
Latin
: disease

lanatoside
\lənatəsīd\
Latin
: compound

landesite
\landəsīt\
Latin
: mineral

landler
\lentlər\
Austrian
: dance

landsturm
\läntshtùrm\
German
: military retreat

lanete
\lanətē\
Tagalog
: tree

langbanite
\lòngbənīt\
geographical name
: mineral

lansdowne
\lanzdaùn\
Trademark
: fabric

lansfordite
\lantsfərdīt\
Latin
: mineral

lanthopine
\lanthəpēn\
Latin
: compound

lapageria
\lapəjirēə\
Latin
: plant

lapeler
\ləpelər\
French
: one that pins

lappeted
\lapədə̇d\
English
: having headgear

lardacein
\lärdāsēən\
ISV
: compound

larderellite
\lärdərelīt\
French
: mineral

larrea
\lərēə\
Latin
: shrub

larsenite
\lärsənīt\
Latin
: mineral

lasiocampid
\lāzēəkampəd\
Latin
: moth

latebra
\ladəbrə\
Latin
: white yolk

latifundiary
\ladəfəndēerē\
Latin
: of landowners

latiplantar
\ladəplantər\
Latin
: having the hinder part

latosol
\ladəsäl\
ISV
: soil

laubmannite
\laủbmənīt\
German
: mineral

laudanosine
\lȯdanəsēn\
Latin
: compound

lauhala
\laủhälə\
Hawaiian
: dried leaves

lauia
\laủēə\
Hawaiian
: parrot fish

laurionite
\lȯrēənīt\
Latin
: mineral

lautarite
\laủdərīt\
Hungarian
: mineral

lavandulol
\ləvanjəlȯl\
Latin
: alcohol

lawrencite
\lȯrənsīt\
Latin
: mineral

lazzi
\lädzē\
Italian
: comic businesses

leasow
\lezə\
English
: rough land

lecanium
\ləkānēəm\
Latin
: plant

lecanomancy
\lekənōmantsē\
Latin
: divination of water basin

lecanoroid
\lekənȯrȯid\
Latin
: pertaining to lichens

ledeburite
\lādəbərīt\
German
: mineral

ledol
\lēdȯl\
Latin
: compound

legantine
\legəntən\
Latin
: of authorities

leguleian
\legyəlēən\
Latin
: pettifogger

lehiite
\lēhīīt\
Latin
: mineral

leifite
\lēfīt\
Swedish
: mineral

leiomyomatous
\līəmïämədəs\
Latin
: of soft muscle tumors

lengenbachite
\lengənbäkīt\
Swiss
: mineral

lennilite
\lenəlīt\
Latin
: mineral

lenticel
\lentəsel\
Latin
: pore

lentiginous
\lentijənəs\
Latin
: freckled

leonhardite
\lāənhärdīt\
Swiss
: mineral

lepadid
\lepədid\
Latin
: barnacle

lepidolite
\ləpidəlīt\
Latin
: mineral

lepisosteid
\lepəsästēəd\
Latin
: fish

leptostaphyline
\leptəstafəlīn\
Latin
: having narrow palates

lerret
\lerət\
Unknown
: boat

lettsomite
\letsəmīt\
German
: mineral

leucaugite
\lükäjīt\
Latin
: mineral

leuchtenbergite
\lȯiktənbərgīt\
German
: mineral

leucocidin
\lükəsīdən\
Latin
: bacterial substance

leukotoxicity
\lükətäksisədē\
Latin
: poison in cells

levyne
\lāvēn\
French
: mineral

leza
\lēzə\
Malay
: wood

libera
\lēbərä\
Latin
: funeral song

libethenite
\libethənīt\
Latin
: mineral

liebenerite
\lēbənərīt\
German
: mineral

liebigite
\lēbəgīt\
German
: mineral

lienee
\lēnē\
English
: one who pays mortgage

lierne
\lēərn\
French
: vault

ligas
\lēgäs\
Tagalog
: tree

lightscot
\lītskät\
English
: tax

lignaloe
\līnalō\
French
: tree

lilas
\lēlä\
French
: color

lilium
\liēəm\
Latin
: plant

lillypilly
\lilēpilē\
Unknown
: plant

limnoria
\limnərīə\
Latin
: isopod

lindgrenite
\lindgrənīt\
French
: mineral

linguatulid
\lingwachəlid\
Latin
: worm

linolenin
\linəlēnən\
Latin
: salt

lipocaic
\lipəkāik\
Latin
: pancreas preparation

lirellate
\lərelāt\
Latin
: elongated lichens

liroconite
\līräkənīt\
Latin
: mineral

lithidionite
\ləthidēənīt\
Latin
: mineral

lithosiid
\lithōsēəd\
Latin
: moth

liveingite
\livingīt\
English
: mineral

livetin
\livədən\
Latin
: egg protein

lobeline
\lōbəlēn\
Latin
: compound

lockram
\läkrəm\
English
: woven cloth

loculament
\läkyələment\
Latin
: ovary cell

loculicidally
\läkyəlisīdəlē\
Latin
: killing capsules in fruits

lodicule
\lädəkyül\
Latin
: fruit body

loessial
\lesēəl\
German
: of decayed matter

lomatiol
\lōmāshēȯl\
ISV
: compound

longeron
\länjərən\
French
: fuselage

loricae
\lərīsē\
Latin
: shells

loseyite
\lōzēīt\
Latin
: mineral

louro
\lōrü\
Portuguese
: tree

loxommoid
\lȯxämȯid\
Latin
: spider

lubritorium
\lübrətȯrēəm\
Latin
: washing station

luetically
\lüedikəlē\
Latin
: affected with congenital
diseases

lukban
\lükbän\
Turkish
: grapefruit

lukiko
\lükēkō\
Ugandan
: chief

luluai
\lüləwī\
geographical name
: head chief

lumberdar
\ləmbərdär\
Hindi
: village chief

lulliloo
\ləlilü\
Afrikaans
: shout joyously

lundyfoot
\ləndēfüt\
Irish
: variety of snuff

lupercalian
\lüpərkālēən\
Latin
: of church festivals

lushburg
\ləshbərg\
Latin
: lightwoven fabric

luteolin
\lüdēələn\
Latin
: pigment

lutjanid
\lüchānəd\
Latin
: beetle

lychnoscope
\liknəskōp\
Latin
: window

lycorine
\līkōrən\
ISV
: alkaloid

lydite
\līdīt\
German
: stone

lyery
\līəri\
English
: fatty

lygaenid
\lījēnəd\
Latin
: true bug

lymnaeid
\limnēəd\
Latin
: snail

lyomerous
\līämərəs\
Latin
: of pelican fish

Lysenkoism
\līsenkōizəm\
Russian
: biological doctrine

lysyl
\līsəl\
ISV
: radical

lyttae
\litē\
Latin
: cartilage

maasbanker
\mäsbankər\
Dutch
: fish

mabuya
\məbüyə\
Spanish
: lizard

macana
\məkänə\
Spanish
: wooden weapon

Macaulayan
\məkälēən\
English
: of the poet

macawood
\məkäwùd\
Spanish
: tree

machairodont
\məkīrədänt\
Latin
: saber-toothed

machree
\məkrē\
Irish
: darling

mackayite
\makēīt\
French
: mineral

macrencephalic
\makrensefəlik\
Latin
: large head

maculicolous
\makyəlikələs\
Latin
: of fungus

macupa
\məküpə\
Spanish
apple

madhuca
\mədükə\
Hindi
: tree

madhyamika
\mədyämikə\
Sanskrit
: adherent of Buddhism

maeandroid
\mēandròid\
Latin
: of coral

Maeonian
\mēōnēən\
Latin
: of Homer's birthplace

Maeterlinckian
\mādərlinkēən\
Belgian
: pertaining to poets

mafite
\mafīt\
Latin
: mineral

maftir
\mäftir\
Hebrew
: reader of scripts

maggiore
\mäjōrē\
Italian
: musical scale

maghemite
\maghemīt\
Latin
: mineral

Maglemose
\magləmōsə\
Swedish
: culture

magnaflux
\magnəfləks\
Trademark
: testing method

mahala
\məhalə\
Yokuts
: figure target

mahasanghika
\məhäsəngəkə\
Sanskrit
: Buddhist

maizer
\māzər\
English
: bird

makutu
\mäkütü\
Maori
: witchcraft

malabathrum
\maləbathrəm\
Latin
: plant

malchus
\malkəs\
Greek
: sword

malikana
\mäləkänə\
Hindi
: fee

maldonite
\mäldənīt\
Greek
: mineral

malebranchism
\maləbrankizəm\
French
: philosophical system

malinowskite
\malənäfskīt\
Russian
: mineral

mallein
\malēən\
ISV
: product

Malpighian
\malpigēən\
Italian
: of cells

mammaplasty
\maməplastē\
Latin
: plastic surgery

mammillation
\maməlāshən\
Latin
: protuberance

mananosay
\manənōsā\
Algonquian
: clam

manasseite
\manasēīt\
Latin
: mineral

mandrin
\mandrən\
French
: stylet

mangabeira
\mangəbärə\
Portuguese
: tree

manganeisen
\mangənīzən\
ISV
: alloy

mangwe
\mangwā\
Afrikaans
: wood

mantelletta
\mantəledə\
Italian
: cloak

maral
\məräl\
Persian
: snowcat

maracan
\merəkan\
Portuguese
: parrot

marara
\mərärə\
Australian
: tree

marcionism
\märshənizəm\
Italian
: doctrine

marica
\mərīkə\
Latin
: plant

marigraphic
\merəgrapfik\
Latin
: self registering gauges

maringouin
\märangwan\
French
: monkey

marli
\märlē\
French
: flat dish

marquisette
\märkwəzet\
French
: meshed fabric

martynia
\märtinēə\
Latin
: plant

mascle
\maskəl\
English
: steel plate

massig
\mäsə<u>k</u>\
German
: moderate

mastaba
\mastəbə\
Egyptian
: tomb

mastomys
\mastōməs\
Latin
: mouse

mateley
\mātlē\
Unknown
: arms spread out

mathemeg
\mathəmeg\
Czech
: fish

matross
\məträs\
English
: gunner mate

maucherite
\maüchərīt\
German
: mineral

mauvine
\mōvən\
French
: color

Mazzinian
\mätsēnēən\
Italian
: patriotic policies

mbalolo
\embəlōlō\
Fiji
: worm

Meccano
\məkanō\
Trademark
: steel construction

mecholyl
\mekəlil\
Trademark
: drug

medaka
\mədäkə\
Japanese
: fish

Medicean
\medəchēən\
Italian
: family

megaron
\megərän\
Latin
: hall

mehari
\məhärē\
Arabic
: camel

meiotaxy
\mīətaksē\
Latin
: whorl

meke
\mākē\
Fijian
: dance

melanian
\məlānēən\
Latin
: black in pigmentation

melatope
\melətōp\
Latin
: point in interference

melilite
\meləlīt\
Latin
: mineral

meliponine
\məlipənīn\
Latin
: of honeybees

mellah
\melə\
Hebrew
: Jewish quarter

melodeon
\məlōdēən\
Latin
: organ

meloe
\meləwē\
Latin
: beetle

melonite
\melənīt\
Latin
: mineral

meneghinite
\menəgēnīt\
Italian
: mineral

menilite
\menəlīt\
Italian
: mineral

meninting
\məninting\
geographical name
: bird

menthadiene
\menthədīen\
ISV
: compound

mentzelia
\mentsēlēə\
German
: plant

meperidine
\məperədēn\
ISV
: compound

meprobamate
\məprōbəmāt\
ISV
: compound

merocerite
\məräsərīt\
Latin
: mineral

mersalyl
\mərsalil\
ISV
: compound

mesabite
\məsäbīt\
geographical name
: mineral

mesatipellic
\məsatipelik\
Latin
: moderate acetabulum size

mesepimeron
\mezəpimərän\
Latin
: wall

mesothesis
\məsäthəsəs\
Latin
: mediating principle

mesoxalyl
\məsäksəlil\
Latin
: compound

metahalloysite
\metəhəlȯisīt\
ISV
: mineral

metamer
\medəmər\
Latin
: chemical compound

metatorbernite
\metətȯrbərnīt\
Latin
: mineral

metavauxite
\metəvȯksīt\
French
: mineral

metayage
\medəyäzh\
French
: farming system

metazeunerite
\metəzȯinərīt\
German
: mineral

metraterm
\mētrətərm\
Latin
: worm

micrinite
\mīkrənīt\
Latin
: mineral

milarite
\mēlärīt\
Italian
: mineral

millegrain
\milgrān\
French
: gems cut perfectly

millet
\məlet\
Turkish
: community

millisite
\miləsīt\
Latin
: mineral

minasragrite
\mēnäsrägrīt\
Turkish
: mineral

Minyan
\minyən\
Greek
: of pottery

mirza
\mirzə\
Arabic
: honored man

mitscherlichite
\michərlikīt\
German
: mineral

modena
\mȯdənä\
Italian
: pigeon

modiolar
\mədīələr\
Latin
: pertaining to ears

moerithere
\mirəthir\
Latin
: animal

moissanite
\moisənīt\
French
: mineral

molle
\mȯyä\
Spanish
: pepper

molysite
\moləsīt\
Italian
: mineral

Monazite
\mänəzīt\
German
: mineral

monetite
\mänətīt\
German
: mineral

moniezia
\mȧnezhə\
German
: plant

monimostylic
\mänəmōstīlik\
Latin
: of reptiles

monoousious
\mänōüziē̇s\
Latin
: of one essence

monosabio
\mänəsäbēō\
Spanish
: bullring fighter

montaignesque
\mäntānesk\
French
: of literary style

montroydite
\mäntrȯidīt\
Latin
: mineral

Moquelumnan
\mōkələmnən\
Spanish
: language family

morada
\mərädə\
Spanish
: chapel

morchelloid
\mȯrkeloid\
Latin
: pertaining to fungi

mordisheen
\mȯrdishēn\
Hindi
: disease

morenosite
\mȯrenəsīt\
Latin
: mineral

moroc
\märäk\
Turkish
: bird

motacilla
\mōdəsilə\
French
: bird

mudejar
\müdhehär\
Arabic
: architecture

mugga
\məgə\
Australian
: bark

muirapiranga
\müəräpərängə\
Portuguese
: tree

mume
\mümē\
Japanese
: apricot

munguba
\məngübə\
Tupi
: tree

murciana
\mərshēänə\
Spanish
: dance

murinus
\myərīnəs\
Latin
: gray

murrnong
\mərnȯng\
Australian
: herb

murshid
\mùrshēd\
Arabic
: religious teacher

murumuru
\mərümərü\
Portuguese
: tree

muthmannite
\müthmənīt\
German
: mineral

mycophthorous
\mīkäfthərəs\
Latin
: parasitizing fungi

myiasis
\mīə̇səs\
Latin
: fly disease

myliobatid
\milēäbȯtəd\
Latin
: sting ray

myoclonus
\mīäklȯnəs\
Latin
: muscle contraction

myristicin
\mə̇ristisin\
Latin
: compound

myrmekitic
\mərməkitik\
Latin
: of minerals

mysophobic
\mīsəfōbik\
Latin
: fear of filth

mystagogue
\mistəgäg\
Latin
: interpreter

mytilaceous
\midəlāshəs\
Latin
: of fish

mytilid
\midələd\
Latin
: mollusk

myzostome
\mīzästōm\
Latin
: worm

nabla
\nablə\
Hebrew
: lute

naboom
\nəbōm\
Afrikaans
: tree

nacarat
\nakərat\
French
: vivid red

nachthorner
\näkhthərnər\
German
: organ stops

nagatelite
\nagətelīt\
German
: mineral

naggar
\nəgär\
Arabic
: boat

nagid
\nägēd\
Hebrew
: ruler

nagyagite
\nagyə̇gīt\
German
: mineral

nahoor
\nəhu̇r\
Hindi
: sheep

nair
\näir\
Hindi
(1): fish
(2): otter

nandine
\nandən\
French
: wildcat

nanger
\nangər\
French
: antelope

nannygai
\nanēgī\
Australian
: fish

nantokite
\nantəkīt\
Spanish
: mineral

naphazoline
\nəfazəlēn\
ISV
: compound

napier
\nāpēər\
Hindi
: grass

narceine
\närsēēn\
ISV
: compound

naringenin
\nerənjenən\
Latin
: compound

nargil
\närgēl\
Hindi
: coconut

narsarsukite
\närsərsəkīt\
German
: mineral

naucorid
\nȯkərid\
Latin
: bug

naumannite
\nȯmənīt\
German
: mineral

necator
\nəkādər\
Latin
: worm

nectopod
\nektəpäd\
Latin
: swimming limb

negre
\negrā\
Unknown
: bird

negundo
\nəgəndō\
Hindi
: tree

nemaline
\neməlīn\
Latin
: fibrous

nemourid
\nəmu̇rəd\
Latin
: stonefly

neper
\nēpər\
English
: logarithmic scale

nephelinic
\nefəlinik\
Latin
: of minerals

nephromixium
\nefrəmixēəm\
Latin
: excretory organ

nepouite
\nəpüīt\
ISV
: mineral

nerine
\nərīnē\
Latin
: plant

nerolidol
\nərälidȯl\
ISV
: compound

nesslerize
\neslərīz\
German
: treat with alkaline solution

netop
\nētäp\
Virginian
: friend

neurinoma
\nyu̇rənōmə\
Latin
: nerve tumor

neuroglia
\nyərōglēə\
Latin
: tissue

nickeliferous
\nikəlifərəs\
Latin
: containing alloys

nicodemite
\nikədēmīt\
biblical name
: secret follower

nidamental
\nīdəmentəl\
Latin
: of nests

nierembergia
\nērəmbərjēə\
German
: plant

nieshout
\nēshau̇t\
German
: weed

nieveta
\nēəvēdə\
Spanish
: herb

nigricant
\nigrəkint\
Latin
: black

nigrine
\nīgrən\
German
: mineral

nipter
\niptər\
Greek
: ceremony

nisi
\nēsē\
Latin
: not absolute

nitrofurazone
\nītrəfyùrəzōn\
ISV
: compound

nivenite
\nivənīt\
Latin
: mineral

nizamate
\nəzämāt\
Hindi
: jurisdiction of soldier

nocerite
\nōsərīt\
Italian
: mineral

nodosaur
\nōdəsòr\
Latin
: dinosaur

noncompos
\nänkompəs\
Latin
: one not of sound mind

noni
\nōnē\
Hawaiian
: pineapple

nonobstante
\nänəbstantē\
Latin
: license

nonylene
\nänəlēn\
ISV
: compound

norit
\nòrət\
Trademark
: carbon

norroy
\näròi\
English
: highest officer

northupite
\nòrthəpīt\
English
: mineral

notalian
\nōtālēən\
Latin
: of south marine temperature

nothocline
\näthəklīn\
Latin
: gradation of forms

notoedric
\nōdəedrik\
Latin
: of rodents

notommatid
\nətämətoid\
Latin
: bug

notostracan
\nətästrəkən\
Latin
: of crustaceans

novodamus
\nōvədāməs\
Latin
: writ

nullisomic
\nələsōmik\
Latin
: of chromosomes

nummulitic
\nəmyəlitik\
Latin
: of minerals

nupercaine
\nyüpərkān\
ISV
: drug

nutrilite
\nyütrəlīt\
ISV
: mineral

nutritory
\nyütrətōrē\
Latin
: healthy

nymphaea
\nimfēə\
Latin
: halls

nytril
\nītrəl\
Latin
: fiber

obeah
\ōbēə\
Afrikaans
: charm

obispo
\ōbispō\
Afrikaans
: ray

obiter
\ōbədər\
Latin
: in passing

objectable
\əbjektəbəl\
Latin
: capable of being opposed

oblationary
\äbləāshəneri\
Latin
: church official

occludent
\əklüdənt\
Latin
: serving to hinder

octastylos
\äktəstīləs\
Greek
: building

octobass
\äktəbās\
Latin
: huge violin

octoechos
\äktōēkäs\
Greek
: liturgical book

octonary
\äktənerē\
Latin
: stanza

odaller
\ōdələr\
Latin
: owner of estate

odonate
\ōdənāt\
Latin
: insect

odoriphore
\ōdärəfōr\
Latin
: group radical

odorophore
\ōdärəfōr\
Latin
: anything carrying a scent

odylic
\ōdilik\
Latin
: of supernatural forces

oecophorid
\ēkäfərid\
Latin
: moth

ogeed
\ōjēd\
Latin
: having moldings

oinochoe
\oinäkəwē\
Greek
: pitcher

okenite
\ōkənīt\
German
: mineral

oldhamite
\ōldəmīt\
Latin
: mineral

olenellid
\ōləneləd\
Latin
: beetle

oleocellosis
\ōlēōsəlōsəs\
Latin
: spotting of citrus

ombu
\ämbü\
Portuguese
: tree

ommochrome
\äməkrōm\
Latin
: pigment

oncidium
\änsidēəm\
Latin
: plant

ondine
\ändēn\
French
: color

ongole
\ängōl\
geographical name
: cattle breed

onychomadesis
\änəkōmədēsəs\
Greek
: shedding of nails

oopoda
\ōäpədə\
Latin
: parts of insect

ootid
\ōətid\
Latin
: egg cell

oozooid
\ōəzōóid\
Greek
: larva

opelet
\ōplət\
Latin
: anemone

opisthaptor
\əpisthaptər\
Latin
: posterior of organ

optogram
\äptəgram\
Latin
: external object

oraria
\òrärēə\
Greek
: vestments

orchesography
\òrkəsägrəfē\
Latin
: directing of dance

organosol
\òrganəsäl\
ISV
: resin

ornithomyzous
\ornithəmīzəs\
Latin
: parasitizing birds

orpine
\òrpən\
Latin
: plant

orthicon
\òrthəkän\
ISV
: camera tube

orthonon
\orthənän\
Latin
: photographic material

ortygan
\òrtəgən\
Hindi
: bird

ossia
\ōsēə\
Latin
: or else

osteopsathyrosis
\ästēäpsathərōsəs\
Latin
: familial disease

ostiary
\ästēeri\
Latin
: doorkeeper

otheoscope
\ōthēəskōp\
Latin
: instrument

otitid
\ōtitəd\
Latin
: fly

Ouija
\wējə\
Trademark
: blackboard letters

ovaloid
\ōvəlòid\
Latin
: shaped like eggs

ovejectoral
\ōvəjektərəl\
French
: of high muscular power

ovomucin
\ōvəmyüsən\
ISV
: compound

oxadiazole
\äksədīəzōl\
ISV
: compound

oxirane
\äksərān\
ISV
: compound

oxyuricide
\äksēyùrəsīd\
Latin
: killing worms

pacaya
\pəkīyə\
Spanish
: palm tree

pactolian
\paktōlēən\
Latin
: golden

paenula
\pēnyələ\
Latin
: coat

paenungulate
\pēnəngyəlāt\
Latin
: mammal

paeonic
\pēänik\
Latin
: of metrical feet

pagurian
\pəgyùrēən\
Latin
: hermit crab

paigeite
\pājīt\
Latin
: mineral

pajitanian
\pajətānēən\
Latin
: of Stone Age

palaeichthyic
\palēikthēik\
Latin
: of ancient fish

palaeocrinoid
\palēōkrīnòid\
Latin
: animal

palaeotheriodont
\palēōthirēədänt\
Latin
: fossil

palamate
\paləmət\
Latin
: web footed

palanka
\pəlankə\
Turkish
: camp

palayan
\pəlīən\
Tagalog
: tree

paleethnology
\palēethnäləjē\
Latin
: of prehistoric men

palila
\pəlēlə\
Hawaiian
: honeycreeper

pallasite
\paləsīt\
Latin
: mineral

pallograph
\paləgraf\
Latin
: vibration instrument

pallometric
\paləmetrik\
Latin
: of earth's surface

palmierite
\palmēərīt\
Italian
: mineral

palmiste
\palmēst\
French
: tree

palmitin
\palmətən\
Latin
: ester

palmodic
\palmädik\
Latin
: jerky

paltock
\paltäk\
English
: tunic

pampean
\pampēən\
Latin
: of the dry lands

panachure
\panəshur\
French
: patchy surface

panaritium
\panərishēəm\
Latin
: inflammation of tissue

pancheon
\panchən\
Latin
: vessel

pandal
\pandəl\
Hindi
: pole

pandita
\pändēdə\
Sanskrit
: priest

pangi
\panjī\
Malay
: tree

Paninean
\pänənēən\
Sanskrit
: adhering to rules

panniculus
\pənikyələs\
Latin
: sheet of tissue

pantine
\pantən\
French
: doll

papale
\pəpälä\
Hawaiian
: hat

papion
\pāpēän\
Latin
: monkey

parachor
\perəkor\
Latin
: constant of change

paragonimiasis
\perəgänəmīəsəs\
Latin
: disease

paralic
\pəralik\
Latin
: of esters

paramylum
\pəramələm\
Latin
: carbohydrate

parastades
\pərastədēz\
Greek
: parts of church

pargasite
\pärgəsīt\
German
: mineral

parlatoria
\pärlətōrēə\
Latin
: scale

parmenidean
\pärmənidēən\
Latin
: of philosophy

paromologia
\pərōməlōjēə\
Latin
: rhetoric

parulis
\pərüləs\
Latin
: abscess in gum

passalus
\pasələs\
Greek
: beetle

paternoite
\pädərnōīt\
Latin
: mineral

pauraque
\paùräkä\
Spanish
: tree

pechay
\pechā\
Chinese
: cabbage

pedalier
\pedəlir\
Latin
: part of piano

pedetid
\pədedəd\
Latin
: rodent

peirameter
\pīramədər\
Latin
: dynamometer

pelidnota
\pelədnōdə\
Latin
: beetle

pelmet
\pelmət\
French
: curtain

pelodytid
\pelōdidəd\
Latin
: of frogs

penaea
\pənēə\
Latin
: plant

penninite
\penənīt\
German
: mineral

pentimento
\pentəmentō\
Italian
: reappearance

pepsigogue
\pepsəgäg\
Latin
: secretes proteins

Perbunan
\pərbyünən\
Trademark
: rubber

percontation
\pərkäntāshən\
Latin
: questioning

perdendosi
\pərdendōsē\
Latin
: dying away

perfilograph
\pərfīləgraf\
Latin
: instrument

periacinal
\perēasənəl\
Latin
: surrounding seeds

periople
\perēōpəl\
Latin
: waxy layer

peristerite
\pəristərīt\
Latin
: gem

perloir
\pərlwär\
French
: steel punch

peropodous
\pəräpədəs\
Latin
: having rudimentary limbs

perrier
\perēər\
French
: engine

persicary
\pərsikerē\
Latin
: plant

peruginesque
\pārüjȧnesk\
Italian
: of the painter

pesante
\pāsäntā\
Italian
: heavily

petalocerous
\petəläsȧrəs\
Latin
: having joints

pethidine
\pethədēn\
ISV
: drug

petromyzont
\petrōməīzänt\
Latin
: eel

petroxolin
\pəträksȧlin\
ISV
: compound

pettah
\pedə\
Tamilian
: curb

peyotism
\pāyōdizəm\
Spanish
: religion

phacelia
\fəsēlēə\
Latin
: plant

phacella
\fəselə\
Latin
: filament

phaeism
\fēizəm\
Latin
: incomplete melanism

phaeophyceous
\fēəfishəs\
Latin
: of animals

phaeosporous
\fēəspōrəs\
Latin
: of algae

phaethontic
\fāəthäntik\
Latin
: of seabirds

phalacrocoracine
\faləkrōkorəsīn\
Latin
: of crows

phalaenopsis
\falənäpsəs\
Latin
: orchid

phalangette
\falənjet\
French
: finger part

phallaceous
\fəlāshēəs\
Latin
: resembling fungi

pharetrone
\ferətrōn\
Latin
: sponge

pharmacon
\färməkän\
Latin
: poison

pharmacopoeial
\färməkəpēyȧl\
Latin
: of books

pharyngognath
\feringȧgnath\
Latin
: fish

phaseolin
\fəsēəlin\
Latin
: kidney bean protein

phellandrene
\felandrēn\
Latin
: chemical

phenacyl
\fenəsil\
Latin
: compound

phenetidine
\fənetədēn\
Latin
: compound

phenetole
\fenətōl\
ISV
: compound

phenytoin
\fənidəwin\
Latin
: compound

phialopore
\fīaləpōr\
Latin
: aperture

phimosis
\fīmōsəs\
Latin
: tightening

phlebotomus
\fləbätəməs\
Latin
: fly

phocaenid
\fōsēnəd\
Latin
: porpoise

pholadid
\fōlədid\
Latin
: mollusk

pholcid
\fälsəd\
Latin
: spider

phoroptor
\fəräptər\
Latin
: instrument

phosphagen
\fäsfəjen\
Latin
: compound

phosphatidyl
\fäsfətīdəl\
Latin
: compound

phrynin
\frīnən\
Latin
: frog poison

phthalimide
\thaləmīd\
Latin
: compound

phthisicky
\tizəkē\
Latin
: wheezy, asthmatic

phycitid
\fisədəd\
Latin
: moth

phylephebic
\filefəbik\
Latin
: of chief leaders

phyletism
\fīlətizəm\
Latin
: racial nationalism

phyllidium
\fəlidēəm\
Latin
: outgrowth

phyllocarid
\filəkerid\
Latin
: crustacean

phyllocyst
\filəsist\
Latin
: cavity

phyllody
\filədē\
Latin
: plant arrangement

phyllorhine
\filərīn\
Latin
: leaf-nosed

physalis
\fīsələs\
Latin
: herb

physharmonica
\fishärmänikə\
Greek
: reed organ

physiologoi
\fisēäləgȯi\
Greek
: philosophers

phytophthora
\fītäfthərə\
Latin
: fungal disease

piceous
\pisēəs\
Latin
: black

picotite
\pikətīt\
Latin
: mineral

picudilla
\pikyədilə\
Spanish
: fish

piedra
\pēädrə\
Spanish
: disease

pierine
\pīərīn\
Latin
: of cabbage

pietoso
\pēətōsō\
Italian
: compassionately

pilastrade
\piləsträd\
Latin
: row of columns

pilocarpidine
\pīləkärpədēn\
Latin
: chemical

pilonidal
\pīlənīdəl\
Latin
: of sinuses

pinkerton
\pinkərtən\
Latin
: detective

pinnatifid
\pənatəfid\
Latin
: cleft

pinnotherid
\pinəthirəd\
Latin
: crab

Pinzgauer
\pintsgaùər\
Austrian
: horse

piperitone
\pīperətōn\
ISV
: compound

piprine
\piprīn\
Latin
: of birds

pirandellian
\pirəndelēən\
Latin
: of the writer

piripiri
\pirəpirē\
Spanish
: herb

piririgua
\pirərēgwä\
Spanish
: rodent

pisanite
\pəzänīt\
German
: mineral

Pisidian
\pəsidēən\
Greek
: of ancient Greece

pistacia
\pistashə\
Greek
: tree

pitahaya
\pidəhīə\
Spanish
: cactus

pitangua
\pitangwä\
Spanish
: flycatcher

piteira
\pəterə\
Portuguese
: tree

pitri
\pitrē\
Hindi
: forefather

pittosporum
\pətäspərəm\
Latin
: tree

placidamente
\plächēdəmentē\
Italian
: calmly

plagionite
\pläjēənīt\
German
: mineral

plancheite
\plänchāīt\
French
: mineral

plandok
\plandäk\
Malay
: goat

planidiiform
\planədīəförm\
Latin
: resembling insects

planigram
\plānəgram\
Latin
: radiograph

planography
\plānōgrəfē\
Latin
: instrument

planont
\planänt\
Latin
: organism

planosol
\planəsäl\
Latin
: intrazonal soil

plasmaphereses
\plazməfərēsēz\
Latin
: blood processes

plastidome
\plastədōm\
French
: cell wall

plastigel
\plastəjel\
Latin
: viscous substance

plataleiform
\pladəlēəförm\
Latin
: spoon-billed

platanna
\plətanə\
Afrikaans
: frog

platiniridium
\platəniridēəm\
ISV
: element

Platonician
\pladōnishən\
Greek
: philosophical

plattnerite
\platnərīt\
German
: mineral

platylepadid
\pladəlepədid\
Latin
: barnacle

platypezid
\pladəpezəd\
Latin
: fly

platyrrhiny
\pladərīnē\
Latin
: broadness of nose

platystencephaly
\pladəstensefəlē\
Latin
: having narrow head

plaudite
\plädədē\
Latin
: appeal

plectomycetous
\plektōmīsēdəs\
Latin
: of fungi

pledget
\plejət\
Unknown
: compress

pleionian
\plīōnēən\
Latin
: of meteorological regions

pleiophylly
\plīəfilē\
Latin
: more leaves

pleonexia
\plēəneksēə\
Latin
: avarice

plerergate
\plirərgāt\
Latin
: worker ant

plethodon
\plethədän\
Latin
: salamander

pleurothotonos
\plùrəthätənəs\
Latin
: tonic spasm

Plexiglas
\pleksəglas\
Trademark
: acrylic resin

pleximetric
\pleksəmetrik\
Latin
: of plates

plexor
\pleksər\
Latin
: hammer

plie
\plēā\
French
: ballet jump

pliotron
\plīəträn\
Latin
: vacuum

ploiariid
\plòierēid\
Latin
: bug

plombage
\pləmbäzh\
French
: feather

plumieride
\plüumirīd\
Latin
: bitter crystalline

plumularia
\plümyəlārēə\
French
: plant

plusiid
\plüzēəd\
Latin
: moth

pluteus
\plüdēəs\
Latin
: low wall

pluvialine
\plüvēəlīn\
Latin
: of plovers

pneumatique
\nyümətēk\
French
: letter

pocan
\pōkən\
Latin
: bush

poched
\pōshād\
French
: resembling parts

pochote
\pəchōdē\
Spanish
: herb

podeones
\pōdēənēz\
Latin
: abdomens

podesta
\pōdəstä\
Italian
: chief magistrate

podetiiform
\pədēshēəförm\
Latin
: resembling an organ

podilegous
\pədiləgəs\
Latin
: pertaining to pollen

podophyllotoxin
\pädəfilətäxin\
Latin
: crystalline

poeciliid
\pēsilēid\
Latin
: fish

podura
\pədyürə\
Latin
: insect

pogge
\päg\
Unknown
: fish

polacca
\pōlakə\
Polish
: dance

polaron
\pōlərän\
ISV
: electron

polemarch
\päləmärk\
Greek
: chief

polilla
\pōlēyə\
Spanish
: tree

polistes
\pōlistēz\
Latin
: wasp

politeia
\pälətīə\
Greek
: constitution

pollam
\päləm\
Tamilian
: district

pollera
\pəyerə\
Spanish
: dress

pollinodium
\pälənōdēəm\
Latin
: branch

pollucite
\pəlüsīt\
Latin
: mineral

polybrid
\pälībrəd\
Latin
: hybrid organism

polyctenid
\pəliktənid\
Latin
: bug

polydymite
\pəlidəmīt\
Latin
: mineral

polygonaceous
\pəligənāshəs\
Latin
: of plants

polygonatum
\pälēgänədəm\
Latin
: plant

polymyodous
\pälēmīōdəs\
Latin
: of birds

polyodont
\pälēədänt\
Latin
: having many teeth

polypean
\päləpēən\
Latin
: resembling coral

polypedatid
\pälēpədādəd\
Latin
: tree frog

polypheme
\päləfēm\
Latin
: giant
(adjective spelled
polyphemian)

polyphloesboean
\päləflesbēən\
Greek
: loud-roaring

poluphloisboian
\pälyəfloisboiən\
Greek
: loud-roaring

polyporoid
\pəlipəroid\
Latin
: pertaining to coral

polystachyous
\pälēstakēəs\
Latin
: having many stalks

polytopy
\pəlidəpē\
Latin
: independent origin

polyxenid
\pəliksənid\
Latin
: millipede

pomacentroid
\pōməsentroid\
Latin
: fish

pomarrosa
\pōmərōsə\
Spanish
: apple

pomatorhine
\pōmadərīn\
Latin
: having nostrils

pomatumed
\pōmādəmd\
Latin
: having ointments

pommee
\pämā\
French
: having the end of each arm
terminated

pommer
\pȯmər\
German
: tuba

pompholyx
\pämfəliks\
Latin
: disease

pompilid
\pämpəlid\
Latin
: wasp

pomster
\pämztər\
Corn
: treat illness

pongol
\pängȧl\
Tamilian
: festival

pontederiaceous
\päntədirēāshəs\
Latin
: of aquatic plants

pontil
\päntəl\
French
: metal rod

pontocaine
\päntəkān\
ISV
: drug

pontonier
\päntənir\
French
: boatman

pontypool
\päntēpül\
Unknown
: metalware

pooli
\pülē\
Mende
: timber tree

poonac
\pünak\
Sinhalese
: coconut cake

Popolocan
\pōpəlōkən\
Spanish
: language family

popotillo
\pōpətēyō\
Spanish
: plant

poppean
\päpēən\
Latin
: pertaining to seeds

porcellanian
\porsəlānēən\
Italian
: of crabs

porcellanite
\pȯrselәnīt\
German
: mineral

poricidal
\porәsīdәl\
Latin
: dehiscing through holes

poritoid
\pәrītȯid\
Latin
: coral

porphyropsin
\pȯrfәräpsәn\
Latin
: pigment

porphyroxine
\porfәräksēn\
Latin
: compound

portamento
\pōrdәmentō\
Italian
: continuous glide

porteous
\pōrtēәs\
Scottish
: roll of offenders

portiforia
\portәfōrēә\
Italian
: ecclesiastical books

portmantologism
\pōrtmantälәjizәm\
Latin
: word derived from other
words

portoise
\pȯrdәs\
Unknown
: upper part of vessel

portolano
\pōrtәlänō\
Italian
: medieval navigation

portunid
\pōrtünid\
Latin
: crab

posada
\pōsädә\
Spanish
: innn

possibile
\pәsibәlē\
Latin
: something conceivable

postament
\pōstәment\
Latin
: frame

postical
\pästәkәl\
Latin
: behind

postiche
\pästēsh\
French
: false hair

potageries
\pōtajәrēz\
French
: garden vegetables

potamobenthos
\pädәmōbenthäs\
Latin
: organism

potamogalid
\pädәmägәlәd\
Latin
: of insectivores

potamogeton
\pōdәmōjētän\
Latin
: plant

potassiferous
\pädәsifәrәs\
Latin
: bearing compounds

potentilla
\pōtәntilә\
Spanish
: tree

potestates
\pōtestätәs\
Latin
: legal authorities

potrack
\pätrak\
Imitative
: make a high shrill

pottah
\pädә\
Hindi
: certificate of lease

potwalloper
\pätwälәpәr\
English
: voter

poulardize
\pülärdīz\
French
: make chicken

pourie
\pōri\
Scottish
: vessel

povidone
\pōvәdōn\
ISV
: compound

powellite
\paὺəlīt\
Latin
: mineral

powitch
\paὺich\
Unknown
: apple

poyou
\pȯiü\
Guarani
: armadillo

practician
\praktishən\
Latin
: pragmatic person

praecognita
\prēkägnidə\
Latin
: something unknown

praedium
\prēdēəm\
Latin
: tenement of land

praenestine
\prēnestən\
geographical name
: of the city

praetextae
\prētekstē\
Latin
: white robes

praetorianism
\prētōrēənizəm\
Latin
: corrupt military

praguian
\prägēən\
Latin
: adherent to WWII

prasinous
\prāzənəs\
Latin
: color of leeks

praxeological
\praksēəläjəkəl\
Latin
: pertaining to human conduct

precedable
\prəsēdəbəl\
Latin
: capable of being introduced

Precipitron
\prēsīpəträn\
Trademark
: apparatus

preconization
\prekənəzāshən\
Latin
: process of becoming bishop

preeclampsia
\prēəklampsēə\
Latin
: toxic conditions

prefixion
\prēfikshən\
Latin
: word placement

pregneninolone
\pregnēninəlōn\
ISV
: compound

prehnitene
\prānətēn\
German
: compound

prelacy
\preləsē\
Latin
: church office

premunitory
\prēmyünətōrē\
Latin
: pertaining to land estates

preparateur
\prepərətər\
French
: laboratory assistant

pressirostral
\presərästrəl\
Latin
: of birds

prestant
\prestənt\
Latin
: metallic stop

pretendant
\prətendənt\
Latin
: one who pretends

preteritness
\predəritnəs\
Latin
: of verbs

priapulid
\prīapyəlid\
Latin
: worm

priceite
\prīsīt\
Latin
: mineral

primipilar
\prīmipələr\
Latin
: constituting the chief centurion

primulaverin
\primyəlavərin\
Latin
: crystalline

priscillian
\prəsilyən\
Latin
: of philosophy

Privine
\privən\
Trademark
: drug

probertite
\präbərtīt\
Latin
: mineral

probit
\präbət\
ISV
: statistical unit

procainamide
\prōkānəmīd\
ISV
: compound

procaviid
\prōkāvēəd\
Latin
: mammal

procidentia
\prōsədenshə\
Latin
: prolapse of organ

proctiger
\präktijər\
Latin
: abdominal segment

proctotrupid
\präktətrüpid\
Latin
: wasp

procureur
\prōkəreur\
French
: agent

prodelision
\prädəlizhən\
Latin
: initial vowel pronunciation

prodigiosin
\prōdijēōsən\
Latin
: pigment

prodromus
\prädrəməs\
Greek
: preliminary publication

profichi
\prōfēkē\
Italian
: fruit

profundal
\prəfəndəl\
Latin
: of lakes

progredien
\prōgrēdēən\
Latin
: bug

promizole
\prōməzōl\
Trademark
: drug

pronuba
\pränyübə\
Latin
: moth

propadrine
\prōpədrən\
Latin
: compound

propendent
\prōpendənt\
Latin
: hanging forward

properdin
\prōpərdən\
Latin
: protein for serum

properispomena
\prōperəspämənə\
Latin
: accented words

propionyl
\prōpēənil\
ISV
: radical

propneustic
\prōnyüstik\
Latin
: of insects

propodus
\präpədəs\
Greek
: crustacean

propylidene
\prōpilədēn\
ISV
: compound

propylite
\präpəlīt\
ISV
: mineral

proquaestor
\prōkwestər\
Latin
: magistrate

prosbul
\präzbul\
Hebrew
: rabbinical statement

prosodetic
\präsədedik\
Latin
: situated anterior of the beak

prosopon
\prəsōpän\
Latin
: insect stage

prosopyle
\präsəpīl\
Greek
: aperture in sponges

prosthion
\prästhēän\
Greek
: teeth

protelid
\prəteləd\
Latin
: mammal

protelytropterous
\prətelēträptərəs\
Latin
: of extinct insects

prothonotarial
\prōtänəterēəl\
Greek
: of church officials

protonotary
\prōtänəterē\
Greek
: official

protolog
\prōdəlȯg\
Greek
: original description of
species

protome
\prətōmē\
Latin
: head representation

Proustian
\prüstēən\
French
: of philosophy

provisorily
\prəvīsərəlē\
Greek
: in a conditional manner

prytaneum
\pritənēəm\
Greek
: long hall

psalterium
\sȯltirēəm\
Latin
: third chamber of stomach

psammosere
\saməsir\
Latin
: sand

pselaphid
\seləfid\
Latin
: beetle

pseudapospory
\südapəspȯrē\
Greek
: production

pseudaxis
\südaksəs\
Greek
: grapevine

pseudojervine
\südəjərvēn\
ISV
: compound

pseudowavellite
\südəwāvəlīt\
Greek
: mineral

pseudoyohimbine
\südəyōhimbēn\
ISV
: compound

psicose
\sīkōs\
Greek
: sugar

psophometric
\sōfəmetrik\
Greek
: measuring noise

psychagogue
\sīkəgäg\
Greek
: guide of souls

psyllid
\siləd\
Greek
: louse

psywar
\sīwär\
ISV
: mental conflict

pteralium
\tərālēəm\
Latin
: insect wing

pterideous
\teridēəs\
Latin
: pertaining to plants

pteromalid
\təräməlid\
Latin
: fly

pteropaedes
\terəpēdēz\
Latin
: birds hatching

pterophorid
\təräfərid\
Latin
: moth

pterygiophore
\tərijēəfȯr\
Latin
: bony element

pterylography
\terəlägrəfē\
Latin
: study of birds

ptilopod
\tiləpäd\
Greek
: having feet feathered
(has homonym: tylopod)

ptilosis
\təlōsəs\
Greek
: plumage

ptychoderid
\tīkädərid\
Latin
: moth

ptychopariid
\tīkəpārēəd\
Latin
: trilobite

ptyxes
\tiksēz\
Latin
: dispositions of leaves

puccinoid
\pəksənȯid\
Greek
: pertaining to fungi

pucherite
\pükhərīt\
German
: mineral

pudor
\pyüdȯr\
Latin
: modesty

pudu
\püdü\
Afrikaans
: deer

pukeko
\pükākō\
Afrikaans
: bark

pulegol
\pyüləgol\
ISV
: compound

pulicidal
\pyüləsīdəl\
Latin
: killing fleas

pulldoo
\pu̇ldü\
French
: hen

pulvillus
\pəlviləs\
Latin
: cushion

pulvinus
\pəlvīnəs\
Latin
: base

pulviplume
\pəlvēplüm\
Latin
: feathers

pumiceous
\pyümishəs\
Latin
: resembling stone

punee
\pünāā\
Hawaiian
: couch

pupunha
\pəpünyə\
Portuguese
: palm tree

purree
\pu̇rē\
Hindi
: yellow

puschkinia
\pu̇shkinēə\
German
: plant

puseyite
\pyüzēīt\
English
: high churchman

pustulant
\pəschələnt\
Latin
: formation agent

pycniospore
\piknēəspōr\
Latin
: fungal seed

pygofer
\pīgəfər\
Latin
: insect abdomen

pyinma
\pēinmä\
Burman
: color

pylstert
\pīlstert\
Afrikaans
: ray

pyocele
\pīōsēl\
ISV
: pus filled cavity

pyracene
\pirəsēn\
ISV
: compound

pyralidid
\pəralədəd\
Latin
: moth

Pyralin
\pirələn\
Trademark
: plastic

pyraloid
\pirəloid\
Latin
: moth

pyrazoline
\pīrazəlēn\
ISV
: compound

pyrazolyl
\pīrazəlil\
ISV
: compound

pyrethrolone
\pīrēthrəlōn\
ISV
: alcohol

pyribenzamine
\pirəbenzəmēn\
Trademark
: drug

pyribole
\pirəbōl\
Latin
: rock

pyridyl
\pirədil\
ISV
: compound

pyrilamine
\pīriləmēn\
ISV
: compound

pyrolusite
\pīrəlüsīt\
German
: mineral

pyroxmangite
\pīräksmanjīt\
ISV
: mineral

pyrrhotism
\pirətizəm\
Latin
: red hair condition

pyrroline
\pirəlēn\
ISV
: compound

pyruvate
\pīrüvāt\
ISV
: salt ester

pyrylium
\pīrilēəäm\
Latin
: element

pythiambic
\pithēambik\
Latin
: of metrical feet

pyxidate
\piksədāt\
Latin
: resembling plantains

pyxides
\piksədēz\
Grek
: containers

quaddle
\kwädəl\
Scottish
: grumbler

quadrature
\kwädrəchὺər\
Latin
: star configuration

quadricycle
\kwädrəsīkəl\
Latin
: object with four wheels

quadrireme
\kwädrərēm\
Greek
: boat

quadrivoltine
\kwädrəvōltēn\
Latin
: producing four generations

quaestiones
\kwīstēōnās\
Latin
: criminal acts

quaestorship
\kwestərship\
Latin
: the state of being detective

quai
\kā\
French
: those lying on the Seine river

quandy
\kwandē\
Imitative
: duck

quaternate
\kwädərnāt\
Latin
: every fourth year

queachy
\kwēchi\
English
: marshy

quelite
\kālēdē\
Spanish
: plant

quenselite
\kwentsəlīt\
German
: mineral

quercimeritrin
\kwərsimerətrin\
ISV
: compound

quesited
\kwēsīdə̇d\
Latin
: astrological

questeur
\kestəur\
French
: member of parliament

quetsch
\kwech\
German
: vat of rollers

quillai
\kēyī\
Spanish
: tree

quillon
\kēyōn\
French
: handle of sword

quinolinyl
\kwinəlinəl\
ISV
: compound

quinton
\kantōn\
French
: violin

quinuclidine
\kwənüklədēn\
ISV
: compound

quiritarian
\kwirəterēən\
Latin
: legal

quite
\kētā\
Spanish
: blow of passes

Quoratean
\kwōrətēən\
Spanish
: language family

qutb
\kûdəb\
Arabic
: saint

raan
\rän\
Scottish
: disease

rabato
\rəbādō\
French
: collar

racemase
\rasəmās\
Latin
: enzyme

rachiform
\rākəform\
Latin
: shaped like spines

Racovian
\rəkōvēən\
Polish
: of the university

radknight
\radnīt\
English
: tenant

raffinase
\rafənāz\
Latin
: enzyme

raguly
\ragyəlē\
French
: notched

raioid
\rāȯid\
Latin
: resembling rays

raisine
\rāzənā\
French
: preserved pears

rajah
\räjə\
Hindi
: silk

ralstonite
\ṙȯlztənīt\
English
: mineral

rameseum
\raməsēəm\
Greek
: temple

rammelsbergite
\raməlsbərgīt\
German
: mineral

ramsayite
\ramzēīt\
English
: mineral

randannite
\randanīt\
German
: mineral

rangatira
\rängətirə\
Maori
: chief

rann
\ran\
Gaelic
: stanza

ranunculaceous
\rənnkyəlāshēəs\
Latin
: pertaining to herbs

Rassenkreise
\räsənkrīzə\
German
: species

rath
\rä\
Gaelic
: earthwork

rathite
\rätīt\
German
: mineral

ratine
\ratənā\
French
: yarn

rauriki
\raurəkē\
Maori
: plant

rauvite
\rȯvīt\
German
: mineral

ravenala
\ravənālə\
Latin
: shrub

raviney
\rəvēnē\
Latin
: resembling gorges

razon
\rāzän\
blend
: bomb

reason
\rezən\
English
: timber

reboise
\rəbȯiz\
Latin
: reforest

rebolera
\rebəlerə\
Spanish
: bullfighting

rechabite
\rekəbīt\
Hebrew
: one who lives in tents

reddendum
\rədendəm\
Latin
: clause

reddition
\rədishən\
Latin
: application of reasoning

redingtonite
\redingtənīt\
geographical name
: mineral

refait
\rəfā\
French
: game

refractometric
\rəfraktəmetrik\
Latin
: of instruments

refrenation
\refrənāshən\
Latin
: failure of aspect

regidor
\rāhēthȯr\
Spanish
: officer

regosol
\regəsäl\
Latin
: soil

reiter
\rīdər\
German
: cavalry soldier

Rellyan
\relēən\
Latin
: minority group

Renanian
\rənanēən\
French
: of the philosopher

rendu
\rändü\
French
: drawing

rengas
\rengäs\
Malay
: tree

reptant
\reptənt\
Latin
: crab

resazurin
\rezazhərin\
ISV
: compound

reserpine
\rəsərpən\
ISV
: alkaloid

responsory
\rəspänsərē\
Latin
: anthem

restionaceous
\restēənāshəs\
Latin
: resembling herbs

retgersite
\retgərzīt\
English
: mineral

reticella
\redəchelə\
Italian
: needlepoint lace

retinalite
\retənəlīt\
ISV
: mineral

retrofection
\retrəfekshən\
Latin
: pinworm infestation

retzian
\retsēən\
Swiss
: mineral

reverable
\rəvirəbəl\
Latin
: meriting honor

rewirable
\rəwīrəbəl\
Latin
: capable of being wired again

reynard
\rānärd\
French
: fox

rhabditid
\rabdīdəd\
Latin
: worm

rhachitome
\rakətōm\
Latin
: amphibian

Rhaetian
\rēshēən\
Greek
: of ancient Greece

rhagades
\ragədēz\
Greek
: linear cracks

rhagon
\rāgän\
Latin
: sponge

rhamnazin
\ramnəzin\
ISV
: compound

rhamnetin
\ramnədən\
ISV
: compound

rhamninose
\ramnənōs\
ISV
: compound

rhamphotheca
\ramfəthēkə\
Latin
: horny sheath

rhapontigenin
\rəpäntəjenən\
ISV
: compound

Rhenish
\renəsh\
German
: on this side of river

rhinocerotiform
\rīnäsərätəfòrm\
Latin
: resembling mammals

rhinolophine
\rīnäləfīn\
Latin
: bat

rhipiphorid
\rəpifərid\
Latin
: beetle

rhizocaline
\rīzəkālēn\
ISV
: compound

rhodora
\rədōrə\
Latin
: plant

rhomboclase
\rämbəklās\
ISV
: mineral

rhopalocercous
\rōpəlōsərkəs\
Latin
: having wide tail

rhumbatron
\rəmbəträn\
blend
: catcher

rhus
\rəs\
Latin
: plant

rhynchoceph
\rinkəsef\
Latin
: reptile

rhynchote
\rinkōt\
Latin
: bug

riceyer
\rīsēər\
Latin
: resembling grains

richellite
\rəshelīt\
geographical name
: mineral

ricinine
\risənēn\
ISV
: compound

ricinolein
\risənōlēən\
ISV
: compound

rickardite
\rikərdīt\
English
: mineral

rickmatic
\rikmətik\
Scottish
: business

ricolettaite
\rikəletəīt\
geographical name
: mineral

riebeckite
\rēbekīt\
German
: mineral

Riemannian
\rēmänēən\
German
: of the mathematician

rillet
\rilət\
English
: small book

rimas
\rēməs\
Tagalog
: fruit

rinkolite
\rinkəlīt\
Russian
: mineral

rinneite
\rinēīt\
German
: mineral

roanoke
\rōənōk\
Virginian
: beads

Robenhausian
\rōbənhaüzēən\
German
: culture

Robespierrist
\rōbspirəst\
French
: follower

roeblingite
\rōblingīt\
German
: mineral

roemerite
\rāmərīt\
German
: mineral

roesslerite
\reslərīt\
German
: mineral

romadur
\rōmədůr\
German
: cheese

rombowline
\rämbōlən\
English
: knot

romeite
\rōmēīt\
French
: mineral

romerillo
\rōmərilō\
Spanish
: rodent

romescot
\rōmskät\
English
: tax

rompu
\rämpü\
French
: heraldic

roneograph
\rōnēəgraf\
Latin
: produce copies

rosasite
\rōzəsīt\
German
: mineral

roscoelite
\räskōlīt\
German
: mineral

roselite
\rōzəlīt\
Spanish
: mineral

rosieresite
\rōzəēerəsīt\
French
: mineral

rosiny
\räzənē\
Latin
: abounding in odor

rostellate
\rästəlāt\
Latin
: resembling necks

rototill
\rōdōtil\
Trademark
: to stir

rottlera
\rätlərə\
ISV
: powder

rouen
\rüän\
French
(1): duck
(2): chinaware

rovescio
\rōveshō\
Italian
: contrarily

roweite
\rōīt\
English
: mineral

royet
\rȯiət\
Scottish
: wild

ruana
\rüänə\
Spanish
: wool

ruckumlaut
\rəkùmlaùt\
German
: vowel

rudistan
\rüdistən\
Latin
: crustacean

rudmasday
\rədməsdē\
English
: festival

runcinate
\rənsənət\
Latin
: worm

ruridecanal
\rùrədəkānəl\
Latin
: of ecclesiastical ranking

rushee
\rəshē\
Scottish
: university student

rustre
\rəstər\
French
: heraldry

rutelid
\rüteləd\
Latin
: beetle

ryanodine
\rīanədēn\
ISV
: compound

ryeland
\rīlənd\
English
: sheep

ryobu
\rēōbü\
Japanese
: Buddhist

sabal
\sābal\
Latin
: plant

sabbat
\sabət\
French
: assembly

sabbatia
\səbāshēə\
Latin
: plant

sabha
\səbä\
Sanskrit
: hall

sabinane
\sabənān\
ISV
: compound

sabra
\säbrä\
Hebrew
: fruit

saccomyoidean
\sakōmīöidēən\
Latin
: rodent

saccorhiza
\sakərīzə\
Latin
: sea anemone

sacculina
\sakyəlīnə\
Latin
: parasite

sadducaic
\sajəkāik\
Latin
: of parties or sects

sadhana
\sädənə\
Hindi
: religious training

safflor
\saflȯr\
Latin
: color

safflorite
\saflərīt\
Italian
: mineral

sagenite
\sajənīt\
French
: mineral

sagittocyst
\səjitəsist\
Latin
: capsule

sahlinite
\sälənīt\
German
: mineral

saithe
\sāth\
Scottish
: fish

sakeen
\səkēn\
Hindi
: goat

sakeret
\sākəret\
Latin
: male falcon

salai
\səlī\
Hindi
: tree

salambao
\säləmbau̇\
Portuguese
: fishing net

salar
\səlär\
German
: depression

salband
\salband, zälbänt\
German
: border

salfern
\salfərn\
Latin
: seed

salmiac
\salmēak\
ISV
: ammonium

salmonsite
\salzmənīt\
Englsh
: mineral

salmwood
\sämwu̇d\
Unknown
: tree

salsuginous
\salsüjinəs\
Latin
: of plants growing in soils

salticid
\saltəsəd\
Latin
: spider

Salvarsan
\salvərsan\
Trademark
: drug

Salyrgan
\salərgən\
ISV
: compound

samaj
\səmäj\
Hindi
: society

sambaqui
\sambəkē\
Tupi
: kitchen

sambuca
\sambyükə\
Arabic
: harp

sambunigrin
\sambyənīgrən\
ISV
: compound

samiresite
\saməresīt\
Japanese
: mineral

samohu
\səmōhü\
geographical name
: gray color

sampleite
\sampəlīt\
English
: mineral

Sampsaean
\sam(p)sēən\
Latin
: member of sect

sanbornite
\sanbərnīt\
English
: mineral

Sandemanian
\sandəmānēən\
Latin
: member of sect

sangreeroot
\sangrērüt\
Latin
: plant

sanidinic
\sanədinik\
German
: of compounds

sanious
\sānēəs\
Latin
: with bloody tinge

sann
\san\
Hindi
: fiber

santalene
\santəlēn\
ISV
: compound

santenone
\santənōn\
ISV
: compound

santolina
\santəlīnə\
Latin
: plant

santon
(1) \santən\ (2) \säntōn\
(1) Spanish, (2) French
(1): saint
(2): clay image

sanvitalia
\sanvətālēə\
Latin
: plant

saperda
\səpərdə\
Latin
: beetle

saphenous
\səfēnəs\
Latin
: of veins

sapin
\sapan\
French
: fir tree

sappho
\safō\
Greek
: bird

saprolegnious
\saprəlegnēəs\
Latin
: of fungi

sarabaite
\sərabəīt\
Latin
: monk

sarada
\shärədə\
Kashmiri
: alphabet

sarangousty
\serəngüstē\
Persian
: stucco work

sarcel
\särsəl\
Latin
: hawk wing

sarcelle
\särsel\
French
: bird

sarcocolla
\särkəkälə\
Latin
: gummy serum

sarcodinian
\särkədinēən\
Latin
: of fish

sardana
\särdänə\
Catalan
: dance

sarkinite
\särkənīt\
German
: mineral

sarmientite
\särmēentīt\
German
: mineral

saron
\särȯn\
Javan
: metallophone

saros
\seräs\
Greek
: unit of time

sarsar
\särsər\
Arabic
: cold wind

sarsen
\särsən\
Alteration
: mass of stone

sartorite
\särdərīt\
German
: mineral

sasin
\sāsən\
German
: black duck

sasine
\sāsən\
Latin
: instrument

Satem
\sädəm\
German
: language family

satisdation
\sadəsdāshən\
Latin
: security

saturae
\sädərī\
Latin
: stage shows

sauconite
\säkənīt\
geographical name
: mineral

Sauraseni
\sorəsānē\
Sanskrit
: language family

saussuritize
\säsərətīz\
Latin
: to convert minerals

sauvegarde
\sōvgärd\
French
: protection

savanilla
\savənilə\
geographical name
: fish

savate
\səvat\
French
: form of boxing

savoyard
\səvȯiərd\
Latin
: devotee to comic operas

sawali
\səwälē\
Tagalog
: matting

saxatile
\saksətīl\
Latin
: living in rocks

saxicavous
\saksēcavəs\
Latin
: boring in rock

saya
\säyə\
Spanish
: skirt

scabies
\skābēz\
Latin
: itch

scacchite
\skakīt\
Italian
: mineral

scaenae
\sēnē\
Latin
: theatres

scalage
\skālij\
Latin
: stocks of wood

scalecide
\skāləsīd\
Trademark
: killing mosquitoes

scamozzi
\skəmätsē\
Italian
: variation of car

scandaroon
\skandərün\
Turkish
: pigeon

scandent
\skandənt\
Latin
: climbing

scapel
\skapəl\
Latin
: small stem

scapolitization
\skapəlitəzāshən\
Latin
: conversion into mineral

scaum
\skȧm\
Scottish
: burn

sceuophorion
\skevəfȯryȯn\
Greek
: receptacle

sceuophylacium
\skyüōfəlāsh(ē)əm\
Greek
: holy place

schairerite
\shīrərīt\
German
: mineral

schallerite
\shalərīt\
English
: mineral

schapbachite
\shäpbäkīt\
German
: mineral

scharf
\shärf\
German
: mixture stop

schepen
\skāpən\
German
: officer

scherm
\ske(ə)rm\
Afrikaans
: fence

schillerize
\shilərīz\
Latin
: impart a mineral

schirmerite
\shərmərīt\
German
: mineral

schistorrhachis
\skistȯrəkis\
Latin
: splitting of spine

schistosomiasis
\shistəsōmīəsəs\
Latin
: disease

schizocoelous
\skitsəsēləs\
Latin
: pertaining to cavities

schizolite
\skizəlīt\
Latin
: mineral

schizont
\skīzänt\
Latin
: cell

schizozoite
\skizəzōīt\
German
: mineral

schnurkeramik
\shnu̇rkärämik\
German
: pottery

schorlomite
\shorləmīt\
German
: mineral

schorly
\shorlē\
German
: resembling tourmaline

schreibersite
\shrībərsīt\
German
: mineral

schreinerize
\shrīnərīz\
German
: press cloth

schultenite
\shu̇ltənīt\
Dutch
: mineral

schwartzembergite
\shwȯrtsəmbərgīt\
German
: mineral

schwarz
\shwȯrts\
German
: bid

sciaenid
\sīēnid\
Latin
: fish

Scillonian
\səlōnēən\
Greek
: of the islands

Scillitan
\silətən\
Latin
: of the ancient city

scintigram
\sintəgram\
Latin
: instrument

sciolto
\shältō\
Italian
: with freedom

scirrhoid
\skiroid\
Latin
: resembling tissue

sciuroid
\sīyùroid\
Latin
: squirrel

scolecidan
\skōlesədən\
Latin
: of invertebrates

scoliid
\skōlēid\
Latin
: wasp

scolithus
\skōləthəs\
Latin
: mineral

scolopendra
\skäləpendrə\
Latin
: centipede

scolytoid
\skälətoid\
Latin
: beetle

scoparin
\skōpərən\
ISV
: compound

scopone
\skəpōnā\
Italian
: game

scorodite
\skorədīt\
Latin
: mineral

scorpaenoid
\skorpēnoid\
Latin
: fish

scorzalite
\skòrzəlīt\
Italian
: mineral

scotodinia
\skätədinēə\
Latin
: vertigo

scotograph
\skädəgraf\
Greek
: x-ray picture

scray
\skrā\
Dutch
: container

scrophularia
\skräfyəlārēə\
Latin
: plant

sculptitory
\skəlptətōrē\
Latin
: of 3-dimensional pictures

scutellerid
\skyütelərid\
Latin
: insect

scutelligerous
\skyüdəlijərəs\
Latin
: bearing shields

scye
\sī\
Unknown
: hole

scyllitol
\silətòl\
ISV
: compound

scyphose
\sīfōs\
Latin
: having cup-like structures

sealch
\selkh\
English
: aquatic mammal

Sebilian
\səbilyən\
Spanish
: culture

sebilla
\səbilə\
French
: receptacle

sebright
\sēbrīt\
English
: bird

secateur
\sekətəur\
French
: scissors

Seconal
\sekənòl\
Trademark
: drug

287

secreta
\səkrätä\
Italian
: prayer

secus
\sēkəs\
Latin
: otherwise

segreant
\səgrēənt\
French
: heraldic

Seitz
\zīts\
Trademark
: fiber

seizor
\sēzȯr\
Latin
: one who takes estate

selensulfur
\selənsəlfər\
Latin
: vitreous mixture

seligmannite
\səligmənīt\
German
: mineral

sellaite
\seləīt\
Italian
: mineral

selvagee
\selvəjē\
Latin
: rope

semeiotics
\səmīädiks\
Latin
: study of signs

semibejan
\semēbājən\
scottish
: second-year student

semidine
\semədīn\
ISV
: compound

semiosis
\sēmīōsəs\
Latin
: functional organ

sempervirine
\sempərvīrēn\
ISV
: compound

semseyite
\sem(p)sēīt\
Hungarian
: mineral

senam
\sənäm\
Arabic
: rock

senarmontite
\senərmäntīt\
french
: mineral

senegin
\senəjən\
Latin
: compound

sensitometer
\sentsətämədər\
Latin
: instrument

sepalody
\sepəlōdē\
ISV
: floral organ separation

sepiolite
\sēpēəlīt\
Latin
: mineral

sepoy
\sēpȯi\
Hindi
: soldier

seppuku
\sepükü\
Japanese
: plant

serandite
\serəndīt\
English
: mineral

serein
\səran\
French
: mist

serendibite
\serəndibīt\
Latin
: mineral

sericin
\serəsən\
Latin
: gelatinous protein

serimpi
\sərimpē\
Javan
: dancer

serow
\sərō\
Arabic
: goat

serradella
\serədelə\
Spanish
: herb

serrasalmo
\serəsalmō\
Spanish
: fish

serricorn
\serəkȯrn\
Latin
: beetle

servitus
\sərvətüs\
Latin
: slavery

sesban
\ses͵ban\
French
: plant

sestetto
\sestedō\
Italian
: lyrical poem

setier
\sətyā\
French
: unit of length

settecentist
\setəchentist\
Italian
: poet

setwall
\setwäl\
Persian
: herb

seybertite
\sībərtīt\
German
: mineral

shahidi
\shähēdē\
Persian
: member of Sikh sect

shallon
\shalən\
Chinook
: fruit

shamir
\shəmi(ə)r\
Hebrew
(1): stone
(2): worm

shangan
\shangən\
Gaelic
: stick

shantung
\shantəng\
Chinese
: fabric

Shapwailutan
\shapwīlütən\
blend
: language family

shechemite
\shēkəmīt\
Hebrew
: native of Palestine

sheder
\shēdər\
English
: female sheep

sheefish
\shēfish\
English
: fish

shelleyesque
\shelēesk\
Italian
: of the writer

shenango
\shənangō\
geographical name
: dock worker

shepstare
\shepstər\
English
: fish

sherardize
\shərärdīz\
French
: coat with zinc

shieling
\shēling\
British
: hill

shikasta
\shəkastə\
Hindi
: broken hand

shilonite
\shīlōnīt\
geographical name
: mineral

shiralee
\shirəlē\
Australian
: cylindrical pack

shittah
\shitə\
Hebrew
: tree

shoder
\shōdər\
French
: instrument

shogaol
\shōgəȯl\
ISV
: compound

shonkinite
\shänkənīt\
geographical name
: mineral

shortia
\shòrtēə\
Latin
: plant

shoyu
\shōyü\
Japanese
: legume

shreadhead
\shredhed\
English
: roof

shropshire
\shräpshi(ə)r\
English
: sheep

shunammite
\shùnəmīt\
Hebrew
: native of Palestine

sicarius
\səkārēəs\
Latin
: terrorist

siddha
\sidə\
Hindi
: rice

siddur
\sədùr\
Hebrew
: prayer book

siderism
\sidərizəm\
Latin
: magnetism

siderotil
\sidərətil\
Latin
: compound

sifatite
\səfädīt\
Arabic
: school

siffleur
\sēflər\
French
: whistler

sigmaspire
\sigməspīr\
Latin
: sponge

signifie
\sēnyfyā\
French
: sign

silesia
\sīlēzhə\
Latin
: cloth

silicle
\siləkəl\
Latin
: small cloth

sillaginoid
\səlajənòid\
Latin
: fish

sillenite
\silənīt\
German
: mineral

sillimanite
\siləmənīt\
German
: mineral

siloxane
\səläksān\
ISV
: compound

silphid
\silfəd\
Latin
: beetle

siluroid
\silyəròid\
Latin
: resembling fish

silyl
\siləl\
ISV
: radical

simal
\sēməl\
Hindi
: tree

simiid
\simēəd\
Latin
: ape

simpliciter
\simplisədər\
Latin
: by itself

sinamay
\sēnəmī\
Tagalog
: fabric

sinapism
\sinəpizəm\
Latin
: counterirritant

sincosite
\sinkəsīt\
German
: mineral

sindico
\sēndəkō\
Italian
: officer

singspiel
\zingshpēəl\
German
: musical

sinigrin
\sinəgrən\
ISV
: glucoside

sinomenine
\sənämənēn\
ISV
: compound

sinsyne
\sintsīn\
Scottish
: ago

siphoneous
\sīfōnēəs\
Latin
: resembling tubes

sippio
\sipēō\
Unknown
: game

sirat
\sərät\
Arabic
: bridge

sirgang
\sərgang\
Sinhalese
: color

siruaballi
\shirəwəbälē\
Hindi
: stree

siserskite
\sisərskīt\
German
: mineral

sisymbrium
\sisimbrēəm\
Latin
: plant

sitio
\sēdēō\
Spanish
: city

sitosterol
\sīdōstiról\
ISV
: compound

sivathere
\sēvəthir\
Latin
: primate

siwash
\sīwäsh\
name
: college

sjogrenite
\shōgrənīt\
Swedish
: mineral

skevish
\skevish\
Unknown
: rodent

skimmity
\skimədē\
English
: parade

sklim
\sklim\
Scottish
: climb

sklodowskite
\sklədäfskīt\
Russian
: mineral

skyr
\skir\
Norwegian
: curd

slaister
\slāstər\
English
: dirt

slavikite
\slavəkīt\
Czech
: mineral

sleekit
\slēkət\
Scottish
: crafty

slommacky
\sləməkē\
English
: messy

slype
\slīp\
Scottish
: narrow passage

smaik
\smāk\
Scottish
: rascal

Smectymnuan
\smektimnyəwən\
Latin
: adherent

smeddum
\smedəm\
Scottish
: powder

smilagenin
\smīləjenən\
Latin
: compound

sminthurid
\sminthyərid\
Latin
: trilobite

Smyrnaean
\smərnēən\
Greek
: inhabitant of Turkey

smytrie
\smītri\
Unknown
: heap

snavvle
\snavəl\
Australian
: get hold of

snoeking
\snüking\
Afrikaans
: fishing

snotziekte
\snätsēktə\
Afrikaans
: sheep disease

soay
\sōā\
English
: sheep

sobrerol
\sōbreròl\
ISV
: crystalline alcohol

societas
\sōkēətäs\
Latin
: association

socle
\säkəl\
French
: member

sodalite
\sōdəlīt\
Latin
: mineral

soddyite
\sädēīt\
Alteration
: mineral

sodoku
\sōdəkü\
Japanese
: rat bite

softa
\sòftə\
Turkish
: theologist

soken
\sōkən\
English
: district

sokol
\sòkòl\
Russian
: gymnastic society

solan
\sōlən\
English
: duck

solanaceous
\sōlənāshəs\
Latin
: of herbs

solanidine
\sōlanədēn\
ISV
: compound

solay
\səlā\
English
: divide

soldanella
\säldənelə\
Latin
: plant

solenacean
\sälənāshən\
Latin
: mollusk

solenette
\sōlnet\
French
: fish

solenostely
\səlēnəstēlē\
Latin
: internal plant xylem and phloem

solentine
\säləntīn\
Latin
: weed

solideo
\sōlədāō\
Italian
: hat

solion
\sälīän\
ISV
: electron

solodize
\sōlədīz\
Russian
: to convert into soil

solonetzic
\sälənetzik\
Russian
: of intrazonal soils

solpugid
\sälpyüjəd\
Latin
: arachnid

somma
\sämə\
Italian
: volcanic crater

sonovox
\sänəväks\
Latin
: sound box

sophora
\səfōrə\
Latin
: plant

sophorine
\säfərēn\
ISV
: compound

sorbitan
\sȯrbətan\
ISV
: alcohol

sorboside
\sȯrbəsīd\
ISV
: compound

soricident
\sərisədent\
Latin
: having teeth

Sorrentine
\sȯrəntēn\
Italian
: of the city

Sotadean
\sōdədēən\
Greek
: of the philosopher

sotie
\sōtē\
French
: play

souchong
\süchȯng\
Chinese
: tea

soulmass
\sȯməs\
English
: all soul's day

soutache
\sütash\
French
: flat braid

Southcottian
\saùthkȯdēən\
Latin
: follower

souzalite
\sōzəlīt\
French
: mineral

sovprene
\sävprēn\
Russian
: rubber

sowlth
\sōlth\
Irish
: ghost

spadaite
\spädəīt\
German
: mineral

spadiciferous
\spədisəfərəs\
Latin
: bearing spikes

spalacid
\spəlasəd\
Latin
: rodent

spanghew
\spanghyü\
English
: throw violently

spangolite
\spangəlīt\
Latin
: mineral

sparterie
\spärdərē\
French
: fabric

spartina
\spärtənə\
Latin
: grass

spavined
\spavənd\
English
: swelling

speerings
\spērəns\
English
: news

spekboom
\spekbüm\
Afrikaans
: tree

speluncar
\spəlnkər\
Latin
: pertaining to caves

speos
\spēäs\
Greek
: tomb

spermaceti
\spərməsetē\
Italian
: wax

spermioteliosis
\spərmēətēlēōsəs\
Latin
: transformation

speronara
\sperənärə\
Italian
: boat

sperrylite
\spārēlīt\
Italian
: mineral

spet
\spā\
French
: fish

sphacelate
\sfasəlāt\
Latin
: mortify

sphaeriaceous
\sfirēāshəs\
Latin
: of parasites

sphaeriid
\sfirēəd\
Latin
: mollusk

sphaerite
\sfirīt\
German
: mineral

sphaeropsidaceous
\sfiräpsədāshəs\
Latin
: pertaining to fungi

sphagnicole
\sfagnəkōl\
Latin
: fungus

sphalerite
\sfalərīt\
German
: mineral

sphecid
\sfēsəd\
Latin
: insect

sphenacodont
\sfənakədänt\
Latin
: reptile

spherulitize
\sfiryələtīz\
ISV
: convert

sphex
\sfeks\
Greek
: wasp

sphingosine
\sfingəsēn\
ISV
: compound

sphyrion
\sfirēän\
Latin
: hammer

spiegeleisen
\spēgəlīzən\
German
: iron

spiflication
\spifləkāshən\
Latin
: violence

Spigelian
\spījēlēən\
Dutch
: of the painter

spilosite
\spīləsīt\
German
: mineral

spinacene
\spīnəsēn\
ISV
: compound

spinasterol
\spīnəsteról\
Latin
: compound

spinifex
\spīnəfeks\
Latin
: grass

spinthariscope
\spinthərəskōp\
Greek
: instrument

spionid
\spīənəd\
Latin
: worm

spirketing
\spərkəding\
English
: planks

spirochetemia
\spīrōkēdēmēə\
Latin
: bacteria in blood

spiroloculine
\spīrōlakyəlīn\
Latin
: divided into chambers

spirometric
\spīrəmetrik\
Latin
: measuring gas

spirotrich
\spīrətrik\
Latin
: protozoan

spiruroid
\spīrüröid\
Latin
: beetle

spitzflote
\shpitsflādə\
German
: instrument

splanchnopleure
\splanknəplùr\
Latin
: layer of tissue

spodogram
\spädəgram\
Latin
: preparation of ash

spongocoel
\späŋgəsēl\
Latin
: cavity

sponsalia
\spänsālēə\
Latin
: writ

spraing
\spräŋ\
Scottish
: stripe

spruit
\sprüt\
Afrikaans
: stream

spurrite
\spərīt\
English
: mineral

squagga
\skwägə\
Australian
: fish

squamipennate
\skwāməpenāt\
Latin
: scaly

squatmore
\skwätmōr\
Latin
: poppy

squattocracy
\skwätäkrəsē\
Latin
: wealthy owners

squillid
\skwiləd\
Latin
: insect

squirish
\skwīrish\
Latin
: of the gentries

staithe
\stāth\
Scottish
: wharf

stakage
\stākəj\
Latin
: channel

stannator
\stanādər\
Latin
: assembly

staphylinid
\stafəlinəd\
Latin
: beetle

stashie
\stashi\
Alteration
: uproar

stasimon
\stasəmän\
Latin
: choral system

statutable
\stachədəbəl\
Latin
: standard

stavesacre
\stāvzākər\
English
: plant

steapsin
\stēapsən\
ISV
: compound

steckling
\stekliŋ\
German
: plant

stedman
\stedmən\
English
: ringing bell

steentjie
\stēnchē\
Afrikaans
: fish

steigerite
\stīgərīt\
German
: mineral

stellionate
\stelyənət\
Latin
: fraud

stemmery
\stemərē\
Latin
: building

stemson
\stem(p)sən\
Latin
: timber

stentorine
\stentərīn\
Latin
: of protozoans

stephanion
\stəfānēən\
Greek
: point in suture

steradiancy
\stərādēənsē\
Latin
: radiant flux

stercobilin
\stərkōbīlən\
ISV
: compound

stercorite
\stərkərīt\
German
: mineral

sterigma
\stirigmə\
Latin
: stalk

sternbergia
stərnbərgēə
Latin
: plant

sternson
stərnsən
English
: boat

Stesichorean
\stəsikərēən\
Greek
: of the composer

stibonium
\stəbōnēəm\
Latin
: univalent ion

stichtite
\stiktīt\
Dutch
: mineral

stictiform
\stiktəförm\
Latin
: resembling lichens

stigmonose
\stigmənōs\
Greek
: disease

stiletted
\stīledəd\
French
: having a probe

stipellate
\stīpelət\
Latin
: having leaflets

stokesia
\stōkēzhə\
Latin
: plant

stokesite
\stōksīt\
German
: mineral

stolzite
\stōlzīt\
German
: mineral

stomochord
\stōməkȯrd\
Latin
: structure

storable
\stōrəbəl\
Latin
: something can be furnished

stradiot
\stradēət\
French
: cavalryman

straffordian
\strəfōrdēən\
English
: follower

strainometer
\stranämədər\
ISV
: minute deformation

strepsinema
\strepsənēmə\
Latin
: threads

strigeid
\strijēəd\
Latin
: trematode

strigovite
\strigəvīt\
German
: mineral

strobilaceous
\sträbəlāshəs\
Latin
: of linear series

stromeyerite
\strōmīərīt\
German
: mineral

sturtite
\stərdīt\
English
: mineral

stylolite
\stīləlīt\
ISV
: mineral

Stymphalian
\stimfālēən\
Greek
: of mythology

styracin
\stirəsən\
German
: compound

styphnate
\stifnāt\
German
: acid

styryl
\stīrəl\
ISV
: compound

suasorium
\swəsōrēəm\
Latin
: oration

subaurale
\səbȯralē\
Latin
: body part

suberylarginine
\sübȧrəlärjənēn\
French
: toxin

subgalea
\səbgālēə\
Latin
: insect part

subopercle
\səbōpərkəl\
Latin
: fish

subpurlin
\səbpərlən\
ISV
: architecture

subsizar
\səbsīzər\
English
: student

succinylsulfathiazole
\səlsinəlsəlfəthīəzōl\
ISV
: compound

suckerel
\səkərəl\
Unknown
: fish

sudburite
\sədbərīt\
German
: mineral

suffete
\səfēt\
Greek
: chief magistrate

sulfasuxidine
\səlfəsəksədēn\
Trademark
: drug

sulfisoxazole
\səlfəsäksəzōl\
Trademark
: drug

sulfydrate
\səlfīdrāt\
Trademark
: drug

sulung
\sülüng\
English
: unit of land

sulvanite
\səlvənīt\
German
: mineral

superoxol
\süpəräksȯl\
ISV
: compound

suprarenalin
\süprərenələn\
ISV
: epinephrine

surah
\sürə\
Alteration
: cloth

surmullet
\sərmələt\
English
: fish

sursassite
\sərsasīt\
German
: mineral

surti
\sərdē\
Hindi
: tree

survigrous
\sərvīgrəs\
Latin
: heraldic

susannite
\süzanīt\
German
: mineral

susuhunan

\süsühünän\

Javan

: ruler

suterberry

\südərbārē\

English

: tree

svanbergite

\sfänbərgīt\

Swedish

: mineral

swainsona

\swānsōnə\

Latin

: plant

swartzite

\swärtsīt\

German

: mineral

sweal

\swēl\

Scottish

: melt

swedenborgite

\swēdənbòrgīt\

German

: mineral

Swinburnian

\swinbərnēən\

English

: of the writer

sycon

\sīkän\

Latin

: sponge

syenite

\sīənīt\

Latin

: mineral

sylphon

\silfän\

Trademark

: tubular bellow

sylvestrene

\silvestrēn\

ISV

: compound

sylviid

\silvēəd\

Latin

: bird

sylvinite

\silvənīt\

Latin

: mineral

symphysion

\simfizēän\

Latin

: part of skull

symplocos

\simpləkäs\

Latin

: plant

synartetic

\sinärtedik\

Latin

: metrically continuous

synaxarist

\sinaksərist\

Greek

: author of narrative

syndet

\sindet\

Latin

: detergent

syneidesis

\sinīdēsəs\

Greek

: practical application

synesis

\sinəsəs\

Greek

: grammatical construction

syngenesious

\sinjənēzēəs\

Greek

: united by anthers

syngenite

\sinjənīt\

Greek

: mineral

synkatathesis

\sinkətathəsis\

Greek

: endorsement

synneurosis

\sinyərōsis\

Greek

: articulation

synodicon

\sənädəkän\

Greek

: decree

synoicous

\sinòikəs\

Latin

: having anthers

synostose

\sinəstōs\

Latin

: unite

syphiloma

\sifəlōmə\

Greek

: tumor

syphilophobe

\sifəlōfōb\

Greek

: one scared of bacteria

syrma
\sᵊrmə\
Greek
: robe

systyle
\sistīl\
Greek
: column

szmikite
\smikīt\
German
: mineral

szomolnokite
\səmälnəkīt\
Hungarian
: mineral

tabernaemontana
\tabərnēmäntanə\
Latin
: plant

taborite
\tābərīt\
German
: mineral

tabun
\täbȯn\
German
: liquid

tacheometer
\takēämədər\
French
: speed indicator

tachysterol
\təkistəròl\
ISV
: compound

taenite
\tēnīt\
German
: mineral

tagal
\təgäl\
Spanish
: straw

tagilite
\tagəlīt\
geographical name
: mineral

tahona
\təhōnə\
Spanish
: mill

tailzie
\tālyē\
Scottish
: restrict property

taisch
\tāsh\
Scottish
: ghost

talitol
\talətȯl\
ISV
: crystalline

tamarix
\taməriks\
Latin
: plant

tamborito
\tämbərēdō\
Spanish
: dance

tampala
\tampalə\
Tagalog
: potherb

tanagra
\tanəgrə\
Latin
: statue

Tanchelmian
\tankelmēən\
Latin
: follower

tanbur
\tanbȯər\
Hindi
: instrument

tangalung
\tangäləng\
Filipino
: wildcat

tangantangan
\tangäntangän\
Tagalog
: oil

Tanquelinian
\tankəlinēən\
French
: follower

tanka
\dängä\
Chinese
: boat

tapeinocephaly
\təpīnōsefəlē\
French
: skull

tapotement
\təpōtmənt\
French
: percussion in massage

tarapacaite
\terəpəkäīt\
Spanish
: mineral

tardamente
\tärdəmentē\
Italian
: slowly

Tardenoisian
\tärdənȯizēən\
French
: of culture

Tarquinian
\tärkwinēən\
Latin
: of Roman kings

tarragona
\terəgōnə\
geographical name
: red color

tarsorrhaphy
\tärsȯrəfē\
Latin
: suturing of eyelids

Tartarean
\tärderēən\
Latin
: infernal

tartine
\tärtēn\
French
: jam

Tasian
\täsēən\
Egyptian
: of culture

tatuasu
\tatüəsü\
Portuguese
: armadillo

taufer
\tȯifər\
German
: denomination

tavistockite
\tavəstäkīt\
German
: mineral

Tayacian
\təyāsēən\
Spanish
: glacial age

Tchefuncte
\chəfünktə\
geographical name
: culture

techne
\teknē\
Greek
: skill

tecoma
\təkōmə\
Latin
: plant

teedle
\tēdəl\
Scottish
: sing

teiid
\tēyəd\
Latin
: reptile

teinite
\tānīt\
Japanese
: mineral

teleblem
\teləblem\
Latin
: universal veil

teleran
\teləran\
blend
: navigation system

temalacatl
\tämələkädəl\
Spanish
: stone

temse
\temz\
English
: sieve

tenendas
\tə'nen͵das\
Latin
: law

teniente
\tenēentē\
Spanish
: official

Tennysonian
\tenəsōnēən\
English
: of the poet

tenuiroster
\tenyəwērästər\
Latin
: bird

tepetate
\tepətädē\
Spanish
: mineral

teraph
\terəf\
Hebrew
: image

terebinthine
\terəbinthən\
ISV
: compound

terebrant
\tərēbrənt\
Latin
: insect

terebratulid
\terəbrachəlid\
Latin
: insect

terlinguaite
\tərlingwāīt\
geographical name
: mineral

ternovskite
\tərnofskīt\
Russian
: mineral

terpadiene
\tərpədīēn\
ISV
: compound

terranean
\tərānēən\
Latin
: of earth

Tertullianist
\tərtəlēənist\
Latin
: follower

teschemacherite
\teshəmakərīt\
German
: mineral

tesota
\təsōdə\
Latin
: wood

tessellar
\tesələr\
Latin
: resembling tablets

testudinate
\təstüdənət\
Greek
: reptile

tethyid
\tethēəd\
Latin
: insect

tetractinellid
\teraktəneləd\
Latin
: sponge

tetradymite
\tertadəmīt\
Greek
: mineral

teuk
tyük\
Imitative
: bird

Thackerayan
\thakərēən\
English
: of the novelist

thalamencephalon
\thaləmənsefälän\
Latin
: part of brain

thalassinid
\thəlasənəd\
Latin
: crustacean

thalenite
\tälənīt\
Swedish
: mineral

thaliacean
\thālēāshən\
Latin
: aquatic organism

thanadar
\tänədär\
Hindi
: chief officer

thanatotic
\thanətädik\
Latin
: of death

Thargelia
\thärgēlēə\
Latin
: festival

thaumasite
\thäməsīt\
ISV
: mineral

thebaine
\thēbəēn\
ISV
: compound

theelol
\thēlòl\
ISV
: compound

thegnly
\thānlē\
English
: of servants

theileria
\thīlirēə\
Latin
: bacterium

theine
\thēēn\
ISV
: compound

thelphusian
\thelfyüzhən\
Latin
: of crabs

thelyphonid
\thəlifənid\
Latin
: wasp

Themistian
\thəmischən\
French
: monk

Theocritean
\thēäkritēən\
Greek
: idyllic

theopaschite
\thēəpaskīt\
Greek
: adherent

Theophrastian
\thēəfrashən\
Greek
: of the philosopher

theopneust
\thēäpnyüst\
Latin
: divinely inspired

theravadin
\terəvädən\
Hindi
: adherent

thermel
\thərmel\
ISV
: temperature measurer

thermidor
\thərmədòr\
Latin
: counterrevolutionary stage

thermistor
\thərmistər\
ISV
: component

thesocyte
\thesəsīt\
Greek
: cell

thevetin
\thəvētən\
ISV
: compound

thianthrene
\thīanthrēn\
ISV
: compound

thiazolidine
\thīəzōlədēn\
ISV
: compound

thienyl
\thīənil\
ISV
: compound

Thiokol
\thīəkäl\
Trademark
: drug

thiophenine
\thīäfənēn\
ISV
: compound

thirlage
\thərlij\
Scottish
: feudal servitude

thitka
\thitkə\
Burman
: tree

thomisid
\thōməsid\
Latin
: crab

thoreaulite
\tōrōlīt\
Belgian
: mineral

threonine
\thrēənēn\
ISV
: compound

thripid
\thripəd\
Latin
: insect

thryonomyid
\thrīänəmīəd\
Latin
: rodent

thucholite
\thükəlīt\
Latin
: mineral

thurberia
\thərbirēə\
Latin
: plant

thymidine
\thīmədēn\
ISV
: compound

thynnid
\thinəd\
Latin
: insect

thyreotropic
\thīrēəträpik\
Latin
: secreting

tiao
\dēaù\
Chinese
: coin

Tiburtine
\tibərtīn\
Latin
: of Italy

Ticinese
\tichənēz\
geographical name
: of Switzerland

tilasite
\tiləsīt\
Latin
: mineral

tillet
\tilət\
English
: fabric

tillicum
\tiləkəm\
Chinook
: friend

tilsit
\tilsət\
geographical name
: cheese

timaliine
\təmālēīn\
ISV
: of birds

timonism
\tīmənizəm\
English
: hating people

tinchel
\tinkəl\
Scottish
: ring hunter

tineal
\tinēəl\
Latin
: of ringworms

tinticite
\tintikīt\
German
: mineral

tinzenite
\tinzənīt\
German
: mineral

tiphiid
\tifēəd\
Latin
: wasp

tirma
\tərmə\
Scottish
: oyster catcher

titillative
\tidəlādiv\
Latin
: tickling

titoki
\tətōkē\
Maori
: tree

titivation
\tidəvāshən\
Latin
: improving

titrant
\tītrənt\
Latin
: substance

tocopherol
\təkäfəräl\
ISV
: compound

tocororo
\tōkərōrō\
Spanish
: tree

togue
\tōg\
French
: fish

toise
\tȯiz\
French
: unit of land

tokay
\tōkā\
Hungarian
(1): dessert
(2): reptile

tolguacha
\tōlwächə\
Spanish
: plant

toloaches
\tōlwächēz\
Spanish
: plants

toluidide
\tälyüədīd\
ISV
: compound

toluquinone
\tälyəkwīnōn\
ISV
: compound

tomtate
\tämtāt\
Spanish
: fish

tonada
\tənädə\
Spanish
: folksong

toorie
\türi\
Scottish
: bonnet

torgoch
\torgōkh\
Welsh
: fish

Torinese
\torənēz\
Latin
: of the Italian city

toringin
\tərinjən\
Malay
: compound

torquate
\torkwāt\
Latin
: collared

torsibility
\torsəbilədē\
Latin
: ability to untwist

torticollis
\tordəkäləs\
\Latin
: abnormal condition

tortile
\tòrtəl\
Latin
: twisted

tortillon
\tordēyän\
French
: stump

torulopsis
\toryəläpsəs\
Latin
: fungus

tostamente
\tōstəmentē\
Italian
: rapidly

totaquine
\tōdəkwēn\
ISV
: drug

Totonacan
\tōtənäkən\
Spanish
: language family

tourte
\türt\
French
: pie

tovariaceous
\tōverēāshəs\
Latin
: of plants

towan
\taüən\
Corn
: hill of sand

trachelate
\trakəlāt\
Latin
: shaped like necks

tractatule
\traktətyül\
Latin
: small essay

traiteur
\trātər\
French
: house

trangam
\trangəm\
English
: trinket

transitron
\tranzəträn\
ISV
: component

transude
\transüd\
Latin
: pass through

traskite
\traskīt\
English
: baptist

tredecile
\trədesəl\
Latin
: astrological aspect

treey
\trēē\
English
: with trees

tremalith
\treməlith\
Latin
: stone

tremelline
\trəmelīn\
Latin
: of fungi

tremex
\trēmeks\
Greek
: wood

trephocyte
\trefəsīt\
Latin
: cell

triaconter
\trīəkäntər\
Greek
: gallery

triakid
\trīəkid\
Latin
: fish

tribon
\tribōn\
Greek
: garment

trichechodont
\trikekədänt\
Latin
: mammal

trichinoscope
\trəkīnəskōp\
Latin
: instrument

trimetrogon
\trīmetrəgän\
ISV
: mapping system

trimyristin
\trīməristən\
ISV
: compound

Triquean
\trēkāən\
Spanish
: language family

tritanopia
\tritənōpēə\
ISV
: blue-yellow blindness

trithionate
\trīthīənāt\
ISV
: compound

tritomite
\tridəmīt\
German
: mineral

tritylodont
\tritələdänt\
Latin
: fossil

trochelminth
\trōkəlminth\
Latin
: worm

troctolite
\träktəlīt\
ISV
: mineral

troilite
\trōəlīt\
ISV
: mineral

trombiculid
\trämbikyəlid\
Latin
: mite

trommel
\träməl\
German
: cylinder

trompil
\trämpəl\
French
: aperture

troodont
\trōədänt\
Latin
: mammal

tropaeolum
\trōpēələm\
Latin
: plant

trophaea
\trōfēə\
Latin
: monument

tropidine
\träpədēn\
ISV
: compound

troupand
\trüpand\
Afrikaans
: bird

trudellite
\trüdelīt\
German
: mineral

Tsakonian
\tsəkōnēən\
Greek
: of the area

tschermigite
\chərməgīt\
Russian
: mineral

Tshiluba
\chəlübə\
Congolese
: major trade language

tubocurarine
\tyübōkyürärēn\
ISV
: compound

tubulure
\tyübyəlur�\
Latin
: short opening

tuille
\twēl\
French
: hinged plate

tulbaghia
\təlbagēə\
Latin
: plant

tupaiid
\tyüpīəd\
Latin
: tree shrew

turpeth
\tərpəth\
Scottish
: root

turrum
\tərəm\
Austrlian
: fish

tutty
\tətē\
(1)Sanskrit (2)English
(1): substance
(2): flower

twatchel
\twachəl\
English
: worm

twayblade
\twāblād\
English
: orchid

Tychonic
\tīkänik\
Greek
: of astronomy

tylus
\tīləs\
Greek
: prominence

tyndallometer
\tindəlämətər\
Latin
: brightness measurer

typhlosolar
\tifləsōlər\
Latin
: of the fold

tyrosinosis
\tīrōsənōsəs\
Latin
: disease

Tyrtaean
\tərtēən\
Greek
: of the Spartan poet

tystie
\tīsti\
Scandinavian
: bird

tzute
\tsütā\
Guatemalan
: patterned square

uang
\wäng\
Javan
: rhinoceros

ubiety
\yübīədē\
Latin
: whereness

ubussu
\übu̇sü\
Portuguese
: tree

ucuuba
\ükyə(w)übə\
Portuguese
: tree

udal
\(y)üdəl\
Scandinavian
: tenure system

Ugaritic
\ügəritik\
geographical name
: language

uji
\üjē\
Japanese
: maggot disease

ulae
\ülī\
Hawaiian
: lizard

ulexine
\yüleksēn\
ISV
: compound

umbellet
\əmbələt\
Latin
: small inflorescence

umbellulate
\əmeblyəlāt\
Latin
: arranged in inflorescences

unamo
\ünämō\
Spanish
: plant

unbonneted
\ənbanətəd\
English
: without headgear

unbrookable
\ənbru̇kə́bəl\
English
: unendurable

undecylenate
\əndesəlenāt\
ISV
: compound

unduly
\əndyülē\
English
: excessively

ungemachite
\əngəmäkīt\
Hungarian
: mineral

unguitractor
\əngwətraktər\
Latin
: insect part

uniatism
\yünēətizə́m\
Russian
: system of faith

unicursal
\yünikərsəl\
Latin
: of one curve

unionides
\yünēänədēz\
Latin
: mollusks

unkar
\ənkär\
geographical name
: culture

unraveler
\ənravələr\
English
: one that disentangles

urachal
\yùrəkəl\
Latin
: of tissue

uracil
\yùrəsil\
ISV
: compound

uramil
\yùrəmil\
ISV
: compound

uranospinite
\yərənäspənīt\
ISV
: mineral

ureaform
\yùrēəfòrm\
ISV
: fertilizer

urfirnis
\ùrfirnəs\
German
: lustrous paint

urinant
\yərinənt\
French
: being in pale

urisk
\ùrisk\
Scottish
: mythical being

urubu
\ùrəbü\
Portuguese
: vulture

ussingite
\əsingīt\
Danish
: mineral

ususes
\yüsəsəz\
Latin
: agreements

utahlite
\yütälīt\
ISV
: mineral

utia
\ütēə\
Spanish
: rodent

valerate
\valərāt\
ISV
: compound

valerian
\vəlirēən\
Latin
: plant

valleriite
\vəlirēīt\
ISV
: mineral

valoniaceous
\vəlōnēāshəs\
Latin
: resembling plants

vanadoan
\vənādəwən\
ISV
: mineral

vannal
\vanəl\
Latin
: of insects

Vansittartism
\vansidərtizəm\
German
: WWII doctrine

vanthoffite
\vanthofīt\
German
: mineral

Varronian
\vərōnēən\
Italian
: people with surnames

vaterite
\vädərīt\
German
: mineral

vauntlay
\vontlā\
French
: hunting dog race

vavasory
\vavəsōrē\
Latin
: of fees

veblenism
\veblənizəm\
German
: doctrine

vellinch
\velinch\
German
: instrument

venereologist
\venirēäləjist\
Latin
: doctor

venesect
\venəsekt\
Latin
: open veins

venturine
\venchərēn\
Italian
: powder

veratroyl
\vəratrəwil\
ISV
: compound

vergence
\vərjənts\
Latin
: turning of eyeballs

vermetus
\vərmēdəs\
Latin
: worm

vernadskite
\vərnadskīt\
German
: mineral

vernonin
\vərnənin\
ISV
: compound

vervain
\vərvān\
French
: plant

vestiture
\vestəchür\
Latin
: clothing

viajaca
\vyəhäkə\
Spanish
: plant

viburnum
\vībərnəm\
Latin
: plant

vidame
\vēdam\
French
: officer

vielle
\vyel\
French
: instrument

vijao
\vēhäō\
Spanish
: tree

villota
\vilōtə\
Italian
: dance

vinquish
\vinkwish\
Scottish
: disease

Vinylite
\vīnəlīt\
Trademark
: resin

vinylogous
\vīniləgəs\
ISV
: of resins

viosterol
\vīästəròl\
ISV
: compound

virama
\vərämə\
Sanskrit
: mark

virgilia
\vərjilēə\
ISV
: compound

viscolize
\viskəlīz\
ISV
: blend into smooth mixture

viseite
\vēzāīt\
French
: mineral

vison
\vizən\
Greman
: mink

vitascope
\vīdəskōp\
ISV
: instrument

vitellarium
\vīdəlerēəm\
Latin
: insect part

vitry
\vitrē\
French
: canvas

vivianite
\vivēənīt\
ISV
: mineral

vizierate
\vəzirət\
Latin
: office

voe
\vō\
Swedish
: inlet

voilier
\vwalēā\
French
: fish

voltzite
\vältsīt\
German
: mineral

volumeter
\vəlümədər\
ISV
: displacement of liquid measurer

vomicine
\väməsēn\
ISV
: compound

vorhand
\fōrhänt\
German
: player in bid

vredenburgite
\vredənbərgīt\
German
: mineral

vulgus
\vəlgəs\
Latin
: short poem

vulpinite
\vəlpinīt\
German
: mineral

wabble
\wäbəl\
English
: butterfly larvae

wadeite
\wādīt\
English
: mineral

wah
\wä\
Nepali
: panda

waldflote
\väldflətə\
German
: flute

wali
\wälē\
Arabic
: saint

waling
\wāling\
English
: bracing vertical members

waltherite
\vältərīt\
German
: mineral

wardmote
\wȯ(ə)dmōt\
English
: fine

warfarin
\wȯrfərin\
ISV
: compound

Washoan
\wäshōən\
geographical name
: language family

wastrife
\wāstrīf\
Scottish
: unhealthy

watchet
\wächət\
English
: blue color

waterie
\wätərē\
English
: bird

Waucobian
\wäkōbēən\
geographical name
: subdivision

wauke
\wau̇kā\
Hawaiian
: berry

Wedgwood
\wejwu̇d\
Trademark
: pottery

weedicide
\wēdəsīd\
Latin
: killing weeds

wehrlite
\werlīt\
German
: mineral

weigela
\wījēlə\
Latin
: plant

weismannian
\vīsmanēən\
German
: adherent

Whatman
\wätmən\
Trademark
: drawing papers

whitling
\hwitling\
Unknown
: salmon

whitlow
\hwitlō\
English
: disease

whyo
\hwīō\
English
: band member

wichuraiana
\wichərēyanə\
English
: rose

wilburite
\wilbərīt\
English
: mineral

willemite
\wiləmīt\
German
: mineral

Wishoskan
\wəshäskən\
Virginian
: language family

wissel
\wisəl\
English
: retribution

Wittgensteinian
\vitgənshtīnēən\
German
: adherent

witwall
\witwȯl\
English
: woodpecker

wolfeite
\wu̇lfīt\
Geran
: mineral

wollomai
\wäləmī\
Australian
: fish

woodhouseite
\wu̇dhau̇sīt\
English
: mineral

wrackful
\rakfu̇l\
English
: destructive

wustite
\wu̇stīt\
German
: mineral

wuther
\wətẖər\
Scottish
: blow

xanthamide
\zanthəmīd\
ISV
: compound

xanthenyl
\zanthənil\
ISV
: radical

xanthin
\zanthən\
ISV
: compound

xanthoconite
\zanthäkənīt\
Latin
: mineral

xanthosine
\zanthəsēn\
ISV
: compound

xanthoxenite
\zanthäksəsīt\
ISV
: mineral

xanthoxylin
\zanthäksələ̇n\
Latin
: bark extract

Xaverian
\zāvirēən\
Spanish
: of the saint

Xenocratean
\zənäkrətēən\
Greek
: of the philosopher

Xerogel
\zirəjel\
Latin
: gummy substance

xiphosure
\zifəsu̇r\
Latin
: crab

xylenol
\zīlənȯl\
ISV
: compound

xylobalsamum
\zīlōbolsəməm\
Latin
: root

Xylonite
\zīlənīt\
Trademark
: plastic

xyloside
\zīləsīd\
ISV
: compound

xylylene
\zīlələen\
ISV
: compound

yacal
\yäkəl\
Spanish
: tree

yaffingale
\yafəngāl\
English
: woodpecker

yair
\yer\
Scottish
: enclosure

yaje
\yähä\
Spanish
: plant

yakin
\yəkēn\
Assamese
: goat

Yakonan
\yakənən\
geographical name
: language family

yampee
\yampē\
Imitative
: plant

Yankeefying
\yankēfīing\
geographical name
: to make similar to New York

yasht
\yasht, 'yəsht\
Avestan
: hymn

yatalite
\yadəlīt\
geographical name
: mineral

Yatren
\yatrən\
Trademark
: drug

yeatmanite
\yātmənīt\
ISV
mineral

yeni
\yenē\
Latin
: bird

yerbal
\yərbäl\
Spanish
: plant

yetzarim
\yātsərim\
Hebrew
: impulses

yite
\yīt\
English
: woodpecker

yockeynut
\yokēnət\
English
: lotus

yod
\yȯd\
Hebrew
: voice glide

yogh
\yōkh\
Hebrew
: letter

yojana
\yōjənə\
Hindi
: unit of length

yomawood
\yōməwůd\
Burmese
: wood

yttrocrasite
\itrōkrāsīt\
ISV
: mineral

yucatan
\yükətan\
geographical name
: orange color

Yukian
\yükēən\
geographical name
: language family

Yunnanese
\yünənēz\
geographical name
: of the Chinese province

Zadokite
\zādəkīt\
biblical name
: line of priests

zakah
\zəkä\
Arabic
: fine

zander
\zandər\
German
: duck

zapodid
\zapədid\
Latin
: rodent

Zapotecan
\zäpōtākən\
geographical name
: language family

zaratite
\zärətīt\
Italian
: mineral

zebub
\zēbəb\
Arabic
: fly

zebulunite
\zebyəlinīt\
Hebrew
: member of tribe

zecchino
\zəkēnō\
Italian
: gold coin

zeiform
\zēəförm\
Latin
: resembling fish

Zechstein
\zekstīn\
German
: geographical period

Zephiran
\zefəran\
Trademark
: drug

zeugite
\zügīt\
Latin
: structure

zeunerite
\zoinərīt\
German
: mineral

ziarat
\zēärət\
Hindi
: tomb

zinkenite
\zinkənīt\
German
: mineral

ziphioid
\zifēȯid\
Latin
: whale

zirklerite
\zərklərīt\
German
: mineral

zoanthodeme
\zōanthədēm\
ISV
: aggregate

zoidiophilous
\zōidēäfələs\
German
: of fertilization

zollverein
\tsȯlfərīn\
German
: gymnastic association

zolotnik
\zälətnēk\
Russian
: unit of length

zooxanthella
\zōəsanthelə\
ISV
: organism

zoozoo
\züzü\
English
: dove

zorillo
\zərilō\
Spanish
: shrub

zoster
\zōstər\
Greek
: disease

zounds
\zwaùndz\
German
: mild oath

zoysia
\zoizēə\
Latin
: grass

zunyite
\zünyīt\
German
: mineral

zygotene
\zīgətēn\
French
: compound

zygotoid
\zīgətȯid\
Latin
: resembling plant spores

zymosan
\zīməsan\
ISV
: compound

Chapter 8: Cosmos

abaxile
\a-ˈbak-səl\
Latin
: facing away from the axis

acanthamoeba
\əˌkanthəˈmēbə\
Latin
: protozoan

achuete
\ä-chə-ˈwā-tē\
Nahuatl
: tropical tree with yellow-brown wood

aclidian
\ā-ˈkli-dē-ən\
Latin
: having no clavicles

acupressure
\a-k(y)ə-ˈpre-shər\
Latin
: massage with therapeutic effects

addossed
\ə-ˈdäst\
Latin>French
: set or turned back to back, used in heraldry

adrenomedullary
\əˌdrēnōˈmedᵊlˌerē\
Latin
: of the spinal cord and kidneys

aegirine
\ā-gə-ˌrēn, ˈē-jə-ˌrēn\
German
: mineral

aeroscepsy
\er-ō-ˌskep-sē\
Greek>Latin
: power of animals to observe quality of air

agalawood
\a-gə-lə-ˌwu̇d\
Malayalam>Portuguese
: tree with dark heartwood

agallochum
\ə-ˈga-lə-kəm\
Greek
: tree with dark heartwood

agar
\ä-gər\
Malay
: resin

Agonothetae
\ˌa-gə-ˈnä-thə-ˌtē\
Greek
: judges of public games

Ahi
\ä-hē\
Hawaiian
: tuna

aislingi
\ī-shliŋ-ē\
Irish Gaelic
: poetical descriptions

aissawa
\ī'säwə\
Arabic
:religious brotherhood

aiwain
\ī-ˌwīn\
unknown
: fruit

ajoure
\ä-ˌzhu̇-ˌrā\
French
: decorated with translucent or pierced designs

Akali
\ə-ˈkä-lē\
Panjabi
: militant sect of Sikhism

akathistoi
\äˈkäthēˌstē\
Greek
: Lenten hymns

akela
\ə-ˈkē-lə\
English geographic name
: leader of cub scout pack

alcmanic
\alk-ˈma-nik\
Greek
: of poems

alectoromancy
\ə-ˈlek-tə-rō-ˌman(t)-sē\
Greek
: divination through kernels

aleuriospore
\ə-ˈlu̇r-ē-ə-ˌspȯr\
Greek
: asexual fungal spore

alfione
\al-fē-ˈō-nē\
Spanish
: bird

algarovilla
\al-gə-rō-ˈvē-ə\
Spanish
: seed

alilonghi
\a-lə-ˈlȯŋ-gē\
Italian
: fish

allectory
\ə-ˈlek-tə-rē\
Greek>Latin
: talismanic stone

allelochemical
\ə¦lelōˈke-mi-kəl\
Greek
: toxic chemical produced by plants as defense

alloiometry
\a-ˌlȯi-ˈä-mə-trē\
Greek
: relative growth of part in relation to an organism

allothogenous
\alə¦thäjənəs\
Greek
: derived from preexisting rocks

Almerian
\almə¦rēən\
Spanish
: of Spanish Neolithic culture

alroot
\älˌrüt\
Hindi
: mulberry

altiplanicie
\al-ti-plə-ˈnē-sē-ˌā\
Latin>Spanish
: plateau

alumite
\a-lə-ˌmīt\
French
: rhombohedral crystal

alypine
\aləpēn\
trademark
: drug

amaas
\äˌmäs\
Afrikaans
: tree

amadavat
\amədəˌvat\
irregular
: weaverbird

amerism
\aməˌrizəm\
Latin
: state of undifferentiated fern

amillenarian
\āmi-lə-¦ner-ē-ən\
Latin
: one that denies older philosophy of peace

ammonoidean
\aməˈnȯidēən\
Latin
: of cephalopods

amphisbaenian
\am(p)-fəs-¦bē-nē-ən\
Latin
: like a serpent

anacahuite
\anəkəˈwētā\
Spanish
: aromatic tree

anagnostae
\aˌnagˈnästē\
Greek
: clerics

anatman
\əˈnätmən\
Sanskrit
: Buddhist doctrine

ancylostomiases
\aŋ-ki-lō-stə-ˈmī-ə-ˌsēz\
Greek
: infestations from hookworms

Andaquian
\ändə¦kē ən\
Spanish
: language

andesitic
\an-di-¦zi-tik\
German
: of grayish rocks

Animiki
\əˈniməkē\
Ojibwe
: of Proterozoic rocks

anorogenetic
\aˌnȯrō¦jenetik\
Greek
: free from mountain making disturbance

antapices
\antapisēz\
Latin
: points in celestial sphere

anticum
\anˈtīkəm\
Latin
: front porch

antiodont
\antēəˌdänt\
Latin
: of dentition where the crests of opposing teeth meet

antiscorbutic
\an-tē-skȯr-¦byü-tik\
Latin
: counteracting scurvy

antisepses
\an-tə-ˈsep-ˌsēz\
Greek
: processes inhibiting growth
of microorganisms

Antoninian
\antəˈninēən\
Italian
: of Roman emperors

apikorsim
\äpēˈkòrsəm\
Hebrwe
: Jews who are lax about
observing Jewish law

apocynaceous
\əˌpäsəˈnāshəs\
Latin
: of plants with milky juice

araphostic
\arəfästik\
Greek
: unsewed

arahant
\a-rə-ˌhant\
Sanskrit
: monk who has attained
moksha

Arcady
\är-kə-dē\
Greek
: ideal place

arillodium
\arəˈlōdēəm\
Greek
: false tissue

artefac
\är-ti-ˌfak\
Latin
: tool

asaron
\asəˌrän\
ISV
: phenolic ether

Asbolan
\azbəˌlan\
German
: mineral aggregate

asfetida
\as-ˈfe-tə-də\
Latin
: dried gum resin

askeses
\ə-ˈskē-sēz\
Greek
: self restraints

astacene
\astəsēn\
ISV
: ketone pigment

astacuran
\astəˈkyùrən\
Latin
: crayfish

atabek
\atəbek\
Russian
: provincial governor

ataunto
\əˈtòntō\
French
: completely in order

Atayal
\atəˈyäl\
Malay
 : Malaysian people on
Taiwan

athetosic
\athətōsik\
Greek>Latin
: of nervous disorders

atokal
\atəkəl\
Greek
: of worm parts

augustale
\aùgəˈstälē\
Italian
: gold coin

aurar
\aùrär\
Norse
: monetary unit of Iceland

avanyu
\əˈvänyü\
Tewa
: sacred serpent

avernian
\əˈvərnēən\
Italian
: of fire

Baalim
\bā-(ə-)ləm\
Hebrew
: idols

babaylanes
\bäbīˈlän äs \
Filipino
: pagan priests

Bablah
\bə-ˈblä\
Sanskrit>Persian
: acacia tree

bacteremic
\bak-tə-ˌrē-mik\
Latin
: with microbes in blood

baetuli
\bēchəl ī \
Greek1>Latin
: stones

baho
\pä͜ˌhō\
Hopi
: prayer stick

Baianism
\bā(y)ə͜ˌnizəm\
French
: doctrine of divine grace

balefire
\bāl-ˌfīr\
English
: signal fire

balimbing
\bəˈlimbiŋ\
Tagalog
: carambola

baluchitherium
\bə͜ˌlüchəˈthirēəm\
Latin
: mammal similar to the rhinoceros

bansalaque
\bän͜ˌsäləˈkē\
Tagalog
: large tree

bantin
\bän-tᵊn\
Malay
: ox

barouchet
\barü¦shā\
French
: small carriage

barytes
\bə-ˈrī-tēz\
Greek
: mineral

batidaceous
\batəˈdāshəs\
Latin
: of shrubs with succulent leaves

bayon
\bī-ˈȯn\
Tagalog
: sack of woven strips

bearbaiting
\ber-ˌbā-tiŋ\
English
: setting dogs on a chained bear

bedeman
\bēd-mən\
English
: licensed beggar

bedgery
\bejərē\
Australian name
: narcotic drug

bekti
\bek-tē\
Bengali
: fish

beglerbey
\be-glər-ˌbā\
Turkish
: governor of province

bersine
\bər-ˈsēn\
Arabic
: clover

bessybug
\be-sē-ˌbəg\
Imitative
: beetle

bhaktic
\bak-tik\
Sanskrit
: of religious devotion

bibliopegist
\bi-blē-ˈä-pə-jist\
Greek>French
: bookbinder

bicuhybao
\bi-ˈkwē-baù\
Portugues
: Brazilian timber tree

bielby
\bēl-bē\
Australian name
: bandicoot

Bigarreau
\bi-gə-¦ro-\
French
: cherry

bilimbing
\bəˈlimb iŋ\
Malay
: tree

birlinn
\bir-lən\
: captain ship

birr
\bər\
Norse>English
: impetus

Biscayneer
\ˈbiskānēr\
Spanish geographical name
: sailor

bismutotantalite
\bizmətəˈtantᵊlˌīt\
Swedish>Latin
: mineral

bivoltinism
\bīvōlˌt-ᵊnizəm\
French>Italian
: producing two broods in a season, as of silkworms

bobeche
\bō-ˈbesh\
French
: collar

Boehmenist
\bāmənȯst\
one who follows
Quakers

Bogomile
\bə-gə-ˈmēl\
Slavic
: Bulgarian

bolases
\bō-lə-səz\
Spanish
: weapons with iron balls

boobook
\bübu̇k\
Imitative
: owl

boojum
\bü-jəm\
English geographical name
: spiny tree

boomkin
\büm-kən\
Dutch>Flemish
: sail

borasque
\bə-ˈrask\
Greek>Spanish
: wind

bordun
\bȯrdᵊn\
French>English
: bass instrument

Bororoan
\bōrəˌrōən\
Portuguese
: Brazilian language

Bourguignon
\bu̇r-gēn-ˌyōⁿ\
French
: native of Burgundy, France

broh
\brō\
Malay
: pig-tailed monkey

bromel
\brō-məl\
Latin
: plant

bronteon
\bränˈtēən\
Greek
: device used in theater

buccin
\bəksən\
Latin
: trumpet

bucrane
\byüˌkrān\
Greek>Latin
: sculptured ornament

burgo
\bərˈgō\
French & Portuguese
: common top shell

burle
\bu̇rlā \
Italian
: musical compositions

burmanniaceous
\bərˌmanēˈāshəs\
Latin
: of tropical herbs

burunduki
\bu̇rənˈdükē\
Russian
: squirrel

butterflyer
\bə-tər-ˌflīr\
English
swimmer who
does a specific stroke

byliny
\bəˈlēnē\
Russian
: folk epics

cabalism
\kabəˌlizəm\
Hebrew>Latin
: adherence to esoteric
doctrine or tenets

cabio
\kä-bē-ō\
Bisayan>Spanish
: large percoid fish

cabossed
\kəˈbäst\
French
: without animal neck
showing

cachexy
\kə-ˈkek-sē\
Greek>Latin
: malnutrition

Caipotorade
\kīpətəˈrädē\
Spanish
: dialect

cajang
\käjəŋ\
Malay
: palm leaf strip

calangall
\kalȧnˌgȯl\
Arabic>French>English
: rhizome

calinda
\kəˈlində\
Spanish
: ceremonial dance

calo
\kə-ˈlō\
Romany>Spanish
: language of gypsies

calomorphic
\kalə¦mòrfik\
Latin
: of intrazonal soils with high calcium content

camelteer
\ka-məl-¦tir\
English
: camel driver

camorristi
\kä-ˌmò-ˈrē-stē\
Italian
: secret organizations

cancellaresca
\kän ˌchelə ˈreskə\
Italian
: cursive script

cannel
\ka-nᵊl\
English
: bituminous coal

capuli
\käpə¦lē\
Nahuatl>Spanish
: Mexican tree

carbonatite
\kärˈbänəˌtīt\
Latin
: rock

cardamom
\kär-də-mən\
Greek>Latin
: capsular fruit

cardita
\kärˈdītə\
Greek
: mollusk

Carolean
\ker-ə-¦lē-ən\
Latin
: relating to Charles

carraran
\kəˈrärən\
Italian
: of marble

Castalie
\kastəlē\
Greek
: source of inspiration

castor
\ka-stər\
Greek
: mineral

casula
\käsu̇ˌlä\
Latin
: shoe

catholicoi
\kə-ˈthò-li-ˌkòi\
Greek
: heads of church

catonic
\käˈtänik\
Italian>Latin
: harsh

caulicolo
\kau̇ˈlēkəˌlō\
French & Italian
: stalk

cauri
\kau̇rē\
French
: monetary unit of Guinea

cautivo
\kau̇ˈtēvō\
Spanish
: tree

cavyyard
\kavəˌyärd\
Spanish
: herd of saddle horses

Cayuvavan
\käyəˈvävən\
Spanish
: language

cellophane
\se-lə-ˌfän\
ISV
: transparent cellulose

cellulifugal
\selyəlif(y)əgəl\
ISV
: conducted away from cell body of nerve impulses

centavo
\sen-ˈtä-vō\
Spanish
: El Salvador monetary unit

ceriantharian
\sirēˌanˈtha(a)rēən\
Latin
: of arthropods

cervalet
\sər-və-ˌlā\
French
: bass instrument

cestodan
\se-¦stō-dᵊn\
Latin
: of tapeworms

cetotolite
\sēˈtōtᵊlˌīt\
Greek
: whale bone fossil

cetraric
\səˈtra(a)rik\
Latin
: of lichens

chelicer
\ke-lə-sər\
Greek>Latin
: appendage

chagigah
\k̲ə'gēgə\
Hebrew
: voluntary sacrifice

cheloniid
\kə'lōnēəd\
Latin
: turtle

cherimoyer
\cher-ə-'mȯi-ər\
Quechua>Spanish
: oblong fruit

chevrotin
\shevrəˌtan\
French
: mammal

chirimoya
\chir-ə-'mȯi-ə\
Quechua>Spanish
: pale green fruit

chiapanecas
\chēˌäpə'nākəs\
Spanish
: girls' dance

Chimakuan
\chiməˌküən\
Native American name
: language

Chimmesyan
\chimsēən\
Native American name
: Indian people

chinacrine/chinacrin
\kinəˌkrēn\
trademark
: antimalarial drug

chinkara
\chiŋ'kärə\
Hindi
: common gazelle

Chiriquian
\chirəˌkēən\
Panama geographic name
: of prehistoric pottery

chiven
\chivən\
English
: chub of Europe

chlordan
\klȯr-ˌdan\
ISV
: insecticide

chloropalladate
\klōrōpalədāt\
ISV
: salt

cholecystis
\kōləˌsistəs\
Greek
: gall bladder

Cholonan
\chə'lōnən\
Spanish
: of Peruvian language

chremslach
\kremzlək\
Yiddish
: pastries

chrimsel
\krimzəl\
Yiddish
: pastry

chromaffin
\krō-mə-fēn
ISV
: of salts

chromonemic
\krō-mə-ˌnē-mik\
Latin
: of coiled threadlike cores

chrysalidian
\kri-sə-ˌli-dē-ən\
Greek
: of pupae

chrysograph
\kri-səgraf\
Greek
: to write in letters of gold

chthonian
\thō-nē-ən\
Greek
: of hell

chytridiose
\kə̇ˌtridē'ōs\
French>Latin
: fungal disease

cigala
\sə̇'gälə\
French
: cicada

cigale
\sə̇'gäl\
French
: insect

cinemazation
\sinəməzāshən\
Latin
: making a motion picture

cinquecentisti
\chiŋ-kwi-chen-'ti-stē\
Italian
: 16th century Italian artists

cinquepas
\saⁿk(ə)pä\
French
: dance

circuiteer
\sərkəti(ə)r\
English
: travel in circuit

cistronic
\si-ˈsträ-nik\
ISV
: segment of DNA

cithren
\si-thrən\
Latin
: guitar

citricola
\sə̇ˈtrikələ\
Latin
: insect

citybilly
\sitē͏̱bilē\
English
: musician

clarionet
\kler-ē-ə-¦net\
French
: wood instrument

Clio
\klī-ō\
Greek
: Muse of history

cloacae
\klō-ˈā-͏̱kē\
Latin
: chambers of birds

cnidosporidian
\nīdəspəˈridēən\
Latin
: of protozoans

coenuriasis
\sēnyəˈrīəsə̇s\
Latin
: disease

cogongrass
\kō-¦gōn-͏̱gras\
Bisayan>Spanish
: grasses

coleophorid
\kōlēäfərid\
Latin
: moth

coleoptilum
\kō-lē-ˈäp-tə-ləm,\
Greek>Latin
: first leaf of moncotyledon

colobomatous
\käləˈbōmətəs\
Latin
: of eye fissures

colossality
\käləˈsalətē\
Latin
: of great size

Comechingon
\kōməchiŋˈgän\
Spanish
: language

commandant
\kä-mən-¦dänt\
French
: officer

comptie
\kämp-tē\
Seminole
: woody plant

condy
\kändē\
English
: disinfectant

cong
\käŋ\
English
: adherent of Communist movement

congener
\kän-jə-nər\
Latin
: one with relationships

conker
\käŋ-kər\
English
: horse chestnut

conoscente
\kōnəˈshentē\
Italian
: smart guy

contorniato
\kənˈtȯ(r)nēätō\
Italian
: medallion

contrahierba
\käntrəˈyərbə\
Spanish
: tropical American herb

coolies
\kü-lēz\
English
: workers

cordaitalean
\kȯ(r)dā͏̱ī'tā͏̱lēən\
Latin
: of Pennsylvanian plants

coria
\kȯr-ē-ə\
Latin
: membranes

cormous
\kȯrməs\
Latin
: bearing scaly leaves

costoxiphoid
\kä-stəzī͏̱fȯid\
Latin
: of cartilage

couguar
\kügwär\
French
: large cat

countercompony
\kaun-tərkəm'pōnē\
French
: of a double row of squares

couxio
\küshēü\
Tupi
: monkey

coyne
\kȯin\
English
: exaction of food

craticular
\krə'tikyələ(r)\
Latin
: of the diatom resting stage

cratonal
\krā-¦tä-nᵊl\
Latin
: of Earth's crust

cremasterial
\kremə¦stirēəl\
Latin
: relating to a thin muscle

crinoidean
\krə'nȯidēən\
Greek>Latin
: of echinoderms

crocoisite
\kräkwə‚zīt\
German
: red lead ore

cromorne
\krō'mȯrn\
French
: woodwind instrument

crosnes
\krōnz\
French
: artichokes

crotalism
\krōtᵊl‚izəm\
Latin
: poisoning

crucian
\krü-shən\
German
: fish

cruisken
\krüskən\
Gaelic
: jug

ctenophorous
\tə-'nä-fə-rəs\
Latin
: of solitary animals

cubically
\kyü-bi-kəlē\
Latin
: in the manner of a cube

cubicly
\kyü-biklē\
Latin
: of the third degree

cudbear
\kəd-‚ber\
English
: coloring material

cumara
\k(y)ümərə\
Spanish>French
: tonka-bean tree

curacao
\k(y)ùr-ə-saù\
Dutch
: liquor

curialism
\kyùr-ē-əlizəm\
Latin
: church doctrine

cyanean
\sī-‚anēən\
Greek
: dark blue

cyclothym
\sīkləthim\
Latin
: temperamental individual

cyperaceous
\sipə'rāshəs\
Latin
: of plants

cyprinodont
\siprə‚nədänt\
Latin
: fish

cyprinoidean
\siprə'nȯidēən\
Latin
: of fish

cyrtoceratite
\sərtə'serə‚tīt\
Latin
: mineral

cystonectous
\sistənectəs\
Latin
: of siphons

cytozym
\sītəzim\
Greek>French
: thromboplastin

dacitic
\dā¦sitik\
Latin
: of minerals

daffodile
\da-fə-‚dī(-ə)l\
Dutch
: yellow color

dancetty
\dan¦setē\
French
: with large decorations

dandiacally
\dan-¦dī-ə-kəlē\
Latin
: of fops

Danlaga
\dān-ˌlä-gə\
Danish
: law

Darghinian
\därˈginēən\
Latin
: language

dasahara
\dəs(h)əˈhərə\
Sanskrit
: festival

daysailer
\dāsālər\
English
: sailboat

debye
\dəˈbī\
Dutch
: electric unit

decating
\dekəˌtiŋ\
French
: textile process

delatorian
\deləˈtōrēən\
Latin
: of accusers

dendrocolaptine
\dendrəkəlaptīn\
Latin
: of birds

deodara
\dēəˈdärə\
Hindi
: cedar

deuton
\d(y)üˌtän\
Greek
: nucleus

devachanic
\dāvə¦chänik\
Sanskrit
: of intermediate
state of ego

diascopy
\dīˈaskəpē\
Greek
: plate of glass

didinium
\dīˈdinēəm\
Latin
: protozoans

didymate
\didəmət\
Greek
: twinfold

dikaryophasic
\dī¦karēə¦fāzik\
Greek
: of fungus life cycle phase

diskography
\dəˈskägrəfē\
Greek
: roentgenogram

dodonaeic
\dōdᵊn¦ēik\
Latin
: of oracle of Zeus

dourade
\dōˈrädə\
Spanish
: dolphin

dryfland
\drifland\
Afrikaans
: land

dubba
\dəbə\
Hindi
: bottle

Dukhobortsy
\dükəˈbȯrtsē\
Russian
: Russian sects

dulzian
\dəlzēən\
Italian
: pipe organ stop

Dyophysitic
\dī¦äfə¦sitik\
Greek
: of doctrine

dysostoses
\disäˈstōsēz\
Greek
: detective bone formations

ephi
\ēfī\
Greek
: unit of measure

epicaridea
\epəkəˈridēə\
Greek>Latin
: parasites

esdragol
\ezdrəˌgȯl\
ISV
: liquid ester

eurobin
\yəˈrōbən\
ISV
: ointment

feriae
\fir-ē-ˌē\
Latin
: days of church

finikin
\finəkən\
English
: finicky

flatbrod
\flat-ˌbrōd\
Old Norse
: wafer

flotorial
\flōˈtōrēəl\
Latin
:running for office

foussa
\fü-sə\
Malagasy
: mammal

foutra
\fütrə\
French
: fig

frati
\frätē\
Italian
: friar

friszka
\frishkə\
Hungarian
: section of dance

gabbart
\gabərd\
French
: ship

galangal
\galən̩ˌgal\
English
: rhizome

galleta
\gə(l)ˈyǀetə\
Spanish
: grass

Gallina
\gəˈlēnə
American geographical name
: relating to Mexican culture

Gallomen
\galōˌmen\
French
: people who like French culture

gammacismus
\gaməˌsizməs\
Greek
: swastika

gammagraphic
\gaməˌgrafik\
Latin
: relating to rays

gaulding
\gȯl(d)ən
Unknown
: heron

gavialoid
\gāvēəlȯid\
Hindi>French
: crocodile

Geatas
\yāətäs\
Swedish
: Scandinavian peoples

genette
\jə-ˈnet\
French
: carnivorous mammal

genipapo
\jenəˈpapō ˌzhenəˈpapü\
Tupi>Portuguese
: tree

genom
\jēˌnäm\
Greek
: chromosome

gentisate
\jentəˌsāt\
Latin
: salt

geodiid
\jēˈōdēə\
Greek>Latin
: root

gharial
\gərēəl\
Hindi>French
: crocodile

gimmaled
\giməld\
English
: made of rings

glomera
\glämərə\
Latin
: tufts

gorcrow
\gȯrkrō\
English
: black bird

grysbuck
\grāsˌbäk\
Afrikaans
: antelope

guativere
\gwäˈtēvə ˌrā\
Spanish
: bird

guglet
\gəglət\
English
: water vessel

Haeckelism
\hekə‚lizəm\
German
: theories

haematinon
\hē'matənän\
Greek>Latin
: glass

Haggadoth
\hə-'gä-‚dōt\
Hebrew
: nonlegal part of Talmud

hamartomatous
\hamə(r)tämətəs\
Greek
: of mass resembling a tumor

Hanafi
\hanəfē\
Arabic
: school

handjar
\han‚jär\
Arabic
: dagger

harmala
\härmələ\
Greek
: herb

Hassunan
\hə'sünən\
Arabic
: culture

helvine
\helvən\
German
: mineral

Herati
\he'rätē\
Afghan geographical name
: silk rug

heretogh
\herə‚tōḵ\
English
: leader of army

hetaira
\hə'tīrə\
Greek
: courtesan

hicotea
\hikə'tāə\
Spanish
: tortoise

Hiodont
\hīə‚dänt\
Greek
: fish

Hivvite
\hi‚vīt\
Hebrew
: Israeli

Hohlflute
\hōl‚flätə\
German
: pipe organ

homoeomeriae
\hōmē¦ämərī‚ē\
Latin
: theories

hoopid
\hüpəd\
unknown
: salmon

hukama
\hə-kə-'mä\
Arabic
: physicians

hyperidrosis
\hī-pərədrōsəs\
Greek
: sweat

hyperpiesis
\hī-pər pī'ēsəs\
Greek
: high blood pressure

hystricomorphous
\histrəkō‚mòrfəs\
Latin
: of rodents

ikmo
\ikmō\
 Tagalog
: betel

isohalsine
\īsōhal‚sēn\
Greek
: line on map

Jagellonian
\yägə¦lōnēən\
Swiss
: relating to dynasty

Jagiello
\yä'gyelō\
Lithuanian
: member of dynasty

Japhetic
\jə'fetik\
Hebrew
: relating to son of Noah

jaspachate
\jaspə‚kāt\
French & Latin
: chalcedony

Jassy
\yä-sē\
Romanian
: city in Romania

javali
\hävə'lē\
Spanish
: peccary

Jeevesian
\jēvzēən\
English
: of butler

jeisticcor
\jēstiˌkȯ(ə)r\
French
: coat

Jivaroan
\hēvəˌrōən\
Spanish
: like people

josup
\jōzəp\
Afrikaans
: fish

jugera
\yügərə\
Latin
: units of land area

Jussieuan
\jəsēyüən\
French
: of French botanist

Kahn
\kän\
German
: serum-precipitation
reaction

kainit
\kīˈnēt\
German
: natural salt

kamanchile
\käməˈchilē\
Spanish
: tree

Kandyan
\kandēən\
Asian geographical name
: of town in Sri Lanka

Kanesian
\kəˈnēzhən\
Turkish
: inhabitant of Asia Minor

kans
\kän(t)s\
Hindi
: grass

karaya
\kəˈrīə\
Hindi
: gum

karrooboom
\kərüˌbüm\
Afrikaans
: plant

kathismata
\kȧˈthēzmətə\
Greek
: sections of Psalter

Kendal
\kendᵊl\
English
: wooden cloth

Kerman
\kərˈmän\
Persian
: carpet

keruing
\kerəwiŋ\
Malay
: tree

ketoxime
\kēˈtäkˌsēm\
ISV
: compound

keur
\kər\
Afrikaans
: shrub

khakibos
\kakēbäs\
Afrikaans
: marigold

kichlach
\kiḵlək\
Yiddish
: baked products

kiering
\kiriŋ\
English
: treating metal vat

kokko
\käkō\
unknown
: leguminous tree

kolace
\kəˈlächē\
Czech
: sweet bun

kolkhozy
\kəlˈkȯzē\
Russian
: farms

Kommandantura
\kämənˌdanˈtůrə\
German
: military government

kootchar
\küchə\
Australian native name
: honeybee

kurakkan
\kůrəˌkän\
Tamil
: cereal grass

labarria
\ləˈbärē\
Spanish
: snake

lanolin
\lanᵊlən\
ISV
: wool grease

lapan
\lapən\
English
: meat

lardoon
\lär¦dün\
French
: strip of material

Lares
\ler-ēz, 'lä-ˌrās\
Latin
: tutelary gods

laurvikite
\laùrviˌkīt\
German
: rock

leathwake
\lēthˌwāk\
English
: supple

leervis
\lir-ˌvis\
Afrikaans
: fish

leke
\le-kə\
Albanian
: monetary units

lenis
\lēnəs, lānəs\
Latin
: smooth pronunciation

lenite
\lə'nīt\
English
: to undergo replacement of consonant

lennoaceous
\lenəwāshəs\
Latin
: of parasitic herbs

leucitic
\lü¦sitik\
Latin
: of minerals

liane
\lē'än\
French
: plant

libidivi
\libēdivē, lēbēdēvē\
Spanish
: tree

limmata
\limətə\
Greek
: scales

lingam
\liŋgəm\
Sanskrit
: symbol

littorinidian
\litərə'nidēən\
Latin
: of snails

lootsman
\lütsmən\
Dutch
: fishe

lotibush
\lōdēbùsh\
English
: shrub

Lucullian
\lü'kəlēən\
Latin
: lavish

ludfisk
\lüdˌfisk\
Norwegian
: stockfish

lyard
\līərd\
English
: streaked with gray

magani
\mə'gänē\
Tagalog
: class of warriors

malacone
\maləˌkōn\
Greek>German
: zircon

mallemuck
\maləˌmək\
Dutch
: bird

mangabey
\maŋgəˌbā\
Malagasy
: monkey

markhoor
\märˌkù(ə)r\
Persian
: wild goat

marsileaceous
\märˌsilē'āshəs\
Latin
: of water ferns

medimn
\mə'dim\
Greek
: unit of capacity

mesdemoiselles
\mādəmə¦zel\
French
: unmarried French women

mestom
\me͵stäm\
Greek>German
: conducting tissue of
vascular plant

metalloenzyme
\mə͵talō'en͵zīm\
Greek
: specific enzyme

methylase
\methə͵lās\
ISV
: enzyme

miguelet
\migə͵let\
Spanish
: soldier

Milanau
\milə͵naủ\
Arawakan
: people

Mohurrum
\mō'hərəm\
Arabic
: first month of Islamic year

moirai
\mói͵rī\
Greek
: individual destinies

moither
\mói͟thə(r)\
unknown
: to perplex

mollah
\mȯ-lə\
Arabic>Turkish
: teacher of Islamic laws

Mombuttoo
\mäm'bətü\
Sudanese
: people

Moog
\mōg, müg\
trademark
: used for a music synthesizer

mooruk
\mü'rủk\
Imitative
: cassowary

morepork
\mȯr͵pōk\
Imitative
: frogmouth

moudiewort
\mōdiwȯrt\
English
: mole

munja
\münjə\
Hindi & Sanskrit
: grass

nandina
\nan'dīnə, -dēnə\
Japanese>Latin
: shrub

Naskhi
\naskē\
Arabic
: Arabic script

necropoleis
\nə'kräpəlīs\
Greek
: cemeteries

Nientsi
\nēentsē\
Russian
: people

Neoteinia
\nēə'tēnēə\ retention of larval
in adulthood

Nijmegen
\nī-͵mā-gən\
Dutch
: city in Netherlands

noir
\nwär\
French
: crime fiction

nomoi
\nō͵mói\
Greek
: laws

norethisterone
\nȯrə'thistə͵rōn\
Trademark
: hormone

numeracy
\n(y)ümərəsē\
capacity of quantitative
thought

nyasalander
\nyas ə͵landə(r)\
Zulu
: inhabitant of a
place in Africa

nye
\nī\
English
: flock of pheasants

oakmoss
\ōkmäs\
English
: lichen

oam
\'ōm\
English
: warm vaporous air

obeli
\ä-bə-͵lī\
Greek>Latin
: symbols in ancient
manuscripts

obi
\ōbē\
Twi>Edo
: voodooism

oblanceolate
\äbˈlan(t)sēələt\
Latin
: inversely tapering

obliterator
\ə-ˈbli-tə-rātər\
Latin
: device canceling postage stamps

obstruent
\äbztrəwənt\
Latin
: stoppage

occlusor
\əklüsə(r)\
Latin
: body part blocking another

octaacetate
\äktəa-sə-ˌtāt\
Latin
: salt

odontocetous
\ōˌdäntəˈsēˌtəs\
Latin
: of suborder

Odontophorus
\ōˌdänˈtäf(ə)rəs\
Latin
: genus of partridges

oeci
\ˈēˌsī\
Latin
: Roman apartments

Ogee
\ōˌjē\
English
: S-shaped molding

Oka
\ōkə\
French
: Quebec cheese

olla
\älə\
Spanish
: earthenware jar

oleocyst
\ōlēōˌsist\
Latin
: diverticulum

oleovitamin
\ōlēōvītəmən\
Latin
: preparation containing derivatives in soil

oliver
\ä-lə-vər\
English
: old form of smith's hammer

Omayyad
\äˈmī(y)əd\
Arabic
: member of a dynasty ruling the Muslim empire

Ommiad
\äˈmīəd\
Arabic
: member of a dynasty ruling the Muslim empire

omphalic
\ämˌfalik\
Latin
: relating to umbilicus

onde
\ōⁿˈdā\
French
: waving

ondy
\ˈändē\
French
: wavy

oo
\ōˌō\
Hawaiian
: honey eater

ophidiid
\ōˈfidēəd\
Latin
: fish

Opisthocomi
\äpəsˈthäkəˌmī\
Latin
: suborder

opisthodomos
\äpəsˈthädəməs\
Greek
: back chamber

ora
\ōrə\
Norse
: money of account

orf
\ȯ(ə)f\
English
: sore mouth

os
\äs\
Greek
: bone

osculant
\äskyələnt\
Latin
: intermediate in character

ostension
\äˈstenchən\
Latin
: process of pointing out

otidine
\ōtə͵dēn\
Latin
: of old birds

otto
\ä-tō\
Arabic>Persian
: perfume

ouphe
\aůf\
English
: elf

overberg
\ō-vərbərg\
Afrikaans
: tramontane

oxgall
\äksˈgȯl\
English
: yellow

oxgoad
\äks-gōd\
English
: rod

oxyluminescence
\äk-sēlüməˈnesəns\
Latin
: illumination through
chemical reaction

oxyrhynchi
\äksə͵riŋkī\
Greek
: crabs

pace
\ˈpā-sē\
Latin
: with all due respect

pahi
\pəˈhē\
Tahitian
: ship

pajahuello
\pähəˈwelō\
unknown
: venomous tick

pala
\palə\
Tswana
:antelope

palaeoniscoid
\pālēōniskȯid\
Latin
: fossil

palaeophile
\pālēōfīl\
Latin
: antiquary

paleothere
\pālēōthir\
Latin
: fossil

palapala
\päləˈpälə\
Hawaiian
: writing

palatogram
\palətə͵gram\
ISV
: impression on the tongue

paleoentomological
\pālēōentəməläjəkəl\
Latin
: studying fossil insects

paleogene
\pālēōjēn\
 part of a time
period

paleopallium
\pālēōpalēəm\
 old part of
cerebral cortex

Palermitan
\pəˈlərmətᵊn\
Italian
: native of Italian city

palla
\päyə\
Spanish
: Incan princess

palladinize
\palədə͵nīz\
Latin
: treat with
metallic element

palmaris
\palˈma(a)rəs\
Latin
: two muscles of the palm

paludous
\palyədəs\
Latin
: of marshes

pampsychism
\pamˈsī͵kizəm\
Greek
: theory of nature

Pandanales
\pandəˈnālēz\
Latin
: plant species

panicle
\panəkəl\
Latin
: racemose inflorescence

panidiomorphic
\panˈidēə͵mȯrfik\
Latin
: with proper form or shape

panir
\päˈnir\
Hindi
: Indian cheese

panmictic
\pan¦miktik\
Greek
: of random mating

Panoan
\pänəwən\
Spanish
: language family

panorpoid
\panȯrˌpȯid\
Latin
: of insects

panth
\ˈpän(t)th\
Sanskrit
: sect

papable
\pāpəbəl\
Italian
: likely to succeed
for the office of pope

paphian
\pāfēən\
Latin
: wanton

papilionoid
\pəˈpilēəˌnȯid\
Latin
: butterfly

para
\pär-ə\
Turkish
: monetary unit

parabrake
\parəbrāk\
English
: parachute

paracystitides
\perəsi-ˈsti-tə-ˌdēz\
Latin
: bladder tissue inflammation

paragonite
\pəˈragəˌnīt\
German
: mica

paralaurionite
\perəˈlȯrēəˌnīt\
Greek
: mineral

paraphysoid
\pəˈrafəˌsȯid\
Latin
: of hyphal threads

parashoot
\parəˌshüt\
English
: to attack parachute invader

paratergite
\perəˈtərˌjīt\
Latin
: lateral part of
the dorsum of an insect

parcenter
\pärsentər\
English
: to align the centers of
optical senses along one axis

Parian
\pa(a)rēən\
Greek
: of ceramic body clay

parishen
\parishən\
English
: ecclesiastical unit
of area

parisite
\parəˌsīt\
English
: mineral

parmelioid
\pär¦mēlēˌȯid\
Latin
: of lichens

parthenopid
\pärˈthenəpid\
Latin
: of spider crabs

particate
\pärtəˌkāt\
Latin
: unit of land area

parulides
\pərüləˌdēz\
Latin
: gumboils

pase
\ˈpäsā\
Spanish
: cape movement by matador

Passeres
\pasəˌrēz\
Latin
: of suborder of birds

patagiate
\pəˈtājēət\
Latin
: of wing membrane

patimokkha
\pətēˈmȯkə\
Sanskrit
: Buddhist rules

patronite
\patrəˌnīt\
English
: mixture of minerals

patteran
\patərən\
Sanskrit>Romany
: handful of leaves

Paulinian
\pȯˈlinēən\
Latin
: relating to an
apostle or his writings

paussid
\pȯsəd\
Latin
: beetle

pavie
\pāvi\
English
: deft motion

pawl
\pȯl\
Dutch
: pivoted tongue

pega
\pāgə\
Spanish
: fishes

Peguan
\peˈgüən\
Burmese
: of place in Burma

pelargonaldehyde
\peˌlärˌgänˈal-də-ˌhīd\
ISV
: organic compound

Pelew
\pəˈlü\
Palauan
: language

pellock
\pelək\
English
: porpoise

peloric
\pəlȯrik\
Latin
: abnormally regular

pendle
\pendᵊl\
French
: pendent object

Pennacook
\penəˌku̇k\
Algonquian
: confederacy of peoples

pentacrinite
\penˈtakrəˌnīt\
Latin
: fossil

pentammine
\penˈtaˌmēn\
Latin
: molecule

pereira
\pəˈrerə\
English
: tree

periostitis
\perēˌäˈstītəs\
Latin
: inflammation of
connective tissues in bones

peripatoid
\pəˈripəˌtȯid\
Latin
: arthropod

peritectic
\perəˌtektik\
Greek
: taking place
between the solid phases of
the liquid melt

peronium
\pəˈrōnēəm\
Greek
: animal tissue of a tentacle

persis
\pərsəs\
German
: cudbear

petala
\petᵊlə\
Latin
: plate of gold

pete
\pēt\
English
: safe

pettiauger
\petēˈȯgə(r)\
Alteration
: canoe

phacelli
\fəˈselī\
Greek>Latin
: rows of filaments

phalanger
\fəˈlanjə(r)\
Latin
: marsupial
mammals

Phallales
\fəˈlālēz\
Latin
: fungi

phanerocryst
\fanərōkrist\
Greek
: crystal

Phascolomys
\faskəˈlōməs\
Greek
: wombats

Phascolosoma
\faˌskōləˈsōmə\
Greek>Latin
: genus of worms

Phaseolus
\fə'sēələs\
Latin
: herb genus

phasianid
\fāzēə'nid\
Latin
: bird

phenanthryl
\fə'nan(t)thrəl\
Latin
: radical

phenmiazine
\fen͵mīā-͵zēn\
Greek
: compound

philippus
\fə'lipəs\
Greek
: gold stater

philydraceous
\filə'drāshəs\
Greek
: of herbs

phoenicochroite
\fēnə'käkrə͵wīt\
German
: mineral

phormium
\fȯ(r)mēəm\
Greek
: herb

phoronid
\fə'rōnəd\
Latin
: marine animal

phosphorroesslerite
\fäsfə(r)reslə͵rīt\
German
: mineral

phosphuranylite
\fäsfyə'ranºl͵īt\
Latin
: mineral

photozincotypy
\fōtōziŋkə͵tīpē\
Latin
: engraving

phragmites
\frag-'mī-tēz\
Greek
: grasses

phyllocaline
\filōkā͵lēn\
Greek
: hormone

phymatid
\fī'matəd\
Latin
: bug

physeterid
\fī'sētə(r)id\
Greek
: whale

pickaternie
\pikə͵tərni\
Unknown
: gull

pignora
\pignərə\
Latin
 pledge

pila
\pīlə\
Latin
: heavy javelin

pileolus
\pī'lēələs\
Latin
: cap of fungi

piley
\pīlē\
English
: having long slender member

pitirri
\pitə|rē\
Spanish
: flycatcher

Platodaria
\platə'da(a)rēə\
Greek
: flatworm genus

porcini
\pȯr'chēnē\
Italian
: mushroom

porpitoid
\pȯ(r)pətȯid\
Latin
: siphonophore

portiones
\pōrshē'ōnēz
Latin
: part

portreeve
\pōrt͵rēv\
English
: bailiff

potassa
\pə'tasə\
Latin
: potash

pottingar
\pätiŋgər\
Scottish
: apothecary

Pourpresture
\pu̇r'pres(h)chər\
French
: wrongful land appropriation

332

pozzuolana
\pätsəwə'länə\
Italian
: aggregate material

printaniere
\praⁿtånyeer\
French
: made with vegetables

prinzwood
\printswu̇d\
German
: elm wood

privatdocenten
\prē¦vätdōt¦sentᵊn\
German
: lecturers

propionibacteria
\prōpē¦änəbak-'tir-ē-ə\
Latin
: types of bacteria

propodeon
\prō'pōdēən\
Latin
: part of thorax

protopoditic
\prōtōpə'ditik\
Latin
: of penultimate joint of leg

psammomatous
\sa¦mōmətəs\
Latin
: of fibrous tumors

pucciniaceous
\pək̦sinē'āshəs\
Latin
: of fungi

Pulesati
\p(y)ülə'sätē\
Egyptian
: people with armor

purdonion
\pər'dōnēən\
English
:coal container

puruloid
\pyu̇r(y)əlȯid\
Latin
: of pus

pyrenomycetous
\pī̦rēnō̦mīsētəs\
Greek
: of fungi

pyridoxal
\pirə'däksəl\
ISV
: aldehyde

pyrocollodion
\pīrōkə-'lō-dē-ən\
Greek
: nitrogen

pyrolaceous
\pīrə'lāshəs\
Latin
: of herbs

pyrophanite
\pī'räfə̦nīt\
German
: mineral

pyrrhichius
\pə'rikēəs\
Latin
: metric foot

qazi
\käzē\
Arabic
: muslim judge

qre
\krē\
Hebrew
: Jewish mode

quamash
\kwä-mish\
Chinook
: plant

queriman
\kwerə'män\
Dutch
: mullet

quinovin
\kwə'nōvən\
ISV
: glycoside

quintolet
\kwintᵊl¦et\
English
: verse of 5 lines

Ramesside
\ramə̦sīd\
Greek
: of kings of Egypt

recco
\re-kō\
English
: preliminary survey

rechate
\ri-'chāt\
English
: hunting call

redargue
\ri-'där-gyü\
English
: disprove

reitbuck
\rēțbäk\
Afrikaans
: antelope

rencontre
\ren'käntə(r)\
French
: combat

ricinus
\ris°nəs\
Latin
: plant

rifampicin
\rifˈampəsən\
ISV
: antibiotic

ripienist
\rəpˈyānəst\
Italian
: one that plays a small
musical instrument

rissoidean
\risəwədēən\
Latin
: of snails

rocou
\rōkü\
Tupi>French
: tree

Rogerene
\räjə¦rēn\
English
: follower of religious leader

rotta
\rä-tə\
English
: musical instrument

sabakha
\sabəkə\
Arabic
: saline plain

sandik
\sänˌdēk\
Hebrew
: person who holds Jewish
infant during a ceremony

sarcocol
\särkəˌkäl\
Greek
: gummy exudate

sceatta
\sha-tə\
Norse
: coin

schlieric
\shlirik\
German
: of small masses in mineral
composition

scirrhi
\s(k)irī\
Greek
: indurated glands

seaux
\sō(z)\
French
: pottery pails

semeed
\səˈmād\
French
: in ornamental pattern

senarii
\səˈna(a)rēī\
Latin
: verses of six feet

senti
\sentē\
Swahili
: monetary value

serrati
\seˈrātī\
Latin
: muscles of the trunk

Sesiidae
\səˈsīəˌdē\
Latin
: genus of moths

Sevin
\sevən\
Trademark
: used for insecticide

Seyfert
\sēfə(r)t\
English name
: class of spiral galaxies

shochtim
\shōḵtəm\
Hebrew
: persons licensed by rabbinic
authority

sicklemic
\sikə¦lēmik\
Latin
: of sickle-cell trait

signori
\sēn¦yȯ(ə)rē\
Italian
: men of rank

siwin
\sēwən\
unknown
: sea trout

sookie
\sùkē\
English
: used as a call to cows

spayad
\spāəd\
English
: male deer in his third year

spicae
\spīˌsē\
Latin
: reverse plains

Sradh
\s(h)räd\
Hindi
: Hindu rite

stoccata
\stəˈkätə\
Italian
: stab

strigilis
\strijələs\
Latin
: ivory instrument

Sufiism
\süfē͟izəm\
Arabic
: Islamic mysticism

sympus
\simpəs\
Greek
: congenital malformation

synoeky
\sə'nēkē\
Greek
: commensalism

takamaka
\takə'makə\
Spanish
: oleoresin

taratantara
\tarətantərə\
Latin
: blare of trumpet

thuya
\th(y)üyə\
Latin
: wood

Tmesipteris
\mə'siptərəs\
Greek>Latin
: fern allies

tompion
\tämpēən\
English
: plug

toroth
\tō'rōt(h)\
Hebrew
: laws

triphylite
\trifə͟līt\
Greek
: green color

Trophis
\trōfəs\
Greek>Latin
: trees

Tsimshian
\chimshēən\
Algonquian
: Indian people

tulare
\tü'lärä\
Spanish
: bush fields

tunu
\tünü\
Spanish
: tree

turpentiny
\tərpəntīnē\
Latin
: oleoresin

tylia
\tilēə\
Greek
: point on the skull

Typhlopidae
\ti'fläpə͟dē\
Greek
: family of snakes

Tyrrhene
\tə'rēn\
Greek
: Etruscan people

unio
\yünē͟ō\
Latin
: mussel

Violle
\vyȯl\
Frenh
: photometric unit

waesuck
\wā͟sək\
Scottish
: expressing grief

waganging
\wā͟gaŋiŋ\
Scottish
: departure

waywode
\wā͟wōd\
Hindi>English
: military commander

wealpublic
\wēlpə-blik\
English
: commonwealth

whatsis
\(h)wätsəs\
English
: mysterious character

whippletree
\hwipəltrē
English
: pivoted swinging bar

windlestrae
\win(d)ᵊl͟strā\
English
: stalk of grass

wincey
\win(t)sē\
English
: fabric

wiver
\wīvə(r)\
English
: fabulous animal

335

writhled
\rith̶əld\
English
: shriveled

Xenurus
\zə̇'n(y)ùrəs\
Greek
: genus of armadillos

Zarvanism
\zərvə͵nizəm\
Latin
: ancient Iranian religion

zine
\zēn\
English
: noncommercial publication

Ziryen
\zir͵yen\
Finnish
: language

Chapter 9: -ible words

These are all the words in the dictionary ending with -ible. We excluded that words that can be spelled with –able as well. If you memorize these 292 words, then you will know that any other word is spelled with –able (or –uble in the case of chasuble).

accessible
adducible
amissible
appetible
apprehensible
assertible
bivisible
coercible
cognoscible
combustible
comestible
commonsensible
compactible
compatible
competible
compossible
comprehensible
compressible
comptible
conceptible
concessible
concupiscible
conducible
constructible
consumptible
contemptible
contrasuggestible
controvertible
convertible
corrigible
corrodible
corrosible
corruptible
credible
crucible
deducible
deductible
defeasible
defectible
defensible
delible
depressible

derisible
descendible
destructible
diffusible
digestible
dirigible
discernible
discerptible
dispersible
disponible
distensible
divertible
divisible
docible
ductible
edible
educible
effectible
effervescible
elidible
eligible
emulsible
erosible
eruptible
eversible
evincible
excerptible
exclusible
exhaustible
exigible
expansible
explosible
exponible
extensible
extravisible
extrusible
fallible
feasible
fencible
fermentescible
flexible
fluidible

fluxible
forcible
frangible
fungible
fusible
gullible
horrible
hypersusceptible
illegible
immarcescible
immersible
immiscible
impartible
impassible
imperceptible
imperfectible
impermissible
implausible
impossible
imprescriptible
imputrescible
inaccessible
inadmissible
inamissible
inaudible
incoercible
incognoscible
incombustible
incommiscible
incompatible
incompatible
incompossible
incomprehensible
incompressible
inconclusible
incontrovertible
inconvertible
inconvincible
incorrigible
incorruptible
incredible
indefeasible

337

indefectible
indefensible
indeflectible
indelible
indestructible
indicible
indiscernible
indiscerptible
indivertible
indivisible
indocible
inducible
inedible
ineligible
ineludible
inevasible
inexhaustible
inexigible
inexpansible
inexpressible
inextensible
infallible
infeasible
infectible
inflexible
infractible
infrangible
infusible
ingestible
insensible
instructible
insubmergible
insubmersible
insubvertible
insuppressible
insusceptible
intangible
intelligible
interconvertible
interruptible
intervisible
intransgressible
intransmissible
introducible
intromissible
introversible
invertible
invincible
irascible
irreducible
irreductible

irrefrangible
irremissible
irreprehensible
irrepressible
irreproducible
irresistible (noun)
irresponsible
irreversible
irruptible
legible
mandible
miscible
noncollectible
noncombustible
nonconvertible
nondeductible
nondiffusible
nondigestible
nonmiscible
nonreversible
offensible
omissible
oppressible
ostensible
partible
passible- capable of feeling
or suffering
partible
perceptible
perfectible
permissible
persuasible
pervertible
plausible
possible
prehensible
prescriptible
previsible
producible
protractible
protrusible
putrescible
receptible
reconstructible
reconvertible
redemptible
reducible
reeligible
reflexible
refrangible

refusible- capable of renewal
with a new fuse
remissible
rendible
repressible
reproducible
rescissible
resistible
responsible
reversible
revertible
revisable
risible
semiflexible
semiresponsible
sensible
sponsible
suasible
subaudible
subdivisible
submergible
submersible
submissible
subsensible
subvertible
subvisible
suggestible
superfusible
supersensible
suppressible
susceptible
suspendible
tangible
tensible
terrible
thurible
transmissible
unaccessible
uncollectible
uncomprehensible
uncontrovertible
unconvertible
uncorruptible
undiscernible
uneligible
unexhaustible
unexpressible
unfallible
unfeasible
unflexible
unimpressible

unintelligible
uninterruptible
unplausible
unpossible
unreducible
unreproducible
unresistible
unresponsible
unsensible
unsusceptible
untangible
unvendible
vendible
vincible
visible
vitrescible
vivisectible

Afterword

By: Roopa Hathwar

As a privileged and proud mother, I am honored to give my insight into the making of two national champions! Our journey to the Scripps National Spelling Bee started in 2007 when Sriram was 7 years old in first grade at the Montessori, when he watched the regional spelling bee in our area. Just watching the regional bee was inspirational for him to want to be part of this someday!

So the following school year, when I approached his English teacher at his school, she kindly obliged and agreed to have Sriram in the mock spelling bee sessions. That, in my opinion, was when the seeds were sown to create these champions. Sriram diligently prepared each week to study the school lists and as his mom, I got to spend a considerable amount of time each day to work with him on different language patterns. His meticulous efforts proved to be fruitful when he won the school bee in 2008. Despite being a school champion, I was told that he would not be eligible to compete at the regional level since the bee was limited to students from 4th to 8th grade. This prompted my appeal to the local sponsor who was then The Corning Leader. I was then told by the sponsor that there is no lower age limit (and rightfully so), for this competition which made Sriram eligible to compete.

Sriram thoroughly enjoyed the preparation and the regional spelling bee that year, since he was going in as a rookie with no expectations or pressure. We as parents were thrilled to pieces to see Sriram be the regional winner and getting a ticket to the National Spelling Bee! However, he did not rest on his laurels for long, for he knew that there awaited a much bigger challenge in DC. We were faced with a monumental task of preparing with the Merriam Webster's 3rd Unabridged Dictionary. As we prepared for the journey to DC, in our first year, we scoured for resources for preparation and could come up with only one book at that time, "How to Spell Like a Champ." So, we decided to get exposed to language patterns and word lists in that book. Soon we realized that while this was a great resource for beginners, we needed to dig deeper in order to advance at the national level. The National Spelling Bee website also provides the link to Consolidated Word List, which was our next level of study source. We realized that while this was an extensive study list, we still needed to prepare for those esoteric words that are asked at the National Spelling Bee. That's what prompted us to dive deep into the dictionary. The word lists got bigger and difficult each time we reviewed the dictionary. It is fair to say that by the time Sriram entered 8th grade, he had gone over the dictionary several times and we were fully satisfied with the preparation to the extent that it did not matter where he placed at the nationals. We knew he was a champion in our books already! So when Sriram was declared the co-champ in 2014, we were delighted to see his years of hard work come to fruition!

That the life of a champion gets hectic in the days, weeks and months after the win is an understatement! With the media tours, local, regional, national and international recognition and of course the unforgettable experience of meeting the president in the White House, you function on very little sleep and a lot of adrenaline!

Just when we thought that we were coming off the gigantic wave of celebrations for Sriram, Jairam expressed an interest to be part of this experience all over again! We commended Jairam for taking on this arduous journey despite having seen his brother go through the roller coaster of wins and losses in the competition! The fact that he even wanted to venture into this journey, knowing fully well what it entailed, was laudatory in our opinion. What works for the goose does not necessarily work for the gander. We realized that Jairam did not have the luxury of having as many years as Sriram did to handle this beast. Also, Jairam's learning style was a bit different from Sriram with Jairam learning more efficiently by typing words in to a computer rather than reading through the dictionary. So, although the curriculum remained unchanged, the learning style was certainly different. This is where I felt we were helpful as parents to identify our children's learning style and vary the learning methods accordingly. Jairam finished with an impressive 22nd place in his rookie performance in 2015. He returned back from the National Spelling Bee with more resolve to better his ranking and possibly win it. He intensified his efforts that school year and prioritized his extracurricular activities, in order to stay focused enough to put in the required time and effort to prepare for the spelling bee. His dream came true when he became a co-champion in 2016. We were celebrating another spelling bee victory! We had to pinch ourselves several times to make sure we were not dreaming!

Both the boys put in a lot of time for the spelling bee, but that was not the only thing they did. We all know that most kids who participate in the National Spelling Bee are well rounded kids and our kids were no different. They both were involved in sports, music, and joined in all family celebrations and vacations, yet made time to prepare for the spelling bee.

The journey to each of their wins were hampered by our local sponsor dropping out of the sponsorship in mid-August of 2012. In a span of 3 weeks, we scoured for sponsors in the area, finally being successful with asking the Corning Rotary Club to be our sponsor. We are deeply grateful to the Corning Leader who sponsored the regional spelling bee for so many years in this area and would like to express our sincere gratitude to the Corning Rotary Club for their sponsorship in the past years. Again, as parents we had a small role in facilitating the reinstatement of sponsorship in the area.

Finally, I would like to conclude by saying that attitude is a choice and it would be prudent if we go with an attitude of learning the language and not necessarily focus only on winning the bee. It takes out that pressure and helps you have fun with it. It did not matter to the boys if the format or rules were changed, if the words got tougher or the competition got stiffer. They were having fun learning and the championship was an icing on the cake! No knowledge is futile and no time spent in learning is ever wasted.

We wish the best of luck to the aspiring spellers out there in pursuing their dreams!

Made in the USA
Las Vegas, NV
25 February 2024

86313608R00188